An Overview of Financial Crises around the World

An Overview of Financial Crises around the World

First Edition

Edited by Antonio N. Bojanic

Tulane University

cognella | ACADEMIC PUBLISHING

Bassim Hamadeh, CEO and Publisher
Angela Schultz, Senior Field Acquisitions Editor
Michelle Piehl, Senior Project Editor
Christian Berk, Associate Production Editor
Emely Villavicencio, Senior Graphic Designer
Stephanie Kohl, Licensing Associate
Natalie Piccotti, Senior Marketing Manager
Kassie Graves, Vice President of Editorial
Jamie Giganti, Director of Academic Publishing

Printed in the United States of America.

ISBN: 978-1-5165-2980-3 (pbk) / 978-1-5165-2981-0 (br)

cognella® | ACADEMIC PUBLISHING

Contents

Introduction

Financial crises have occurred in every country ever since people started living in communities and engaged in written contracts between those with an excess of capital and those with a shortfall of funds. Though there are no two financial crises that are exactly alike—in terms of its causes, evolution, and consequences—they are all likely to share some common features, including abrupt drops in asset prices and increases in uncertainty.

In the United States, the first financial crisis happened soon after independence, in 1792. The result of speculative trading and a faulty design for the first central bank established in the country, this crisis will also be remembered as the one where government bailouts of financial institutions started to happen. Other crises followed—between 1797 and 1800, 1857–1859, 1873–1879, 1893–1897, 1907, 1929–1941, 1973–1975, 1981–1982, 1986–1989, and 2007–2009—but the one that began in 1929 holds a special place in US economic history. The unemployment rate rose from 3 percent in 1929 to 25 percent in 1933, and it was still 15 percent in 1940. The depression pushed millions of middle-class families into poverty. By comparison, during the 2007–2009 crisis, unemployment peaked at 10.1 percent in October 2009. The fall in asset prices started with the stock market crash of October 1929. Increases in uncertainty and a wave of bank failures came next, precipitating an unanticipated drop in prices across the country. The economy got caught up in a tailspin for more than 10 years and didn't quite recover until well into the 1940s.

This book presents a sample of articles that analyzes different episodes of crises both in the United States and in other countries and regions around the world. The objective is to understand the principal causes, consequences, and policy responses that have emerged as a result of financial crises. An added objective is to highlight the similarities across nations. A lesson that may emerge after reading the experiences of several countries is that we are not that different after all and that the same kind of folly is likely to cause financial turmoil in the US and in every other nation on earth.

The articles have been organized into four broad categories. In the first one—articles by Mishkin (1990) and Summers (2000)—an overview of the theoretical reasons that explain financial crises is provided. The second section describes two great crises, the Great Depression in the United States, as detailed by Irving Fisher (1933), and the Asian crisis of the 1990s, described by Chowdhry and Goyal (2000). Country-specific crises are presented in the third section, with Bojanic (2013) concentrating on Bolivia and its experiences with inflation; Wade and Sigurgeirsdottir (2012) describing Iceland's recent banking crisis; Tornell (1995) utilizing the Mexican experience and arguing that economic crises are oftentimes needed in order to push through painful trade liberalization and fiscal reforms; Leightner (2007) focusing on Thailand; and Feldstein (2002) describing Argentina's crisis during the late 1990s and early 2000s. The final section and the last two articles—Lal (2010) and Lastra and Wood (2010)—concentrate on the 2007–2009 financial crisis, with an emphasis on the causes and consequences of this latest episode of financial turmoil.

While the book is targeted to economics and finance undergraduate students, it is accessible to anyone with a general interest in the aggregate economy and a particular interest in financial markets.

PART I

Overview of Theoretical Reasons that Explain Financial Crises

READINGS

FREDERIC S. MISHKIN (1991)
Asymmetric Information and Financial Crises: A Historical Perspective

LAWRENCE H. SUMMERS (2000)
International Financial Crises: Causes, Prevention, and Cures

CHAPTER 1

Asymmetric Information and Financial Crises: A Historical Perspective

Frederic S. Mishkin (1991)

I. INTRODUCTION

In recent years there has been a growing concern with the fragility of the financial system. Increasing defaults on junk bonds and the stock market crash of October 1987 have raised the specter of major financial crises which might inflict severe damage on the economy. Policymakers, particularly those in the central bank, are faced with the questions of what should they do to prevent financial crises and what should be their response when a financial crisis appears imminent. In order to start providing intelligent answers to these questions, we must first understand what is the nature of financial crises and how they might affect the aggregate economy.

This paper seeks to understand the nature of financial crises by examining the history of financial crises in the United States using the new and burgeoning literature on asymmetric information and financial structure, which has been excellently surveyed recently by Gertler (1988a). After describing how an asymmetric information approach helps to understand the nature of financial crises, the paper focuses on a historical examination of a series of financial crises in the United States, beginning with the panic of 1857 and ending with the stock market crash of October 19, 1987. The asymmetric information approach explains the patterns in the data and many features of these criseswhich are otherwise hard to explain. It also suggestswhy financial crises have had such important consequences for the aggregate economy over the past one hundred and fifty years.

II. THE NATURE OF FINANCIAL CRISES

There are two polar views of the nature of financial crises existent in the literature. Monetarists beginning with Friedman and Schwartz (1963) have associated financial crises with banking panics. They stress the importance of banking panics because they view them as a major source of contractions in the money supply which, in turn, have lead to severe contractions in aggregate economic activity in the United States. Their view of financial crisis leads monetarists to advocate a central bank lender-of-last-resort role to prevent banking panics so that monetary instability will be prevented. Monetarists do not view events in which there is a sharp drop in wealth but there is no potential for a banking panic and a resulting sharp decline in the money supply as real financial crises that require any central bank intervention. Indeed, Schwartz (1986) characterizes these situations as "pseudo financial crises". Central bank intervention in a pseudo-financial crisis is unnecessary and can indeed be harmful since it leads to a decrease in economic efficiency because firms that deserve to fail are bailed out or because it results in excessive money growth that stimulates inflation.

An opposite view of financial crises is held by Kindleberger (1978) and Minsky (1972) who have a much broader definition of what constitutes a real financial crisis than monetarists. In their view, financial crises either involve sharp declines in asset prices, failures of both large financial and nonfinancial firms, deflations or disinflations, disruptions in foreign exchange markets, or some combination of all of these. Since they perceive any of these disturbances as having potential serious consequences for the aggregate economy, they advocate a much expanded role for government intervention when a financial crisis, broadly defined, occurs.

One problem with the Kindleberger-Minsky view of financial crises is that it does not supply a rigorous theory of what characterizes a financial crisis, and it thus lends itself to'being used too broadly as a justification for government interventions that might not be beneficial for the economy. Indeed, this is the basis of Schwartz's (1986) attack on the Kindleberger-Minsky view. On the other hand, the monetarist view of financial crises is extremely narrow because it only focuses on bank panics and their affect on the money supply. The recent literature on asymmetric information and financial structure, on the other hand, does provide a broader view of the nature of financial crises, but it supplies a theory which does not automatically justify government interventions when their is a sharp drop in wealth as the Kindleberger-Minsky view might.

The asymmetric information literature which looks at the impact of financial structure on economic activity focuses on the differences in information available to different parties in a financial contract. Borrowers have an informational advantage over lenders because borrowers know more about the investment projects they want to undertake than do lenders. This informational advantage leads to adverse selection and a classic "lemons" problem first described by Ackerloff (1970). A lemons problem occurs in the debt market because lenders have trouble determining whether a lender is a good risk (he has good investment opportunities with low risk) or, alternatively, is a bad risk (he has poorer investment projects with high risk). If the lender cannot distinguish between the borrowers of good quality and bad quality (the lemons) he will only make the loan at an interest rate that reflects the average quality of the good and bad borrowers. The result is that high-quality borrowers will be paying a higher interest rate than they should because low-quality borrowers pay a lower interest rate than they should. One result of this lemons problem is that some high-quality borrowers may drop out of the market and so profitable investment projects that should be undertaken will not be.[1]

1 The lemons problem also can be important in equity markets. Myers and Majluf (1984) and Greenwald, Stiglitz and Weiss (1984) describe how the inability of investors to distinguish between good and bad issuers of equity means that the price they will pay for shares will reflect the average quality of the issuers. The result

Another result, as demonstrated by Stiglitz and Weiss (1981), is that information asymmetry can lead to credit rationing in which some borrowers are arbitrarily denied loans. This occurs because a higher interest rate leads to even greater adverse selection: the borrowers with the riskiest investment projects will now be the likeliest to want to take out loans at the higher interest rate. If the lender cannot discriminate who are the borrowers with the riskier investment projects, he may want to cut down the number of loans he makes, which causes the supply of loans to decrease with the higher interest rate rather than decrease.[2] Thus, even if there is an excess demand for loans, a higher interest rate will not be able to equilibrate the market because additional increases in the interest rate will only decrease the supply of loans and make the excess demand for loans increase even further. Indeed, as Mankiw (1986) has demonstrated, a small rise in the riskless interest rate can lead to a very large decrease in lending and even a possible collapse in the market.

The adverse selection-lemons analysis above indicates how a disruption can occur in financial markets that adversely affects aggregate economic activity. If market interest rates are driven up sufficiently because of increased demand for credit or because of a decline in the money supply, the adverse selection problem might dramatically increase and there will be a substantial decline in lending, which. in turn. leads to a substantial decline in investment and aggregate economic activity. In addition, if uncertainty increases in a financial market so it is now harder for lenders to screen out good borrowers from bad borrowers, the adverse selection problem also increases-dramatically and again can lead toasharp decline in investment and aggregate activity.

These mechanisms suggest that an important manifestation of a financial crisis would be a large rise in interest rates to borrowers for which there is substantial difficulty in obtaining reliable information about their characteristics, that is, for which there is a serious asymmetric information problem. On the other hand, there would be a much smaller effect on interest rates to borrowers for which there is almost no asymmetric information problem because it is easy to obtain information about their characteristics. Since low-quality borrowers are more likely to be firms for which information about their characteristics is difficult to obtain, while high-quality borrowers are more likely to be ones for which the asymmetric information problem is least severe, a rise in the spread between interest rates on low-quality versus high-quality bonds can provide information on when the adverse selection problem becomes more severe in debt markets.

One way that lenders can reduce the adverse selection problem in debt markets is to have the borrower provide collateral for the loan. With collateral, even if the borrower defaults on the loan, the lender will take title to the collateral which can be sold to make up the loss. Thus if the collateral is of good enough quality, then it is no longer as important whether the borrower is of good or bad quality since the loss incurred by the lender if the loan defaults is substantially

---

is that high-quality firms receive a lower price for their shares than their fair market value, while low-quality firms receive a price above their fair market value. As a result, some high-quality firms will not issue shares and so investment projects with a positive net present value will not be undertaken.

2 Asymmetric information can also explain credit rationing in which there are restrictions On the size of loans, as in Jaffee and Russell (1976).

reduced. The fact that there is asymmetric information between the borrower and lender is no longer as important a factor in the market.

The importance of collateral for reducing the adverse selection problem in debt markets provides another mechanism whereby financial disruption adversely affects aggregate economic activity. As emphasized by Calomiris and Hubbard (1990) and Greenwald and Stiglitz (1988). a sharp decrease in the valuation of firms' assets in a stock market crash lowers the value of collateral and thereby makes adverse selection a more important problem for lenders since the losses from loan defaults are now higher. Note that this decline in asset values could either occur because of expectations of lower future income streams from these assets or because of a rise in market interest rates which lowers the present discounted value of future income streams. The lemons problem analysis indicates that the increased importance of adverse selection will lead to a decline in lending and therefore a decline in investment and aggregate economic activity. Again we would expect that this increase in the adverse selection problem would affect interest rates for lower quality firms more than it would affect interest rates for higher quality firms for which there is better information about their characteristics. Hence, it would be manifested by an increase in the interest rate spread for high versus low quality borrowers.

Asymmetric information between borrowers and lenders also results in a moral hazard problem which affects the efficiency of financial markets. Because lenders have trouble in ascertaining the quality of investment projects that borrowers undertake, the borrower has incentives to engage in activities that may be personally beneficial but will increase the probability of default and thus harm the lender. For example, the borrower has incentives to cheat by misallocating funds for his own personal use, either through embezzlement or by spending on perquisites which do not lead to increased profits (F. Ross Johnson, the former CEO of RJR-Nabisco is reputed to have had RJR-Nabisco pay for two personal maids, two dozen country club memberships, and a fleet of ten corporate planes nicknamed the "RJR Airforce"). Also the borrower has incentives to undertake investment in unprofitable projects that increases his power or stature, or to invest in projects with higher risk in which the borrower does well if the project succeeds but the lender bears most of the loss if the project fails. In addition, the borrower has incentives to shirk and just not work very hard. The conflict of interest between the borrower and lender (the agency problem implies that lending and investment will be at suboptimal levels. Indeed, as indicated by Bernanke and Gertler (1989), a lower amount of a borrowers' net worth increases the agency problem because the borrower has less to lose by engaging in moral hazard. Hence, a decline in borrowers net worth leads to a decrease in lending, and thus a decline in investment and aggregate economic activity.

The agency and adverse selection problems provide additional mechanisms for effects from financial crises on the aggregate economy. An unanticipated deflation or a disinflation redistributes wealthfrom debtors to creditors by increasing the realvalue of debt and thereby reducing borrowers' net worth. The resulting increase in adverse selection and agency problems causes a decline in investment and economic activity.[3] The presence of asymmetric information thus

3 Calomiris and Hubbard (1989) emphasize this mechanism in their econometric analysis of the 1894–1909 period.

provides a rationale for Irving Fisher's (1933) debt-deflation analysis of depressions which points to a decreasing price level and increased real indebtedness as a major source of the economic contraction during the Great Depression. In a multi-period context, Gertler (1988b) shows that the concept of a borrower's net worth can be broadened to include the discounted value of future profits. Thus a stock market crash which represents a decreased valuation of firms' discounted future profits also increases adverse selection and agency problems and can lead to a decline in investment and a business cycle contraction.

Firms with high net worth and which have a high value of discounted future profits, that is, high-quality firms, are much less likely to have greatly increased agency costs (costs due to asymmetric information in the market) when a stock market crash or a deflationary shock occurs, while the opposite is the case for low quality firms with low net worth and a low value of discounted future profits. An increase in agency costs stemming from either disinflation or a stock market crash, therefore, should also be reflected in a rise in the interest rate spread for high versus low quality borrowers.

An important feature of the recent literature on asymmetric information and financial structure is that it suggests why banks play a prominent role in financial markets. Banks are eminently well suited to solve many of the adverse selection and moral hazard problems inherent in credit markets. They have expertise in information collection about firms and thus are better able to screen good borrowers from bad borrowers at low cost. This is particularly the case since they are not as subject to the free-rider problemwhich exists for individual purchasers of marketable securities who can costlessly take advantage of information that other purchasers of marketable securities produce. Their advantages in information collection activities are also enhanced by their ability to engage in long-term customer relationships and to issue loans using lines of credit arrangements. They also can engage in lowercost monitoring than individuals, as is demonstrated in Diamond (1984). and also have advantages in enforcement of restrictive covenants, both of which reduce the potential for moral hazard by borrowers.[4] The existence of asymmetric information in credit markets provides a compelling rationale for the importance of banks in getting funds from savers to borrowers who have the most attractive investment opportunities, thereby enhancing economic efficiency.

The importance of asymmetric information provides another mechanism by which financial crises lead to reduced economic activity. The analysis above indicates that banks perform an important role in generating productive investment for the economy. Thus, as is described in Bernanke (1983), disturbances in financial markets that reduce the amount of financial intermediation that can be undertaken by banks, will lead to a reduction in lending to borrowers with profitable investment opportunities and will result in a contraction of economic activity.

4 In addition, as pointed out by Stiglitz and Weiss (1983), banks have an advantage in minimizing moral hazard on the part of borrowers because banks can use the threat of cutting off lending in the future to improve borrower's behavior.

Bank panics are clearly one major way in which banks may find themselves unable to fully perform their intermediation role.[5] In a panic depositors, fearing the safety of their deposits, withdraw them from the banking system, causing a contraction in loans and a multiple contraction in deposits. Here again an asymmetric information problem is at the source of the financial crisis because depositors rush to make withdrawals from solvent as well as insolvent banks since they cannot distinguish between them. Furthermore, banks' desire to protect themselves from possible deposit outflows leads them to increase their reserves relative to deposits, which also produces a contraction in loans and deposits. The net result is that a bank panic reduces the funds available to banks to make loans and the cost of financial intermediation rises, causing a reduction in investment and a decline in aggregate economic activity.

A bank panic also has the feature of decreasing liquidity which will lead to higher interest rates. As we have seen before, this rise in interest rates directly increases adverse selection problems in credit markets and also can reduce the value of firms' net worth, which also increases adverse selection as well as agency problems. Thus, since bank panics have the secondary effect of increasing adverse selection and agency problems in financial markets, bank panics lead to economiccontraction through these channels as well. We should then also expect to see that bank panics are associated with a larger interest rate spread between higher and lower quality debt instruments.

The monetarist literature on the role of bank panics in economic contractions adds an additional channel to how financial crises affect the aggregate economy. Friedman and Schwartz (1963) document how bank panics in the United States led to sharp contractions in the money supply as a result of depositors movement out of deposits into currency and banks movement out of loans into reserves. These contractions in the money supply then are seen as being responsible for substantial declines in economic activity and the price level.

The view in the recent literature on asymmetric information and its impact on aggregate economic activity is complementary to the monetarist view of the importance of bank panics. Indeed, the asymmetric information approach provides a transmission mechanism for how a decline in the money supply leads to a decline in aggregate economic activity. The deflation that stems from a decline in the money supply increases adverse selection and agency problems which cause a decline in investment and aggregate economic activity. However, the asymmetric information approach suggests that the impact of a decline in the money supply as a result of a financial crisis is not the whole story of why financial crises affect the aggregate economy. Instead it takes a much broader view of what a financial crisis is and puts a very different light on when a financial crisis is real rather than a pseudo-crisis.

5 Credit controls, such as those imposed in 1980, or disintermediation arising out of depositrate ceilings are another possible way in which banks may find themselves unable to fully perform their intermediation role.

III. A HISTORICAL ANALYSIS OF PRE WORLD WAR II FINANCIAL CRISES

To obtain evidence on how we should characterize financial crises, we examine a series of episodes in the 1857–1941 period in which it is clear that financial crises occurred. Then in the next section we will examine two postwar episodes where there was Federal Reserve intervention to prevent a financial crisis.

The analysis in the previous section suggests that a critical variable for assessing the nature of a particular financial crisis is the spread between interest rates for high and low-quality borrowers. For the period beginning in 1919, the analysis uses the spread between Moody's Baa corporate bond rate and the long-term Treasury bond rate averaged over the month the same spread variable used by Bernanke (1983). This variable is denoted as SPREADB. However, since this series is not available before 1919, another alternative measure must be used before that date. Macaulay (1938) provides monthly yield data for high-grade railroad bonds from 1857 to 1935 which are essentially averages over the month–they are calculated from the average of the high and low bond price for that month. The spread measure was constructed from this data by subtracting the average yield on the best one-fourth of the bonds from the average yield on the worst one-fourth of the bonds. (I.e., three bonds in the best and worst categories were used for 1857 to 1866, five bonds from 1867 to 1881, eight bonds from 1882 to 1887 and ten bonds from 1888 to 1935.[6]) One-fourth as the fraction of bonds in the best and worst categories was chosen because this fraction led to the highest correlation of the Macaulay spread variable with the Bernanke spread variable in the 1919 to 1935 period when the two series overlap. However, the effect of the choice of the fraction of bonds to include in each category is not crucial. The correlation coefficient between Macaulay spread variables using a different choice for the number of bonds in each category is always above .95 in the 1857 to 1918 period, and the conclusions for each episode studied are not affected by a different choice for the number of bonds in each category.

The Macaulay spread variable has several problems in comparison with the Bernanke spread variable. First, there is no guarantee in the Macaulay variable that the worst or the best bonds remain in the same rating class throughout the time period studied. This cannot be helped because bond ratings for these bonds are not available. It should also be realized that the Bernanke spread variable is not perfect on these grounds either because, as Temin (1976) points out, during periods when default risk was changing rapidly, it is not clear that the Moody's ratings continued to have the same meaning. Another potential problem is that the Macaulay bonds are all of fairly high grade: In the 1919 to 1935 period the worst Macaulay bond still has an interest rate below the Moody's Baa corporate bond rate, while the best bond has a rate below the Aaa corporate bond rate. There is a possibility that the Macaulay bonds might not have a sufficient difference in their grades to pick up the changes in the interest rates for high and low-quality borrowers.

6 Note that the dates when the number of bonds in each category changes do not fall within any of the subsamples analyzed in the paper. This avoids the potential for any discootinuities in the interest rate spread series during the episodes studied.

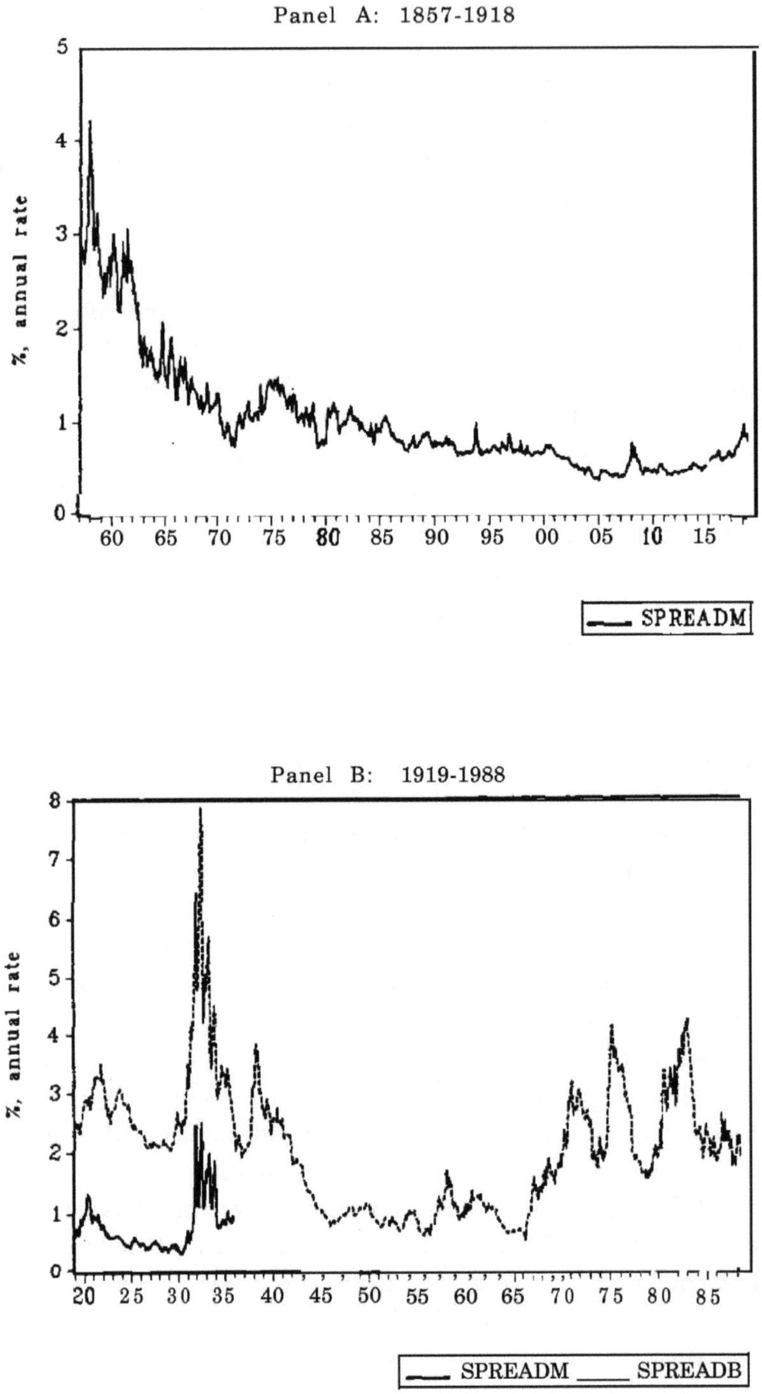

FIGURE 1.1 Interest Rate Spreads

Despite these limitations, the Macaulay measure seems to perform well. The Macaulay spreadvariable, denoted as SPREADM, is plotted for the 1857 to 1918 period in Figure 1.1, Panel A. Panel B plots the Bernanke spread variable, denoted as SPREADB, over the 1919 to 1988 period along with the Macaulay variable from 1919 to 1935. As is visible in Panel B, the Macaulay variable is highly correlated with the Bernanke variable: the correlation coefficient between the two variables over the 1919 to 1935 period is 0.88. Both tell similar stories in that period: they both rise during the 1920–21 recession, decline thereafter to a low point in the late twenties, climb dramatically with the onset of the banking panics in late 1930, and then fall to substantially lower levels by the end of 1935. Furthermore, as we will see, the Macaulay spread variable seems to have a consistent relationship with stock market and commercial paper rate variables in the pre-1919 episodes studied below, adding further confidence in its validity.

The analysis of the nature of financial crises in the previous section also suggests that we should look at stock prices and interest rates when we analyze the individual episodes of financial crisis. The level of stock prices, denoted as STOCK, is constructed as the cumulative geometric sum of the stock market return series from Wilson, Sylla and Jones (1990),[7] and is thus meant to be an end of monthly series. However, the earlier data in the stock market series (up until the 1920s) are made up of monthly averages or the averages of the high and low stock prices for the month. Thus even though the stock price series used here is meant to be thought of as an end of month series, it is actually closer to a monthly average up until the 1920s. Furthermore, up until 1890, the stock price series is primarily made up of railroad stocks.

The interest rates examined are those on high grade commercial paper, denoted by RCP, and those on call loans to stock and bond brokers in New York, denoted by RCALL. For the period 1857 to 1918, the commercial paper rate series is choice 60–90 day two name paper from Macaulay (1938), while after this date it is the rate on 4-6 month commercial paper obtained from Banking and Monetary Statistics, 1914–1940 and 1941–1970, arid from the Federal Reserve Bulletin of various years. The call loan rate series is taken from Wilson, Sylla and Jones (1990) and it along with the commercial paper rate series are monthly averages of daily rates. In the analysis of the financial crises to follow, more attention will be focused on the commercial paper rate when discussing interest rate movements. This makes sense because commercial paper rates should be closer to the interest rates that affect business firms' decisions to invest, while call loan rates are influenced by peculiarities of events in the stock market.

There are clearly many other variables that we might want to examine in order to better understand what is going on during financial crises—such as business failures, the price level, commodity prices, industrial production, to name a few. However, in this paper I will be conducting a more preliminary analysis and will only be examining financial market variables. In future work, I hope to be able to use such data to engage in a fuller treatment of the financial crisis phenomenon.

7 The stock price series developed by Schwert (1989b) is very close to that of Wilson, Sylla and Jones (1990) and its use would not change any conclusions in the analysis here.

Now that we understand the data we are looking at, we can turn to discussion of particular episodes of financial crises. We will focus especially on the timing of events and financial variables during these episodes, because the timing will enable us to distinguish between different views of the nature of financial crises. The crises we will examine first are the pre-World War II episodes that are most prominent in discussions by Sprague (1910). Kindleberger (1978), Bordo (1986), Gorton (1987) and Schwert (1989a).[8] Historical descriptions of these episodes are found in Sprague (1910), Collman (1931), Smith and Cole (1935), Friedman and Schwartz (1963), and Sobel (1968).

THE PANIC OF 1857

The stock price, interest rate spread and commercial paper rate data for the two-year period surrounding the panic in October 1857 are reported in Figure 1.2. Panel A plots the Macaulay interest rate spread variable, denoted by SPREADM and the stock price index denoted by STOCK. The left-hand vertical axis corresponds to the spread variable, while the right-hand vertical axis corresponds to the stock price index. The stock price index is normalized to equal 100 at its peak value. Panel B plots the commercial paper rate. In both panels, the NBER date for the beginning of the 1857-58 recession. July 1857, is marked on the horizontal axis with an "R", while the October 1857 date for the banking panic is marked by a "P". This general format is used in the figures for the other episodes discussed later.

The interest rate spread variable along with the commercial paper rate begins to climb beginning in July of 1857, three months before the banking panic, while the stock market is falling from the beginning of the year. On August 25. the Ohio Life Insurance & Trust Company, a major financial institution which had made substantial investments in western land and railroads as well as in commodity futures, failed. This was then followed by a major stock market crash in September and October. The market return of 14.46% in September and –15.26% in October were the tenth and eleventh worst monthly returns tabulated by Wilson, Sylla and Jones (1990) for their entire sample period form January 1834 through August 1988. With the failure of the Ohio Life & Trust Company, reserves began to be pulled from New York and the first bank failures there occurred in September. Interest rates shot through the roof with the commercial paper rate rising to 18% in September and a peak of 24% in October. Thinly capitalized railroads, such as the Delaware, Lackawanna & Western, and the Fond du Lac and several smaller railroads went bankrupt in September. Major runs on the New York banks began in October, finally culminating in a suspension of specie payments in mid-October, and bank panics spread throughout the country. Failures of major railroads such as the Erie & Pittsburgh, the Fort Wayne & Chicago, the Reading and Illinois Central occurred in October. The outcome was a severe recession whic h ended in December 18.58.

8 The financial crisis associated with the beginning of World War I in August 1914 is not examined below because the data for this period are not available from August to November 1914 when the New York Stock Exchange was closed.

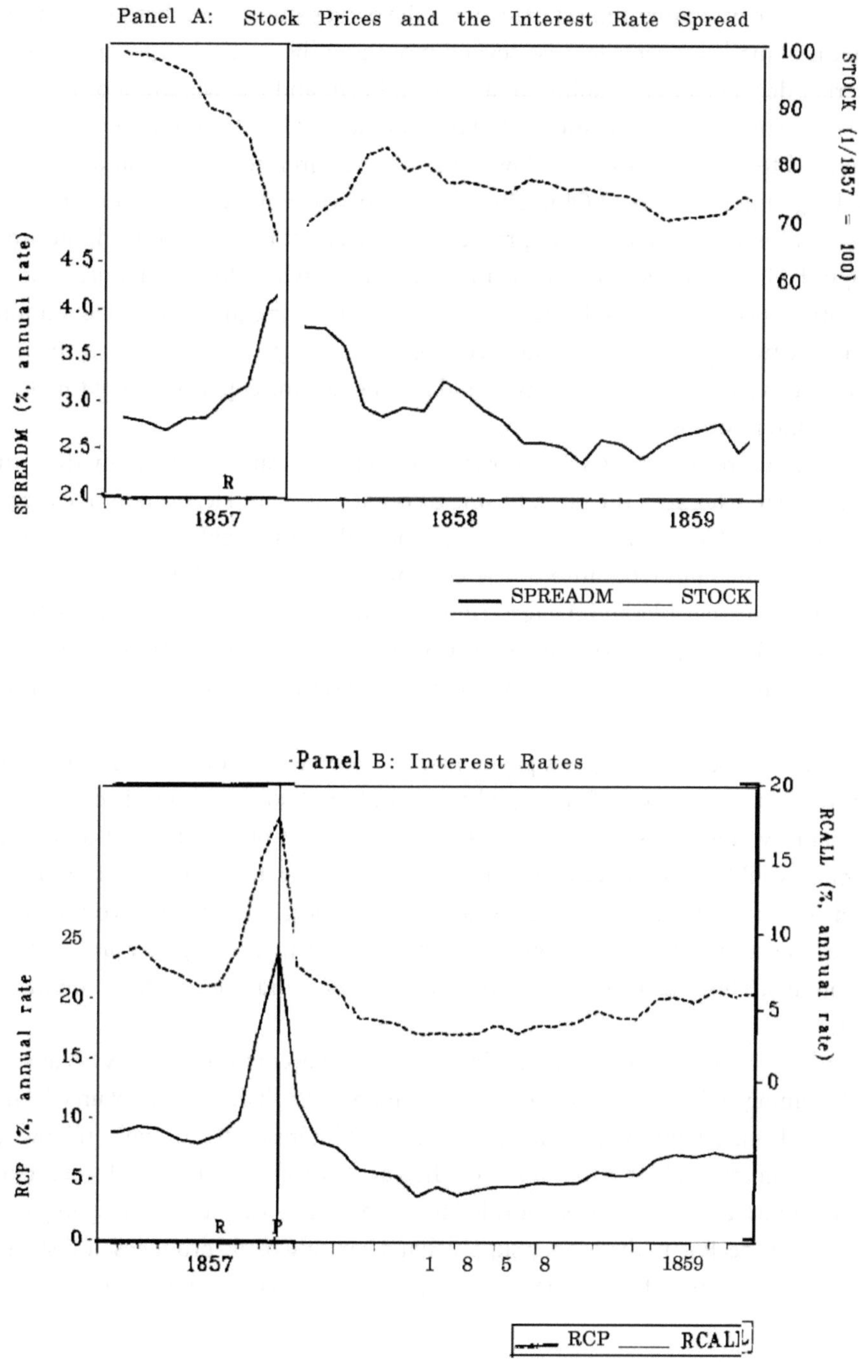

FIGURE 1.2 The Panic of 1857

The timing of events in the panic of 1857 seem to fit an asymmetric information interpretation of the financial crisis. Rather than starting with the bank panic in October 1857, the disturbance to the financial markets seems to arise several months earlier with the rise in interest rates, the stock market decline, a major failure of a financial firm and the widening of the interest rate spread. The asymmetric information story provides an explanation of how the financial crisis could have led to a severe economic downturn. The rise in interest rates and the stock market decline, alongwith the failure of Ohio Life & Trust Co. which increased uncertainty, would magnify the adverse selection and agency problems in the credit markets. Indeed, the stock market crash might be linked to the general rise in interest rates which lowers the present discounted-value of future income streams. In this case, the panic of 1857 can be viewed as a liquidity crisis. The net result from the increase in adverse selection and agency problems is that investment activity and aggregate economic activity would decline causing expectations of further economic contraction and business failures.

As pointed out in Gorton (1987), depositors would now want to withdraw their funds from the banking system because the bleak business conditions would lead them to expect losses on deposits left in the banks, and this would be especially undesirable at a time when their consumption might be falling because of the economic downturn. The outcome of the process would be a run on the banks and the resulting panic would raise interest rates further, cause the stock market to decline even more and worsen agency and adverse selection problems even more in the credit markets. That a severe economic contraction would develop is a logical outcome of this process.

Finally, after suspension of specie payments. the intervention of clearing house associations, as is pointed out in Gorton (1985), helped to separate out solvent from insolvent banks.[9] The banking panic would then subside, and with the restoration of liquidity in the banking system, interest rates would fall, the stock market might undergo a recovery, and if economic uncertainty and deflation were not too severe, agency and adverse selection problems would diminish, leading to a decline in the interest rate spread variable and setting the stage for an eventual recovery of the economy. This scenario seems to describe the data and the events in the 1857-58 period quite well.

A monetarist interpretation cannot explain these set of events as effectively because it does not explain the timing of the events and the financial variables: i.e., it does not explain why the banking panic occurred when it did and why the spread between interest rates for high and low-quality borrowers rises dramatically before the panic and then declines after the panic subsides. However, the asymmetric information story does not rule out important consequences on aggregate economic activity from the decline in the money supply that a banking panic produces. It just suggests that there is more to the story of a financial crisis than its affects on the money supply.

9 Another important role of the clearing house associations mentioned by Gorton (1985) is that they would provide liquidity to the banking system by issuing clearing-house certificates during a panic. However, the clearing house associations had not yet taken on this role in 1857, but did so in later banking panics.

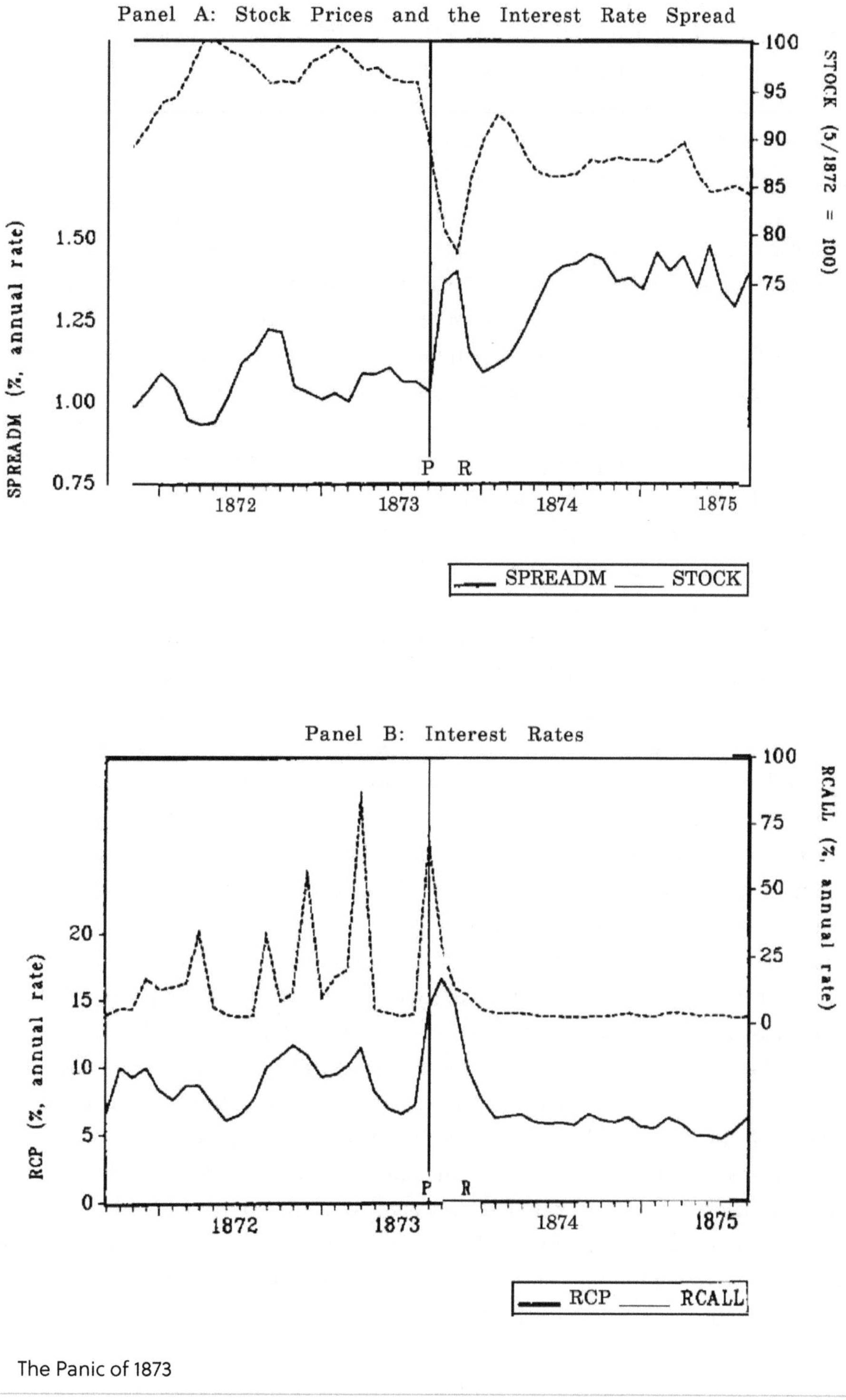

FIGURE 1.3 The Panic of 1873

THE PANIC OF 1873

The data for the two year period spanning the banking panic of September 1873 is found in Figure 1.3, Panels A and B. The format is identical to that in Figure 1.2. Of all the panics studied in this paper, the panic of 1873 is somewhat unusual. First, it occurs before the business cycle peak, as can be seen in Figure 1.3, and second, it was apparently quite unpredictable since it was not preceded by a rise in the in terest rate spread.

The initial disturbance for the panic seems to have originated with the financial difficulties of the railroad sector. On September 8, 1873, the New York Warehouse & Security Company, who had made substantial loans to the Missouri, Kansas & Texas Railroad as well on grain and produce, suspended. This suspension was soon followed by the failure of the banking house of Kenyon, Cox & Co. as a result of endorsements on $1.5 million of paper issued by the Canada Southern Railroad. At the time neither of these failures were considered to be of major importance, but they were soon followed by the suspension of Jay Cooke & Co. on September 18, one of the most respected and important financial institutions in the United States, and the suspension of Fisk & Hatch the next day. The collapse of Jay Cooke & Co. also stemmed from financial difficulties in the railroad sector, specifically problems with its loans to Northern Pacific Railroad which Jay Cooke controlled. With the announcement of the Jay Cooke & Company failure, the stock market went into a nose dive, with the result that September 18, 1873 was dubbed "Black Thursday", and the decline in stock prices was over 7% in the month of September. Immediately, runs began on the Fourth National Bank and the Union Trust Company. By Saturday, September 20, both the Union Trust Company and the National Bank of the Commonwealth had failed and a major banking panic was in full swing. On the same day the New York Stock Exchange took the unprecedented step of closing, not to reopen until September 30. On September 20, the New York Clearing House began to issue clearing-house loan certificates to its member banks, and the decision to suspend specie payments was made on September 24. Over the next several days, suspension of specie payments spread nationwide. Only by the end of October had banks almost fully resumed specie payments to depositors.

In Figure 1.3, Panel A, we see that the spread between interest rates on high and low-quality borrowers jumped in the month immediately following the banking panic and stock market crash. We also see in Panel B that interest rates began to rise one month before the crash, and thus the higher interest rates may have been one source of increased adverse selection and agency problems that helped cause the panic. However, the abruptness of the panic suggests that major failures of financial firms such as Jay Cooke & Co. may have increased informational uncertainty, depressed the value of net worth relative to liabilities, and thereby increased adverse selection and agency costs. The runs on banks which occurred immediately after the failure of Jay Cooke & Co. reduced the ability of the banks to perform their intermediation role and are another potential factor in inducing an investment decline and a general economic contraction, which began, according to the NBER dating, in November 1873.[10]

10 A similar phenomenon can also affect consumer spending, as is discussed in Mishkin (1978).

Again the sorting out process of insolvent from insolvent banks and insolvent from solvent business firms after the panic would reduce informational uncertainty. The decline in interest rates and the recovery of the stock market after November 1873, would also help reduce adverse selection and agency problems. Consistent with this view, the spread variable does decline immediately after November 1873. However, in contrast to the 18.57 episode, the spread variable begins to rise in 1874, and for the last half of 1874 and all of 1875 is at levels near the peak value reached in October and November of 1873. The high values of the interest rate spread in 1874 and 1875 are explained by the substantial deflation that sets in after the 1873 panic. As we have seen, a sharp deflation transfers wealth from borrowers to creditors which causes a deterioration in business firms' net worth. The resulting increase in asymmetric information problems, which is reflected in the rise in the interest rate spread, can thus be a major propagation mechanism during the recession." The recession which began in November 1873 was especially long lived, and, according to NBER dating, did not end until March 1879. It is often considered to be one of the more severe economic contractions in U.S. history, and by some writers is categorized as being the second most severe, only to be outdone by the Great Contraction of 1929-33.

The data in Figure 1.3 is quite consistent with an asymmetric information interpretation of the 1873 panic and the severe recession following. However, it gives a prominent role to the bankingpanic and affects on the economy from declines in the money supply. As Friedman and Schwartz (1963) point out the period from 1873 to 1879 has an unusual number of years in which declines in the money supply occur. These declines in the money supply were likely to have been an important factor in the decline in aggregate demand in this period. The resulting extraordinary and prolonged deflation of the period was then likely to have been an important factor in the rise of asymmetric information problems because of the resulting deterioration in firms balance sheet positions, which further encouraged a contraction in aggregate economic activity.

THE PANIC OF 1884

We will devote somewhat less discussion to the panic of May 1884 because it was not a particularly severe crisis. However, the patterns in the data in Figure 1.4 around the panic date are very similar to the patterns we see in other financial crises. A recession had begun in April 1882, well before the panic, and the interest rate spread variable had been declining with the exception of one large upward blip toward the beginning of 1884. With the decline of stock prices after February 1884, the spread variable again begins to rise. Then, as Sprague (1910) puts it, "Within little more than a week an astonishing series of instances of fraud and defalcation, unexplained in our history,were brought to light.[11]" On May 8, the firm of Grant & Ward, in which the son of Ulysses S. Grant was a major partner, failed. When audited the firm was found to have assets of only $67,174 and liabilities of $16,792,640. The Marine National Bank, whose president, James D. Fish, was a partner in Grant & Ward, failed immediately when it came to light that the bank

11 Sprague (1910), page 110. For those who like myself do not know the meaning of the word "defalcation", it means a misappropriation of funds held by a trustee or other fiduciary.

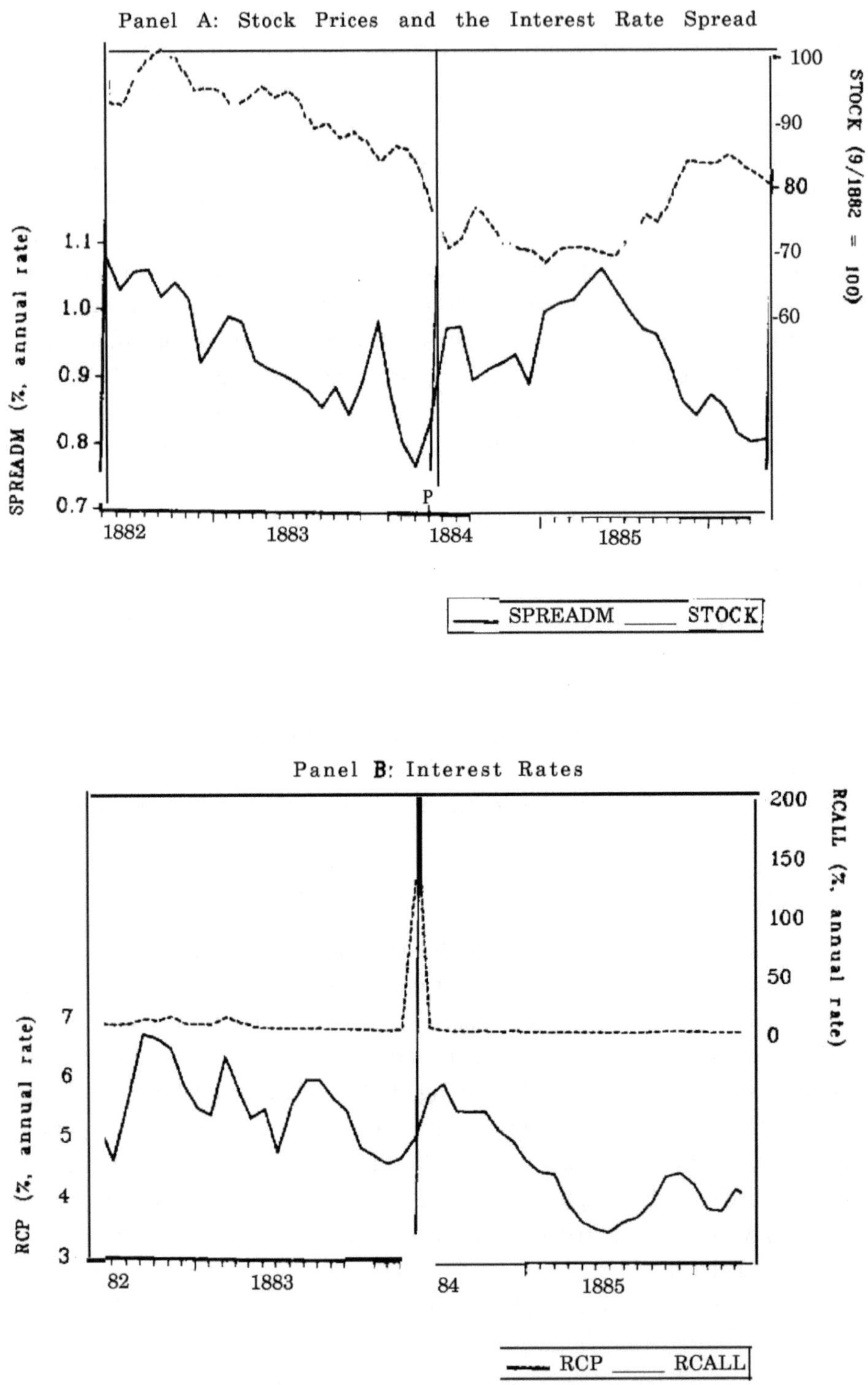

FIGURE 1.4 The Panic of 1884

had illegally certified one of Grant & Ward's check for $750,000. On May 13, it became known that John C. Eno, the president of the Second National Bank had absconded with over $3 million of the bank's securities. The next day, the Metropolitan National Bank closed its doors when it was learned that its president, George Seney, had used bank funds to speculate in railroad stocks which had declined precipitously in value. On the morning of May 16, A.W. Dimock & Co. failed, while in the afternoon Fisk & Hatch (which was able to reopen after the panic of 1873) followed suit, taking down with it several banks connected with the firm.

The conditions seemed ripe for a full-scale panic, and we see in Panel A of Figure 1.3 the typical pattern associated with a panic of a sharp increase in interest rates, especially for call loans, a sharp decline in stock prices (over 8% in May). and a sharp rise the interest rate spread. However, a panic of the 1873 magnitude was avoided by the timely action of the New York Clearing House Association. On the afternoon of May 14, the New York Clearing House met and approved the issue of clearing house certificates to the Metropolitan National Bank. The bank was thereby enabled to resume operations the next day and was reorganized with a new president. In addition. the Second National Bank was able to meet all payments because the father of the bank's president repaid the funds stolen by his son. The net result was that the bank panic subsided and there was no general suspension of specie payments in the banking system. In the aftermath of the financial crisis, we see the usual pattern that interest rates decline along with the interest rate spread. We also see a pattern that was found after the 1873 panic: the interest rate spread rose again after the decline immediately following the panic. The continuing deflation which caused a deterioration of firms' balance sheet positions and continuation of the recession which increased uncertainty help explain this rise in the interest rate spread.

THE PANIC OF 1890

The panic of 1890, like that of 1884, was only a minor crisis, in large part because of the swift action by the Clearing House Association. In Figure 1.5, we see the usual pattern of stock prices, the interest rate spread and interest rates before the panic in November 1890. Interest rates begin to rise and the stock market begins to fall several months before the panic, and at the same time the interest rate spread begins to widen. On November 7, the Bank of England raised its discount rate from five to six percent which created concern in the New York money market. Heavy selling in the London stock market on November 10 was followed by substantial declines in stock prices in New York, and at 2 P.M. the failure of Decker, Howell & Co. was announced, which also involved the Bank of North America. The Clearing House Association then immediately decided to issue clearing-house certificates, although this action did not become known until after the close of business on the eleventh, Although the next day the brokerage firm of J.C. Walcott & Co. suspended and the North River Bank closed, confidence was restored with the knowledge that clearing-house certificates were being issued. When knowledge of Baring Brothers & Co.'s failure in London reached New York early on November 15, stocks fell sharply. However, despite almost thirty failures of brokerage houses, a major panic was avoided. The rise in the interest rate spread was quite small and by the end of November when Wall Street recognized that the Bank

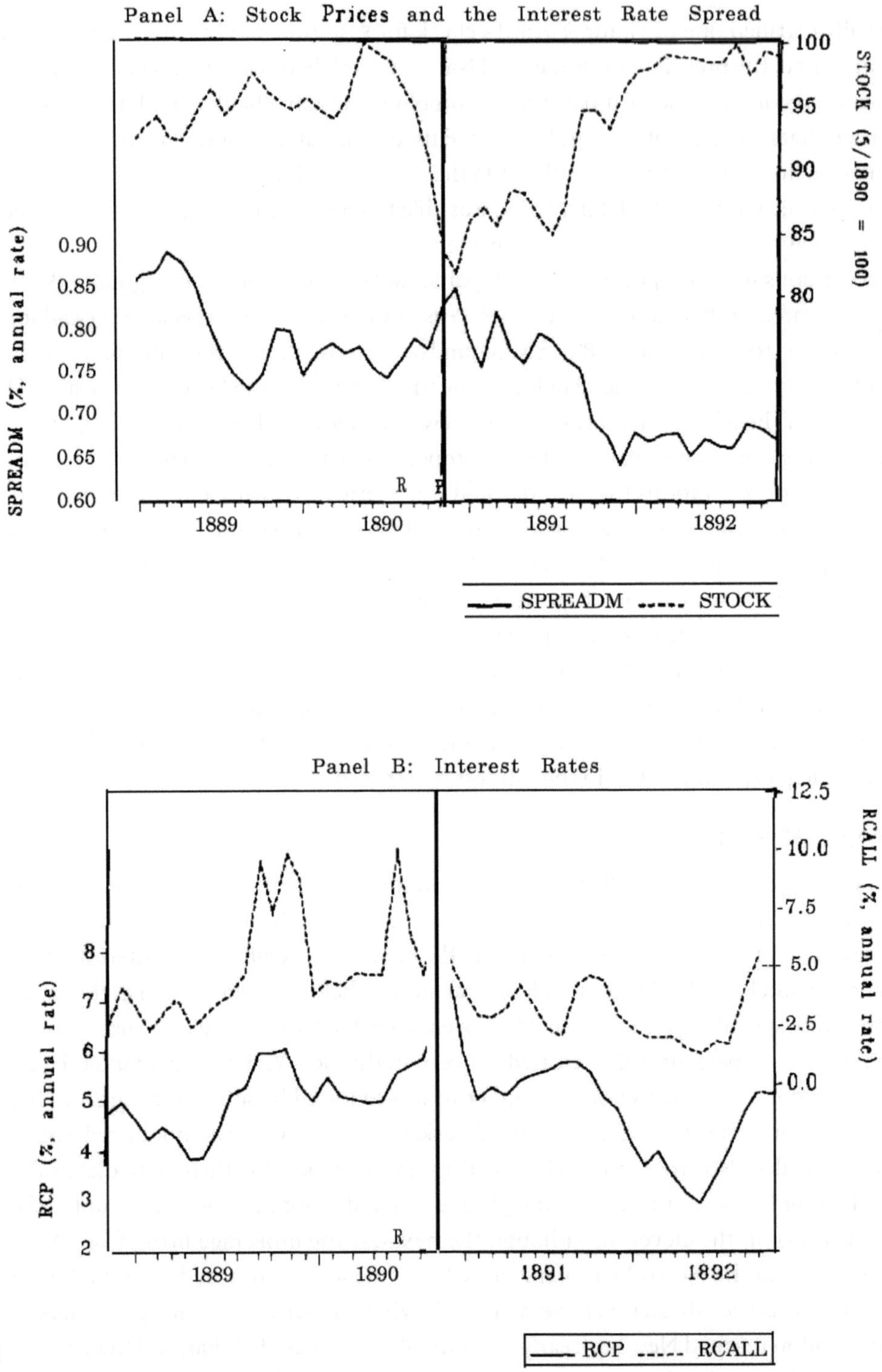

FIGURE 1.5 The Panic of 1890

of England and a syndicate of bankers were providing support to the London money market, stock prices were recovering. The banking system weathered the panic nicely and was able to continue full payments of specie to their depositors. After December, the commercial paper rate declined along with the interest rate spread. The recession, which lasted until May 1891. remained a mild one.

THE PANIC OF 1893

The panic of 1893, in contrast to the two previous panics of 1884 and 1890. was a severe one. As we can see in Figure 1.6, after the onset of the recession in February 1893, interest rates rose and the stock market began to decline. Business conditions were very unsettled and nonfinancial business failures were substantial. Sprague (1910) reports that the number and the amount of liabilities of mercantile failures in the period from January to July 1893 were unprecedented. In addition, deflation had set in at the beginning of the year which was producing a deterioration in business firms' net worth. Given the climb in interest rates and fall in stock prices, along with uncertainty about the health of business firms and the deterioration in firms' balance sheets, the adverse selection and agency problems began to increase and the spread between interest rates on high versus low quality borrowers began to rise, as is indicated by the increase in the interest rate spread variable.

On February 26, the Philadelphia and Reading Railroad went into receivership, but more importantly on May 4 the stock market received word of the failure of the National Cordage Co., a stock market favorite, and a stock market crash ensued. At this stage of the crisis, the New York banks appeared to be weathering the crisis. However, banks in the West and the South. who were burdened with many problem loans, began to face bank runs and in June this led to substantial withdrawal of funds by these banks from the banks in New York. Although the wave of bank failures was subsiding by the beginning of July, a second wave of panic hit the western and southern banks in the third week of July. On July 25, the New York, Lake Erie & Western Railroad and the Wisconsin Marine & Fire Insurance Company suspended and there was another sharp drop in the stock market. The bank panics in the South and West, the resulting withdrawals by these banks from the New York banks, and the loss of confidence in the New York banks meant that they too would succumb to the crisis despite provisions by the Clearing House Association to issue loan certificates early on. Finally, by the beginning of August there was a general suspension of specie payments to bank depositors.

The contraction of lending by the banking system as a result of its troubles reduced its role in solving adverse selection and agency problems and clearly made these problems worse in the financial markets. The seriousness of these asymmetric information problems is reflected in the high values of the interest rate spread variable in Panel A, which peaked in August 1893. Our asymmetric information analysis indicates that the events of the 1893 panic were then a major factor in the very severe economic contraction that occurred from February 1893 to June 1894. Sobel (1968) reports that besides the over 600 bank failures as a result of the panic (five percent of American banks). there were over 15,000 commercial bankruptcies which included

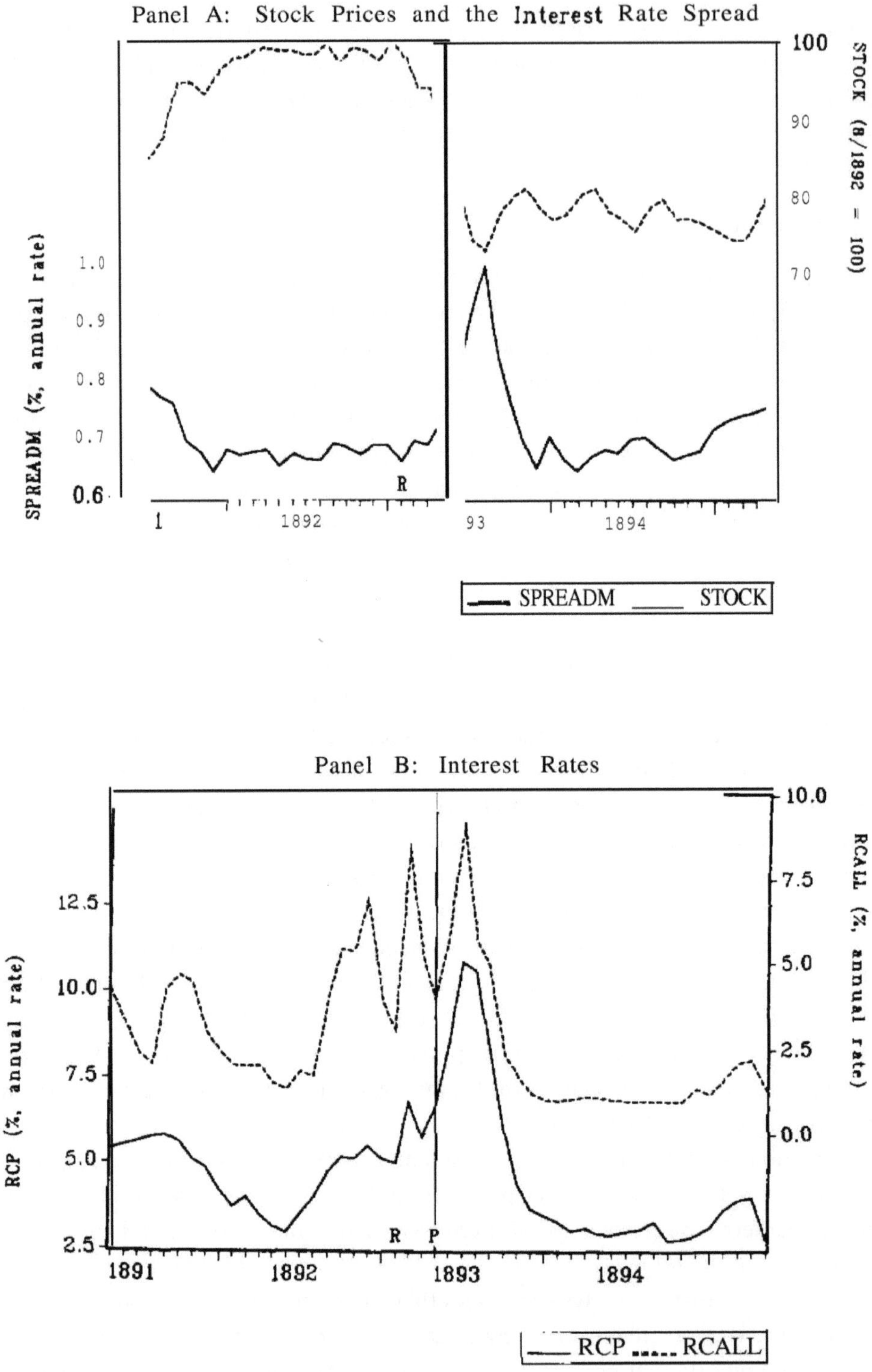

FIGURE 1.6 The Panic of 1893

such prominent railroads as the Northern Pacific, the Atchison, Topeka & Santa Fe, and the New York & New England.

THE 1896 PANIC

Little seems to be written about the panic of 1896, but since Gorton (1987) includes it in his listing of bank panics, the data surrounding his date for the panic in October 1896 is reported in Figure 1.7. The data show the typical patterns found in the other panics. Interest rates rise and stock market prices fall several months prior to the panic date, and as our asymmetric information story indicates, there is also a rise in the interest rate spread variable. After the panic subsides, interest rates and the interest rate spread fall, while stock prices recover. Another typical pattern is that the panic occurs after the onset of the recession in January 1896, which ends in June 1897. Both the panic and the recession are mild ones, and there is no suspension of specie payments as in the panic of 1893.

THE PANIC OF 1907

The panic of October 1907 was one of the more severe panics discussed in this paper. The traditional story about the beginning of this panic, for example in Sprague (1910), Collman (1931). Friedman and Schwartz (1963) and Sobel (1968), emphasizes the difficulties of a group of banks associated with F.A. Heinze, C.F. Morse, and E.R. and O.F. Thomas, who used them to finance their speculative activities. Their grand scheme was to establish a corner in the United Copper Company, which they owned, and to make a killing by squeezing the short sellers. When they suffered large losses with the collapse of the corner on Monday, October 14, the eight banks associated with their activities came under suspicion and were forced to seek assistance from the New York Clearing House Association during that week. By Monday, October 21, the Clearing House had appeared to put the affairs of these banks in order, when it was learned that the president of the Knickerbocker Trust Company, the third largest trust company in New York, was involved with Morse's investment activities. The distrust of Knickerbocker Trust resulted in unfavorable clearing balances and the National Bank of Commerce announced that it would no longer continue to clear for Knickerbocker Trust on the following day, October 22. The Clearing House Association did not extend assistance to Knickerbocker Trust, and this is generally viewed as having been a serious mistake. The ensuing run on Knickerbocker Trust forced the bank to close its doors on October 22. The following day, a run began on the second largest trust company, the Trust Company of America, and on October 24, the Lincoln Trust Company was also subjected to a run. Although these trust companies were provided with assistance, the steps taken were too slow and were not sufficiently dramatic to restore confidence, as Sprague (1910) and Friedman and Schwartz (1963) indicate. The stock market crashed on October 24 and the monthly return for October 1907 was –10.9% the thirty-first largest negative return for the 1834–1988 period documented by Wilson, Sylla and Jones (1990). With the assistance of J.P. Morgan, $35 million was raised by the end of the week to assist the Trust Company of America and the bank panic in New York seemed to be under control. By now, however. fear had spread

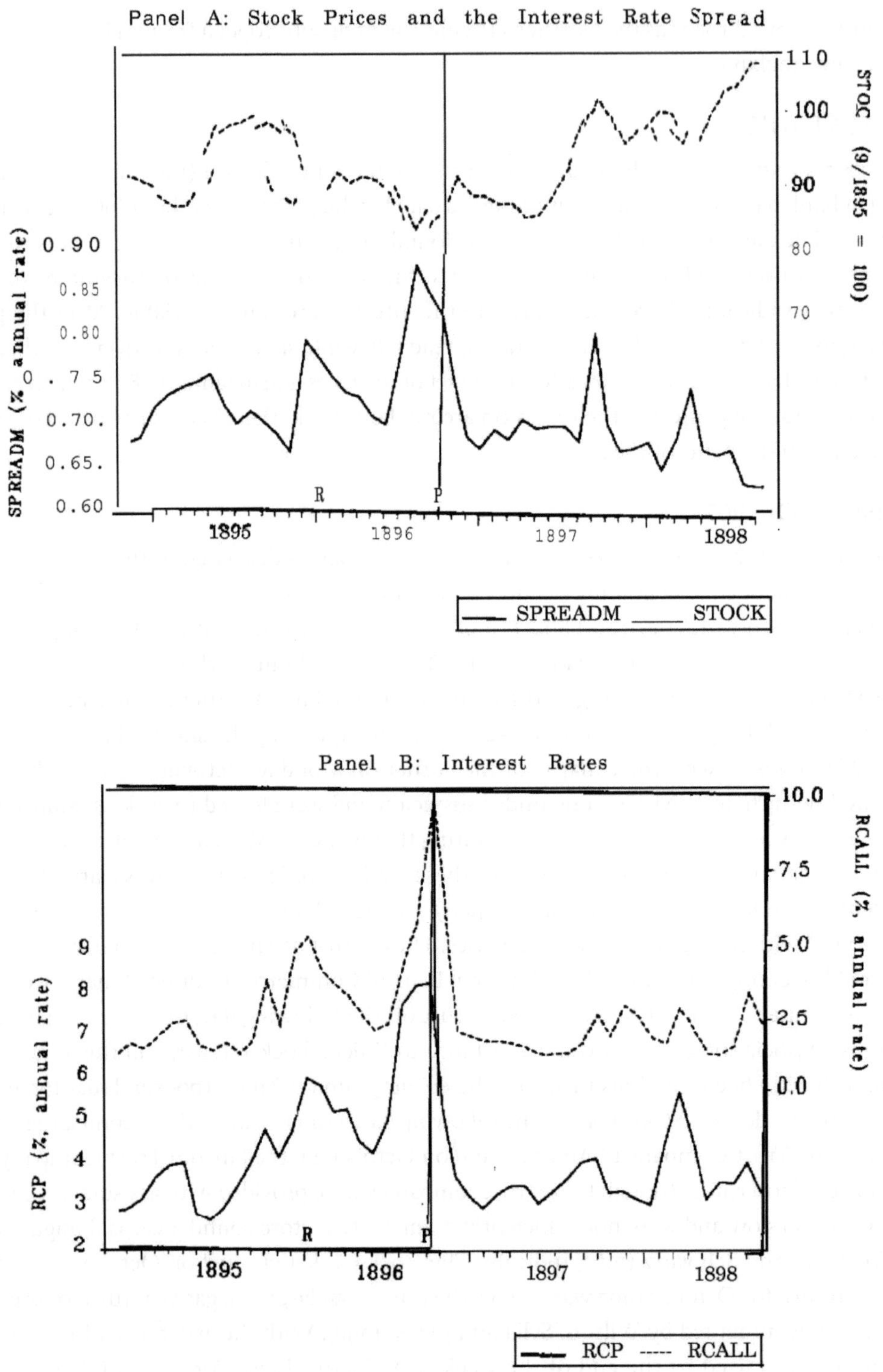

FIGURE 1.7 The Panic of 1896

throughout the United States, and country banks withdrew large amounts of funds from their New York correspondent banks. Only when the situation was grave for the New York banks did the Clearing House Association finally issue clearing-house loan certificates on October 26. This action was too late because the New York banks still suspended payments of specie to depositors and the suspension of specie payments then spread nationwide. Payments of specie to depositors was not resumed until the beginning of January 1908.

The traditional story about the 1907 panic places much of the responsibility on securities manipulation and inadequate action by the Clearing House Association to prevent a major disruption of the banking system. Friedman and Schwartz (1963) view the substantial decline in the money supply that followed the panic to have turned a mild recession into the severe recession extending from June 1907 to June 1908. The data in Figure 1.8 suggest that there may be more to the story. The most striking feature of the data, as can be seen in Panel A, is the substantial increase in the interest rate spread variable that begins in early 1907, six months before the panic. Indeed, most of the rise in the spread variable has already occurred by the time of the October banking panic. As can be seen in Panel A, the banking panic apparently raised the interest rate spread higher and helped prolong its high values in the first half of 1908, but most of the rise cannot be attributed to the bank panic itself.

The rise in the spread variable before the bank panic is easily explained by our asymmetric information story. The stock market begins to decline starting at the end of 1906, and the negative return in March of −9.8% is the fortieth largest negative return in the 1834-1988 period. Before the panic begins in October, the stock market has declined even further, by twenty-five percent from its peak in late 1906. As we have discussed previously, the decline in the valuation of firms by this substantial amount raises adverse selection and agency problems for borrowing firms because it has in effect lowered their net worth.

The onset of the recession in June 1907 before the panic, which raised uncertainty about the quality of firms' investment projects, also increased the adverse selection problem. In addition, the rise in the commercial paper rate starting in June of 1907 from 5.4% to 6.8% by September, further worsened the potential for adverse selection. The resulting increases in the degree of asymmetric information problems, even before the October banking panic, should raise the spread between interest rates for high and low-quality borrowers and hence the SPREADM variable. Indeed, since most of the rise in the commercial paper rate and decline in the stock market has already occurred before the onset of the panic. not surprisingly most of the rise in the SPREADM variable has already occurred. The presence of severe asymmetric information problems, even before the banking panic, suggests that they were also potentially important factors in creating a severe business cycle contraction. The decline in the money supply resulting from the bank panics is almost surely another important factor in the severity of the contraction, but the evidence here suggests that it is far from being the whole story.

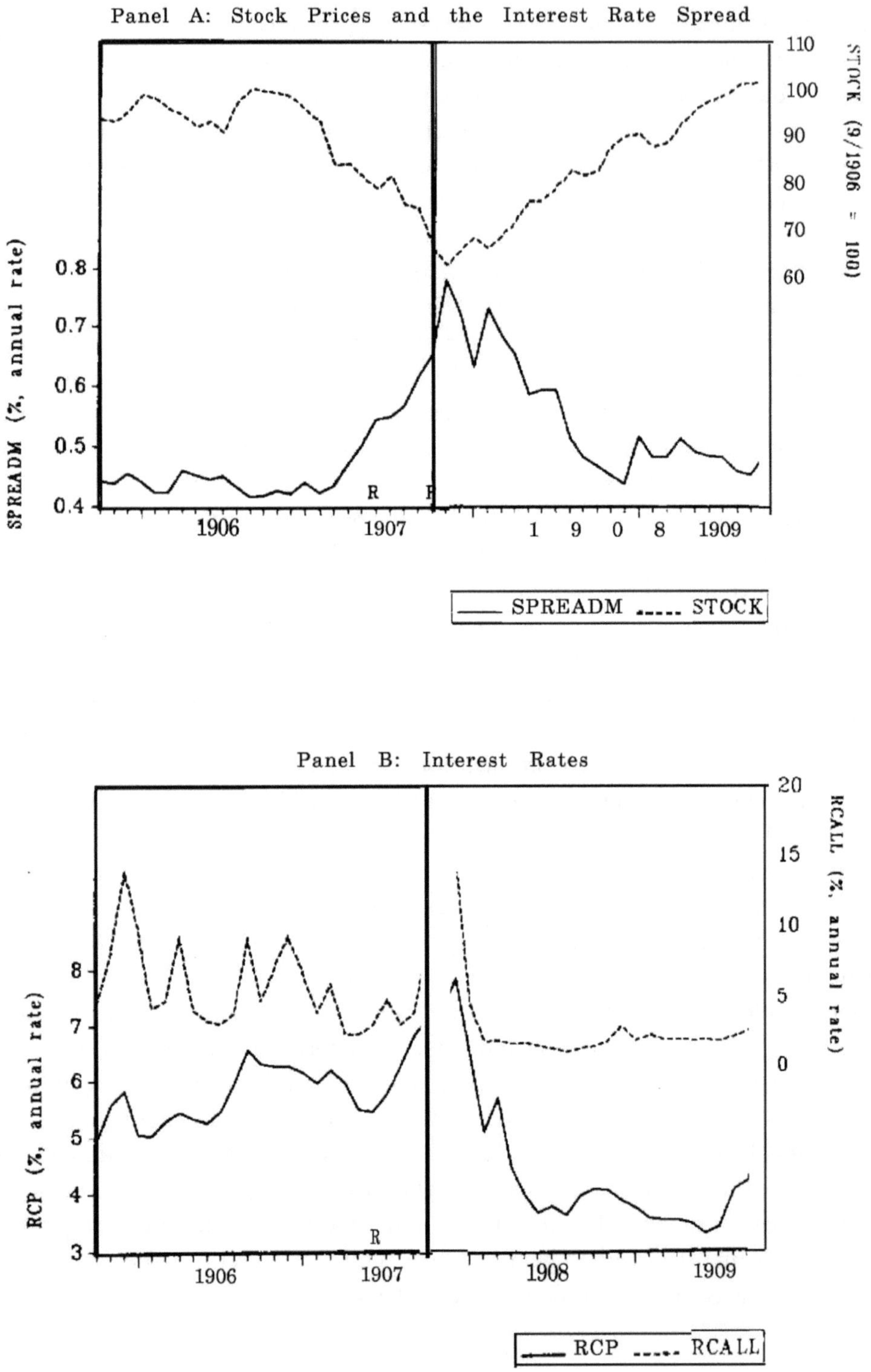

FIGURE 1.8 The Panic of 1907

THE GREAT DEPRESSION PERIOD

A major difference for the Great Depression period from other periods of financial panic analyzed above is the presence of the Federal Reserve System. which began its operations in 1914. Although the Great Depression is dated by the NBER as beginning in September 1929, the public always associates the beginning of the Depression with the stock market crash of October 1929. The outcome of the panic period starting October 23 and culminating in the crash on October 29 was a negative return for the month of October of close to 20%. This was the largest monthly negative return in the stock market up to that time. The data in Figure 9, however, indicate that this financial panic differed substantially from those in previous periods.

Because of the large swing in the interest rate spread variable in the 1929-35 period, it is hard to discern its movements in the early phase of the Great Depression in Panel A. Thus, an extra panel, Panel C, has been added to Figure 1.9 that shows the stock price and interest rate spread data for the 1929-30 period. In the panels of Figure 1.9, "C" marks the October 1929 stock market crash, "P1" the first banking panic of November 1930, "P2" he second banking panic of March 1931, "P3" Britain's departure from gold in September 1931, and "PHI" the bank holiday of March 1933.

As we have seen in our analysis of previous panics, the usual pattern is for a stock market crash to be accompanied by a sharp rise in both the level of interest rates and the interest rate spread. Although in Panel C of Figure 1.9 there is some rise in the interest rate spread when the crash occurs, the increase is fairly small. In addition, Panel B indicates that interest rates did not rise, the commercial paper rate held steady, while call loan rates even fell. Although the stock market crash had such a great impact on the minds of a whole generation, it does not appear to have developed into a full fledged financial crisis as in the other episodes we have examined. The credit for this development goes to the prompt action by the Federal Reserve Bank of New York to provide reserves to the New York banks. During the panic period. banks and lenders outside of New York rushed to liquidate their call loans to brokers. In order to keep market conditions from getting more unsettled, the Federal Reserve Bank of New York, as described by its president, George L. Harrison, kept its "discount window wide open and let it be known that member banks might borrow freely to establish the reserve required against the large increase in deposits resulting from the taking over of loans called by others." In addition, the New York Fed made open market purchases of $ 160 million during this period, even though this amount was far in excess of what was authorized by the Federal Reserve System's Open Market Investment Committee.

In the aftermath of the New York Fed's action to provide sufficient liquidity for the economy is a decline of the interest rate spread to levels below those before the stock market crash and a continuing low level up until October 1930. What is quite remarkable about the level of the interest rate spread before October 1930 is that it remains so low despite the sharp economic contraction up to that point and the over 40% decline in the value of common stocks. Friedman and Schwartz (1963) state that, from the peak in August 1929 through October 1930, industrial

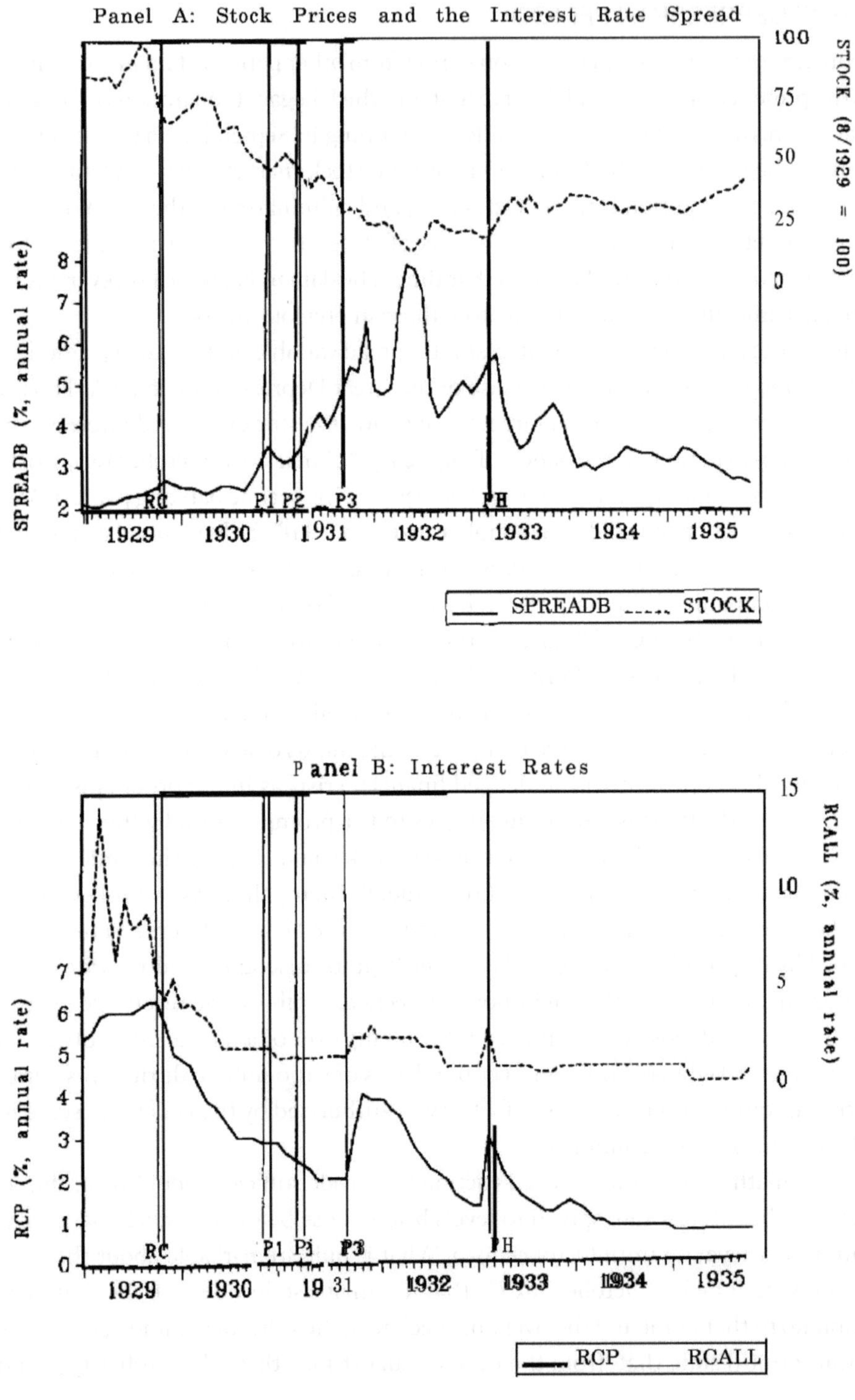

FIGURE 1.9 The Great Depression

Panel C: Stack Prices and the Interest Rate Spread 1/1929 to 2/1931

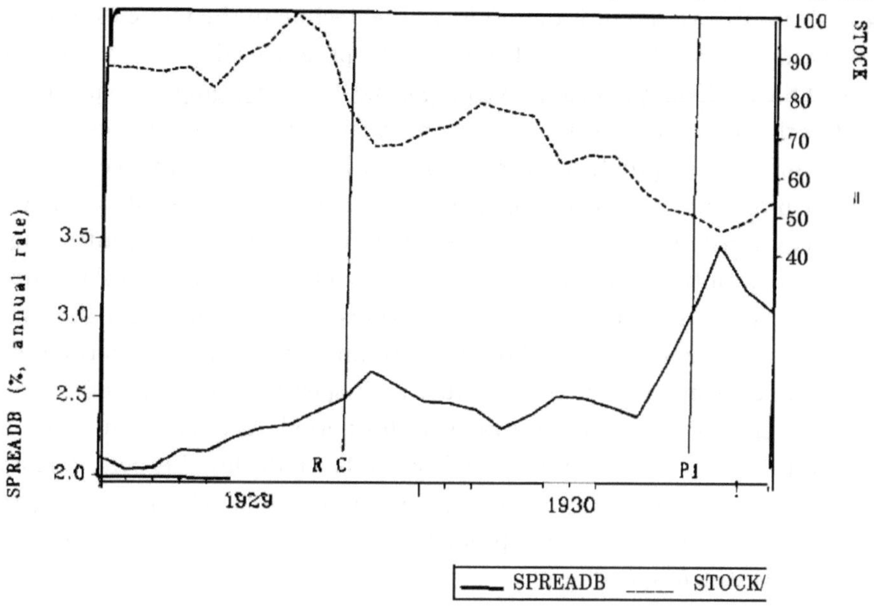

FIGURE 1.9 *(continued)*

production fell 26%, wholesale prices by 14% and personal income by 16%.[12] The failure of the interest rate spread to rise seems to indicate that asymmetric information problems had not yet become severe in financial markets." [13]

Just prior to the first banking panic in November-December 1930, the interest rate spread begins to increase and reaches a temporary peak at the height of the bank panic in December 1930. The first banking panic is described by Friedman and Schwartz (1963) as starting in agricultural regions, where a "contagion of fear spread among depositors" led to the failure of 256 banks with $ 180 million of deposits in November and the failure of 352 banks with over $372 million of deposits in December, including the failure on December 11 of the Bank of United States with over $200 million in deposits. Friedman and Schwartz (1963) viewed the nature of the economic contraction as changing at this stage. The continuing bank panics, which by the time of the Banking Holiday in March 1933 had reduced the number of banks by over a third, was the unique feature of the Great Depression period that they saw as the force behind a steep but normal recession turning into the largest economic contraction ever experienced in U.S. history.

12 Friedman and Schwartz (1963), page 339.

13 The failure of the interest rate spread to rise also casts some doubt on the story put forward by Romer (1988) that the initial severity of the Great Depression may have resulted from increased uncertainty. Since such uncertainty should increase adverse selection and thereby increase the interest rate spread. and yet this does not seem to happen before October 1930, it is not at all clear that uncertainty rose appreciably in this period.

An asymmetric information analysis of the Great Depression, first outlined in Bernanke (1983), agrees with this view, but it does not see the decline in the money supply resulting from the banking panics as being the sole cause of the prolonged depression.[14] Instead it sees the collapse of the banking system as preventing banks from engaging in financial intermediation activities that would reduce asymmetric information problems. The resulting increase in asymmetric information problems in credit markets led to a decline in investment by those with otherwise profitable investment opportunities. Further, the debt-deflation in which the decline in prices transfers resources from debtors to creditors and the continuing decline in the stock market until the middle of 1932 led to a deterioration infirms' balance sheets, which increased adverse selection and agency problems so that lending decreased and hence investment fell. In addition, as pointed out by Mishkin (1978) a similar deterioration in the balance sheets of consumers led them to reduce their spending. A further effect could have come from the behavior of real interest rates in this period. As is shown in Mishkin (1981), although nominal interest rates on high-quality bonds fell during this period, real interest rates climbed to exceedingly high levels during the 1931-33 period.[15] The high level of real interest rates increased the adverse selection problem in credit markets and is one further reason for a decline in investment spending.

All of these effects helped make the Great Depression the most severe in U.S. history. Consistent with this story is the increase in the spread variable to unprecedented levels. By the middle of 1932, the spread between interest rates on corporate Baa and Treasury bonds had risen to above 7.5%, over 5 percentage points higher than the level before October 1930. Indeed, it was not until the end of 1936, that the spread variable falls to levels below those found before October 1930. The fact that the spread between interest rates for low versus high-quality borrowers remained so high for so long indicates that asymmetric information problems were severe in this period. The continuing severity of asymmetric information problems provides an explanation for why the Great Depression was so prolonged.

The fact that aggregate output remained so far below its potential for such a long period of time has always been a puzzle for neoclassical analysis. Bernanke's (1983) documentation of the disruption of the credit markets during the 1931-35 period and the attendant asymmetric information problems provides one explanation. An overlooked fact, however, is that another financial crisis appears to have occurred in the 1937-38 period. From its peak in February 1937 until its trough in March 1938, the stock market declined by over 50%. Indeed, four of the largest

---

14 Also see Hamilton (1987).

15 Hamilton (1987) disputes the view that real interest rates were high during this period because he finds that futures prices in commodity markets were not indicating an expected deflation in this period. Mishkin (1990), however, demonstrates that futures prices in commodity markets are not capable of informing us about expected inflation for aggregate price indices. Cecchetti (1989) using additional evidence also criticizes Hamilton's position that the deflation in this period was not anticipated. More rccent work by Hamilton (1990) is more favorable to the view that real interest rates rose during the 1931-33 period. Indeed, an interesting finding in the Hamilton paper is that substantial anticipated deflation and hence high real rates did not occur until late 1930 and this is exactly when we start to see evidence that serious asymmetric information problems are beginning to appear in the U.S. economy.

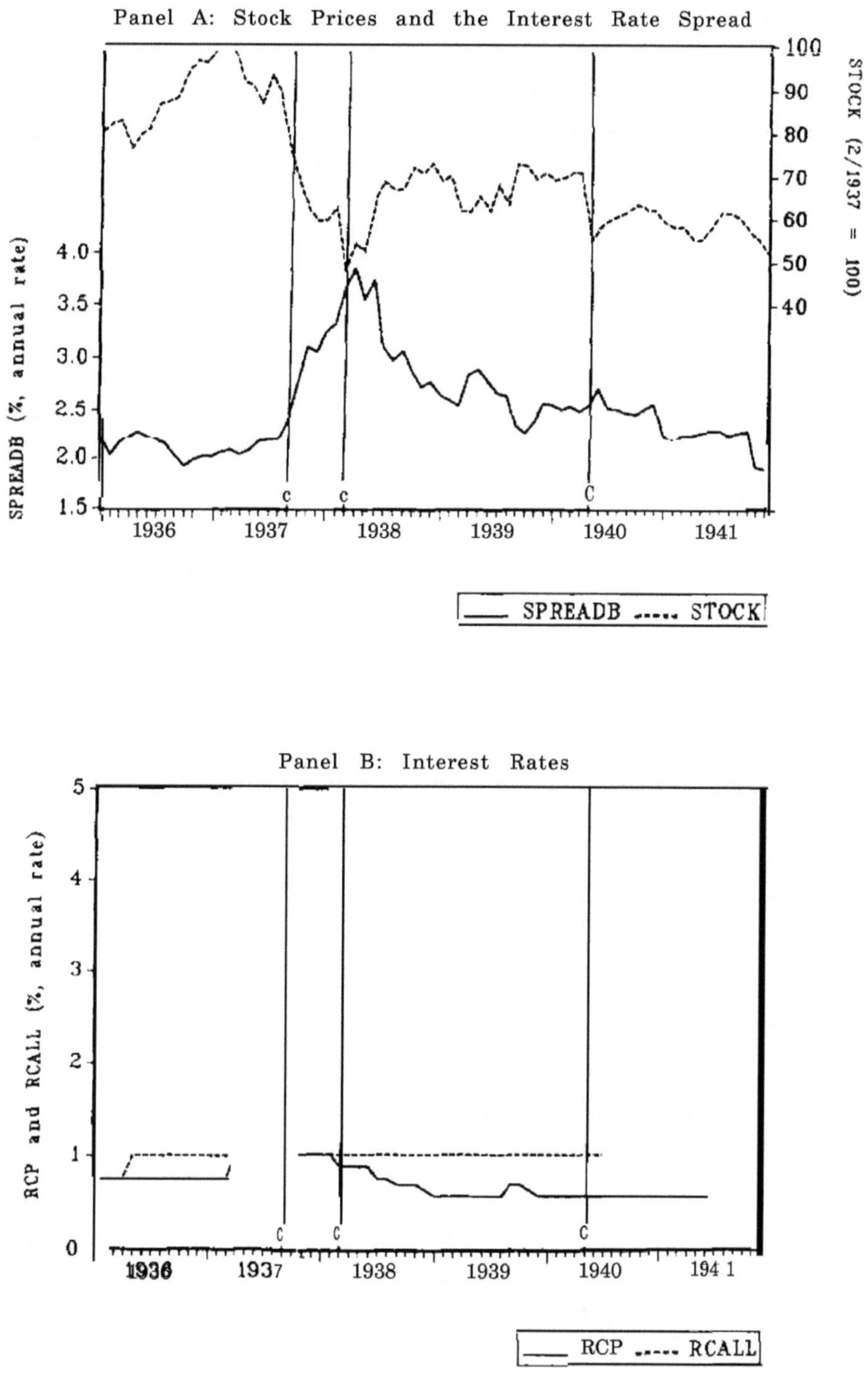

FIGURE 1.10 The 1936–41 Period

fifty negative monthly returns in the 1834 to 1988 period tabulated by Wilson, Sylla and Jones (1990) are found in this one year period. Indeed the stock market return of –23.9% in March 1938 is the second largest negative return (September 1931 is the largest with a return of –29.3%). As we can see in Figure 1.10, which plots the data for the 1936-1941 period, there is another rapid run up of the interest rate spread, which peaks in April 1938, one month after the stock market trough. Indeed in the first half of 1938, the interest rate spread is back at the levels found in 1934. The large spread between interest rates on low and high-quality borrowers suggests that asymmetric information problems were again becoming major in the 1937–38 period, and this helps explain why the economic contraction during this recession was so severe.

The source of the difficulties in financial markets at this time is not absolutely clear. The increase in reserve requirements in August 1936, March 1937 and May 1937 is one possibility, either through its effects on the money supply which declined from March 1937 until May 1938. or by decreasing the ability of the banks to extend loans because of their need to increase the ratio of their reserves to deposits. Regardless of the cause, the financial disruption in 1937-38 may help to explain why the U.S. economy did not really come out of the shadow of the Depression period until World War II.

There is one last episode in the 1936-41 period depicted in Figure 1.10 that deserves some comment. May 1940 has a larger decline in stock market prices than in October 1929. Indeed the negative return of –22.6% in May 1940 is the third largest monthly negative return in the 1834–1988 period. Although the interest rate spread rises in May and June 1940. the magnitude of the rise is very slight and it is also very temporary. The downward trend in the spread variable which started after April 1938 continues after this episode, leading to a spread below 1% by the end of World War II. This illustrates the following important point: a stock market crash by itself does not necessarily imply that a financial crisis has occurred. There is no evidence that there was a serious disruption in financial markets after the May 1940 crash which could have created difficulties for the economy.

AN OVERVIEW OF THE FINANCIAL CRISIS EPISODES

Now that we have analyzed a whole series of financial crises, it is worth asking what do they have in common and what does this tell us about the nature of financial crises. The following facts emerge from our study of episodes in the last half of the nineteenth century and the first half of the twentieth.

1. With one exception in 1873, financial panics always occurred after the onset of a recession.
2. With the same exception in 1873, stock prices decline and the spread between interest rates on low and high-quality bonds rises before the onset of the panic.
3. Many panics seem to have features of a liquidity crisis in which there are substantial increases in interest rates before the panic.

4. The onset of many panics follows a major failure of a financial institution, not necessarily a bank. Furthermore this failure is often the result of financial difficulties experienced by a nonfinancial corporation.
5. The rise in the interest rate spread associated with a panic is typically soon followed by adedine. However, in several cases, most notably after the 1873 panic. the 1907 panic and the Great Depression, the interest rate spread rises again when there is deflation and a severe recession.
6. The most severe financial crises are associated with severe economic contractions. The most severe panic episodes are in 1857. 1873, 1893, 1907 and 1930–33. while 1857–58, 1873–79. 1893–94, 1907–08, and 1929–33 are all considered to be among the most severe economic contractions.
7. Although stock market crashes often appear to be a major factor in creating a financial crisis, this is not always the case. Both the stock market crash in October 1929 and in May 1940 did not have appreciable effects on the interest rate spread. Therefore, the evidence that there was a serious disruption in financial markets after these crashes is weak.

There are several conclusions that can be drawn from the facts listed above. The timing and the pattern of the data in the episodes studied here seem to fit an asymmetric information interpretation of financial crises. Rather than starting with bank panics, most of the financial crises begin with a rise in interest rates, a stock market decline and the widening of the interest rate spread. Furthermore, a financial panic frequently is immediately preceded by a major failure of a financial firm which increases uncertainty in the marketplace. The increase in uncertainty and the rise in interest rates would magnify the adverse selection-lemons problem in the credit markets, while the decline in the stock market increases agency as well as adverse selection problems, both of which are reflected in the rise in the spread between interest rates for low and high-quality borrowers. The increase in adverse selection and agency problems would then lead to a decline in investment activity and aggregate economic activity.

Depositors would now want to withdraw their funds from the banking system because the poor business conditions would lead them to expect losses on deposits left in the banks. The resulting bank panic would raise interest rates further, cause the stock market to decline even more and worsen agency and adverse selection problems even more in the credit markets. This would further encourage a severe economic contraction.

Finally, there would be a sorting out of solvent from insolvent firms by bankruptcy proceedings and sorting out of solvent from insolvent banks, often with the help of public authorities and clearing house associations. The panic would then subside, the stock market might undergo a recovery, interest rates would fall, and if economic uncertainty and deflation were not too severe. adverse selection and agency problems would diminish, leading to a decline in the interest rate spread variable and setting the stage for an eventual recovery of the economy. This process might get short circuited if a substantial deflation sets in, leading to a debt-deflation process which transfers resources from debtors to creditors, thereby leading to a deterioration in business firms' net worth. The deterioration of firms' balance sheet position would then lead to increased asymmetric information problems, reflected by a continuation of a large spread between interest rates for low and high-quality borrowers. Investment spending and aggregate economic activity would then remain depressed for a prolonged period of time.

A monetarist interpretation of financial panics cannot explain the events and their timing as effectively as the asymmetric information approach because the monetarist view does not explain why the spread between interest rates for high and low-quality borrowers rises dramatically before the panic and then declines after the panic subsides. However, the asymmetric information story does not rule out important consequences on aggregate economic activity from the decline in the money supply that a banking panic produces. It just suggests that there is more to the story of a financial crisis than its affects on the money supply.

A monetarist explanation of financial panics is also not able to explain the timing of banking panics, that is, why they occurred when they did. The facts about the panic episodes discussed in this paper are entirely consistent with Gorton's (1987) view that bank panics are predictable. His analysis also depends on asymmetric information because he sees a bank panic as occurring as a result of the inability of depositors to evaluate the risk in individual bank liabilities and so they cannot easily screen out good from bad banks. Hence when aggregate information such as high interest rates, a major failure of a corporation, or weak business conditions stemming from a recession occurs, depositors worry about potential losses on their deposits and withdraw funds from the banking system, precipitating a panic. Gorton (1987) finds that unanticipated changes in the liabilities of failed businesses is the best predictive variable for the occurrence of a bank panic. The analysis in this paper suggests that since stock market declines and widening of the interest rate spread often precede bank panics, stock price and interest rate spread variables, which were not used in Gorton's (1987) analysis. might also appreciably help in the prediction of bank panics.

The successful intervention of the New York Clearing House Association in the 1884 and 1890 episodes and the New York Federal Reserve Bank during the October 1929 stock market crash illustrate how an effective lender-of-last resort role can minimize the impact of a financial crisis on the economy. We now turn to two postwar episodes of financial disturbances in which the Federal Reserve actively performed this role even though the banking system was not directly threatened.

IV. TWO POSTWAR EPISODES OF FINANCIAL DISTURBANCES

The postwar period differs from the pre-World War II period in one important respect. Since 1945. the banking system has not been subjected to a banking panic and in no instance has there been a financial crisis that has had serious adverse consequences for the aggregate economy. Examining episodes of financial disturbances in the postwar period in which banking panics were not an issue should be particularly instructive because the monetarist interpretation does not view them as real financial crises. However, if we do find that these financial disturbances have many of the same patterns in the data as prewar financial crises and thus appear to exhibit the potential for serious asymmetric information problems in credit markets, this would lend additional support to the asymmetric information approach to financial crises. Two episodes, the Penn Central bankruptcy of June 1970 and the stock market crash of October 19, 1987, are postwar examples of financial disturbances in which banking panics were not an issue. In both episodes the Federal Reserve actively provided liquidity to a specific financial sector outside of the banking system and thus engaged in a broader lender-of-last resort role.

THE PENN CENTRAL BANKRUPTCY

Prior to 1970, commercial paper was considered one of the safest money market instruments because only corporations with very high credit ratings issued it. It was common practice for corporations to continually roll over their commercial paper, that is, issue new commercial paper to pay off to be old, Penn Central Railroad was a major issuer of commercial paper, with more than $200 million outstanding, but by May 1970 it was on the verge of bankruptcy and it requested federal government assistance from the Nixon administration.[16] Despite administration support for a bailout of Penn Central, after six weeks of debate Congress decided not to pass bailout legislation. Meanwhile, the Nixon administration asked the Board of Governors to authorize a direct loan from the Federal Reserve Bank of New York Fed to Penn Central. However, on Thursday, June 18, the New York Fed informed the Board of Governors that its staff studies indicated that Penn Central would not be able to repay the loan, and as a result the Board decided not to authorize the loan. Without this loan, Penn Central was forced to declare bankruptcy on Sunday, June 21.

Once the Federal Reserve made the decision to let Penn Central go into bankruptcy, it was concerned that Penn Central's default on its commercial paper would, as Brimmer (1989) puts it, have had a "chilling effect on the commercial paper market" (p. 6), making it impossible for other corporations to roll over their commercial paper. The Penn Central bankruptcy, then, had the potential for sending other companies into bankruptcy which, in turn, might have triggered further bankruptcies—leading to a full-scale financial panic. To avoid this scenario, the New York Fed got in touch with a number of large money center banks on Saturday and Sunday, June 20 and 21, alerted them to the impending Penn Central bankruptcy on June 22, encouraged them to lend to their customers who were unable to roll over their commercial paper, and indicated that the discount window would be made available to the banks so that they could make these loans.[17] Indeed, the banks did as they were told and made these loans, receiving as much as $575 million through the discount window for this purpose. In addition, on June 22 the Fed decided to suspend Regulation Q ceilings on deposits of $100,000 and over in order to keep short-term interest rates from rising, and the formal vote was taken the next day to allow the FDIC and the

16 See Maisel (1973) and Brimmer (1989) for further discussion of the Penn Central bankruptcy episode.
17 It is noteworthy that when the Fed advanced discount loans to banks lending to customers who needed to role over their commercial paper, the banks were told that they would be responsible for the credit risk involved in this lending. See Brimmer (1989), page 6.

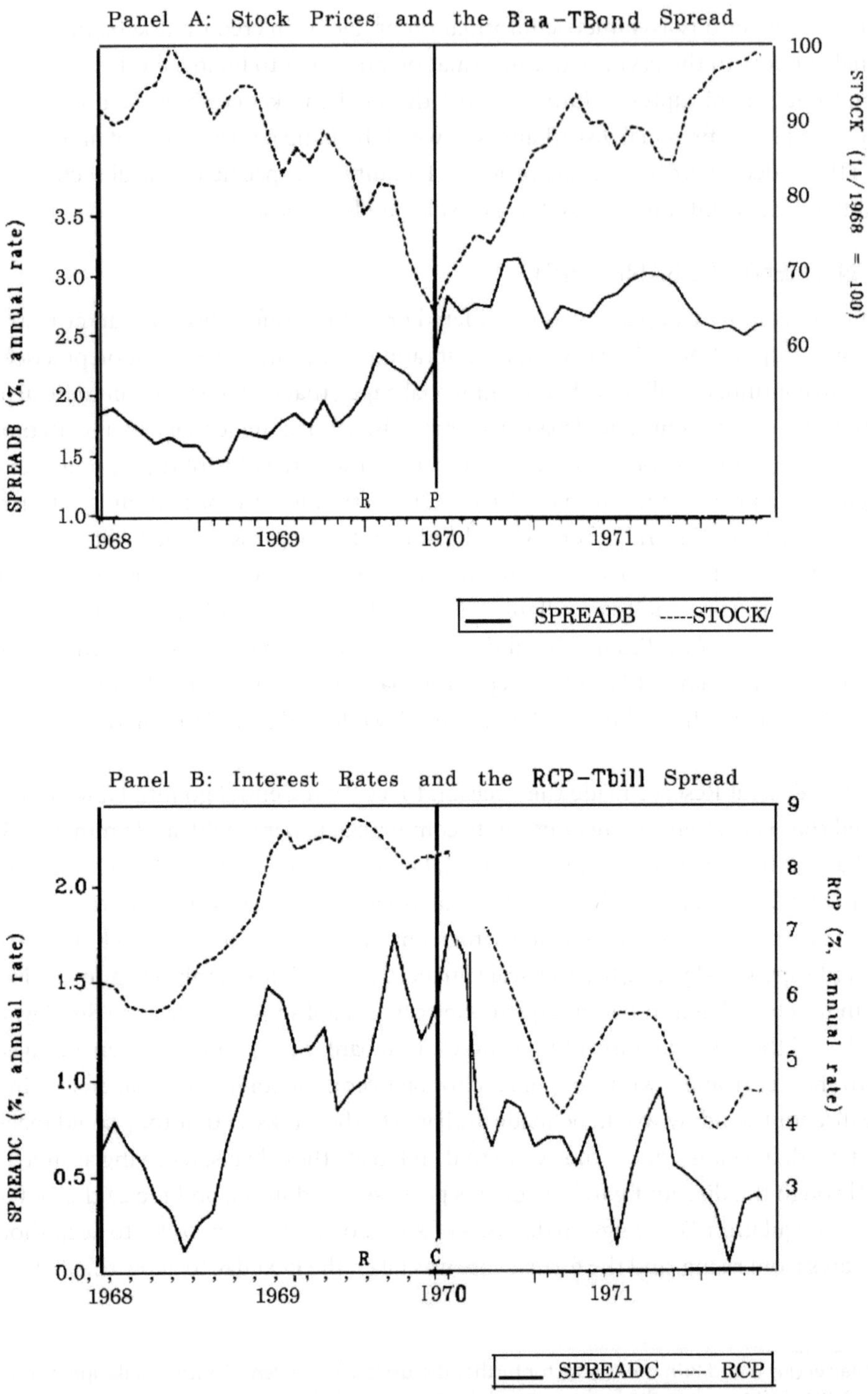

FIGURE 1.11 The Penn Central Bankruptcy

FHLBB to take parallel action. The net result was that the Federal Reserve provided liquidity so that the commercial paper market would keep functioning.

The rationale for the Fed's action was that lenders would not be able to screen out good borrowers in this market from bad borrowers. Was this rationale plausible? The data in Figure 1.11 are suggestive that it was. Panel A has the same format as previous figures, with the onset of the recession in January 1970 marked with an "R", the Penn Central bankruptcy date marked by a "P", and data on the stock market and the SPREADB interest rate spread variable. Panel B contains data on the commercial paper rate and on the interest rate spread between commercial paper (4-6 month) and the six month Treasury bill, denoted by SPREADC (replacing the rate on call loans, which were no longer a major element in money markets).

The data in Panel A display the typical pattern that we saw for prewar financial crises. The high level of interest rates reached in late 1969-early 1970 and the increase in uncertainty with the onset of the recession in January 1970 are likely to have increased the adverse selection problem in the credit markets. Furthermore, by May 1970 the stock market had declined over 35% from its peak value in November 1969. This decline in the valuation of firms resulted in a decrease in net worth and further increased agency and adverse selection problems in the credit markets. Consistent with the rise in asymmetric information difficulties for the credit markets we do see a rise in both of the interest rate spread variables, SPREADB (for long-term bonds) and SPREADC (for commercial paper). Furthermore, despite the Fed's actions we also see a jump in the interest rate spread variables at the time of the Penn Central bankruptcy in June 1970. The fact that the spread between interest rates on corporate Baa and Treasury bonds, rises along with the commercial paper-Treasury spread variable indicates that the problems in the commercial paper market did have a potential for spreading to other sectors of the capital market. As we saw after other financial disturbances, the interest rate spread does decline after the crisis, and this pattern is especially pronounced for the commercial paper-Treasury spread variable in Panel B, which returns to 1968 levels by the end of 1970. The SPREADB variable, on the other hand, continues to remain high for over two years after the Penn Central bankruptcy. However, the increase in the SPREADB variable resulting from the Penn Central bankruptcy was not large by the standards of earlier financial crises. A major disturbance to the credit markets as a result of increased asymmetric information problems seems to have been avoided by the Fed's willingness to perform its lender-of-last resort function.

THE STOCK MARKET CRASH OF OCTOBER 19, 1987

The causes of the stock market crash are still being hotly debated, but the biggest danger to the economy appears not to have come from the decline in wealth resulting from the crash itself, but rather from the threat to the clearing and settlement system in the stock and futures markets.[18] From the peak on August 25, 1987 until October 16, just prior to the crash, the Dow

18 See the Wall Street Journal (1987) and Brimmer (1989) for a description of the events surrounding the stock market crash.

Jones Industrial Average had declined 17.5%. On Monday, October 19, the market fell by 22.6% (as measured by the DJIA) on record volume of 604 million shares. Although October 19, 1987, dubbed "Black Monday", will go down in history as the largest one-day decline in stock prices to date, it was on Tuesday, October 20, 1987, that financial markets received their worst threat. In order to keep the stock market and the related index futures market functioning in an orderly fashion, brokers needed to extend massive amounts of credit on behalf of their customers for their margin calls. The magnitude of the problem is illustrated by the fact that just two brokerage firms, Kidder, Peabody and Goldman, Sachs, had advanced $1.5 billion in response to margin calls on their customers by noon of October 20. Clearly, brokerage firms as well as specialists were severely in need of additional funds to finance their activities. However, understandably enough, banks were growing very nervous about the financial health of securities firms and so were reluctant to lend to the securities industry at a time when it was most needed.

Upon learning of the plight of the securities industry, Alan Greenspan and E. Gerald Corrigan, the president of the New York Federal Reserve Bank and the Fed official most closely in touch with Wall Street, began to fear a breakdown in the clearing and settlement systems and the collapse of securities firms. To prevent this from occurring, Alan Greenspan announced before the market opened on Tuesday, October 20, the Federal Reserve System's "readiness to serve as a source of liquidity to support the economic and financial system." In addition to this extraordinary announcement, the Fed encouraged key money center banks to lend freely to their brokerage firm customers, and, as in the Penn Central bankruptcy episode, made it clear that it would provide discount loans to banks so that they could make these loans. Again, the banks did as they were told and by October 21 had increased by $7.7 billion their loans to brokers and to individuals to purchase or hold securities, As a result, the markets kept functioning on Tuesday. October 20 and a market rally ensued that day, raising the DJIA by over 100 points (over 5%). This action by the Fed is reminiscent of the actions taken by the Fed during the October 1929 panic period in which it provided liquidity to enable money center banks to take over call loans which had been called by others.

The data for the period surrounding the October stock market crash are found in Figure 1.12. Panels A and B have the same format as those in Figure 1.11, while an additional panel, Panel C, has been added which contains weekly data on interest spread variables for the six months surrounding the crash. Panel C plots an additional series obtained from weekly issues of Barrons. the spread between interest rates on junk bonds (those with ratings below Baa) and Treasury bonds.

The data in Figure 1.12 again display patterns seen in other financial crises. The commercial paper rate had been rising for a year before the stock market crash because of the tight money policy followed by the Fed, while stock prices began a decline over a month earlier. The evidence for increased asymmetric information problems in credit markets before the crash, however, is not particularly strong. The commercial paper-Treasury bill interest rate spread variable, SPREADC, also had been rising for a year before the crash, and yet the junk bond-Treasury and Baa-Treasury spread variables, SPREADJ and SPREADB, did not rise until the stock market crash, when they immediately jumped. Not surprisingly, given that asymmetric information

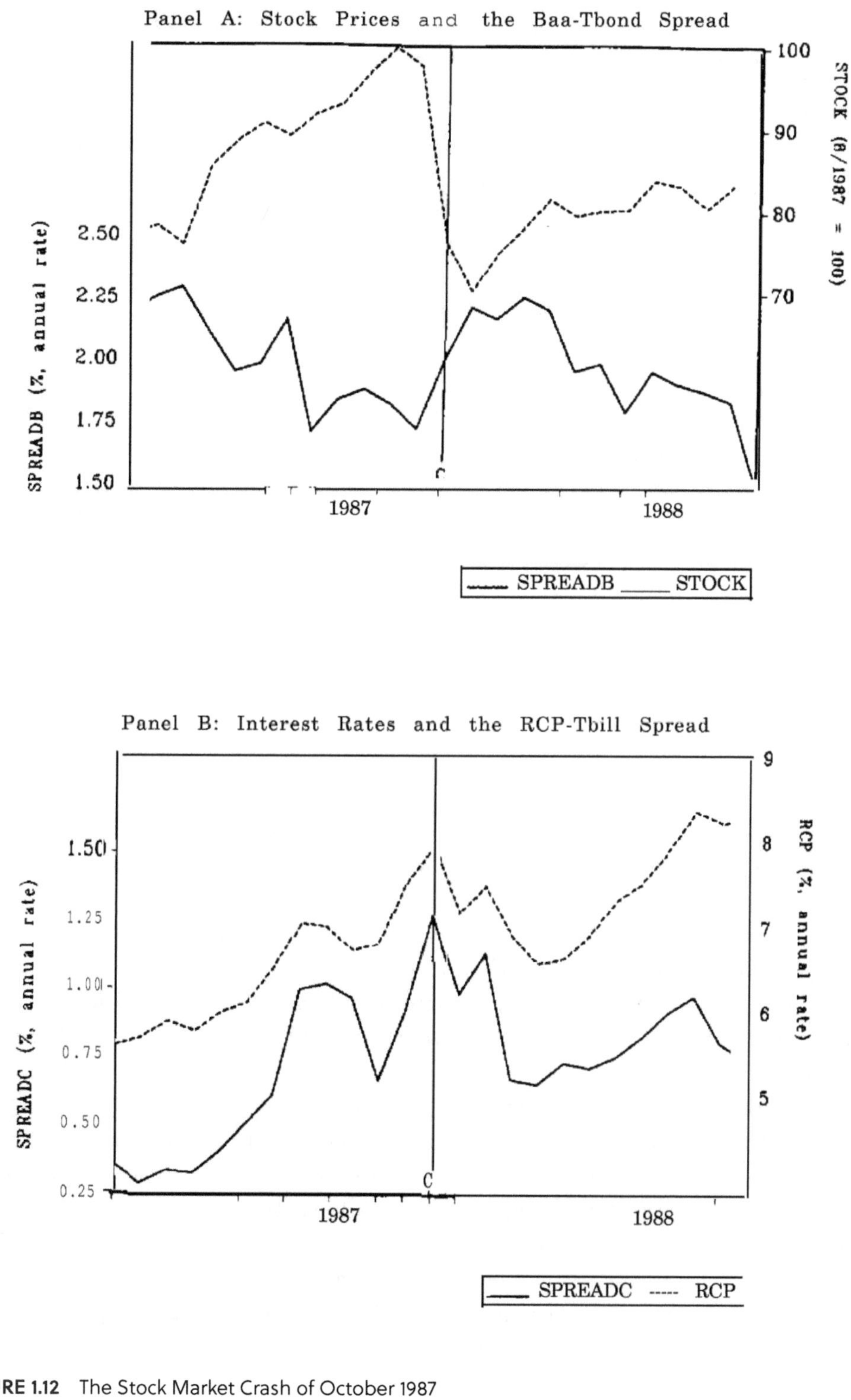

FIGURE 1.12 The Stock Market Crash of October 1987

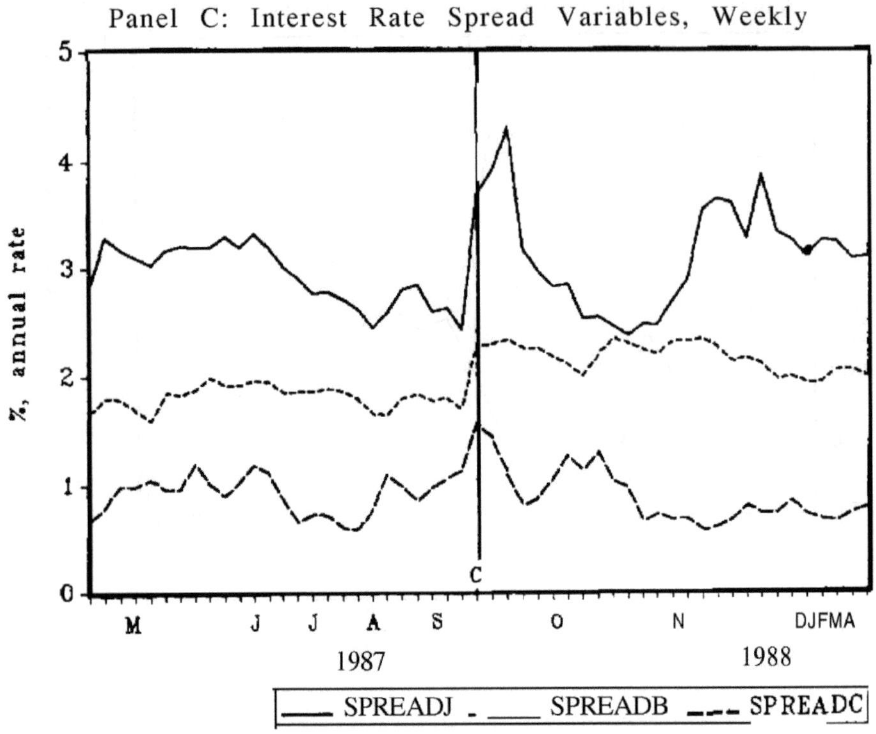

FIGURE 1.12 *(continued)*

effects should impact more on low quality borrowers than on high quality borrowers, the junk bond-Treasury spread shows the largest jump. In the week of the stock market crash, it jumped by 130 basis points (1.3 percentage points) and rose another 60 basis points over the next two weeks. However, as usually occurs after a panic, the junkbond-Treasury spread fell quickly there after and within two months of the crash was back to pre crash levels. The commercial paper-Treasury spread, SPREADC, followed a similar pattern by returning quickly to its pre crash levels, but the Baa-Treasury spread, SPREADB, declined more slowly and only reached its pre crash level six months after the crash.

The fact that the spread variables seem to fit a classic pattern for financial crises suggests that the October 1987 stock market crash did have the potential to create major asymmetric information problems in the credit markets. However, the prompt action by the Fed to perform its lender-of-last resort role kept the asymmetric information problem from getting out of hand, as is indicated by the moderate increase in the Baa-Treasury spread relative to earlier financial panics. The failure to enter a recession after the stock market crash, despite many forecasters predictions along these lines, is consistent with the view that the Fed's actions prevented the development of serious asymmetric information problems in the credit markets.

AN OVERVIEW OF THE POSTWAR EPISODES

The key fact that emerges from the postwar episodes analyzed here is that they both display the typical timing patterns in the data visible in the prewar financial crises, although with a much muted amplitude. This fact suggests that these episodes did have the potential to create a major disturbance to the credit markets by substantially increasing asymmetric information problems. Furthermore, the small magnitude of the effects on the interest rate spread variables suggests that the quick and decisive action by the Federal Reserve to perform a lender-of-last resort role prevented more serious asymmetric information disturbances to the credit markets which could have had significant adverse consequences for the aggregate economy.

V. CONCLUSIONS

The asymmetric information approach to financial crises explains the timing patterns in the data and many features of these crises which are otherwise hard to explain. It also suggests why financial crises have had such important consequences for the aggregate economy over the past one hundred and fifty years. The evidence thus seems to favor an asymmetric information view of financial crises over a monetarist view.

However. the asymmetric information approach can be viewed as complementary to the monetarist view of financial crises since it provides an important transmission mechanism for how banking panics and monetary disturbances affect aggregate economic activity. Yet. the asymmetric information approach does not vie—banking panics and money supply declines as the only financial disturbances that can have serious adverse effects on the aggregate economy. Financial crises have effects over and above those resulting from banking panics and analysis of such episodes as the stock market collapse in the 1937-38 period suggests that a financial crisis which has serious adverse consequences for the economy can develop even if there is no threat to the banking system. The asymmetric information approach also suggests that financial disturbances outside of the banking system in the postwar period have had the potential to have serious adverse effects on the aggregate economy.

This analysis in this paper suggests that there could be benefits to a lender-of-last-resort role for the central bank to provide liquidity to nonbanking sectors of the financial system in which asymmetric information problems have developed. However, there are also potential costs to such an expanded lender-of-last-resort role since it might encourage too much risk taking on the part of nonfinancial corporations. There are thus complex issues in deciding whether an expanded lender-of-last-resort role will on the whole be beneficial and how it should be executed. This is a topic that I plan to pursue in further research.

REFERENCES

Ackerloff, George, "Thc Market for Lemons: Quality Uncertainty and the Market Mechanism," *Ouarterly Journal of Economics* 84 (August 1970): 488–500.

Bernanke, Ben S., "Non-Monetary Effects of the Financial Crisis in the Propagation of the Great Depression," *American Economic Review* 73 (June 1983): 257–76

Bernanke, Ben S. and Mark Gertler, "Agency Costs. Collateral, and Business Fluctuations," *American Economic Review* (1989).

………………………………………………………, "Financial Fragility and Economic Performance," *Ouarterly Journal of Economics* (February 1990).

Bordo. Michael D., "Financial Crises, Banking Crises, Stock Market Crashes and the Money Supply: Some International Evidence, 1870–1933," in F. Capie and G. E. Wood (eds.) *Financial Crises and the World Banking System* (London: MacMillan 1986): 190–248.

Brimmer, Andrew F., "Distinguished Lecture on Economics in Government: Central Banking and Systemic Risks in Capital Markets," *Journal of Economic Perspectives* 3 (Spring 1989): 3–16.

Calomiris, Charles W. and R. Glenn Hubbard, "Price Flexibility, Credit Availability, and Economic Fluctuations: Evidence from the United States, 1894-1909," *The Ouarterly Journal of Economics* 54 (August 1989): 429–52.

………………………………………………………, "Firm Heterogeneity, Internal Finance, and 'Credit Rationing'," *Economic Journal* (March 1990).

Cecchetti, Steven, "Prices During the Great Depression: Was the Deflation of 1930-32 Really Unanticipated?' National Bureau of Economic Research Working Paper No. 3174 (November 1989).

Collman, Charles Albert, *Dur Mysterious Panics* (New York: William Morrow & Co. 1931).

Diamond, Douglas, "Financial Intermediation and Delegated Monitoring," *Review of Economic Studies* 51 (July 1984): 393–414.

Fisher, Irving, "The Debt-Deflation Theory of Great Depressions," Econometrica 1 (October 1933): 337–57.

Friedman, Milton and Anna J, Schwartz, *A Monetary History of the United States.* 1867–1960. (Princeton: Princeton University Press 1963).

Gertler, Mark, "Financial Structure and Aggregate Economic Activity: An Overview," *Journal of Money Credit and Banking* 20 (August 1988a, Part 2): 559–88.

………………………………………………………, "Financial Capacity, Reliquification, and Production in an Economy with Long-Term Financial Arrangements," University of Wisconsin, mimeo. (October 1988b)

Gorton, Gary, "Clearing Houses and the Origins of Central Banking in the U.S." *Journal of Economic History* 45: 277.84

………………………………………………………, "Banking Panics and Business Cycles." Oxford Economic Papers 40 (1988): 751.81.

Greenwald, Bruce and Joseph E. Stiglitz, "Information. Finance Constraints, and Business Fluctuations." in Meir Kahn and S. C. Tsiang, eds. (Oxford: Oxford University Press 1988).

Greenwald, Bruce, Joseph E. Stiglitz and Andrew Weiss. "Information Imperfections in the Capital Market and Macroeconomic Fluctuations," *American Economic Review* 74 (May 1984): 194–99.

Hamilton, James. "Monetary Factors in the Great Depression," *Journal of Monetary Economics* 19 (March 1987): 145–70.

………………………………………………………, "'Was the Deflation During the Great Depression Anticipated? Evidence from the Commodity Futures Market." University of Virginia mimeo, March 23, 1990.

Jaffee, Dwight and Thomas Russell, "Imperfect Information, Uncertainty, and Credit Rationing," *Ouarterly Journal of Economics* 90 (November 1976): 651.66.

Kindleberger. Charles P., *Manias. Panics and Crashes* (London: MacMillan 1978).

Macaulay, Frederick R., *The Movements of Interest Rates. Bond Yields and Stock Prices in the United States Since 1856* (New York: National Bureau of Economic Research 1938).

Maisel, Sherman J., *Managing the Dollar* (New York: Norton 1973).

Mankiw. N. Gregory. "The Allocation of Credit and Financial Collapse." *Quarterly Journal of Economics* 101 (August 1986): 455–70.

Minsky, Hyman P., "Financial Stability Revisited: The Economics of Disaster," in Board of Governors of the Federal Reserve System. *Reappraisal of the Federal Reserve Discount Mechanism,* vol. 3 (Washington, D.C. 1972): 95-136.

Mishkin, Frederic S., "The Household Balance Sheet and the Great Depression," *Journal of Economic History* 38 (December 1978): 918–37.

………………………………………………………, "The Real Rate of Interest: An Empirical Investigation," in *The Cost and Consequences of Inflation,* Carnegie-Rochester Conference Series on Public Policy. 15 (1981): 151–200.

...., "Can Futures Market Data Be Used to Understand the Behavior of Real Interest Rates," Journal (March 1990).

Myers, Steward C. and N. S. Majluf, "Corporate Financing and Investment Decisions When Firms Have Information that Investors Do Not Have," *Journal of Financial Economics* 13 (June 1984): 187–221.

Romer, Christina, "The Great Crash and the Onset of the Great Depression,' National Bureau of Economic Research Working Paper No. 2639 (June 1988).

Schwartz. Anna J., "Real and Pseudo-Financial Crises," in F. Capie and G. E. Wood (eds.) *Financial Crises and the World Banking System* (London: MacMillan 1986): 11–31.

Schwert, G. William, "Business Cycles, Financial Crises and Stock Volatility,' National Bureau of Economic Research Working Paper # 2957 (May 1989a).

...., "Indexes of United States Stock Prices From 1802 to 1987," National Bureau of Economic Research Working Paper # 2985 (May 1989b).

Smith, Walter B. and Arthur H. Cole, *Fluctuations in American Business 1790-180* (Cambridge: Harvard University Press 1935).

Sobel, Robert, *Panic on Wall Street: A History of America's Financial Disasters* (London: MacMillan 1968).

Sprague, O. M. W., *History of Crises under the National Banking System* (Washington, D.C.: National Monetary Commission, U. S. Government Printing Office 1910).

Stiglitz, Joseph and Andrew Weiss, "Credit Rationing in Markets with Imperfect Information," *American Economic Review* 71 (June 1981): 393-410.

...., "Incentive Effects of Terminations: Applications to Credit and Labor markets,' *American Economic Review* 73 (December 1983): 912–27.

Temin, Peter, *Did Monetary Forces Cause the Great Depression?* (New York: W. W. Norton & Co. 1976).

Wall Street Journal, "Terrible Tuesday: How the Stock Market Almost Disintegrateda Day After the Crash," *Wall Street Journal* (November 20.1987).

Wilson, Jack, Richard Sylla and Charles P. Jones, "Financial Market Volatility, Panics Under the National Banking System Before 1914, and Volatility in the Long Run, 1830-1988," in Eugene N. White, ed., *Crashes and Panics: A Historical Perspective* (Dow Jones/Irwin: Hamewood 1990).

END-OF-CHAPTER QUESTIONS

1. Why do monetarists believe that a sharp drop in wealth may not be a sign of a financial crisis? Why do they stress that a bank panic is the true sign of a financial crisis?
2. Explain the "lemons problem" in debt markets and why this problem may precipitate high-quality borrowers to drop out of the credit markets.
3. How is it possible that higher interest rates may cause good financial risks to drop out of credit markets?
4. Why does collateral reduce adverse selection—a type of asymmetric information problem—in credit markets? What happens to adverse selection as the value of collateral increases? Why? What happens to adverse selection when the value of collateral decreases? Why?
5. Unexpected drops in the price level and stock market declines increase asymmetric information problems in credit markets both before (adverse selection) and after (moral hazard) the transaction takes place. Explain the reasoning behind this statement.
6. Explain why a decline in a borrower's net worth increases the problem of asymmetric information and, hence, lead to a decline in lending.

7. Why do traditional banks play a prominent role in reducing the asymmetric information problem in credit markets? What would happen to the problem of asymmetric information during bank panics?
8. During the 1857 crisis, the stock market declined significantly over a short period of time. What caused the decline in the stock market, and what were the consequences of it in terms of asymmetric information and the level of economic activity?
9. Explain how the collapse of Jay Cooke & Co—one of the most respected financial institutions at the time—in September 18, 1873 ("Black Thursday"), may have contributed to the panic of 1873.
10. Before 1913, when the Federal Reserve System was created, the New York Clearing House Association played a major role in the US economy. Briefly describe what was the role of this association in times of financial crises.
11. Explain how the scheme to establish a corner in the United Copper Company may have unleashed the severe financial crisis of 1907.
12. Explain why the failure of the Knickerbocker Trust on October 22, 1907, may have helped in convincing the nation that a central bank was needed to avert financial panics.
13. Describe what are the principal differences between financial crises before 1929 and the financial crisis in 1929 that led to the Great Depression of the twentieth century.
14. Describe the role of the newly created Federal Reserve System during the banking panic that started in the Fall of 1930.
15. How are the crises of 1970 and 1987 different from previous ones, particularly with respect to the role that the Fed played out during both crises.

CHAPTER 2

International Financial Crises: Causes, Prevention, and Cures

Lawrence H. Summers*

Dale Jorgenson has bestowed a great honor and no small challenge by inviting me to give this lecture: a great honor because of the distinguished list of economists who have preceded me; a challenge because of the standard they have set, and because there is no greater challenge for any economist than providing a coherent account of significant events to his scientific peers.

I am sometimes asked by friends about the differences between academic life and life as a public official. There are many. Two stand out. First, as an academic, the gravest sin one can commit is to sign one's name to something one did not write. As a public official it is a mark of effectiveness to do so as often as possible. Second, as an academic, if a problem is too hard and does not admit of a satisfactory solution, there is an obvious response: work on a different problem. That is not a luxury that one has in government.

I have been reminded of this often in recent years as we have grappled with financial crises in a number of what had previously been considered emerging markets with unrestrained futures. Anyone who doubts the social importance of what economists do should consider the debates surrounding these crises. Hundreds of millions of people who expected rapidly rising standards of living have seen their living standards fall; hundreds of thousands if not millions of children have been forced to drop out of school and go to work; hundreds of billions of dollars of apparent wealth has been lost; the stability of large nations as nations has been called into question; and the United States has made its largest nonmilitary foreign-policy-related financial commitments since the Marshall Plan.

Almost all the issues involved in understanding, preventing, and mitigating these crises are the stuff of economics courses and research: fixed versus flexible exchange rates, moral hazard and multiple equilibria, speculation and liquidity, fiscal and monetary policies, regulation and

*U.S. Department of the Treasury, 1500 Pennsylvania Avenue, Washington, DC 20005. This lecture reflects many things I have learned from experiences I have shared with colleagues in the United States government and governments around the world. I thank Brad DeLong, Marty Feldstein, Stephanie Flanders, Ken Rogoff, Andrei Shleifer, and Ted Truman for useful comments and suggestions. I am especially grateful to Nouriel Roubini and Stephanie Flanders for valuable discussions and assistance in the preparation of this lecture. The usual disclaimer applies.

Lawrence H. Summers, "International Financial Crises: Causes, Preventions, and Cures," *The American Economic Review*, vol. 90, no. 2, pp. 1-16.

competition. What economists think, say, and do has profound implications for the lives of literally billions of their fellow citizens. Whether it is discussing the role of derivatives in signaling exchange-rate commitments with Chinese Premier Zhu Rongji, or discussing an NBER working paper on inflation targeting with the Brazilian central bank governor Arminio Fraga, or discussing alternative approaches to bankruptcy law with Indonesia's economic team, or optimal debt durations with the Mexican authorities, I am consistently struck by the impact of the kind of research discussed at the AEA meetings.

The future well-being of the world's people in large part will depend on how the ongoing process of global integration works out. This is a strong statement, but one that is supported by the global economy's post-World War I failure and its post-World War II success. Central to global integration is financial integration: the flow of funds and of capital across international borders. And as the events of the late 1920's and early 1930's remind us, central to global disintegration can be international financial breakdowns.

Today, I want to reflect on the issue of global financial integration in light of the dramatic and largely unpredicted events of recent years. It is perhaps a good time for reflection: there has been enough repair that priority can shift from immediate crisis management, but the crises are sufficiently recent that the sense of urgency that they create to improve the system has not been lost.

I shall address four issues:

(i) what it means to have an efficient financial system, highlighting the important fact that accident prevention is only one aspect of how that system performs;
(ii) the alternate sources of financial crises in general, and roots of the recent crises in particular;
(iii) the best ways to design a system, both at the national and the international level, that will work well and more effectively prevent crises;
(iv) the question of effective crisis response, again, both at the level of national policies and the response of the international community.

I. THE GOAL OF AN EFFICIENT GLOBAL FINANCIAL SYSTEM

Receet years have witnessed a sea change in the global financial system, as the flow of private capital from industrial to developing countries has mushroomed from $174 billion in the 1980's to $1.3 trillion during the 1990's. In 1990, one emerging-market economy issued sovereign Eurobonds. By 1998, 40 or so emerging-market economies had issued them over the course of the 1990's. And the incidence of major financial accidents has risen sharply, to the point where in the fall of 1998 we experienced what many regarded as the worst financial crisis of the last 50 years following Russia's default, leading many to question the premise that an integrated global financial system is desirable.

The question is an important and a fair one. But it can be answered. There is much about a market economy that we take for granted. One of the more remarkable aspects is the work of a well-functioning financial system. On the one side there are consumers who want to set aside resources to prepare for their retirement, or to prepare for a rainy day, or to accumulate resources to purchase a car but who have essentially no productive opportunities for investment. On the other side there are those with opportunities to use resources today to produce more resources tomorrow by investing in equipment, structures, or schooling, or to permit consumers to smooth their consumption streams. It is the task of the financial system to bring the wants and the opportunities together.

When this is done better, a number of benefits result. An economy grows because investments earn higher returns. Scarce capital is put to its best use. Consumers benefit from more future consumption in return for consumption opportunities forgone. Risks are better shared, and individuals face less volatility in the amounts they are able to consume. These are real and tangible benefits, and so it is appropriate that financial systems absorb real resources.

As is now widely understood, the abstract argument for a competitive financial system parallels the argument for competitive markets in general. As the textbooks teach, the appropriate rates of substitution and transformation are equated. Intermediation activity will be profitable when it is efficient; that is, when the gains generated outweigh the costs of the activity. Thus, for example, specialists who provide liquidity to a market will earn profits that reflect the benefit they are bringing buyers and sellers, just as those who transport goods between high-and low-price regions can earn revenues that reflect the benefits they are providing.

In the United States economy today, 7 percent of GNP is devoted to financial intermediation, more than double the share 40 years ago. And this takes no account of the large effort within nonfinancial corporations that is devoted to raising and allocating capital. It is tempting but, I have become convinced, wrong to think of all this intermediation activity as deadweight loss efforts to win zero-sum games.[1] While there may be some elements of this kind of thing, the larger point is this: even small increases in tlre efficiency with which capital is allocated have enormous social benefits. If a typical economy has a capital output ratio of 3:1, it follows that an increase in the efficiency with which capital is allocated of 2 percent or roughly 20 basis points has a social benefit equivalent to that of 6 percent of GNP in forgone consumption.

What does all this have to do with the international financial system or with international financial crises? The implication is that, insofar as international financial integration represents an improvement in financial intermediation (whether because of the transfer of saving from low- to high-return jurisdictions, because of better risk-sharing, or because institutions involved in the transfer of capital across jurisdictions improve the efficiency with which capital is allocated), it offers a potentially significant increase in economic efficiency with benefits both for consumers and for investors around the world. Just as trade in

1 This conclusion reflects evolution in my thinking. Summers and Victoria P. Summers (1989) takes a rather dimmer view of the financial system. While the arguments made there regarding elements of rent-seeking still seem valid, the discussion there did not do justice to the benefits that liquid markets provide.

goods across jurisdictions has benefits, so too will intertemporal trade and trade that shares risks across jurisdictions have benefits.

These are not just abstractions. There are a priori reasons to suppose that the gains from intertemporal trade and from trade in financial services have the potential to be very large. Essentially all of the growth in the world's labor force over the next few decades will take place in the developing world, as the industrialized world ages. Yet most of the world's saving will take place in industrialized countries. And the abundant evidence of unutilized steel mills and what Federal Reserve Chairman Alan Greenspan has called "conspicuous construction" speaks to the potential for improved systems of intermediation to allocate capital more efficiently within developing countries, as well as between the developed and the developing world.

Some, notably Jagdish Bhagwati (1998), have taken the position that these benefits apply only to long-term direct investment. But while, as I will discuss, there are certainly dangers from creating excessive biases in favor of financial flows, one should remember that in the right kind of environment financial flows can also provide important benefits. First, they are the outcome of transactions that finance real trade and related financial transactions and provide cross-border liquidity to the interbank market. Second, they provide capital to local businesses on what are often the best available terms. Third, they are closely associated with the presence of foreign businesses and foreign financial institutions, which themselves bring significant benefits. More generally, generic attempts to distinguish between good (direct) and bad (financial) capital flows remind me of attempts to distinguish between good and bad imports of goods and services in international trade—and may prove equally counterproductive.

While all that potential is certainly there, words like "moral hazard," "adverse selection," "noise trading," and "herding" remind us that economic theory has identified many reasons why financial markets do not always perform perfectly. And the centuries-long history of financial crises teaches us no less clearly that the flows of capital driven by financial markets can be very different from an efficient and optimal allocation of savings to the right investment projects.

How best to think about financial innovation? An analogy may be helpful. The jet airplane made air travel more comfortable, more efficient, and more safe, though the accidents were more spectacular and for a time more numerous after the jet was invented. In the same way, modern global financial markets carry with them enormous potential for benefit, even if some of the accidents are that much more spectacular. As the right public policy response to the jet was longer runways, better air-traffic control, and better training for pilots, and not the discouragement of rapid travel, so the right public policy response to financial innovation is to assure a safe framework so that the benefits can be realized, not to stifle the change.

That said, the development of a proper air transport system also depended on understanding and addressing the reasons for crashes. In the same way, the development of the right kind of international financial system will depend on understanding the causes of crises, a topic to which I now turn.

II. UNDERSTANDING INTERNATIONAL FINANCIAL CRISES

Leo Tolstoy famously observed that "every happy family is the same. Every unhappy family is miserable in its own way." Every financial crisis is different and involves its own distinctive elements. There are, however, some elements that are common to many of the emerging-market financial crises we have seen in recent years.

International financial crises can be defined in many ways and can take many forms. What I mean by an international financial crisis is a situation where the international dimension substantially worsens a crisis in ways that would not occur in a closed economy. By this definition, I do not mean to understate the major role that domestic fundamental weaknesses can play in bringing on a crisis. I do mean to exclude situations where it is primarily poor domestic economic performance that leads to debt-servicing problems.[2] I also mean to exclude currency crises in which countries are forced to adjust exchange rates although, as we shall. see, devaluations can frequently presage international financial crises.

If we are to prevent accidents as effectively as possible, and mitigate them where we cannot prevent them, it is important to understand how they happen and the nature of their antecedents. There have been six major international financial crises during the 1990's: Mexico in 1995; Thailand, Indonesia, and South Korea in 1997–1998; Russia in 1998; and Brazil in 1998–1999. Table 2.1 provides some information on these crises. Elements in common include a dramatic swing in the current account, a large real depreciation, and a significant decline in real output. With some differences between cases, the pattern in all these crises, and indeed, a number of crises historically, appears to involve three broad elements.

First, after a period of substantial capital inflows, investors (both domestic and foreign) decided to reduce the stock of their assets in the affected country in response to a change in its fundamentals. This can have many sources: concern about the viability of the exchange-rate regime, as in most of these cases; concern about large fiscal deficits, as in Russia and Brazil; concern about large current-account deficits, as in Thailand and Brazil; and the increasing salience of long-standing financial-sector weaknesses, arising from some combination of insufficient capitalization and supervision of banks and excessive leverage and guarantee—the combination that, along with directed lending, has been captured in the term "crony capitalism."[3]

Second, after this process went on for some time in these emerging-market countries, investors shifted their focus from evaluating the situation in the country to evaluating the behavior of other investors. The rate of withdrawal increased as a bank-run psychology took hold, and investors

2 While elements of domestic and policy vulnerability were present in the international financial crises under consideration (e,g., the fiscal problems of Russia and Brazil). we like to distinguish episodes like those in the 1990's where capital-account developments had a central role (even if it fed on some fundamental weaknesses) from many episodes in the 1980's where systematic poor policies (large and structural fiscal deficits; high inflation caused by monetization of such deficits; persistently unsustainable external imbalances; and systemic distortions in goods, services, and capital markets) had a greater role in triggering a traditional currency and financial crisis.

3 See Ronald McKinnon and Huw Pill (1996), Morris Goldstein (1998), Paul Krugman (1998), Giancarlo Corsetti et al. (1999a, b), and Council of Economic Advisers (1999) for analyses stressing the role of fundamentals and distortions created by guarantees and weaknesses in the financial sector.

TABLE 2.1 Satistics for "crisis" countries

STATISTIC	COUNTRY					
	BRAZIL	INDONESIA[c]	SOUTH KOREA	MEXICO	THAILAND[d]	RUSSIA
Quarterly real GDP (percentage change)						
Peak to trough	2.6	(18.9)	(7.5)	(9.7)	(13.6)	(4.3)
Trough plus 12 months	4.0[e]	7.5	9.9	6.6	7.4	2.0
Trough plus 24 months	8.7[e]	n.a.	n.a.	15.6	n.a.	n.a.
Quarterly current account ($ billion)						
Peak	(11.5)	(2.4)	(7.4)	(7.9)	(4.8)	(3.6)
Trough	(4.6)	1.8	10.9	0.3	4.2	6.6
12 months after trough	(3.8)[e]	1.8	6.2	(1.2)	3.5	3.5
24 months after trough	n.a.	n.a.	n.a.	(3.0)	n.a.	n.a.
Quarterly current account (percentage of GDP)						
Peak	n.a.	(3.8)	(6.3)	n.a.	(10.7)	n.a.
Trough	n.a.	8.6	16.1	n.a.	16.4	n.a.
12 months after trough	n.a.	3.4	6.9	n.a.	10.8	n.a.
24 months after trough	n.a.	n.a.	n.a.	n.a.	n.a.	n.a.
Change in net international reserves ($ billion)[a]						
Peak to trough	(14.5)	(15.3)	(25.7)	(19.5)	(36.0)	(18.0)
Trough plus 12 months	8.8[e]	52.5	44.8	6.6	13.8	0.4
Trough plus 24 months	13.5[e]	n.a.	69.8	15.7	24.8	n.a.
Change in nominal exchange rate (percent)[b]						
Peak to trough	−41.0	−526.5	-57.2	−54.0	−58.3	−76.0
Trough plus 12 months	13.0[e]	53.5	62.7	−10.0	52.2	n.a.
Trough plus 24 months	4.0[e]	n.a.	73.6	−15.0	47.5	n.a

Notes: Dates of crises are as follows: Brazil, January 1999; Indonesia, October 1997; South Korea, December 1997; Mexico, December 1994; Thailand, July 1997; Russia, August 1998.Quarterly GDP "peak" is assumed to be the quarter in which the "crisis" occurred. "Peaks"for other statistics are assumed to occur in the quarter one year before the crisis quarter in most cases. The designation "n.a." indicates that data are not available. Quarterly real GDP and quarterly current account data are seasonally adjusted.

[a] Net of IMF/BIS loans.
[b] Negative entries indicate depreciation.
[c] Reserve data are gross reserves less gold.
[d] Quarterly current-account balances are not seasonally adjusted.
[e] Based on IMF projections.

sought to avoid being the last ones in as they saw the country's reserves being depleted.[4] This was manifested in the shift of the mode of investment analysis from economics to hydraulics, with an accounting-spreadsheet exercise that made no reference to prices on the sources and uses of funds. Rumors of drastic action (a moratorium, capital controls, or some such) began to circulate, and a panic mentality developed. This phenomenon was particularly evident in Mexico in early 1995 and in South Korea between Thanksgiving and Christmas in 1997, and it seems a particularly pervasive feature of recent emerging-market crises. No one, after all, raised questions about debt rollover in the United Kingdom following sterling's exit from the European Exchange Rate Mechanism (ERM) in 1992, or in continental Europe after the breakdown of the ERM in 1993.

Third, the withdrawal of capital and the associated sharp swing in the exchange rate and reduced access to capital exacerbated fundamental weakness, in turn exacerbating the financial-market response. The real depreciation of the exchange rate reduced real incomes and spending. Extrapolative expectations regarding a falling exchange rate increased pressure for capital flight. And, most importantly, the increased domestic value of foreign-currency liabilities and reduced creditworthiness of domestic borrowers further degraded an already ailing financial system, in turn causing further reductions in lending and worsening of the fundamentals.[5]

In order to understand the economics of the crises we have seen, each of these three critical elements is essential. Without a change in sentiment, driven by a weakening in the economic fundamentals, it is not possible to account for decisions to withdraw capital. Without the bank-run psychology, it is not possible to account for the scale of the change in investors' allocation decisions, which seem so discontinuous with respect to any easily observable aspects of fundamentals. Without reference to the strains on domestic financial systems and corporate firms, it is hard to account for the magnitude of the observed declines in economic performance and the failure of real exchange-rate depreciations to trigger large immediate increases in exports in a number of cases.

Another feature of the 1990's episodes of turmoil is the presence of international "contagion," seen in the ERM crisis of 1992–1993, the "tequila" effects of the Mexican peso crisis of 1994–1995, the "yellow fever" effects of the Asian crisis of 1997–1998, and the asset-market contagion following the Russian devaluation and default in August 1998 and the Brazilian devaluation in January 1999.

4 The role of bank runs/panic and an interpretation of the crisis in terms of an international liquidity crisis has been stressed by Guillermo Calvo (1998), Roberto Chang and Andres Velasco (1998, 1999), Jeffrey Sachs and Steven Radelet (1998, 1999), and Dani Rodrik and Velasco (1999).

5 See Philippe Aghion et al. (1999) and Krugman (1999) for formal models of such balance-sheet effects. These effects may also help to explain why currency crises are often associated with financial/banking crises, a phenomenon referred to as "twin crises." Indeed, in five out of the six international financial crises considered in this paper, currency crises were associated with banking crises. However, the interaction between currency and banking crises is complex. While balance-sheet effects may explain why currency crises lead to banking crises, evidence also suggests that, at times, banking crises precede currency crises and are an early warning signal of future currency crises. The analytical and empirical complex interactions between banking and currency crises have been recently studied by a number of authors, including Barry Eichengreen and Andy Rose (1998), Ilan Goldfajin and Rodrigo O. Valdes (1998), Corsetti et al. (1999b), Goldstein et al. (1999), and Graciella Kaminsky and Carmen Reinhart (1999).

There are many explanations and models of contagion:[6]

(i) It can be due to common shocks (like terns of primary commodity price shocks) that simultaneously hurt the commodity-exporting countries.

(ii) Trade linkages transfer relative price and income (demand) shocks from one country to the other.

(iii) Competitive devaluations among countries competing among themselves or in third markets may explain excessive currency depreciation of many currencies.

(iv) Financial linkages lead to asset-market correlations: if one country invests in and lends to another one, poor economic news in the latter will also affect asset markets in the former.

(v) Market illiquidity may have exacerbated contagion. For example, when some highly leveraged institutions experienced significant losses following the Russian crisis, margin calls and lack of liquidity may have led them or forced them to reduce their positions in other markets, thus feeding contagion.

(vi) Some elements of investors' irrationality; may have been at work; panic, herding, and positive feedback trading may partly explain why investors withdrew indiscriminately from many markets without careful distinction among different emerging markets based on their fundamentals.

(vii) Finally, and in my view, more importantly, "reputational externalitiesn"[7] were almost certainly at work. A crisis in one country can affect investors' expectations and perceptions about common structural conditions and vulnerabilities in other countries and the likely policy response to such vulnerabilities.[8]

From the perspective of actual experience, analytical distinctions between "multiple-equilibrium crises" and "fundamentals-driven crises" seem less sharp than they sometimes do in the academic literature. It seems difficult to point to any emerging-market economy that experienced a financial crisis but did not have significant fundamental weaknesses that called into question the sustainability of its policies. Yet it seems equally difficult to avoid the judgment that, in many of these recent cases, the punishment was in a sense disproportionate to the crime, with the process of capital withdrawal greatly exacerbating any underlying weakness.

6 The theoretical and empirical literature on contagion is vast; many recent contributions were presented at the IMF and World Rank-sponsored conference on International Financial Contagion (3-4 February 2000) (papers available online at (http://www.worldbank.org/research/interest/confs/upcoming/papersfeb3-4/papers.htm)).Good recent surveys are by Rudiger Dornbusch et al. (2000) and Matthew Prisker (2000).

7 This is a concept developed by Richard Zeckhauser (1986).

8 Quoting the 1999 Economic Report of thc President (Council of Economic Advisers, 1999 p. 244): "For example investors' belief in the strength of the Asian cconomic model may have changed when one of the star performers stumbled. The failure of financial institutions in one country may lead investors to believe, in the absence of better information to the contrary, that institutions in similar countries in the same region might be facing the same problems. Similarly, the unwillingness or inability of several Asian economies to defend their currencies more aggressively may have altered investors' views concerning the policy preferences of other economies in the region."

A crude but simple game, related to Douglas Diamond and Philip Dybvig's (1983) celebrated analysis of bank runs, illustrates some of the issues involved here. Imagine that everyone who has invested $10 with me can expect to earn $1, assuming that I stay solvent. Suppose that if I go bankrupt, investors who remain lose their whole $10 investment, but that an investor who withdraws today neither gains nor loses. What would you do? Each individual judgment would presumably depend on one's assessment of my prospects, but this in turn depends on the collective judgment of all of the investors.

Suppose, first, that my foreign reserves, ability to mobilize resources, and economic strength are so limited that if any investor withdraws I will go bankrupt. It would be a Nash equilibrium (indeed, a Pareto-dominant one) for everyone to remain, but (I expect) not an attainable one. Someone would reason that someone else would decide to be cautious and withdraw, or at least that someone would reason that someone would reason that someone would withdraw, and so forth. This phenomenon, which Douglas Hofstadter has labeled "reverberant doubt," would likely lead to large-scale withdrawals, and I would go bankrupt. It would not be a close-run thing. John Maynard Keynes's beauty contest captures a similar idea.

Now suppose that my fundamental situation were such that everyone would be paid off as long as no more than one-third of the investors chose to withdraw. What would you do then? Again, there are multiple equilibria: everyone should stay if everyone else does, and everyone should pull out if everyone else does, but the more favorable equilibria seems much more robust.

I think that this thought experiment captures something real. On the one hand, bank runs or their international analogues do happen. On the other hand, they are not driven by sunspots: their likelihood is driven and determined by the extent of fundamental weaknesses. These questions of equilibrium selection can be and indeed have been more formally analyzed.[9] For my purposes, the point is that preventing crises is heavily an issue of avoiding situations where the bank run psychology takes hold, and that will depend heavily on strengthening core institutions and other fundamentals.

III. CRISIS PREVENTION AT THE NATIONAL AND INTERNATIONAL LEVEL

A. NATIONAL CRISIS-PREVENTION EFFORTS

Many countries experience major shocks—to their terns of trade, to investor confidence, or within their domestic financial systems. Relatively few of them have major financial crises. Why? Table 2.2 provides subjective ratings of the importance of various factors as antecedents to the six major emerging-market financial crises of the 1990's.

9 Stephen Morris and Hyun Song Shin (1998) provide a novel analysis of how weak fundamentals, uncertainty of the type I discussed in Hofstadter's "wolf's dilemma" game, and private information in a standard multiple-equilibrium model can produce a unique equilibrium. This work suggests the fragility of many multiple-equilibria results and the crucial role of fundamental weaknesses. The challenge is now to model these phenomena in more realistic dynamic settings.

TABLE 2.2 Sources of vulnerabilities in recent major capital-account crises

	COUNTRY					
SOURCE	BRAZIL	INDONESIA	SOUTH KOREA	MEXICO	THAILAND	RUSSIA
Pegged exchange rate (reserve depletion)	1	0.5[a]	0.5	1	1	1
Current-account deficit	0.5	2	3	1	1	3
Fiscal deficit	1	3	3	3	3	1
Banking and financial-sector weakness	3	1	1	1	1	1
Government short-term debt	1	3	3	1	2	1
Total short-term foreign indebtedness	2	1	1	2	1	1
General governance	2	1	2	2	2	1

Notes: Key to table entries: 1, very serious; 2, serious; 3, not central.
[a]Indonesia let its exchange rate float in August 1998, did exhibit strong signs of real exchange-rate misalignment, and did not expend reserves defending the rate. However, the inflexible exchange-rate regime does seem to have encouraged a large buildup of foreign currency debt in the private sector.

Four primary conclusions emerge:

(i) In nearly all the cases, serious banking and financial-sector weaknesses played an important role.
(ii) Fixed exchange rates without the concomitant monetary-policy commitments were present as antecedents to crisis in all the cases.
(iii) Traditional macroeconomic fundamentals, in the form of overly inflationary monetary policies, large fiscal deficits, or even large current account deficits, were present in several cases but are not necessary antecedents to crisis in all episodes.
(iv) National balance-sheet weaknesses, including large short-term liabilities either of government or the private sector, were important elements in each of the crises.

A substantial literature has sought more systematically to analyze the antecedents and non-antecedents of financial crises with broadly similar conclusions to my crude table.[10] These

10 There is a vast econometric literature on the causes of recent crises and early-warning indicators of future crises. Recent contributions include Jeffrey Frankel and Rose (1996), Sachs et al. (1996), Andrew Berg and Catherine Pattillo (1998), Goldstein et al. (1999), Sachs and Radelet (1999), and Corsetti et al. (1999c).

four observations, in turn, help identify the four elements of an effective national strategy for minimizing the risk of this kind of crisis.

First, and easier said than done, is maintaining a strong domestic financial system. While many authors emphasize vulnerability measures comparing the level of foreign reserves to measures of short-term liabilities, the work of Simon Johnson et al. (2000) is particularly persuasive in highlighting the strength of domestic financial systems and institutions. When well capitalized and supervised banks, effective corporate governance and bankruptcy codes, and credible means of contract enforcement, along with other elements of a strong financial system, are present, significant amounts of debt will be sustainable. In their absence, even very small amounts of debt can be problematic.

The second element is the choice of appropriate exchange-rate regime, which, for economies with access to international capital markets, increasingly means a move away from the middle ground of pegged but adjustable fixed exchange rates toward the two corner regimes of either flexible exchange rates or a fixed exchange rate supported, if necessary, by a commitment to give up altogether an independent monetary policy. The practical choice between these two poles, for emerging-market economies today, probably has less to do with Robert Mundell's traditional optimal-currency-area considerations than with a country's capacity to operate a discretionary monetary policy in a way that will reduce rather than increase variance in economic output.

Third, a sound and stable macroeconomic policy environment is needed where monetary-policy and fiscal-policy vulnerabilities are minimized, including especially the avoidance of fiscal deficits that are substantially beyond a country's sustainable domestic financing capacity. What this deficit level will be will depend on a country's savings behavior and the quality of its capital markets.

Fourth, countries should reduce their vulnerabilities to liquidity/rollover risk and balance-sheet risk. Foreign reserves need to be compared to meaningfull measures of liabilities that can become a claim against a country's reserves; traditional ratios of reserve to imports are thus of little use. Also, policy biases toward short-term capital need to be avoided.

This last point deserves emphasis because we have seen this kind of bias time and time again in the recent crises:

(i) We saw it in Mexico, with the increasing resort to issuing dollar-denominated Tesobonos in the lead-up to crisis.
(ii) We saw it in Thailand, in the tax breaks on offshore foreign borrowing and the government's decision to mortgage all of its reserves on forward markets.
(iii) We saw it in South Korea, where discriminatory controls kept long-term capital out and ushered short-term capital in.
(iv) And we saw it in Russia, in the government's determined efforts to attract international investors to the market for rubledenominated GKO's.

In this context the question naturally arises of controls on short-term capital inflows as a crisis-avoidance measure. But the first and usually neglected point is that, just as economists usually recommend that efforts to reduce energy consumption should start with the elimination of energy subsidies rather than the introduction of new energy taxes, so the first priority with regard to capital flows must be to do no harm: that is, to avoid policies that reach excessively for short-term capital, such as those we have seen in recent crisis economies.

A measure of sound management of short-term flows is implicit in any prudential regulation of banks. Where controls are in place it is a mistake to be theological about their removal; but experience suggests that such controls tend to become more ineffective over time, create their own costs and distortions, and discourage the integration of financial services that can be an important source of stability. They are no panacea and indeed can degrade the performance of the very functions of the financial system described in Section I.

Still, policy biases that lead to an excessive accumulation of short-term debt should be addressed via policy changes that eliminate such biases, including: the distortions that can result from restrictions on foreign direct investment, inward equity portfolio investment, or the access of nonresidents to long-term bond markets; or policy distortions and tax incentives that can lead to an excessive reliance on debt relative to equity finance. Of course, underdeveloped capital markets, where long-term forms of finance (i.e., equity, long-term bonds) are not widely available, will themselves create a bias in favor of short-term capital flows in the right environment. When we consider the recognized role that efficient capital markets can play in providing finance for long-term growth, it is clear that their development should be given high priority in the process of domestic and international capital-market liberalization.

Just as better airplanes and airports are good in ways that go beyond accident-prevention, all of these steps are valuable not simply as crisis prevention measures, but in their own right, as proven strategies for promoting economic efficiency and growth.

B. INTERNATIONAL CRISIS-PREVENTION EFFORTS

Ultimately, the likelilhood of plane crashes depends on the training and judgment of pilots and sound manufacture of planes. But the system in which pilots operate will equally be important and demands careful consideration. The same applies to the international dimension of crisis prevention.

The overwhelming contribution that the international community can make toward preventing crises is to succeed in encouraging sound national economic policies. And the most important thing that the international community can do in achieving this goal is to promote transparency.

If one were writing a history of the American capital market, I think one would conclude that the single most important innovation shaping that market was the idea of generally accepted accounting principles. The transparency implicit in the generally accepted accounting principles (GAAP) promotes efficient market responses to change, and it supports stability. Furthermore, if as Ken Galbraith has observed, conscience is the fear that someone may be watching, it may be the single most effective means of promoting self-regulation. Very much the same kind of transparency is nceded in the emerging economies.

There is also an important role for better international surveillance of the quality of national policies in the areas just described. This is a role that is increasingly being taken on by the IMF in a broader range of areas, as it moves away from the time when it could be said that IMF stood for "It's Mostly Fiscal."[11] International forums such as the G-7, the new G-20, the APEC finance ministers, and so forth can also be helpful. Indeed, their major accomplishment is not the specific decisions that are taken when they meet—sometimes there are none. Rather, it is the gradual spread of common ways of thinking about and responding to economic developments. The value of the diffusion of best practice, or at least, better practice, is not to be discounted. Over time these forums provide important opportunities to use political pressure to nudge national policies in the right direction.

Beyond the approbation of their peers, the question does arise as to what will motivate countries to pursue stronger policies. The basic answer has to be self-interest. The ultimate reward for countries with improved policies will be better economic outcomes and a higher standard of living for their citizens. The proximate and more immediate indicator and incentive can be the lower borrowing costs that come from being well-regarded by the market.

There are some who suggest that systematic augmentation of countries' foreign reserves, through the availability of generalized, unconditional emergency finance, would make accidents less likely by reducing the risk of the kind of self-fulfilling expectations-driven crises that I have discussed. While conditioned, precalutionary financial support is constructive in some cases, the risk inherent in systematic availability of unconditional credit to countries can be sum" marized in two words: moral hazard. Crises are typically preceded by significant depletion of reserves. There is the real prospect that automatic availability of reserves would simply delay necessary adjustments and thereby prove highly destructive.

While the best preventive policies would minimize the chance that crises would occur, they would never eliminate them entirely. When they do occur, it will be important to follow policies that minimize their virulence and consequences.

IV. NATIONAL AND INTERNATIONAL CRISIS RESPONSE

Crisis response, like crisis prevention, has two dimensions: national policies that can restore confidence and international efforts to finance a credible path out of crises. Of these, by the far the most important is the response of national authorities in the countries concerned. If there is one lesson that has been brought home most forcefully by the events of recent years, it is that countries shape their own destinies—and the international community can never want sound policies or economic stability more than the government and people of the country itself.

11 See my speech on IMF reform (Summers, 1999) for an elaboration of these ideas.

A. EFFECTIVE CRISIS RESPONSE AT THE NATIONAL LEVEL

The best national response to crisis is not to have one. The next best is to have a sufficiently robust set of domestic institutions and national economic system that the crisis is contained and self-limiting and does not reach the stage where a country's capacity to meet its international obligations comes into question. This goes back to questions of crisis-prevention. Here I am talking about full-blown crises of the kind suggested by the six examples we have seen in the 1990's.

In my experience, policymakers in a country facing such a crisis tend to go through stages reminiscent of the five stages of grief. First, there is the denial that a crisis could be taking place. Second, we see anger, with a rush to blame speculators and other outside forces, and often, domestically, a change in government. Third, there is the bargaining: the desperate search for magic bullets that we saw, for example, in the pressure for a currency board in the depth of the crisis in Indonesia. Fourth comes despair, leading eventually to the decision to call in the IMF. Finally, in the fifth stage, there is acceptance and the agreement of a credible plan.

As an academic I used to be impatient with the seemingly mundane advice of former officials and worldly sorts who counseled the victims of financial crisis to communicate with their creditors, get the bad news out early, take decisive steps early to resolve a crisis, and so forth. More recently, I have come to appreciate more keenly that propositions become clichés because they capture truth. In situations where confidence is central, it is a mistake to think that it is only the substance of what national authorities do that matters.

Perhaps the best advice that I have heard about the right policy following a crisis is President Ernesto Zedillo's admonition, based on his experience leading Mexico out of crisis in 1995, that markets overreact, so policy needs to overreact as well.

All of this speaks to the form of an effective policy response to crises. What about its content? It will vary from case to case. But experience suggests some important lessons:

(i) Providing confidence to markets and investors that a credible path out of crisis exists and will be followed is essential. That requires transparency (providing all relevant information to markets so that risk-averse investors are not uncertain about how deep and serious problems are), consistent and credible commitment to a coherent policy-adjustment package (so that political and policy uncertainty does not undermine investors' confidence), and close consultation with creditors (so that sudden negative policy and informational surprises are minimized, and so that creditors are reassured that cooperative approaches to debt servicing difficulties will be pursued).

(ii) If lax fiscal policy is a contributor to the crisis, then tightening will be a key part of restoring confidence, but in a situation in which large-scale outflows of capital are likely to have their own contractionary effect, it is neither necessary nor desirable to tighten fiscal policy solely in response to the crisis itself. Indeed, since devaluation may be deflationary in the short run (through its expenditure reduction effects) rather than expansionary (via the expenditure switching effect that kicks in the medium run), less stress may have to be put on other forms of expenditure-reduction in the adjustment process (i.e., fiscal contraction) when these are not warranted based on fundamentals. And, in fact, fiscal policy was allowed to loosen in several Asian crisis economies when the depth of the recession emerged in early 1998.

(iii) Countries need to ser the right monetary policy to establish confidence, and in a situation in which a currency is in free-fall it is difficult to believe that the way to restore stability is to produce more of that currency. The right monetary policy at times of crisis has to be one that will minimize the average interest rate over the medium term; and where confidence is at issue, that may imply a significant tightening in the short run. Given the free fall of currencies (and ensuing exacerbation of contractionary balance-sheet effects) in cases such as Indonesia, where monetary conditions were kept lax at the onset of the crisis, the argument that lower interest rates early on would have strengthened currencies seems neither convincing nor supported by the evidence. Indeed, currencies stabilized and recovered in Asiancrisis economies after a period of tight money restored confidence in early 1998, paving the way for a rapid and significant reduction in interest rates in the second part of the year.

(iv) Prompt action needs to be taken to maintain financial stability, by moving quickly to support healthy institutions and by intervening in unhealthy institutions. The loss of confidence in the financial system and episodes of bank panics were not caused by early and necessary interventions in insolvent institutions. Rather, these problems were exacerbated by (a) a delay in intervening to address the problem of mounting nonperforming loans; (b) implicit bailout guarantees that led to an attempt to "gamble for redemption"; (c) a system of implicit, rather than explicit and incentive-compatible, deposit guarantees at a time when there was not a credible amount of fiscal resources available to back such guarantees; and (d) political distortions and interferences in the way interventions were carried out (as when an Indonesian bank owned by a son of Presi-. dent Soeharto was closed one day only to be reopened the next, under a different name in the same premises).

(v) Strong and effective social safeguards need to be in place. Effective social policy and spending can ease the task of adjustment during times of crisis, help build support for necessary reforms, and ensure that the burden of adjustment does not fall disproportionately on the poorest and most vulnerable groups in society. This is a moral imperative. It can also be a political imperative if strong adjustment policies are to be sustained. Countries need to own the adjustment program, and governments have to be democratic and have popular support for policies that are painful in the short run but necessary to restore growth in a rapid manner. Indeed, in several Asian countries (Thailand, South Korea, and Indonesia), the process of confidence-restoration and asset-price recovery was associated with the rise to power of new governments that had greater political legitimacy and popular support.

Clearly, in all of these judgments there will be difficult issues of balance, and we can never guarantee that they will be made correctly in every case. But there can be no question (and there has not been any question) that the goal is to restore confidence and stability as rapidly as possible and so to pave the way for renewed growth.

B. INTERNATIONAL CRISIS RESPONSE[12]

As I noted earlier, a hallmark of crisis in its most virulent phase is that a country's creditors come to focus on hydraulics, not economics, looking to see whether there are adequate resources to finance all obligations coming due. Absent this assurance, the restoration of confidence will not be possible.

The central task for the international response to a crisis is the establishment of a path that will see a country and its creditors out of the crisis through a series of mutually consistent and reinforcing actions. The goal must be the restoration of confidence and the normal flow of private capital.

This goal can be addressed in two broad ways in the context of credible policy adjustment:

(i) through the provision of official finance; or
(ii) through some coordination of private creditors to reduce outflows or roll over obligations coming due.

Along with spurring sound policy in the affected country, the crucial objective of the international community in responding to crisis is using these two tools to promote the restoration of confidence.

The provision of emergency finance in support of credible policy adjustment can, in principle and in practice, be highly effective in restoring confidence. Unlike in the 1980's when the international financial institutions and bilaterals provided only relatively minor sums to countries in crisis, large-scale provision of emergency finance has been a central part of the international financial community's response to the crises of the 1990's. The approach followed, as embodied in the IMF's Supplemental Resources Facility, has had something in common with Walter Bagehot's dictum of lending freely at penalty rates on collateral that is sound in normal times. While the counterfactual is not available, I believe that the availability of substantial resources has contributed to the relatively rapid recovery from deep crises in countries such as Mexico and

12 There are many academic and policy contributions to the debate on the reform of the international financial system aimed at preventing crises from occurring and resolving with minimal costs those that do occur. Such contributions include, but are not limited to, work by the Council on Foreign Relations (1999), Eichengreen (1999), Martin Feldstein (1999), and Kenneth Rogoff (1999). Recently, researchers have also started to develop analytical models of architecture to consider the implications and effects (sometimes perverse) of a number of policy proposals, such as partial or full international lender of last resort, capital controls, rollover options, and temporary suspension of external debt payments. These analytical contributions to the architecture debate include work by Goldfajin and Valdes (1999), Olivier Jeanne (1999), Jeanne and Charles Wyplosz (1999), and Jeronim Zettelmeyer (1999).

South Korea which were successful in carrying out their policy commitments. Korea's economy, for example, is currently growing by around 9 percent.

The provision of conditioned finance at premium rates to respond to crises does raise certain difficulties. First, there is the real question of balancing the desire to apply conditionality to country policies with the desire to add confidence to the market. The former requires uncertainty as to whether resources will be forthcoming; the latter is best served by confidence, so the balance that must be struck in a transparent world where national authorities and the market hear the same message is a complicated one.

Second, there is the issue of moral hazard and the possible systemic implications of the expectations of bailouts. There is considerable debate about the importance of this issue. While many disagree, I think it is hard to make the case that investments in emerging markets have been heavily influenced by the expectation of the availability of official resources for bailouts.

For example, there is no systematic evidence that flows to official creditors rose relative to flows to private creditors following the official response to the Mexican financial crisis. Furthermore, there is the analytical point that, if official-sector lending into financial crises is judged properly and is paid back at premium interest rates, it can benefit the lenders, creditors, and countries involved and does not impose a taxpayer cost in the same way that deposit insurance does. Indeed, a well-designed official lending facility that is profitable and makes all relevant agents better off is a clear pareto-improvement.[13] However, as in the case of an efficient and incentive-compatible deposit-insurance and safety-net scheme, possible moral-hazard distortions induced by automatic guarantees need to be avoided to ensure that the scheme does not lead to systemic losses and distortions. Thus, it is certain that a healthy financial system cannot be built on the expectation of bailouts.

The third question raised by large-scale official lending as a response to crisis is one of feasibility. As capital markels integrate and capital flows increase, in at least some cases it may well become impossible for official finance to fill gaps entirely or restore confidence.

These considerations lead to private-sector coordination as an alternative response to crisis. Coordination of bank creditors played a crucial role in the resolution of the South Korean financial crisis and a significant role in Brazil. Private-sector involvement as an approach to crisis resolution has the virtues of avoiding the need for public-sector money and of reducing moral hazard. But it too raises difficulties.

There is the question of achieving coordination. Individual creditors have little incentive to cooperate in reschedulings or debt reductions, and ample opportunities to free ride if approaches based on voluntarism are pursued. At the same time, if approaches based on coercion

13 However, as shown by Neil Wallace (1988), optimal partial suspension schemes during a bank run may dominate a government lender-of-last-resort (or deposit-insurance) scheme unless the government has superior information about the nature and size of the bank run. This leaves open the issue of whether the creditor-coordination problem that leads to self-fulfilling runs could be addressed via appropriate private-sector involvement (a mechanism lo coordinate creditors' actions and avoid a run or, in the extreme, a debt suspension) rather than via large amounts of official support. This is a most complex issue analytically, and even more so in a policy context.

are pursued, there are real questions of fairness: for example, how should a country's domestic debts be treated? And what about efforts on the part of local residents to convert domestic into foreign currency? There is also the real risk of the destruction of confidence undermining new flows, either to the country in question or to its neighbors. For these and other related reasons, the question of private-sector involvement in crisis resolution has rightly been treated with some delicacy.

What is the right mix of private-sector involvement and financing in response to crisis? While case-by-case judgmental approaches are rarely satisfying to analysts, they will, I expect, be pursued by the international community for some time to come. Cases will differ in the nature of the debts coming due, the likelihood that they can ultimately be paid, the ease with which creditors can be organized, the magnitude of contagion risks, and the availability of financial resources, to mention just a few factors. For all these reasons, the G-7 has rightly laid out principles but not detailed procedures for handling issues of private-sector involvement.

V. CONCLUDING REMARKS

I will conclude where I began. Sound financial systems can contribute enormously to economic development around the world, and the flow of capital across international borders can confer enormous benefits. And yet as we have seen, there is the potential for massive accidents.

Some, remembering Jim Tobin's admonition, that it takes a heap of Harberger triangles to fill an Okun gap, conclude that the game is not worth the candle and so the flow of capital should systematically be discouraged. I think the right lesson is the more optimistic one, that with good sense and hard work, and a great deal of creative thought, the Okun gaps can be avoided, and the gains from capital flows can tanslate into what is most important for any economy: namely, changes in its long-term growth rate.

I have described here some of the thinking that has guided the international community in responding to the dramatic developments of reccnt years. I do so not in the conviction that we have all the answers, but in the certainty that the questions are profoundly important. If I have provoked further thought on a set of issues that economists are uniquely qualified to address, I will have succeeded in my purpose.

REFERENCES

Aghion, Philippe; Banerjee, Abhijit and Bachetta, Philippe. "A Simple Model of Monetary Policy and Currency Crises." Mimeo, University of Lausanne, Switzerland, September 1999.

Berg, Andrew and Pattillo, Catherine. "Are Currency Crises Predictable? A Test." International Monetary Fund (Washington, DC) Working Paper No. 98/154, December 1998.

Bhagwati, Jagdish. "The Capital Myth." *Foreign Affairs,* May/June 1998.

Calvo, Guillermo "Capital Flows and Capital-Market Crises: The Simple Economics of Sudden Stops." Mimeo, University of Maryland, July 1998.

Chang, Roberto and Velasco, Andres. "The Asian Liquidity Crisis." National Bureau of Economic Research (Cambridge, MA) Working Paper No. 6796, November 1998.

______. "Liquidity Crises in Emerging Markets: Theory and Policy." National Bureau of Economic Research (Cambridge, MA) Working Paper No. 7272, July 1999; in Ben Bernanke and Julio Rotemberg, eds., *NBER macroeconomics annual* (forthcoming).

Corsetti, Giancarlo; Pesenti, Paolo and Roubini, Nouriel. "What Caused the Asian Currency and Financial Crisis?" *Japan and the World Economy,* September 1999a, *11*(3), pp. 305–73.

______. "Paper Tigers? A Model of the Asian Crisis." *European Economic Review,* June 1999b, *43*(7), pp. 1211–36.

______. "Fundamental Determinants of the Asian Crisis: The Role of Financial Fragility and External Imbalances." Unpublished manuscript, Yale University, 1999c.

Council of Economic Advisers. Economic report of the President. Washington, DC: U.S. Government Printing Office, 1999.

Council on Foreign Relations. "Safeguarding Prosperity in a Global Financial System: The Future International Financial Architecture." Report of an Independent Task Force sponsored by the Council on Foreign Relations, Institute for International Economics, Washington, DC, 1999.

Diamond, Douglas and Dybvig, Philip. "Bank Runs, Deposit Insurance, and Liquidity." *Journal of Political Economy,* June 1983, *91*(3), pp. 401–19.

Dornbusch, Rudiger; Park, Yung Chul and Claessens, Stijn. "Contagion: How It Spreads and How It Can Be Stopped?" Unpublished manuscript, Massachusetts Institute of Technology, January 2000.

Eichengreen, Barry. *Toward a new international financial architecture: A practical post-Asia agenda.* Washington, DC: Institute for International Economics, 1999.

Eichengreen, Barry and Rose, Andy. "The Empirics of Currency and Banking Crises." Mimeo, University of California–Berkeley, 1998.

Feldstein, Martin. "Self-Protection for Emerging Market Economies." National Bureau of Economic Research (Cambridge, MA) Working Paper No. 6907, January 1999.

Frankel, Jeffrey and Rose, Andy. "Currency Crashes in Emerging Markets: An Empirical Treatment." *Journal of International Economics,* November 1996, 41(3–4), pp. 351–66.

Goldfajin, Ian and Valdes, Rodrigo O. "The Twin Crises and the Role of Liquidity." Mimeo, International Monetary Fund, Washington, DC, 1998.

______. "Liquidity Crises and International Financial Architecture." Unpublished manuscript, Central Bank of Chile, Santiago, July 1999.

Goldstein, Morris. *The Asian Financial crisis: Causes, cures, and systemic implications.* Washington, DC: Institute for International Economics, 1998.

Goldstein, Morris; Kaminsky, Graciella and Reinhart, Carmen. "Assessing Financial Vulnerability: An Early Warning System for Emerging Markets." Mimeo, Institute for International Economics, Washington, DC, 1999.

Jeanne, Olivier. "Sovereign Debt Crises and the Global Financial Architecture." Unpublished manuscript, International Monetary Fund, Washington, DC, November 1999.

Jeanne, Olivier and Wyplosz, Charles. "The International Lender of Last Resort: How Large Is Large Enough" Mimeo, International Monetary Fund, Washington, DC, September 1999.

Johnson, Simon; Boone, Peter; Breach, Alastar and Friedman, Eric. "Corporate Governance in the Asian Financial Crisis." *Journal of Financial Economics,* 2000 (forthcoming).

Kaminsky, Graciella and Reinhart, Carmen. "The Twin Crises: The Causes of Banking and Balance-of-Payments Problems." *American Economic Review,* June 1999, *89*(3), pp. 473–500.

Krugman, Paul. "What Happened to Asia?" Unpublished manuscript, Massachusetts Institute of Technology, January 1998.

______. "Balance Sheets, the Transfer Problem, and Financial Crises," in Peter Isard, Assaf Razin, and Andrew K. Rose, eds., *International finance and international crises: Essays in honor of Robert Flood, Jr.* Washington, DC: International Monetary Fund, 1999.

McKinnon, Ronald and Pill, Huw. "Credible Liberalization and International Capital Flows: The 'Overborrowing Syndrome'," in T. Ito and A. O. Krueger, eds., *Financial deregulation and integration in East Asia.* Chicago: University of Chicago Press, 1996, pp. 7–42.

Morris, Stephen and Shin, Hyun Song. "Unique Equilibrium in a Model of Self-Fulfilling Currency Attacks." *American Economic Review,* June 1998, *88*(3), pp. 587–97.

Prisker, Matthew. "The Channels for Financial Contagion." Unpublished manuscript, Board of Governors of the Federal Reserve System, Washington, DC, January 2000.

Rodrik, Dani and Velasco, Andres. "Short-Term Capital Flows." National Bureau of Economic Research (Cambridge, MA) Working Paper No. 7364, September 1999.

Rogoff, Kenneth. "International Institutions for Reducing Global Financial Instability." *Journal of Economic Perspectives,* Fall 1999, *13*(4), pp. 21–42.

Sachs, Jeffrey and Radelet, Steven. "The Onset of the East Asian Financial Crisis." National Bureau of Economic Research (Cambridge, MA) Working Paper No. 6680, August 1998.

______. "What Have We Learned, So Far, from the East Asian Financial Crisis?" Mimeo, Harvard University, January 1999.

Sachs, Jeffrey; Tornell, Aaron and Velasco, Andres. "Financial Crises in Emerging Markets: The Lessons from 1995." *Brookings Papers on Economic Activity,* 1996, (1), pp. 147–98.

Summers, Lawrence H. "The Right Kind of IMF for a Stable Global Financial System." Speech presented at the London School of Business, London, U.K., 14 December 1999.

Summers, Lawrence H. and Summers, Victoria P. "When Financial Markets Work Too Well: A Cautious Case for a Securities Transaction Tax." *Journal of Financial Services Research,* December 1989, *3*(2–3), pp. 261–86.

Wallace, Neil. "Another Attempt to Explain an Illiquid Banking System: The Diamond and Dybvig Model with Sequential Servicing Taken Seriously." *Federal Reserve Bank of Minneapolis Quarterly Review,* Fall 1988, *12*(4), pp. 3–16.

Zeckhauser, Richard, "The Muddled Responsibilities of Public and Private America," in Winthrop Knowlton and Richard Zeckhauser, eds., *American society: Public and private responsibilities.* Cambridge, MA : Ballinger, 1986, pp. 45–77.

Zettelmeyer, Jeronim, "On the Short-Run Effectiveness of Official Crisis Lending." Unpublished manuscript, International Monetary Fund, Washington, DC, December 1999.

END-OF-CHAPTER QUESTIONS

1. Explain the principal reasons behind the significant increase in private capital flows from industrial to emerging economies since the 1980s.
2. Explain what the real, tangible benefits are of a well-functioning financial system.
3. If international financial integration represents an improvement in financial intermediation, explain why international financial integration offers a potentially significant increase in economic efficiency, with benefits both for consumers and for investors around the world.
4. Comment on the implications of the following fact: all of the growth in the world's labor force over the next few decades will take place in the developing world, as the industrialized world ages, yet most of the world's saving will take place in industrialized countries.
5. From the perspective of developing economies, explain the benefits that can be obtained when international financial flows are efficient and occur in the right kind of environment.
6. Besides the fact that it involves more than one country, how does an international financial crisis differ from a traditional financial crisis that erupts in a particular country?
7. What are some of the common features in countries that were affected by the international financial crises of the 1990s?

8. Describe the term "crony capitalism," an important source of financial instability in emerging economies.
9. What is capital flight? Explain why it is more common in financial crises in emerging economies than it is in more developed, mature economies.
10. Twin crises—currency and banking crises—are common in emerging economies. Explain why currency crises tend to accompany banking crises in developing economies.
11. Another characteristic of financial crises in developing economies is "contagion." Explain the meaning of this concept in light of the ERM crisis of 1992–93, the Mexican peso crisis of 1994–95, the Asian crisis of 1997–98, and the Russian crisis of 1998.
12. What were the major antecedents for the crises in Brazil, Indonesia, South Korea, Mexico, Thailand, and Russia during the 1990s? Which were the most important ones?
13. Explain the four elements of an effective national strategy for minimizing the risk of financial crises in emerging economies.
14. Explain the pros and cons of controls on short-term capital inflows as a crisis-avoidance measure.
15. Comment on the importance of generally accepted accounting principles as an instrument to promote transparency and efficiency in financial markets.
16. Explain the reasons why the International Monetary Fund (IMF) must act in ways that will not worsen the problem of moral hazard in countries that rely on this institution.
17. What are the actions that a credible, coherent policy response must have in order to control an ongoing crisis?
18. What role and what actions should be played by international creditors in times of financial crises in developing countries? Are there best practices that should be followed? Are there practices and demands that should never happen?

PART II

Great Financial Crises

READINGS

IRVING FISHER (1933)
The Debt-Deflation Theory of Great Depressions

BHAGWAN CHOWDHRY AND AMIT GOYAL (2000)
Understanding the Financial Crisis in Asia

CHAPTER 3

The Debt-Deflation Theory of Great Depressions

Irving Fisher

INTRODUCTORY

In *Booms and Depressions,* I have developed, theoretically and statistically, what may be called a debt-deflation theory of great depressions. In the preface, I stated that the results "seem largely new," I spoke thus cautiously because of my unfamiliarity with the vast literature on the subject. Since the book was published its special conclusions have been widely accepted and, so far as I know, no one has yet found them anticipated by previous writers, though several, including myself, have zealously sought to find such anticipations. Two of the best-read authorities in this field assure me that those conclusions are, in the words of one of them, "both new and important."

Partly to specify what some of these special conclusions are which are believed to be new and partly to fit them into the conclusions of other students in this field, I am offering this paper as embodying, in brief, my present "creed" on the whole subject of so-called "cycle theory." My "creed" consists of 49 "articles" some of which are old and some new. I say "creed" because, for brevity, it is purposely expressed dogmatically and without proof. But it is not a creed in the sense that my faith in it does not rest on evidence and that I am not ready to modify it on presentation of new evidence. On the contrary, it is quite tentative. It may serve as a challenge to others and as raw material to help them work out a better product.

Meanwhile the following is a list of my 49 tentative conclusions.

"CYCLE THEORY" IN GENERAL

1. The economic system contains innumerable variables—quantities of "goods (physical wealth, property rights, and services), the prices of these goods, and their values (the quantities multiplied by the prices). Changes in any or all of this vast array of variables may be due to many causes. Only in imagination can all of these variables remain constant and be kept in equilibrium by the balanced forces of human desires, as manifested through "supply and demand."

2. Economic theory includes a study both of (a) such imaginary, ideal equilibrium—which may be stable or unstable—and (b) disequilibrium. The former is economic statics; the latter, economic dynamics. So-called cycle theory is merely one part of the study of economic dis-equilibrium.

Irving Fisher, "The Debt-Deflation Theory of Great Depressions," *Econometrica*, vol. 1, no. 4, pp. 337-357.

3. The study of dis-equilibrium may proceed in either of two ways. We may take as our unit for study an actual historical case of great dis-equilibrium, such as, say, the panic of 1873; or we may take as our unit for study any constituent tendency, such as, say, deflation, and discover its general laws, relations to, and combinations with, other tendencies. The former study revolves around events, or *facts;* the latter, around *tendencies.* The former is primarily economic history; the latter is primarily economic science. Both sorts of studies are proper and important. Each helps the other. The panic of 1873 can only be understood in the light of the various tendencies involved—deflation and other; and deflation can only be understood in the light of the various historical manifestations—1873 and other.

4. The old and apparently still persistent notion of "the" business cycle, as a single, simple, self-generating cycle (analogous to that of a pendulum swinging under influence of the single force of gravity) and as actually realized historically in regularly recurring crises, is a myth. Instead of one force there are many forces. Specifically, instead of one cycle, there are many co-existing cycles, constantly aggravating or neutralizing each other, as well as co-existing with many non-cyclical forces. In other words, while a cycle, conceived as a *fact,* or historical event, is non-existent, there are always innumerable cycles, long and short, big and little, conceived as *tendencies* (as well as numerous non-cyclical tendencies), any historical event being the resultant of all the tendencies then at work. Any one cycle, however perfect and like a sine curve it may tend to be, is sure to be interfered with by other tendencies.

5. The innumerable tendencies making mostly for economic dis-equilibrium may roughly be classified under three groups: (a) growth or trend tendencies, which are steady; (b) haphazard disturbances, which are unsteady; (c) cyclical tendencies, which are unsteady but steadily repeated.

6. There are two sorts of cyclical tendencies. One is "forced" or imposed on the economic mechanism from outside. Such is the yearly rhythm; also the daily rhythm. Both the yearly and the daily rhythm are imposed on us by astronomical forces from outside the economic organization; and there may be others such as from sun spots or transits of Venus. Other examples of "forced" cycles are the monthly and weekly rhythms imposed on us by custom and religion.

The second sort of cyclical tendency is the "free" cycle, not forced from outside, but self-generating, operating analogously to a pendulum or wave motion.

7. It is the "free" type of cycle which is apparently uppermost in the minds of most people when they talk of "the" business cycle. The yearly cycle, though it more nearly approaches a perfect cycle than any other, is seldom thought of as a cycle at all but referred to as "seasonal variation."

8. There may be equilibrium which, though stable, is so delicately poised that, after departure from it beyond certain limits, instability ensues, just as, at first, a stick may bend under strain, ready all the time to bend back, until a certain point is reached, when it breaks. This simile probably applies when a debtor gets "broke,"or when the breaking of many debtors constitutes a "crash," after which there is no coming back to the original equilibrium. To take another simile, such a disaster is somewhat like the "capsizing" of a ship which, under ordinary conditions, is always near stable equilibrium but which, after being tipped beyond a certain angle, has no longer this tendency to return to equilibrium, but, instead, a tendency to depart further from it.

9. We may tentatively assume that, ordinarily and within wide limits, all, or almost all, economic variables tend, in a general way, toward a stable equilibrium. In our classroom expositions of supply and demand curves, we very properly assume that if the price, say, of sugar is above the point at which supply and demand are equal, it tends to fall; and if below, to rise.

10. Under such assumptions, and taking account of "economic friction," which is always present, it follows that, unless some outside force intervenes, any "free" oscillations about equilibrium must tend progressively to grow smaller and smaller, just as a rocking chair set in motion tends to stop. That is, while "forced" cycles, such as seasonal, tend to continue unabated in amplitude, ordinary "free" cycles tend to cease, giving way to equilibrium.

11. But the exact equilibrium thus sought is seldom reached and never long maintained. New disturbances are, humanly speaking, sure to occur, so that, in actual fact, any variable is almost always above or below the ideal equilibrium.

For example, coffee in Brazil may be over-produced, that is, may be more than it would have been if the producers had known in advance that it could not have been sold at a profit. Or there may be a shortage in the cotton crop. Or factory, or commercial inventories may be under or over the equilibrium point.

Theoretically there may be—in fact, at most times there must be—over- or under-production, over- or under-consumption, over- or under-spending, over-or under-saving, over-or under-investment, and over or under everything else. It is as absurd to assume that, for any long period of time, the variables in the economic organization, or any part of them, will "stay put," in perfect equilibrium, as to assume that thc Atlantic Ocean can ever be without a wave.

12. The important variables which may, and ordinarily do, stand above or below equilibrium are: (a) capital items, such as homes, factories, ships, productive capacity generally, inventories, gold, money, credits, and debts; (b) income items, such as real income, volume of trade, shares traded; (c) price items, such as prices of securities, commodities, interest.

13. There may even be a *general* over-production and in either of two senses: (a) there may be, in general, at a particular point of time, over-large inventories or stocks on hand, or (b) there may be, in general, during a particular period of time, an over-rapid flow of production. The classical notion that over-production can only be relative as between different products is erroneous. Aside from the abundance or scarcity of particular products, relative to each other, production as a whole is relative to human desires and aversions, and can as a whole overshoot or undershoot the equilibrium mark.

In fact, except for brief moments, there must always be some degree of general over-production or general under-production and in both senses—stock and flow.

14. But, in practice, general over-production, as popularly imagined, has never, so far as I can discover, been a chief cause of great dis-equilibrium. The reason, or a reason, for the common notion of over-production is mistaking too little money for too much goods.

15. While any deviation from equilibrium of any economic variable theoretically may, and doubtless in practice does, set up some sort of oscillations, the important question is: Which of

them have been sufficiently great disturbers to afford any substantial explanation of the great booms and depressions of history?

16. I am not sufficiently familiar with the long detailed history of these disturbances, nor with the colossal literature concerning their alleged explanations, to have reached any definitive conclusions as to the relative importance of all the influences at work. I am eager to learn from others.

17. According to my present opinion, which is purely tentative, there is some grain of truth in most of the alleged explanations commonly offered, but this grain is often small. Any of them may suffice to explain *small* disturbances, but all of them put together have probably been inadequate to explain *big* disturbances.

18. In particular, as explanations of the so-called business cycle, or cycles, when these are really serious, I doubt the adequacy of over-production, under-consumption, over-capacity, price-dislocation, mal-adjustment between agricultural and industrial prices, over-confidence, over-investment, over-saving, over-spending, and the discrepancy between saving and investment.

19. I venture the opinion, subject to correction on submission of future evidence, that, in the great booms and depressions, each of the above-named factors has played a subordinate rôle as compared with two dominant factors, namely *over-indebtedness* to start with and de*flation* following soon after; also that where any of the other factors do become conspicuous, they are often merely effects or symptoms of these two. In short, the big bad actors are debt disturbances and price-level disturbances.

While quite ready to change my opinion, I have, at present, a strong conviction that these two economic maladies, the debt disease and the price-level disease (or dollar disease), are, in the great booms and depressions, more important causes than all others put together.

20. Some of the other and usually minor factors often derive some importance when combined with one or both of the two dominant factors.

Thus over-investment and over-speculation are often important; but they would have far less serious results were they not conducted with borrowed money. That is, over-indebtedness may lend importance to over-investment or to over-speculation.

The same is true as to over-confidence. I fancy that over-confidence seldom does any great harm except when, as, and if, it beguiles its victims into debt.

Another example is the mal-adjustment between agricultural and industrial prices, which can be shown to be a result of a change in the general price level.

21. Disturbances in these two factors—debt and the purchasing power of the monetary unit—will set up serious disturbances in all, or nearly all, other economic variables. On the other hand, if debt and deflation are absent, other disturbances are powerless to bring on crises comparable in severity to those of 1837, 1873, or 1929-33.

THE ROLES OF DEBT AND DEFLATION

22. No exhaustive list; can be given of the secondary variables affected by the two primary ones, debt and deflation; but they include especially seven, making in all at least nine variables, as

follows: debts, circulating media, their velocity of circulation, price levels, net worths, profits, trade, business confidence, interest rates.

23. *The chief interrelations between the nine chief factors may be derived deductively,* assuming, to start with, that general economic equilibrium is disturbed by only the one factor of over-indebtedness, and, in particular, assuming that there is no other influence, whether accidental or designed, tending to affect the price level.

24. Assuming, accordingly, that, at some point of time, a state of over-indebtedness exists, this will tend to lead to liquidation, through the alarm either of debtors or creditors or both. Then we may deduce the following chain of consequences in nine links: (1) *Debt liquidation* leads to *distress setting* and to (2) *Contraction of deposit currency,* as bank loans are paid off, and to a slowing down of velocity of circulation. This contraction of deposits and of their velocity, precipitated by distress selling, causes (3) *A fall in the level of prices,* in other words, a swelling of the dollar. Assuming, as above stated, that this fall of prices is not interfered with by reflation or otherwise, there must be (4) *A still greater fall in the net worths of business,* precipitating bankruptcies and (5) *A like fall in profits,* which in a " capitalistic," that is, a private-profit society, leads the concerns which are running at a loss to make (6) *A reduction in output, in trade and in employment* of labor. These losses, bankruptcies, and unemployment, lead to (7) *Pessimism and loss of confidence,* which in turn lead to (8) *Hoarding and slowing down still more the velocity of circulation.*

The above eight changes cause (9) *Complicated disturbances in the rates of interest,* in particular, a fall in the nominal, or money, rates and a rise in the real, or commodity, rates of interest.

Evidently debt and deflation go far toward explaining a great mass of phenomena in a very simple logical way.

25. The above chain of causes, consisting of nine links, includes only a few of the interrelations between the nine factors. There are other demonstrable interrelations, both rational and empirical, and doubtless still others which cannot, yet, at least, be formulated at all.[1] There must also be many indirect relations involving variables not included among the nine groups.

26. One of the most important of such interrelations (and probably too little stressed in my *Booms and Depressions)* is the direct effect of lessened money, deposits, and their velocity, in curtailing trade, as evidenced by the fact that trade has been revived locally by emergency money without any raising of the price level.

27. In actual chronology, the order of the nine events is somewhat different from the above "logical" order, and there are reactions and repeated effects. As stated in Appendix I of *Booms and Depressions:*

1 Many of these interrelations have been shown statistically, and by many writers. Some, which I have so shown and which fit in with the debt-deflation theory, are: that price-change, after a distributed lag, causes, or is followed by, corresponding fluctuations in the volume of trade, employment, bankruptcies, and rate of interest. The results as to price-change and unemployment are contained in Charts II and III, pp. 352–3. See references at the end of this article; also footnote 2, page 345, regarding the charts.

The following table of our nine factory, occurring and recurring (together with distress selling), gives a fairly typical, though still inadequate, picture of the cross-currents of a depression in the approximate order in which it is believed they usually occur. (The first occurrence of each factor and its sub-divisions is indicated by italics. The figures in parenthesis show the sequence in the original exposition.)

I. (7) Mild *Gloom* and Shock to *Confidence*
(8) Slightly *Reduced Velocity* of Circulation
(1) Debt *Liquidation*

II. (9) *Money Interest* on Safe Loans Falls
(9) But Money Interest on Unsafe Loans Rises

III. (2) *Distress Selling*
(7) More Gloom
(3) Fall *in Security Prices*
(1) More Liquidation
(3) *Fall in Commodity Prices*

IV. (9) *Real Interest Rises;* REAL DEBTS INCREASE
(7) More Pessimism and Distrust
(1) More Liquidation
(2) More Distress Selling
(8) More Reduction in Velocity

V. (2) More Distress Selling
(2) *Contraction of Deposit Currency*
(3) Further Dollar Enlargement

VI. (4) *Reduction in Net Worth*
(4) Increase in *Bankruptcies*
(7) More Pessimism and Distrust
(8) More Slowing in Velocity
(1) More Liquidation

VII. (5) *Decrease in Profits*
(5) *Increase in Losses*
(7) Increase in Pessimism
(8) Slower Velocity
(1) More Liquidation
(6) *Reduction in Volume of Stock Trading*

VIII. (6) *Decrease in Construction*
(6) *Reduction in Output*
(6) *Reduction in Trade*
(6) *Unemployment*
(7) More Pessimism

IX. (8) *Hoarding*

X. (8) *Runs on Banks*

(8) *Banks Curtailing Loans* for Self-Protection

(8) *Banks Selling Investments*

(8) *Bank Failures*

(7) Distrust Grows

(8) More Hoarding

(1) More Liquidation

(2) More Distress Selling

(3) Further Dollar Enlargement

As has been stated, this order (or any order, for that matter) can be only approximate and subject to variations at different times and places. It represents my present guess as to how, if not too much interfered with, the nine factors selected for explicit study in this book are likely in most cases to fall in line.

But, as has also been stated, the idea of a single-line succession is itself inadequate, for while Factor (1) acts on (2), for instance, it also acts *directly* on (7), so that we really need a picture of subdividing streams or, better, an interacting network in which each factor may be pictured as influencing and being influenced by many or all of the others.

Paragraph 24 above gives a logical, and paragraph 27 a chronological, order of the chief variables put out of joint in a depression when once started by over-indebtedness.

28. But it should be noted that, except for the first and last in the "logical" list, namely debt and interest on debts, *all the fluctuations listed come about through a fall of prices*.

29. When over-indebtedness stands alone, that is, does *not* lead to a fall of prices, in other words, when its tendency to do so is counteracted by inflationary forces (whether by accident or design), the resulting "cycle" will be far milder and far more regular.

30. Likewise, when a deflation occurs from other than debt causes and without any great volume of debt, the resulting evils are much less. It is the combination of both—the debt disease coming first, then precipitating the dollar disease—which works the greatest havoc.

31. The two diseases act and react on each other. Pathologists are now discovering that a pair of diseases are sometimes worse than either or than the mere sum of both, so to speak. And we all know that a minor disease may lead to a major one. Just as a bad cold leads to pneumonia, so over-indebtedness leads to deflation.

32. And, vice versa, deflation caused by the debt reacts on the debt. Each dollar of debt still unpaid becomes a bigger dollar, and if the over-indebtedness with which we started was great enough, the liquidation of debts cannot keep up with the fall of prices which it causes. In that case, the liquidation defeats itself. While it diminishes the number of dollars owed, it may not do so as fast as it increases the value of each dollar owed. Then, *the very effort of individuals to lessen their burden of debts increases it, because of the mass effect of the stampede to liquidate in swelling each dollar owed.* Then we have the great paradox which, I submit, is the chief secret of most, if not all, great depressions: *The more the debtors pay, the more they owe.* The more the economic boat tips, the more it tends to tip. It is not tending to right itself, but is capsizing.

33. But if the over-indebtedness is not sufficiently great to make liquidation thus defeat itself, the situation is different and simpler. It is then more analogous to stable equilibrium; the more the boat rocks the more it will tend to right itself. In that case, we have a truer example of a cycle.

34. In the "capsizing" type in particular, the worst of it is that real incomes are so rapidly and progressively reduced. Idle men and idle machines spell lessened production and lessened real income, the central factor in all economic science. Incidentally this under-production occurs at the very time that there is the illusion of over-production.

35. In this rapid survey, I have not discussed what constitutes over-indebtedness. Suffice it here to note that (a) over-indebtedness is always relative to other items, including national wealth and income and the gold supply, which last is specially important, as evidenced by the recent researches of Warren and Pearson; and (b) it is not a mere one-dimensional magnitude to be measured simply by the number of dollars owed. It must also take account of the distribution in time of the sums coming due. Debts due at once are more embarrassing than debts due years hence; and those payable at the option of the creditor, than those payable at the convenience of the debtor. Thus debt embarrassment is great for call loans and for early maturities.

For practical purposes, we may roughly measure the total national debt embarrassment by taking the total sum currently due, say within the current year, including rent, taxes, interest, installments, sinking fund requirements, maturities and any other definite or rigid commitments for payment on principal.

ILLUSTRATED BY THE DEPRESSION OF 1929–33[2]

36. The depression out of which we are now (I trust) emerging is an example of a debt-deflation depression of the most serious sort. The debts of 1929 were the greatest known, both nominally and really, up to that time.

They were great enough not only to "rock the boat" but to start it capsizing. By March, 1933, liquidation had reduced the debts about 20 per cent, but had increased the dollar about 75 per

2 Note the charts, pp. 352–7:

Chart I shows: (1) the price level (*P*) and (2) its percentage rate of rise or fall (*P'*). When the last named is lagged with the lag distributed according to a probability curve so that the various *P'*'s overlap and cumulate we get $\bar{P}'$, as in Charts II and III. This $\bar{P}'$ is virtually a lagged average of the P''s.

Charts II and III show: $\bar{P}'$ contrasted with employment (E). $\bar{P}'$ may be considered as what employment would be if controlled *entirely* by price-change.

Chart IV shows the Swedish official (retail) weekly index number contrasted with the American weekly wholesale and monthly retail indexes.

Chart V shows the estimated internal debt in the United States contrasted with the estimated total money value of wealth. The unshaded extensions of the bars upward show what the 1933 figures would be if enlarged 75 per cent to translate them into 1929 dollars (according to the index number of wholesale commodity prices).

Chart VI shows estimated "fixed" annual charges (actually collected) contrasted with estimated national income. The unshaded extensions of the bars upward show what the 1932 figures would be if enlarged 56 per cent to translate them into 1929 dollars.

Charts VII and *VIII* show the chief available statistics before and after March 4, 1933, grouped in the order indicated in Article 27 above.

cent, so that the *real* debt, that is the debt as measured in terms of commodities, was increased about 40 per cent [(100% – 20%) × (100% + 75%) = 140%]. Note Chart V.

37. Unless some counteracting cause comes along to prevent the fall in the price level, such a depression as that of 1929-33 (namely when the more the debtors pay the more they owe) tends to continue, going deeper, in a vicious spiral, for many years. There is then no tendency of the boat to stop tipping until it has capsized. Ultimately, of course, but only after almost universal bankruptcy, the indebtedness must cease to grow greater and begin to grow less. Then comes recovery and a tendency for a new boom-depression sequence. This is the so-called "natural" way out of a depression, via needless and cruel bankruptcy, unemployment, and starvation.

38. On the other hand, if the foregoing analysis is correct, it is always economically possible to stop or prevent such a depression simply by reflating the price level up to the average level at which outstanding debts were contracted by existing debtors and assumed by existing creditors, and then maintaining that level unchanged.

That the price level is controllable is not only claimed by monetary theorists but has recently been evidenced by two great events: (1) Sweden has now for nearly two years maintained a stable price level, practically always within 2 per cent of the chosen par and usually within 1 per cent. Note Chart IV. (2) The fact that immediate reversal of deflation is easily achieved by the use, or even the prospect of use, of appropriate instrumentalities has just been demonstrated by President Roosevelt. Note Charts VII and VIII.

39. Those who imagine that Roosevelt's avowed reflation is not the cause of our recovery but that we had "reached the bottom anyway" are very much mistaken. At any rate, they have given no evidence, so far as I have seen, that we had reached the bottom. And if they are right, my analysis must be woefully wrong. According to all the evidence, under that analysis, debt and deflation, which had wrought havoc up to March 4, 1933, were then stronger than ever and, if let alone, would have wreaked greater wreckage than ever, after March 4. Had no "artificial respiration" been applied, we would soon have seen general bankruptcies of the mortgage guarantee companies, savings banks, life insurance companies, railways, municipalities, and states. By that time the Federal Government would probably have become unable to pay its bills without resort to the printing press, which would itself have been a very belated and unfortunate case of artificial respiration. If even then our rulers should still have insisted on "leaving recovery to nature" and should still have refused to inflate in any way, should vainly have tried to balance the budget and discharge more government employees, to raise taxes, to float, or try to float, more loans, they would soon have ceased to be our rulers. For we would have insolvency of our national government itself, and probably some form of political revolution without waiting for the next legal election. The mid-west farmers had already begun to defy the law.

40. If all this is true, it would be as silly and immoral to "let nature take her course" as for a physician to neglect a case of pneumonia. It would also be a libel on economic science, which has its therapeutics as truly as medical science.

41. If reflation can now so easily and quickly reverse the deadly down-swing of deflation after nearly four years, when it was gathering increased momentum, it would have been still

easier, and at any time, to have stopped it earlier. In fact, under President Hoover, recovery was apparently well started by the Federal Reserve open-market purchases, which revived prices and business from May to September 1932. The efforts were not kept up and recovery was stopped by various circumstances, including the political "campaign of fear."

It would have been still easier to have prevented the depression almost altogether. In fact, in my opinion, this would have been done had Governor Strong of the Federal Reserve Bank of New York lived, or had his policies been embraced by other banks and the Federal Reserve Board and pursued consistently after his death.[3] In that case, there would have been nothing worse than the first crash. We would have had the debt disease, but not the dollar disease—the bad cold but not the pneumonia.

42. If the debt-deflation theory of great depressions is essentially correct, the question of controlling the price level assumes a new importance; and those in the drivers' seats—the Federal Reserve Board and the Secretary of the Treasury, or, let us hope, a special stabilization commission—will in future be held to a new accountability.

43. Price level control, or dollar control, would not be a panacea. Even with an ideally stable dollar, we would still be exposed to the debt disease, to the technological-unemployment disease, to over-production, price-dislocation, over-confidence, and many other minor diseases. To find the proper therapy for these diseases will keep economists busy long after we have exterminated the dollar disease.

DEBT STARTERS

44. The over-indebtedness hitherto presupposed must have had its starters. It may be started by many causes, of which the most common appears to be *new opportunities to invest at a big prospective profit,* as compared with ordinary profits and interest, such as through new inventions, new industries, development of new resources, opening of new lands or new markets. Easy money is the great cause of over-borrowing. When an investor thinks he can make over 100 per cent per annum by borrowing at 6 per cent, he will be tempted to borrow, and to invest or speculate with borrowed money. This was a prime cause leading to the over-indebtedness of 1929. Inventions and technological improvements created wonderful investment opportunities, and so caused big debts. Other causes were the left-over war debts, domestic and foreign, public and private, the reconstruction loans to foreigners, and the low interest policy adopted to help England get back on the gold standard in 1925.

Each case of over-indebtedness has its own starter or set of starters. The chief starters of the over-indebtedness leading up to the crisis of 1837 were connected with lucrative investment

3 Eventually, however, in order to have avoided depression, the gold standard would have had to be abandoned or modified (by devaluation); for, with the gold standard as of 1929, the price levels at that time could not have been maintained indefinitely in the face of: (1) the "scramble for gold" due to the continued extension of the gold standard to include nation after nation; (2) the increasing volume of trade; and (3) the prospective insufficiency of the world gold supply.

opportunities from developing the West and Southwest in real estate, cotton, canal building (led by the Erie Canal), steamboats; and turnpikes, opening up each side of the Appalachian Mountains to the other. For the over-indebtedness leading up to the crisis of 1873, the chief starters were the exploitation of railways and of western farms following the Homestead Act. The over-indebtedness leading up to the panic of 1893 was chiefly relative to the gold base which had become too small, because of the injection of too much silver. But the panic of 1893 seems to have had less of the debt ingredient than in most cases, though deflation played a leading rôle.

The starter may, of course, be wholly or in part the pendulum-like back-swing or reaction in recovery from a preceding depression as commonly assumed by cycle theorists. This, of itself, would tend to leave the next depression smaller than the last.

45. When the starter consists of new opportunities to make unusually profitable investments, the bubble of debt tends to be blown bigger and faster than when the starter is great misfortune causing merely non-productive debts. The only notable exception is a great war and even then chiefly because it leads *after it is over* to productive debts for reconstruction purposes.

46. This is quite different from the common naïve opinions of how war results in depression. If the present interpretation is correct, the World War need never have led to a great depression. It is very true that much or most of the inflations could not have been helped because of the exigencies of governmental finance, but the subsequent undue deflations could probably have been avoided entirely.

47. The public psychology of going into debt for gain passes through several more or less distinct phases: (a) the lure of big prospective dividends or gains in *income* in the remote future; (b) the hope of selling at a profit, and realizing a *capital* gain in the immediate future; (c) the vogue of reckless promotions, taking advantage of the habituation of the public to great expectations; (d) the development of downright fraud, imposing on a public which had grown credulous and gullible.

When it is too late the dupes discover scandals like the Hatry, Krueger, and Insull scandals. At least one book has been written to prove that crises are due to frauds of clever promoters. But probably these frauds could never have become so great without the original starters of real opportunities to invest lucratively. There is probably always a very real basis for the "new era" psychology before it runs away with its victims. This was certainly the case before 1929.

48. In summary, we find that: (1) economic changes include steady trends and unsteady occasional disturbances which act as starters for cyclical oscillations of innumerable kinds; (2) among the many occasional disturbances, are new opportunities to invest, especially because of new inventions; (3) these, with other causes, sometimes conspire to lead to a great volume of over-indebtedness; (4) this, in turn, leads to attempts to liquidate; (5) these, in turn, lead *(unless counteracted by reflation)* to falling prices or a swelling dollar; (6) the dollar may swell faster than the number of dollars owed shrinks; (7) in that case, liquidation does not really liquidate but actually aggravates the debts, and the depression grows worse instead of better, as indicated by all nine factors; (8) the ways out are either *via laissez faire* (bankruptcy) or scientific medication (reflation), and reflation might just as well have been applied in the first place.

49. The general correctness of the above "debt-deflation theory of great depressions" is, I believe, evidenced by experience in the present and previous great depressions. Future studies by others will doubtless check up on this opinion. One way is to compare different countries simultaneously. If the "debt-deflation theory" is correct, the infectiousness of depressions internationally is chiefly due to a common gold (or other) monetary standard and there should be found little tendency for a depression to pass from a deflating to an inflating, or stabilizing, country.

SOME NEW FEATURES

As stated at the outset, several features of the above analysis are, as far as I know, new. Some of these are too unimportant or self-evident to stress. The one (No. 32 above; also 36) which I do venture to stress most is the theory that when over-indebtedness is so great as to depress prices faster than liquidation, the mass effort to get out of debt sinks us more deeply into debt.[4] I would also like to emphasize the whole logical articulation of the nine factors, of which debt and deflation are the two chief (Nos. 23, 24, and 28, above). I would call attention to *new investment opportunities* as the important "starter" of over-indebtedness (Nos. 44, 45). Finally, I would emphasize the important corollary, of the debt-deflation theory, that great depressions are curable and preventable through reflation and stabilization (Nos. 38–42).

Yale University

4 This interaction between liquidation and deflation did not occur to me until 1931, although, with others, I had since 1909 been stressing the fact that deflation tended toward depression and inflation toward a boom.

This debt-deflation theory was first stated in my lectures at Yale in 1931, and first stated publicly before the American Association for the Advancement of Science, on January 1, 1932. It is fully set forth in my *Booms and Depressions*, 1932, and some special features of my general views on cycle theory in "Business Cycles as Facts or Tendencies" in *Economische Opstellen Aangehoden aan Prof. C. A. Verrijn Stuart*, Haarlem, 1931. Certain sorts of disequilibrium are discussed in other writings. The rôle of the lag between real and nominal interest is discussed in *The Purchasing Power of Money*, Macmillan, New York, 1911; and more fully in *The Theory of Interest*, Macmillan, New York, 1930, as well as the effects of inequality of foresight. Some statistical verification will be found in "Our Unstable Dollar and the So-called Business Cycle," *Journal of the American Statistical Association*, June, 1925, pp. 179–202, and "The Relation of Employment to the Price Level" (address given before a section of the American Association for the Advancement of Science, Atlantic City, N. J., December 28, 1932, and later published in *Stabilization of Employment*, edited by Charles F. Roos, The Principia Press, Inc., Bloomingdale, Ind., 1933, pp. 152–159). See Charts I, II, III. Some statistical verification will be found in *The Stock Market Crash and After*, Macmillan, New York, 1930.

A selected bibliography of the writings of others is given in Appendix III of *Booms and Depressions*, Adelphi Company, New York, 1932. This bibliography omitted Veblen's *Theory of Business Enterprise*, Charles Scribner's Sons, New York, 1904, Chapter VII of which, Professor Wesley C. Mitchell points out, probably comes nearest to the debt-deflation theory. Hawtrey's writings seem the next nearest. Professor Alvin H. Hansen informs me that Professor Paxson, of the American History Department of the University of Wisconsin, in a course on the History of the West some twenty years ago, stressed the debt factor and its relation to deflation. But, so far as I know, no one hitherto has pointed out how debt liquidation defeats itself via deflation nor several other features of the present "creed." If any clear-cut anticipation exists, it can never have been prominently set forth, for even the word "debt" is missing in the indexes of the treatises on the subject.

CHARTS

The following eight charts are all on the "ratio scale" excepting Charts II, III, V, VI, and curve *P*' of Chart I. The particular ratio scale used is indicated in each case.

It will be noted that in Charts VII and VIII all curves have a common ratio scale, as indicated by the inset at the right in both charts, except "Brokers' Loans" in Chart VII and "Failures Numbers," "Failures Liabilities," and "Shares Traded" in Chart VIII, which four curves have another, "reduced" i.e., smaller, common scale, as indicated by the inset at the left of Chart VIII.

It will be further noted that "Money in Circulation," "Failures Numbers," and "Failures Liabilities" are inverted.

The full details of how $\bar{P}'$ in Charts II and III is derived from *P*' in Chart I and also how P' in Chart I is derived from *P* are given in "Our Unstable Dollar and the So-Called Business Cycle," *Journal of the American Statistical Association*, June, 1925.

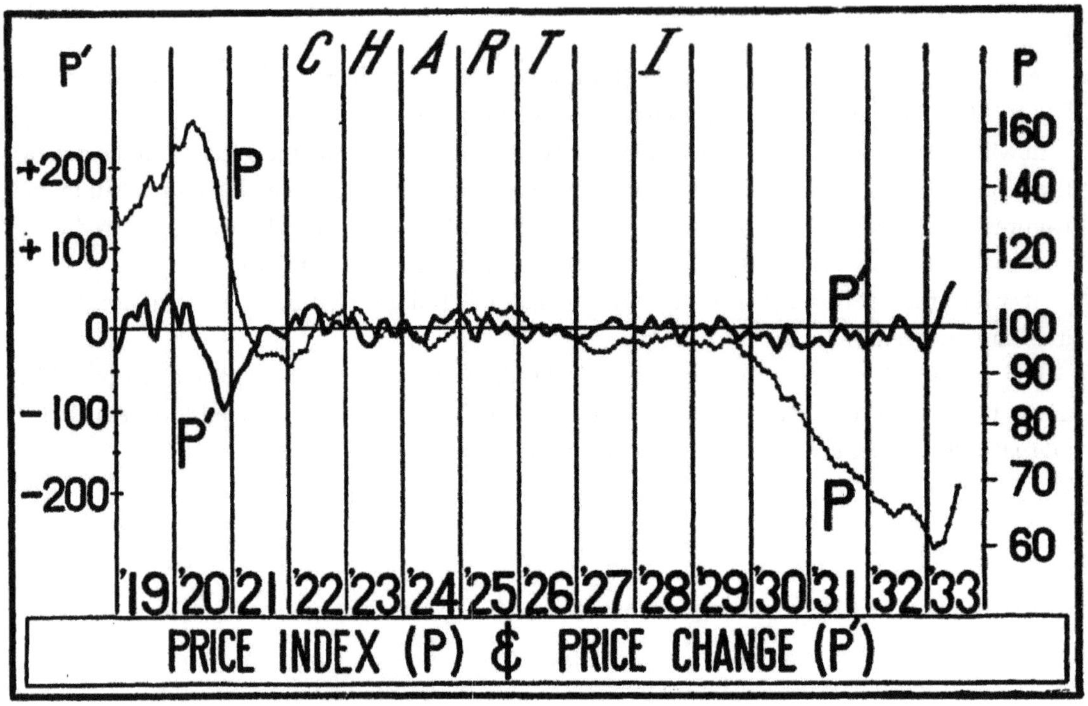
CHART I
P'
P
+200
+100
0
-100
-200
160
140
120
100
90
80
70
60
P
P'
P'
P
'19 '20 '21 '22 '23 '24 '25 '26 '27 '28 '29 '30 '31 '32 '33
PRICE INDEX (P) & PRICE CHANGE (P')

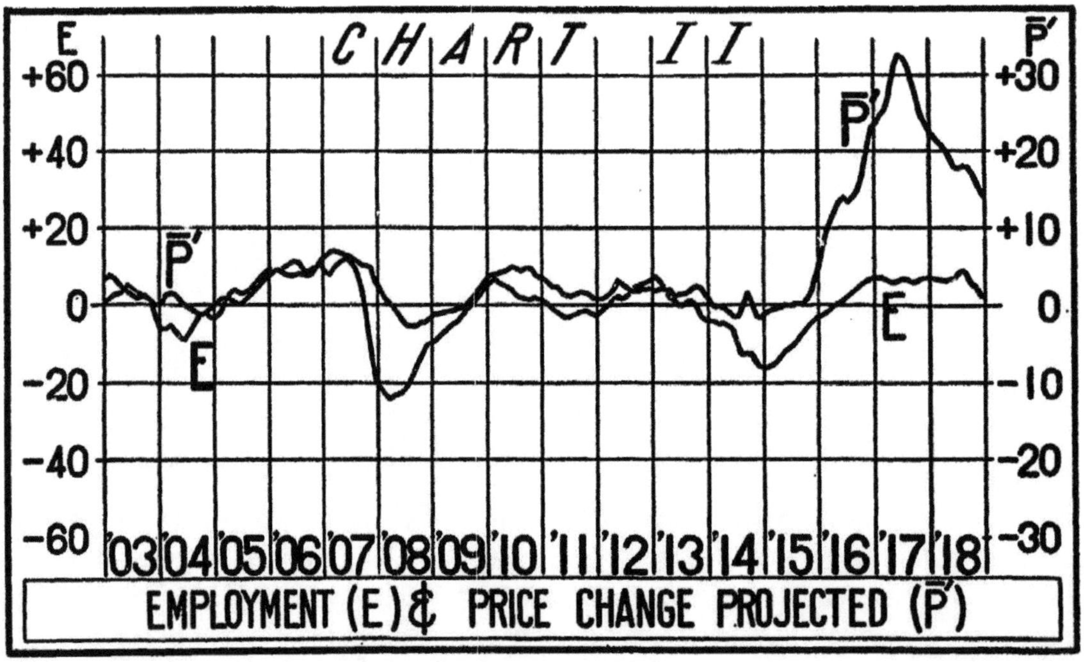
CHART II
E
+60
+40
+20
0
-20
-40
-60
+30
+20
+10
0
-10
-20
-30
E
E
'03 '04 '05 '06 '07 '08 '09 '10 '11 '12 '13 '14 '15 '16 '17 '18
EMPLOYMENT (E) & PRICE CHANGE PROJECTED

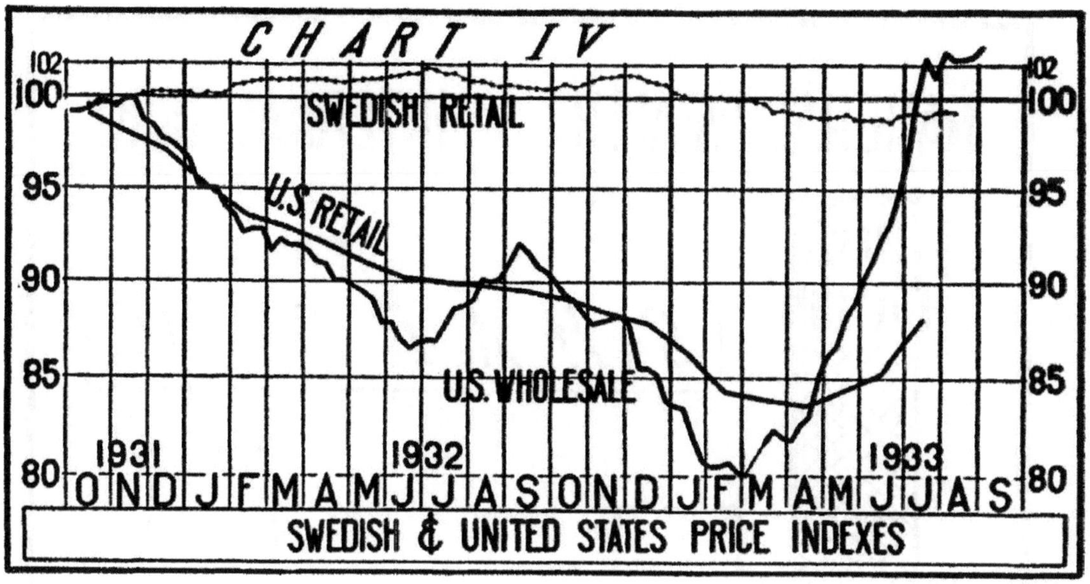
CHART IV
SWEDISH RETAIL
U.S. RETAIL
U.S. WHOLESALE
102
100
95
90
85
80
1931
1932
1933
O N D J F M A M J J A S O N D J F M A M J J A S
SWEDISH & UNITED STATES PRICE INDEXES

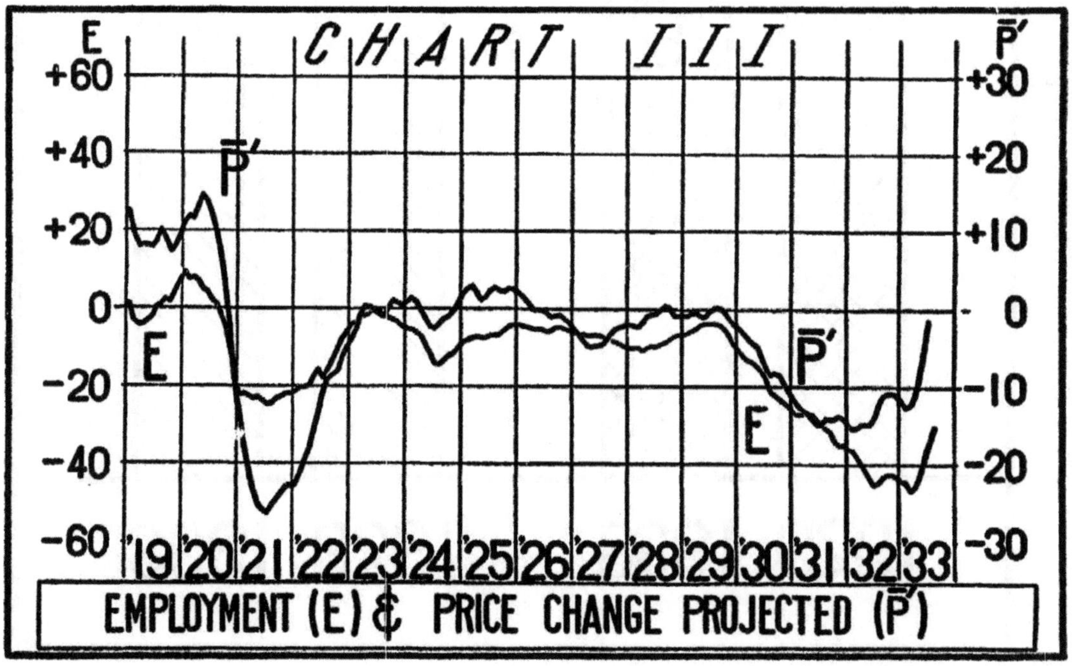
CHART III
E
P̄′
+60
+40
+20
0
-20
-40
-60
+30
+20
+10
0
-10
-20
-30
'19 20 21 22 23 24 25 26 27 28 29 30 31 32 33
EMPLOYMENT (E) & PRICE CHANGE PROJECTED (P̄′)

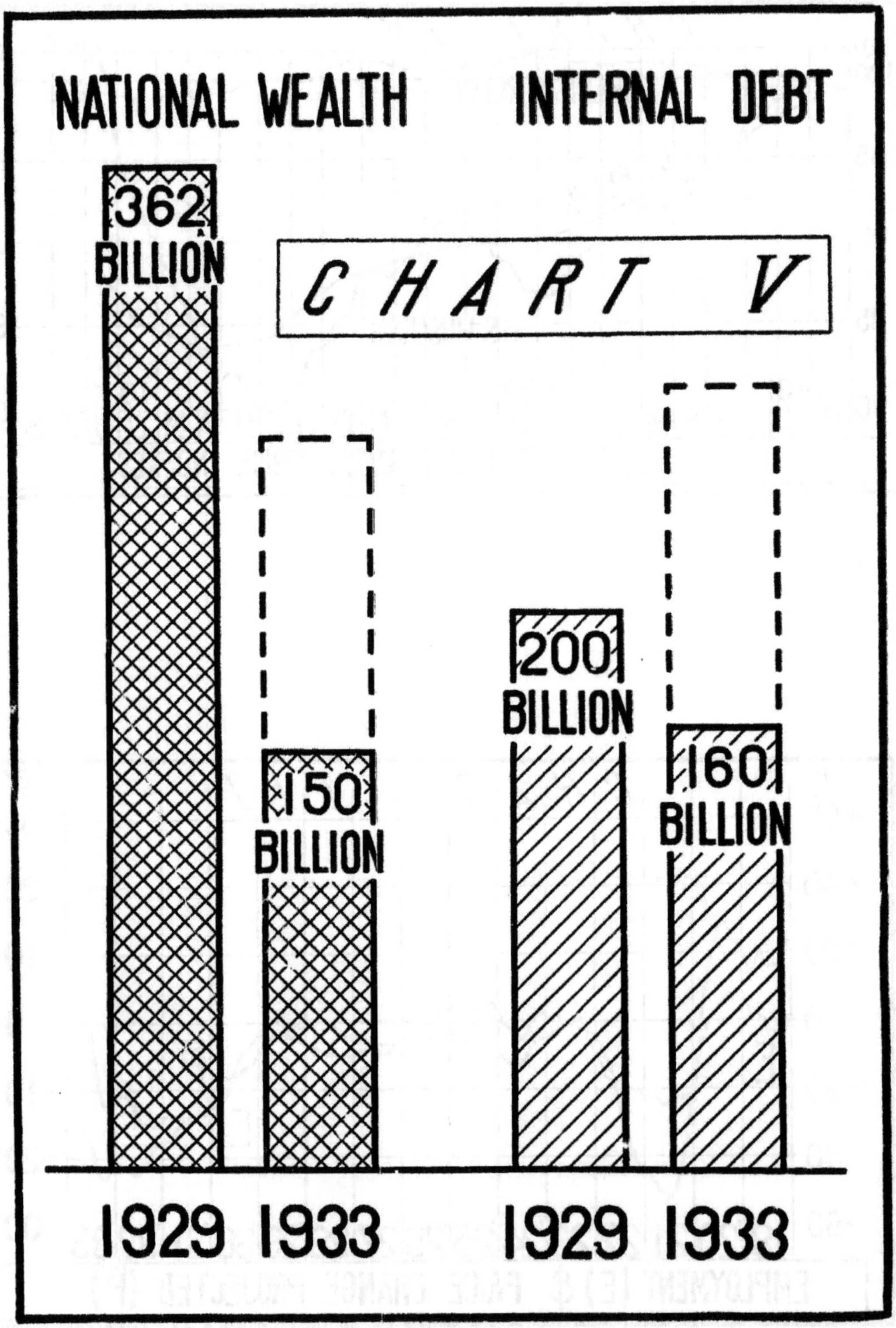
NATIONAL WEALTH
INTERNAL DEBT
CHART V
362 BILLION
150 BILLION
200 BILLION
160 BILLION
1929
1933
1929
1933

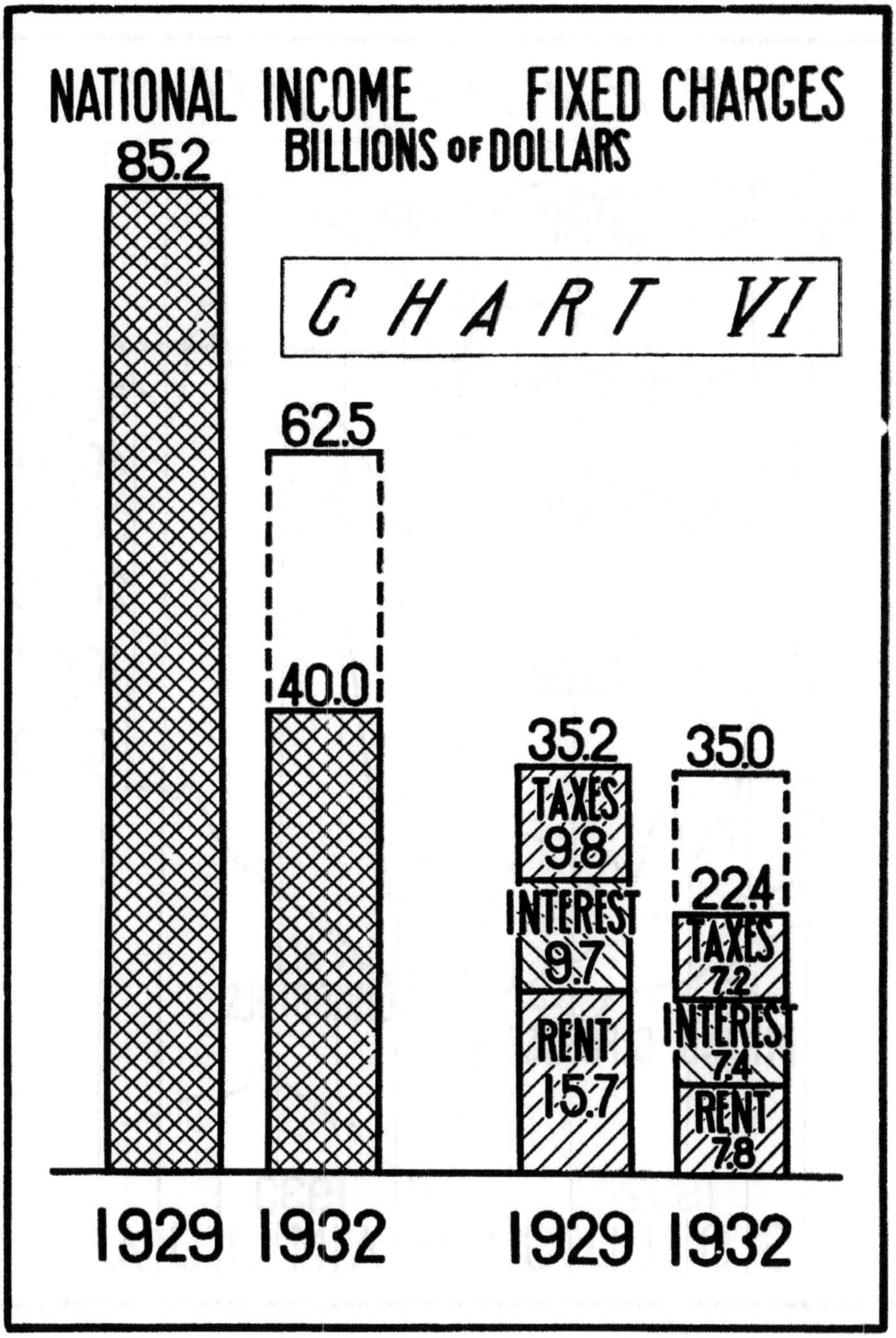
NATIONAL INCOME
FIXED CHARGES
BILLIONS OF DOLLARS
CHART VI
85.2
62.5
40.0
35.2
TAXES 9.8
INTEREST 9.7
RENT 15.7
35.0
22.4
TAXES 7.2
INTEREST 7.4
RENT 7.8
1929
1932
1929
1932

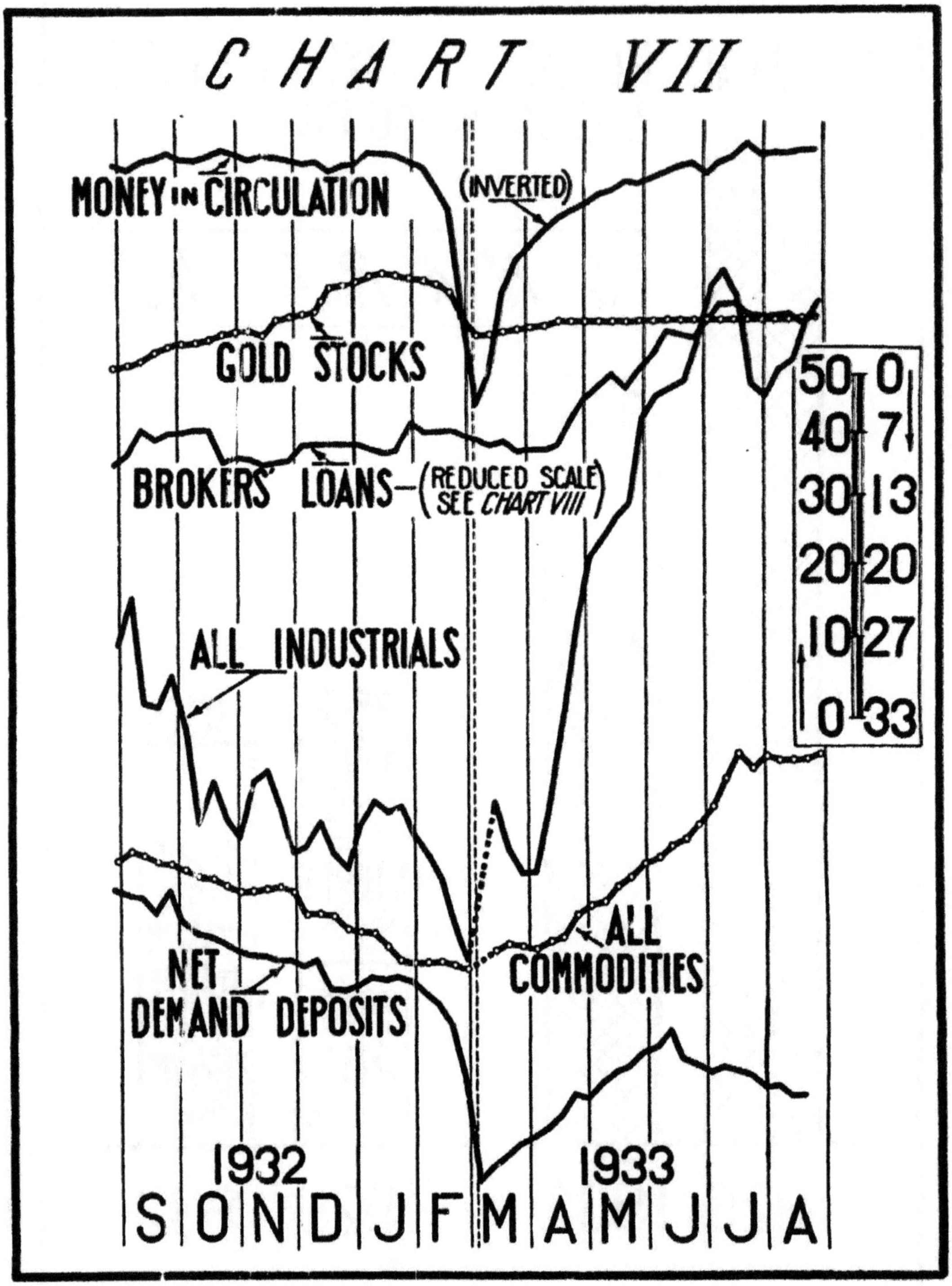
CHART VII
MONEY IN CIRCULATION
(INVERTED)
GOLD STOCKS
BROKERS' LOANS—(REDUCED SCALE SEE CHART VIII)
ALL INDUSTRIALS
NET DEMAND DEPOSITS
ALL COMMODITIES
50 40 30 20 10 0
0 7 13 20 27 33
1932
1933
S O N D J F M A M J J A

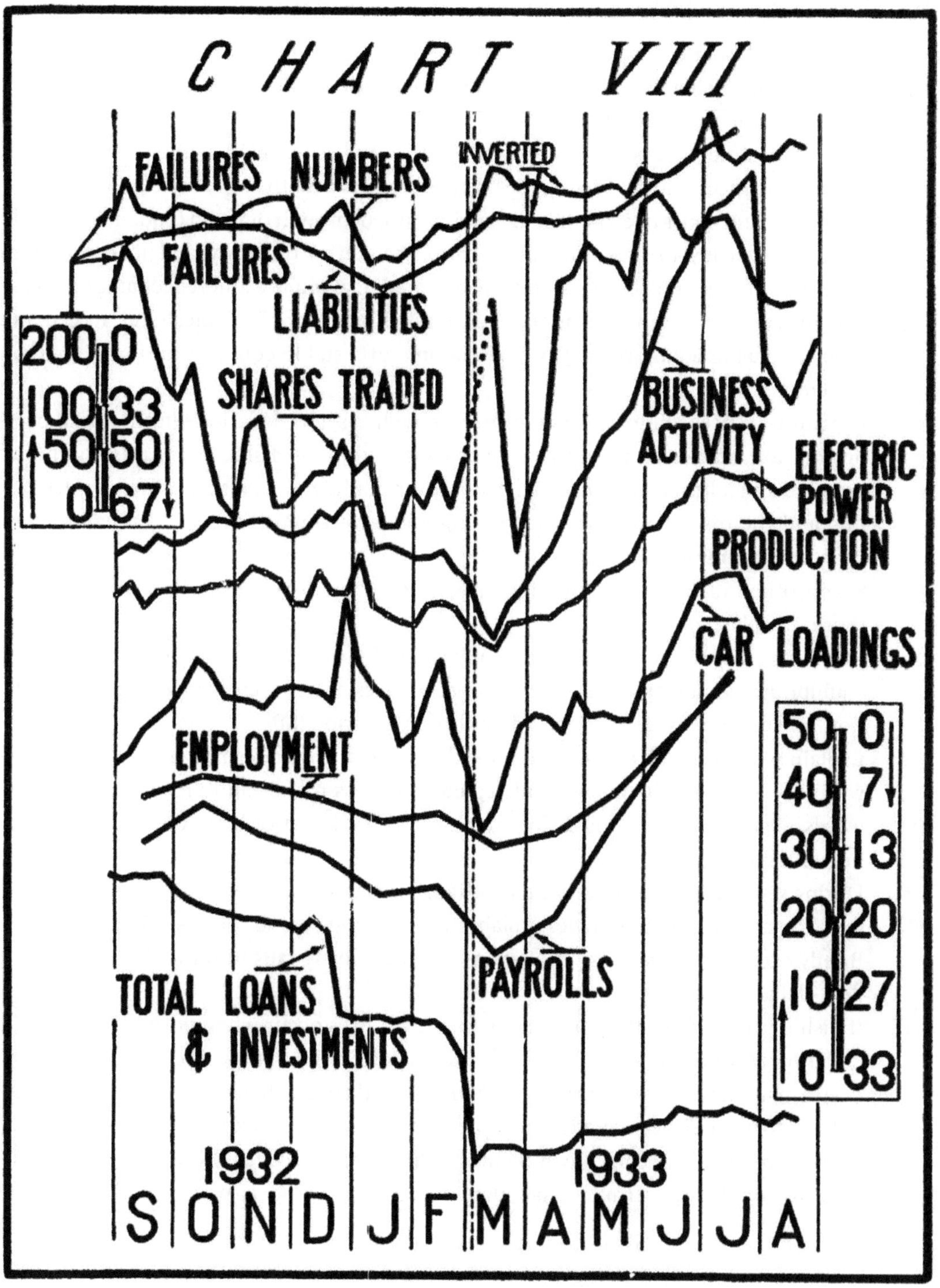
CHART VIII
FAILURES NUMBERS
INVERTED
FAILURES
LIABILITIES
SHARES TRADED
BUSINESS ACTIVITY
ELECTRIC POWER PRODUCTION
CAR LOADINGS
EMPLOYMENT
PAYROLLS
TOTAL LOANS & INVESTMENTS
200 0
100 33
50 50
0 67
50 0
40 7
30 13
20 20
10 27
0 33
1932
1933
S O N D J F M A M J J A

END-OF-CHAPTER QUESTIONS

1. Explain the Fisher theory of debt-deflation.
2. Explain what Fisher means when he states that cycle theory is merely one part of the study of economic disequilibrium.
3. What is the difference between economic history and economic science?
4. Explain why, according to Fisher, the business cycle is a myth.
5. There are three types of economic disequilibrium: (i) growth or trend tendencies, which are deemed steady; (ii) haphazard disturbances, which are unsteady; and (iii) cyclical tendencies, which are unsteady but steadily repeated. Explain the differences among them.
6. Explain why it is assumed that all, or almost all, economic variables tend, in general, toward a stable equilibrium. Give an example of a stable equilibrium in the market for lemons.
7. Explain why, according to Fisher, over-indebtedness and deflation—rather than over-production, under-consumption, over-capacity, price-dislocation, misalignment between agricultural and industrial prices, over-confidence, over-investment, over-saving, and the discrepancy between saving and investment—are the real culprits of economic booms and recessions.
8. Seven other variables are significantly affected by debt and deflation. What are those variables?
9. Assuming an economy in long-run equilibrium, if over-indebtedness altered the initial equilibrium, what would the chain of consequences be between unstainable debt, deflation, and the other seven variables described in question (8)?
10. Explain why over-indebtedness alone—that is, debt that does not lead to deflation—will only lead to a far milder and regular business cycle—and vice versa. In other words, explain why debt and deflation must act together in order to create a significant financial crisis.
11. During severe financial crises, when both high debt and deflation are at work, the more debtors pay, the more they owe. Explain the reasoning behind this assertion.
12. Briefly explain why the crisis that started in 1929 neatly falls into the description of a debt-deflation depression
13. If Fisher is right in stating that severe financial crises occur when both high debt and deflation occur at the same time, how could central banks stop or prevent crises from occurring? Have the response of governments and central banks to recent crises been witness to what Fisher was advocating almost a century ago? Explain.
14. What were the reasons for the over-indebtedness that preceded the stock market crash in 1929? Could the government have done something in order to prevent such high debt?

CHAPTER 4

Understanding the Financial Crisis in Asia

Bhagwan Chowdhry*, Amit Goyal
The Anderson Graduate School of Management at UCLA, 405 Hilgard Avenue, Los Angeles, CA 90095-1481, USA

ABSTRACT

The financial crisis of East Asia in 1997 was largely unanticipated and was characterized by sharp falls in asset prices and currency values in several countries simultaneously. Many empirical models have been developed to predict the occurrence of such crisis. However, the out-of-sample performance of these models is disappointing. Most theoretical explanations of the crisis emphasize the role of banking sector and revolve around models of moral hazard or self-fulfilling runs on liquidity. Empirical tests of the models are, however, rare. Much work remains to be done to explain the contagion, and the effects of equity capital flows. ©2000 Elsevier Science B.V. All rights reserved.

JEL classification: F30; G15; G21; G31

Keywords: Financial crisis; Real exchange rate; Moral hazard; Run; Liquidity; Capital flows

1. INTRODUCTION

The financial crisis that engulfed much of East Asia in 1997 and thereafter appeared to be largely over by the dawn of the new millennium. However, the analysis of the causes and the consequences of the crisis, of the lessons we have learned, and of the policy implications one can derive from such analyses, is likely to continue unabated well into the new millennium. Much has been written and debated about the crisis, in academic circles as well as in the popular press.[1] The articles that appear in this issue contribute to the scholarly research on this topic by providing us with novel insights and empirical analyses that add to our understanding of the many complex

* Corresponding author. Tel.: +1-310-825-5883; fax: +1-209-315-6446.
E-mail address: bhagwan@anderson.ucla.edu (B. Chowdhry).

1 See Prof. Nouriel Roubini's amazingly comprehensive website at www.stern.nyu.edu/~nroubini/asia/AsiaHomepage.html.

Bhagwan Chowdhry and Amit Goyal, "Understanding the Financial Crisis in Asia," *Pacific-Basin Finance Journal*, vol. 8, no. 2, pp. 135-152. Copyright © 2000 by Elsevier B.V. Reprinted with permission.

issues involved. In this article, we attempt to gain a perspective by making sense of the growing scholarly research on this topic. The reading of the literature uncovers several unanswered questions in our minds and thus, we hope to provide not only an understanding of the extant literature but also a research agenda for scholars in the field to take up in their research endeavors.

2. CHARACTERIZING THE CRISIS

The two most visible defining characteristics of a country that experiences a financial crisis are a large drop in the value of its currency and a large drop in its traded equity prices (Figure 4.1). In fact, the event that appears to have triggered the crisis in East Asia was the announcement on July 2, 1997 that the Thai baht would be allowed to float, effectively devaluing the baht by about 20%. Philippines, Malaysia, Indonesia and South Korea abandoned the defense of the currency soon thereafter. By January of 1998, currencies of all of these countries had suffered a tremendous decline.[2] Even Taiwan and Singapore devalued their currency in what is termed as *competitive* devaluation.[3] Hong Kong is the only country in East Asia that successfully defended its currency against speculative attacks and has maintained its parity with the U.S. dollar. The stock markets in all these countries in Asia plunged as the currency crisis engulfed most of East Asian countries.[4] One of the biggest challenges facing scholars studying the East Asian financial crisis is to explain this contagion in which crisis emanating from one country soon swept across all countries in the region.

Currency crises are usually (but not always) preceded by a gradual deterioration in economic fundamentals, such as a significant expansion in money supply, or some other significant events in the economy. In the Thai case, for instance, several finance companies failed immediately prior to the baht devaluation. In fact, Kaminsky and Reinhart (1998) systematically analyze the links between banking and currency crisis and document that problems in the banking sector typically precede a currency crisis.

What are the indicators in the economy that can suggest that a currency crisis may be brewing? Kaminsky et al. (1998), in surveying the literature and based on their own empirical analysis, conclude that two of the most important variables that have proven particularly useful in anticipating currency crises are the level of international reserves and the real exchange rate.

2 See the appendix in Kho and Stulz (2000) for a chronology of various relevant news announcements.

3 The idea behind competitive devaluation is that exports of countries, whose currencies undergo a devaluation to world markets, become more competitive compared to the exports of countries whose currencies do not undergo a devaluation to the same extent. This then puts pressure on countries with stable currencies to devalue in order to make their exports competitive in the world markets. This argument requires that prices in local currencies be sticky; otherwise, exporters could just as well alter their prices to make their products more or less competitive. Most of the articles in the literature fail to discuss this simple, but obvious, point. To what extent is the assumption of sticky prices, especially in midst of a big financial crisis, tenable is not obvious to us, even though the received view in the literature appears to take it for granted.

4 Chander and Patro (2000) document that country fund prices are less sensitive than the local indices to sharp falls in currency prices, resulting in substantial country fund premiums during the crises.

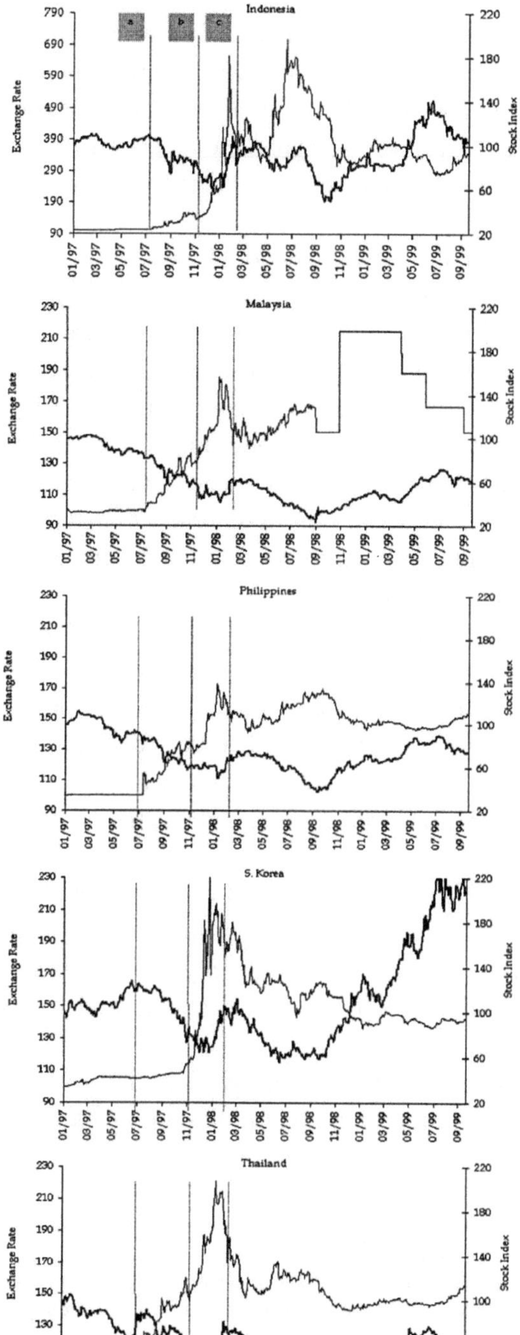

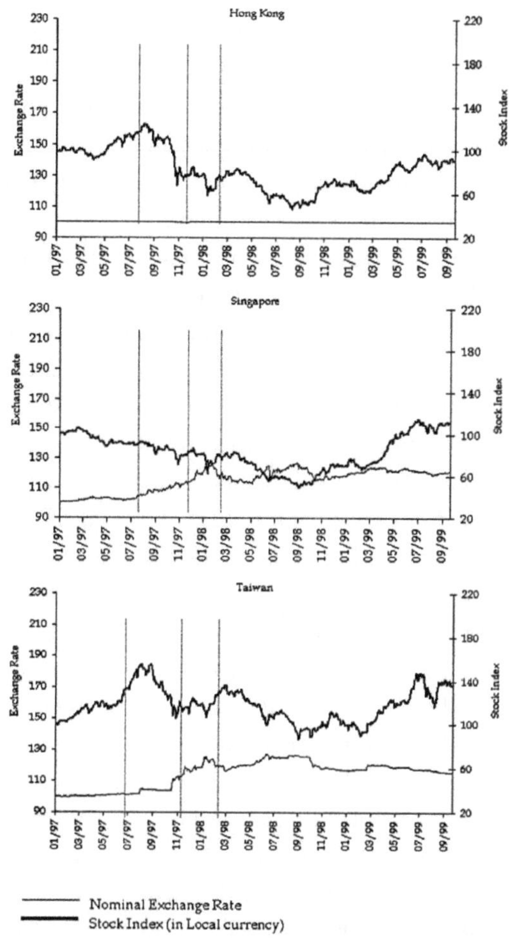

FIGURE 4.1 Nominal exchange rates and stock indices. This figure plots the variation in the exchange rate and the stock indices fin local currency) of five crisis countries (Indonesia, Malaysia, Philippines, South Korea, Thailand) and three non-crisis countries (Hong Kong, Singapore, Taiwan) assuming a base level of 100 on January 1, 1997. The left axis is for the exchange rate and the right axis is for the stock index (note that the exchange rate scale for Indonesia is different from that of the rest of the countries). The three vertical lines represent three significant events: (a) July 2, 1997, when Bank of Thailand announced a managed float; (b) November 17, 1997, when South Korea abandoned its defense of the won; and (c) February 16, 1997, when reports emerged that IMF had threatened to withdraw support.

Source: Datastream.

It is easy to see why depleting international reserves indicate balance of payment problems that can lead to currency crisis. The problem, of course, is that accurate information about the level of international reserves is usually available only with a long lag. Indeed, in the Mexican peso crisis in 1994, the position of the international reserves was a guarded secret of the central bank; the Mexican peso crashed immediately when the market learned that the reserves had fallen to precariously low levels.[5]

Given that timely information about international reserves may not be easily available, an alternative is to examine the behavior of inflation differentials or equivalently the behavior of real exchange rates. The reason is that a large difference in inflation rates, if it were caused by expansionary monetary policy in the country, together with managed exchange rates would generally lead to a significant loss in international reserves. One needs to be careful, however, in using an appropriate measure of inflation in computing the real exchange rate if one is to infer that a large rise in the real exchange rate implies a loss of international reserves. It is the attempt by the central bank to keep nominal exchange rates away from the equilibrium exchange rate by intervening in the market that leads to loss of international reserves. Since the equilibrium exchange rate is defined by the ratio of the price levels of *traded* goods, the appropriate inflation measures must compute price level changes of a basket of goods that contains largely traded goods.[6]

To see this more clearly, look at the real exchange for Hong Kong in Figure 4.2. The real exchange rate calculated using the consumer price index (CPI) shows a consistently rising real exchange rate. However, real exchange rate calculated using PPIs, which are heavily weighted towards traded goods, suggests no appreciable rise and consequently no significant loss in international reserves. For Hong Kong, the prices of non-traded goods increased much more rapidly compared to the prices of traded goods.

Contrast this with the behavior of the real exchange rate in case of the Mexican peso in Figure 4.3. The real exchange rate appears to have increased before the devaluation at the end of 1994 regardless of whether we use CPIs or WPIs to calculate the price levels. This suggests that there must not be a significant difference in inflation rates between traded and non-traded goods for Mexico.[7]

Using the CPI to calculate the real exchange rate can thus be misleading. However, with the exception of Chinn (1998), most of the scholars attempt to account for real exchange rate

5 See Edwards (1997).

6 See Chowdhry and Titman (1999) for elaboration of this point.

7 More generally, if price levels for two indices, such as the CPI and the WPI, and the relative weights each index places on traded and non-traded goods are available, it is simple to infer the inflation in traded goods alone. Formally, if

$$\pi_1 = \theta_1 \pi_T + (1 - \theta_1)\pi_{NT},$$
$$\pi_2 = \theta_2 \pi_T + (1 - \theta_2)\pi_{NT},$$

where π_1 and π_2 represent inflation calculation using the two indices, θ_1 [or $(1 - \theta_1)$] and θ_2 [or $(1 - \theta_2)$] represent the weights on traded [or non-traded] goods inflation π_T [or π_{NT}], then the two equations above can be used to infer π_T in calculating the real exchange rate change.

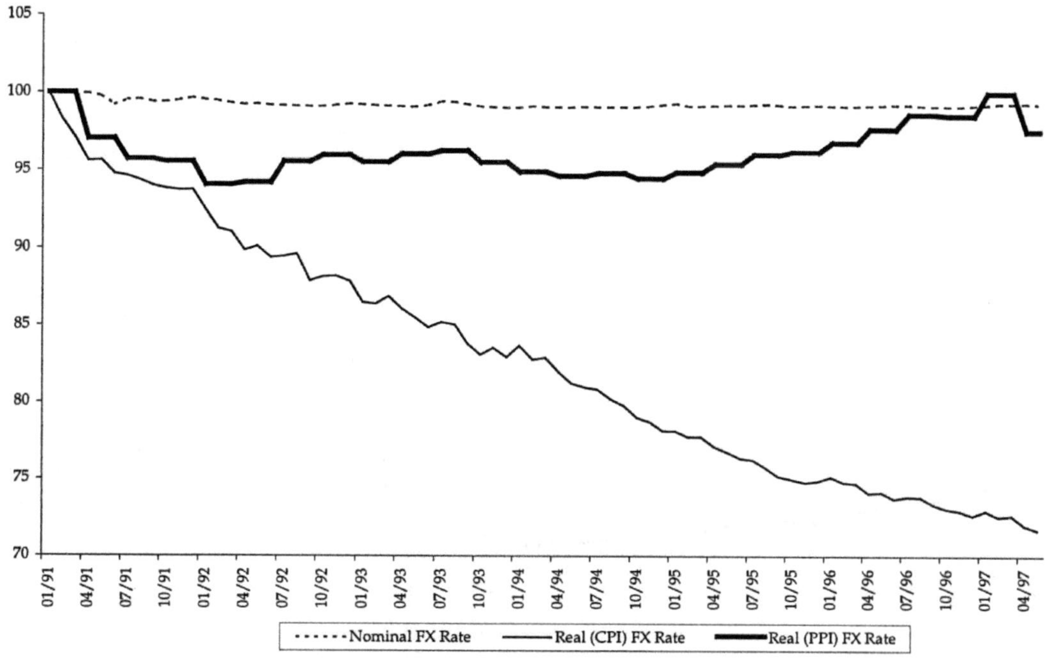

FIGURE 4.2 Nominal and real exchange rate, Hong Kong.

appreciation due to factors such as productivity increases by calculating the deviation from trend. Chinn (1998) points out that this is likely to result in conclusions that are incorrect and misleading.

Figure 4.4 plots nominal and real exchange rates using both CPI and WPI (or PPI) as the price indices, with 1991 first quarter as the base. On the eve of the crisis in July 1997, the real exchange rate using the WPI or the PPI as the relevant index suggests possible balance of payments problems for only Malaysia, Philippines and Thailand. For Indonesia, South Korea, Hong Kong, Singapore and Taiwan, the real exchange rate on the eve of the 1997 crisis does not suggest any balance of payments problems. It appears that real exchange rate would have had a very limited success in predicting the impending currency crisis.

Other variables that appear to indicate impending financial (banking and/or currency) crises relate to the level of debt and lending activity in the economy (as measured by domestic credit or M2) and the level of *external* short-term debt, as a fraction of international reserves.[8] The intuition is that a run, either by foreign lenders or because of capital flight by local investors, can leave the economy vulnerable if it does not possess sufficient international reserves to cushion sudden outflows of funds. Figure 4.5 shows a sharp increase in measures of domestic credit and M2 in many of the crisis countries in Asia prior to the crisis. Figure 4.5 also shows that the level of short-term external debt exceeded the level of international reserves in Indonesia, the Philippines and Thailand. This has led several scholars to blame short-term *debt flows* for the crisis in

8 See Furman and Stiglitz (1998), Kaminsky et al. (1998) and Rodrik and Velasco (1999).

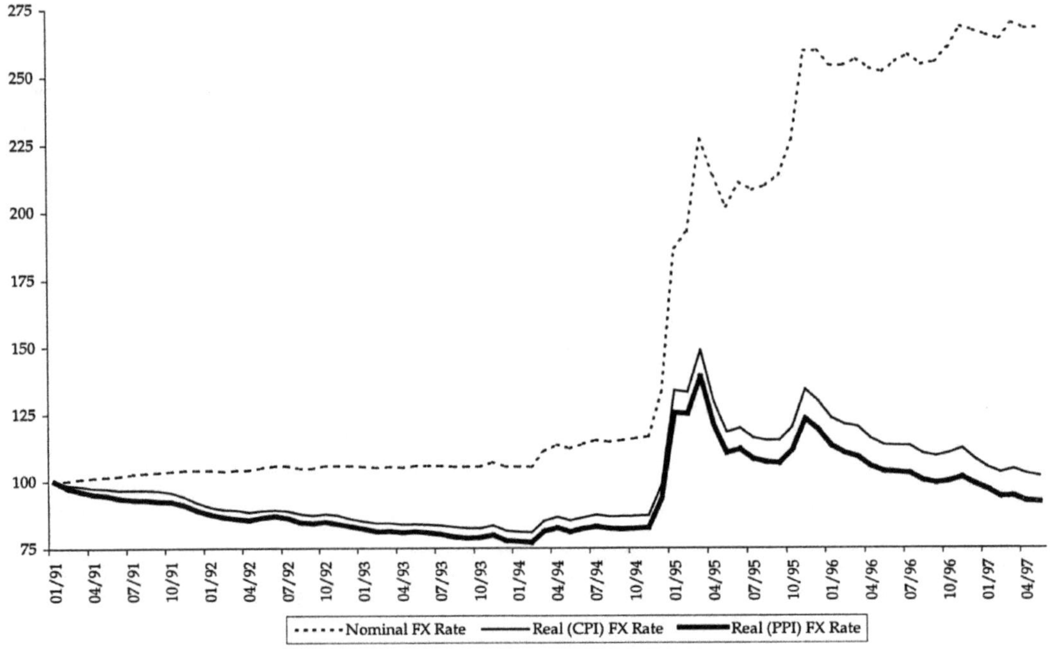

FIGURE 4.3 Nominal and real exchange rate, Mexico.

East Asia.[9] Many take a further leap (without documenting any evidence and without making a persuasive argument) by stating that short-term *capital flows* (debt *and* equity) were responsible for the meltdown we witnessed in East Asia.

It is one thing to *characterize* a crisis ex post and quite another to develop an early warning model that does a reasonable job of predicting crises ex ante. Several scholars have made attempts to build empirical models that would predict crises in advance,[10] but their out-of-sample performance in predicting the Asian crisis, argue Berg and Pattillo (1999), is largely negative. Furman and Stiglitz (1998) note that even the model of Kaminsky et al. (1998), which is somewhat successful in predicting the Asian Crisis, is biased towards predicting a crisis when none occurred (a false alarm); this is, in fact, confirmed in Berg and Pattillo (1999).

3. THEORETICAL EXPLANATIONS OF THE CAUSES OF THE CRISIS

We now review various theoretical explanations that have been offered to explain the crisis in East Asia, the empirical implications that follow from these explanations, the evidence and the policy implications. In our reading of the literature, we find that, in general, theoretical explanations and policy implications are plentiful but relatively little attention is paid to the empirical

9 Furman and Stiglitz (1998), Radelet and Sachs (1998) etc.

10 Frankel and Rose (1996), Sachs et al. (1996), and Kaminsky et al. (1998).

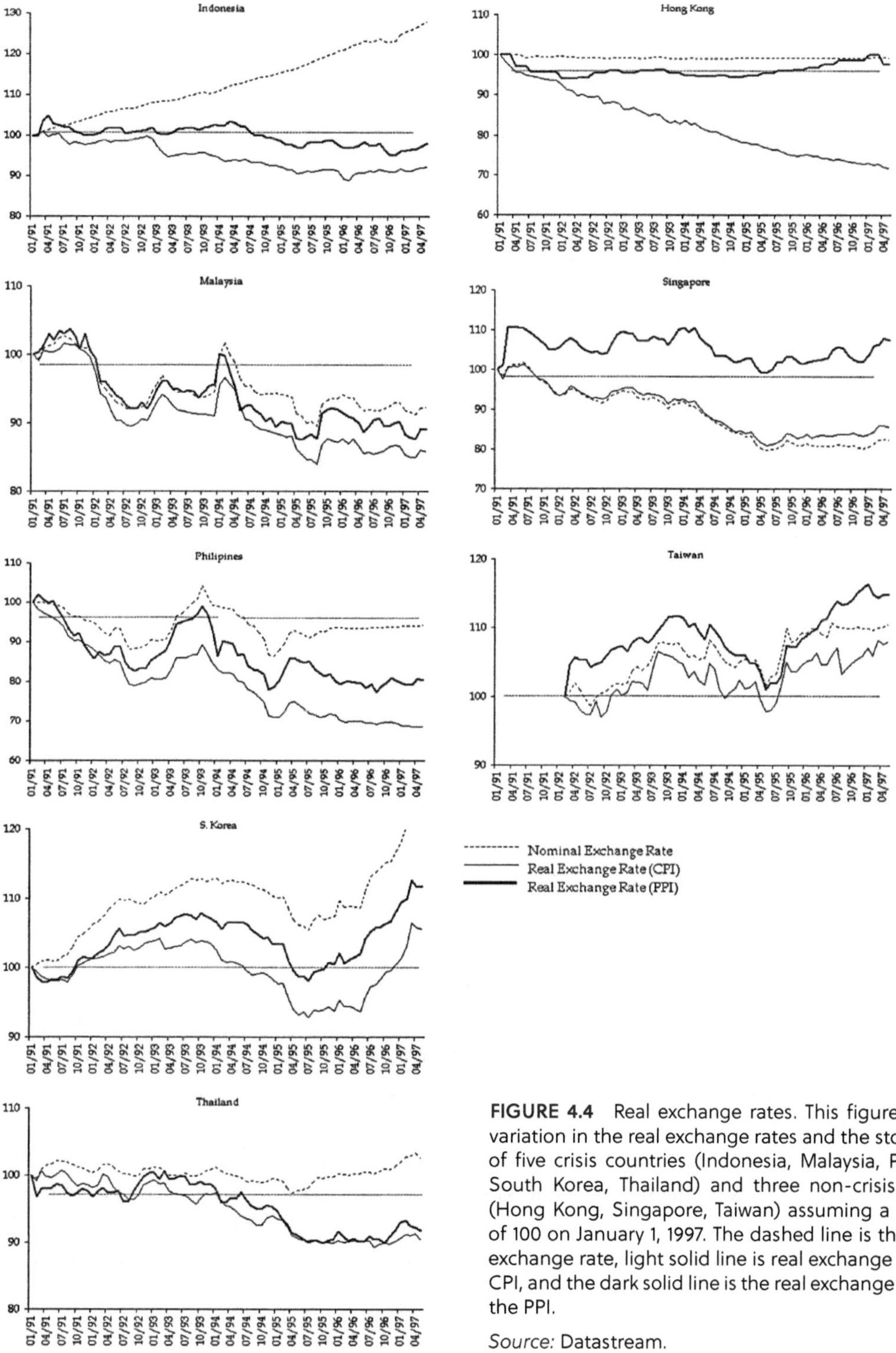

FIGURE 4.4 Real exchange rates. This figure plots the variation in the real exchange rates and the stock indices of five crisis countries (Indonesia, Malaysia, Philippines, South Korea, Thailand) and three non-crisis countries (Hong Kong, Singapore, Taiwan) assuming a base level of 100 on January 1, 1997. The dashed line is the nominal exchange rate, light solid line is real exchange rate using CPI, and the dark solid line is the real exchange rate using the PPI.

Source: Datastream.

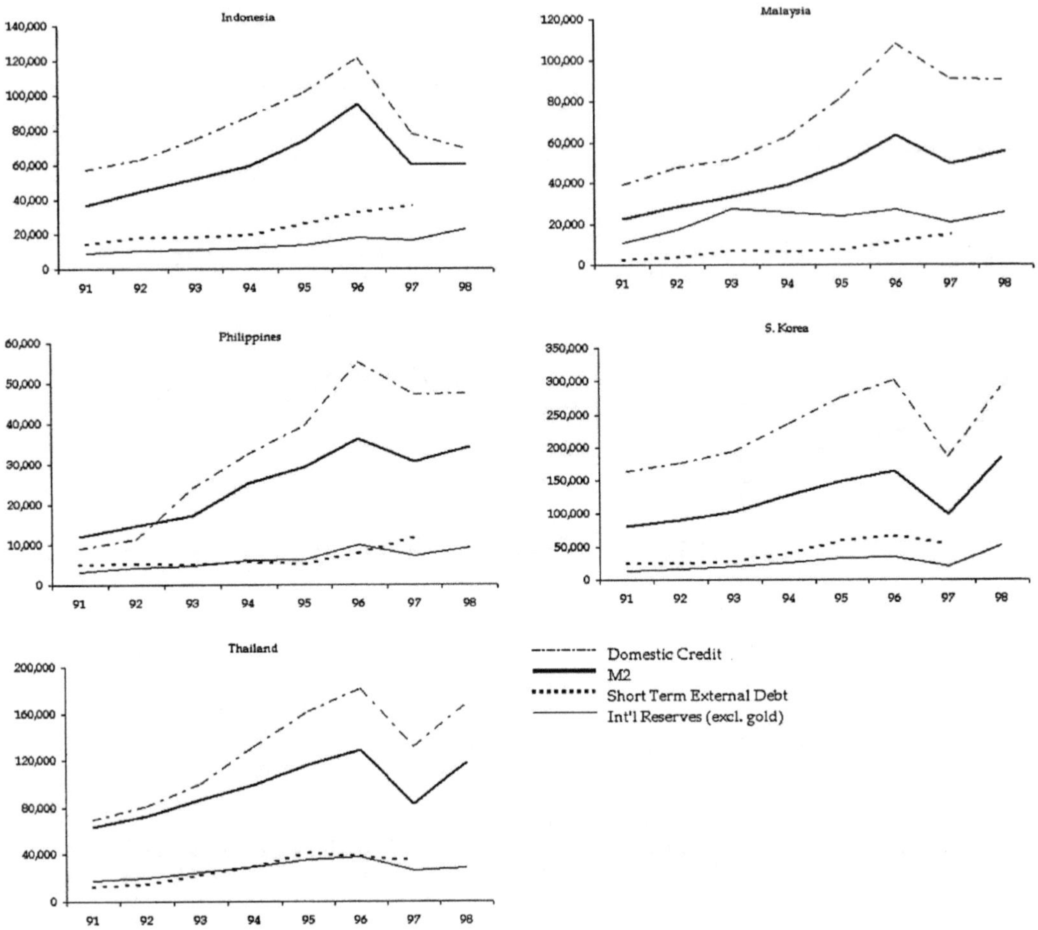

FIGURE 4.5 Money, debt and reserves. All figures in millions of U.S. dollars. All data, except short-term debt, are from IFS. Short-term debt is from World Bank (data for 1998 not available).

implications of the theories and actual empirical tests are rare as of now.[11] In general, the various explanations that have been discussed in the literature can be classified into four broad categories, with several scholars emphasizing more than one of these as being important in explaining the severity of the crisis.

1. Fundamentals: These explanations are variations of the classic, often termed as "first-generation" models, following the seminal papers by Krugman (1979) and Flood and Garber (1984). In these models, the local governments pursue fiscal and monetary policies that are inconsistent with fixed exchange rates, leading to balance of payments problems and depleting reserves. At

11 The article by Kho and Stulz (2000) is an exception.

some point, speculators realize that the central bank will not be able to maintain exchange rate parity and this leads to a speculative attack on the currency.

2. *Second-generation models:* These are variations of the Obstfeld (1984) model. These models are characterized by a tension between the willingness of the government to depreciate and, at the same time, the desire to maintain a fixed exchange rate. The government may want to depreciate because of either high levels of domestic debt or because of the need for expansionary monetary policy due to high unemployment. It may also feel the need to maintain a fixed exchange rate (for facilitating international trade or as a guard against inflation or as a sort of national pride). When speculators realize that it has become costly to maintain the parity, they attack as soon as they think the attack will succeed.

In both the first- and the second-generation models, the crisis is ultimately the result of flawed government policies, with the speculators merely forcing government's hand. However, these models are essentially models of *currency* crisis. The theoretical arguments advanced for the East Asian crisis go beyond the standard currency crisis models and involve other institutions (namely, banks and other financial intermediaries) and other variables (namely, asset prices and corporate borrowing) to explain the crisis.

3. *Moral hazard:* At the heart of these models are structural distortions caused by implicit guarantees to financial institutions such as banks. These implicit guarantees come either from local treasury or from international organizations such as the IMF and they take the form of assuring depositors (and in some cases, equityholders) of banks that they will bail out should the financial institution fail. This provides adverse incentives to financial institutions to make loans that are imprudent. This bids up prices of risky assets beyond their fundamental values, leading to an "asset bubble" in the economy. As potential losses from these loans start to accumulate, at some point, investors realize the infeasibility of *all* implicit guarantees being honored and the asset bubble bursts, bringing down the value of assets in the economy.

4. *Self-fulfilling run on liquidity:* These models emphasize the role of short-term *debt* flows with fixed contractual repayment values that are *not fully* insured. These short-term debt inflows are transformed by local banks into long-term illiquid loans, i.e., the local banks perform the classical maturity transformation. This mismatch of maturity and liquidity between deposits and loans creates a possibility of a run described in the seminal paper by Diamond and Dybvig (1983). A loss of confidence, possibly irrational, on the part of short-term debt holders causes them to withdraw their funds en masse, causing the local banks to fail and the level of intermediation in economy to fall drastically. This leads to real contraction in the economy[12], causing asset prices and currency values to plummet.

There is a widespread consensus among scholars that the "generation" models, by themselves, with emphasis only on fundamentals, such as current account deficits, inflation, real exchange rate appreciation, etc., or on policy inconsistencies, cannot explain the recent financial crises in Asia and Latin America. The empirical evidence is, in fact, consistent with this view; (as discussed

12 See Bernanke (1983).

in Section 2) the out-of-sample performance of most models attempting to predict the crisis is largely negative. Thus, most scholars adopt elements of either the moral hazard explanation or the self-fulfilling run explanation in explaining the East Asian crisis. This makes the role of banks and financial institutions central in almost all plausible explanations advanced so far. This gives rise to a cross-sectional prediction that the depth of the crisis is likely to be larger for countries where banking supervision and regulation were weaker. Tornell (1999) purports to find evidence consistent with this prediction. The August 21–27, 1999 issue of *The Economist* (on p. 17) speculates that "Singapore and the Philippines were spared disaster partly because they prevented their banks from getting into trouble."

The most notable, and perhaps the most comprehensive, analysis incorporating elements of both fundamentals and structural distortions caused by moral hazard is provided in Corsetti et al. (1998). Krugman (1998) emphasizes moral hazard problems as the main explanation. Kane (2000) also relies on moral hazard with a somewhat different notion of a "silent" run by investors to explain the timing of the crisis and the contagion. Chang and Velasco (1998), Furman and Stiglitz (1998) and Radelet and Sachs (1998) emphasize the run on liquidity as the major explanation of the crisis in East Asia. Caballero and Krishnamurthy (1999) assume that there is an *exogenous* fall in international liquidity, but go on to explore how inefficiencies in collateral aggregation exacerbate the allocation of resources and adversely affect financial intermediation and real activity in the economy.

3.1 MORAL HAZARD

There are several dimensions to the explanations that emphasize moral hazard as the central explanation for the crisis.

Krugman (1998) illustrates how financial intermediaries who receive implicit guarantees will *rationally* choose investments that are "too" risky. In addition, argue Corsetti et al. (1998) and Kane (2000), there was often political pressure on domestic financial institutions to direct credit to *local* favored firms and/or industries. Implicit guarantees also provided adverse incentives to international lenders to lend without implementing adequate supervisory, control and risk management systems in place. What were the implications of such distortionary investments? One, there was "overinvestment" caused by "excessive lending" as many projects with negative net present value were financed and undertaken. Two, prices of local assets rose beyond their true economic value leading to "overvaluation" of asset prices. These overinvestment and overvaluation may have given the appearance of spectacular economic growth in many economies in the region before the crisis.

What then triggered the crisis? As the size of the guarantees, caused by mounting losses accumulated by financial intermediaries lending to unprofitable projects, grew, it became clear to investors in the market that all guarantees cannot, or will not, in fact, be honored. This caused a downward spiral in asset and currency prices.

What can explain the timing of the crisis in several countries in the region almost simultaneously (i.e., the appearance of the contagion)? If the implicit guarantees were from an international institution such as the IMF, then the simultaneity of the crisis is a consistent implication of these explanations. The empirical evidence in Kho and Stulz (2000), however, is not very promising in this regard; they document that the bailouts by the IMF were not fully anticipated and that the IMF actions do not appear to have significant systemic effects. If the implicit guarantees were from local authorities, then the simultaneity of the crisis is even more difficult to explain with the above explanation, which would require that aggregate guarantees cross the threshold value simultaneously in all countries in the region. Absent was a fundamental shock (which most scholars agree was not present) that would have affected the profitability of projects in all crisis countries, explaining the need for further analysis of the contagion.

A question that arises with explanations suggesting overinvestment and overvaluation caused by moral hazard is if the market is aware of these distortions and if that gets reflected in market prices somehow. The problem with looking at stock prices alone is that they are the sum of the negative effects of imprudent investment decisions and the option value of the implicit guarantees. It is difficult to disentangle these two opposing effects. Fixed exchange rate regimes further cloud transparency in the economy by making another publicly observable asset price, the exchange rate, uninformative. Future research can focus on understanding what public signals in the market can reflect the information about distorted investment policies and the size of the growing liabilities of the guaranteeing institution.

3.2 SELF-FULFILLING RUN ON LIQUIDITY

Scholars, who emphasize a self-fulfilling run by short-term debt holders sharply reversing debt flows into the crisis countries, point to two empirical characteristics of the crisis that support their view. One, the crisis appears to have been largely unexpected, and, two, the variable short-term debt flows/international reserves explain the cross-sectional variation in the severity of the crisis remarkably well (Furman and Stiglitz, 1998; Rodrik and Velasco, 1999). The remarkable rebound of asset prices in most of the countries in the region (see Figure 4.1) in just a year or so after the crisis lends further support to their view, as it will be implausible to argue that the problems related to inefficiencies in the banking industries in these countries were resolved in such a short period of time. Radelet and Sachs (1998) point to the rebound of the Mexican asset prices after the tequila crisis of 1994 as a support for the self-fulfilling run explanations of such crises.

One might be tempted to argue that perhaps both elements, moral hazard and self-fulfilling run, were present in the East Asian financial crisis. Such equivocation, however, is not particularly insightful and helpful in this case because the policy implications arising from the two views are diametrically opposite. If one believes the moral hazard story, the prescription will call for removing implicit guarantees that lead to adverse incentives. If, however, these crises were caused by a run by short-term debt holders, then the presence of a deposit insurance type scheme is required to calm the nerves of panic-prone short-term depositors (see Diamond and Dybvig, 1983). This, of course, makes the lessons learned from the debate on reform of deposit insurance in the aftermath of the savings and loans crisis in the U.S. useful in this context as well.[13] It appears to us that a judicious mix might entail having *fully insured* short-term depositors—to prevent a self-fulfilling run—and *uninsured* long-term investors (who should not be bailed out ex post either)—to provide incentives for them to put in place sound risk management and control systems[14] that curb the problems caused by moral hazard.

4. FLOWS OF EQUITY CAPITAL AND ITS IMPLICATIONS

The authors of numerous articles (e.g., Corsetti et al., 1998; Furman and Stiglitz, 1998; Radelet and Sachs, 1998; Ito, 1999; Rodrik and Velasco, 1999) have taken the view that short-term capital flows—both debt as well as equity flows—can increase financial fragility and be destabilizing. What is remarkable to us is that none of the theoretical arguments that were built around implications of short-term debt flows applies to equity flows. Furthermore, there is no persuasive empirical evidence in support of this position either; Edwards (1999) casts serious doubts on the oft-cited evidence from the benefits of controls instituted in Chile.

Two of the most voiced concerns over equity flows (other than direct foreign investment flows) are that, one, these equity flows merely cause an increase in prices of existing assets without any corresponding increase in real activity and, two, these equity flows can reverse easily, leaving the real economy in shambles when that happens. First, it is worth noting that these two concerns contradict each other. If, in fact, equity flows do not lead to any increased real activity in the economy, their absence cannot have significant real consequences when these flows get reversed. Second, it should not matter for real activity whether or not the flows are in the form of direct investment or in the form of portfolio investment. This is because when stock prices of existing assets rise as a result of equity flows, this would spur real economic activity as more and more companies would want to issue securities (IPOs and secondary offers) to take advantage of falling cost of equity capital.[15] There appears to be considerable evidence in the finance literature (see for instance Fama, 1990) documenting a positive association between stock price rises and real activity. In fact, many of the authors who voice the first concern also note that moral hazard problems led to increasing asset prices and increased real activity (although not necessarily of the right kind), thus acknowl edging the positive link between stock prices and real activity. The concern about the economy being left in shambles when equity capital flows reverse perhaps stems from the intuition that investment in real capital may be relatively irreversible. However, with irreversible investment, the economy is also less likely to build a large investment in the first place when asset prices are rising.[16]

---

13 See references on Nouriel Roubini's website on the deposit insurance reform debate, http://www.stern.nyu.edu/~nroubini/asia/AsiaHomepage.htm#DEPINS. Also, the Federal Reserve Bank of Minneapolis has the following website: http://woodrow.mpls.frb.fed.us/sylloge/TBTF/index,html.

14 See Ho et al. (2000) who argue that properly modeled value at risk measures would significantly increase the amount of capital needed to meet the revised Basle requirements.

15 See Lucas and McDonald (1990) and Choe et al. (1993).

16 See Pindyck (1988, 1991) and Bertola and Caballero (1994).

TABLE 4.1 Five Asian economies[a]: external financing, e = estimate, f = forecast. ***Source:*** IIF, "Capital Flows to Emerging Market Economies", April, 1999

	1995	1996	1997	1998[e]	19991[f]
Current account balance	−40.6	−54.8	−26.1	−69.2	44.6
External financing, net	83.0	99.0	28.3	−4.2	7.8
Private flows, net	80.4	102.3	0.2	−27.6	0.3
Equity investment, net	15.3	18.6	4.4	13.7	18.5
Direct equity, net	4.2	4.7	5.9	9.5	12.5
Portfolio equity, net	11.0	13.9	−1.5	4.3	6.0
Private creditors, net	65.1	83.7	−4.2	−41.3	−18.2
Commercial banks, net	53.2	62.7	−21.2	−36.1	−16.0
Non-banks, net	12.0	21.0	17.1	−5.3	−2.3
Official flows, net	2.6	−3.3	28.1	23.4	7.6
International financial institutions	−0.3	−2.0	22.4	19.3	−1.7
Bilateral creditors	3.0	−1.3	5.7	4.1	9.3
Resident lending/other, net[b]	−28.3	−27.3	−33.7	-22.9	−21.0
Reserves excluding gold (− = increase)	−14.1	−16.9	31.5	−42.1	−31.4

[a]Indonesia, Malaysia, Philippines, South Korea, Thailand.
[b]Including resident net lending, monetary gold, and errors and omissions.

Empirically, we do observe a positive association between price changes and international equity capital flows. In fact, the sensitivity of these flows to price changes appears to be quite high (see Table 4.1); this has led many observers to label international flows as "hot money". Brennan and Cao (1997) develop a formal model in which foreign investors are relatively less informed than local investors about fundamentals. A negative signal about the fundamentals thus causes foreign investors to revise their estimate of expected returns downward much more than local investors whose prior information was much more precise. This causes foreign investors to sell local assets to local investors, leading to a net outflow of equity capital.[17] Even though the presence of less informed foreign investors may cause equity capital flows to be "fickle", it does not, however, follow that it should result in large swings in *prices* as critics of "hot money" (e.g., Furman and Stiglitz, 1998) seem to imply. This is because with a large fraction of traders being

17 This argument is described informally in Furman and Stiglitz (1998). Brennan and Aranda (1999) show that there will be a net debt outflow as well and that debt flows will be even more volatile than equity flows. The empirical evidence in Table 1 is, in fact, consistent with this argument.

uninformed, a large sell (or buy) order conveys relatively less information about fundamentals and thus, prices set by rational agents should react less to this order flow information.[18]

Our view, therefore, is that there is no persuasive theory and scant empirical evidence to suggest that equity capital flows—"hot money"—cause pernicious effects on the economy. Policy implications suggesting measures to curb equity flows can therefore be considered to be ill founded and premature, at best.

5. CONCLUDING REMARKS

The East Asian crisis of 1998 was remarkable in that it came soon after public pronouncements of the efficacy of the economic models of the Asian tigers. It is no exaggeration to say that the crisis caught everyone unawares with rare warning signals from academic quarters. The aftermath of the crisis has not only led to correction in structural deficiencies of the Asian economies but has also led to correction in the academic literature analyzing the defects in the Asian model.

Whatever may be the final explanation for the immediate reasons for the crisis, there appears to be wide consensus that the crisis reflected some institutional inefficiencies in the Asian economies. Excessive and politically motivated lending, lax banking supervision, inadequate apparatus for handling bankruptcy are just some of the features that highlight what was wrong with these economies. The reforms initiated under the aegis of World Bank, IMF and the foreign investors were intended not only to stem the contagion but also to improve the efficiency of the real and financial sectors of the economy. Although most of the central banks seem to have learned the lesson of not pursuing misguided monetary policies, there are still significant obstacles in the way of cleaning up the banking systems and freeing the capital markets from (implicit) controls. IMF has come in for some criticism for the implicit guarantees it provided to the international lenders, causing the moral hazard problem. The idea of "bailing in" the private creditors seems to be in vogue.[19] Others have expressed a need for some contingent financing facility in times of crisis to stem the flight by private creditors.

There is a general agreement about the need for greater transparency in accounting systems at both the corporate and the country levels. International accounting standards are being developed by the International Accounting Standards Committee. The current capital adequacy norms are seen as too lax (for instance, the riskiness of a loan is measured by whether it is made to a country inside or outside the OECD) although the Basle Committee is trying to update these standards. The governments, however, need to clean up the root causes of banking messes by recapitalizing good banks, forcing the closure of underperforming banks, and generally changing the banking culture. The foreign investors would also welcome fuller and timely information

18 This intuition can be verified with a simple Kyle (1985) type framework.

19 Ecuador defaulted on its Brady bonds in October, 1999. Foreign creditors suspect IMF of complicity, as a way of 'Teaching" them that their loans are not guaranteed.

about the level of international reserves of the country,[20] the extent of forward transactions undertaken by the central banks, and the levels of short-term debt in the economy.

One crucial facet of the crisis seems to have been not given adequate attention by the researchers. The crisis was characterized by huge outflows of *both* the debt capital and equity capital. Models built around the debt flight do not explain the concurrent flight of equity capital. Informational differences between foreign and domestic appear to be important factors in explaining the flows (both the inflows and the outflows) of equity capital. These equity flows cannot explain the large swings in prices, however. We need to understand the effects of equity capital flows better before we can seriously entertain the advice offered by many, most notably Paul Krugman, that suggests capital controls as the least painful way of saving the country from crisis-like situations. Controls on capital not only discourage foreign investors from investing in the country, but also encourage capital flight by domestic investors.

We hope that the collection of articles in this issue would provide a new impetus to research by not only revealing new insights but also setting a challenging future research agenda.

ACKNOWLEDGEMENTS

We thank Felipe Aguerrevere, Michael Brennan, Arvind Krishnamurthy and Richard Roll for helpful comments.

REFERENCES

Berg, A., Pattillo, C., 1999. Are currency crises predictable? A test. IMF Staff Papers 46, 107–138, (http: / /www.imf.org/external/pubs/ft/staffp/1999/06-99/pdf/berg.pdf).

Bernanke, B., 1983. Non-monetary effects of the financial crisis in the propagation of the great depression. American Economic Review 73, 257–276.

Bertola, G., Caballero, R., 1994. Irreversibility and aggregate investment. Review of Economic Studies 61, 223–246.

Brennan, M.J., Aranda, C., 1999. What makes hot money hot? The relative volatility of international flows of debt and equity capital. Working Paper, UCLA, Los Angeles, CA.

Brennan, M.J., Cao, H.H., 1997. International portfolio investment flows. Journal of Finance 52, 1851–1880.

Caballero, R., Krishnamurthy, A., 1999. Emerging markets crises: An asset markets perspective. Working Paper, Northwestern University, Evanston, IL (http://www.kellogg.nwu.edu/faculty/krisharvind/papers/emergmkts.pdf).

Chander, N., Patro, D., 2000. Why do closed-end country funds trade at enormous premiums during currency crises? Pacific-Basin Finance Journal 8 (2), this issue.

Chang, R., Velasco, A., 1998. Financial crises in emerging markets: A canonical model. Working Paper 98-10, Federal Reserve Bank of Atlanta, Atlanta, CA (http://frbatlanta.org/publica/work_papers/wp98/wp9810.pdf).

Chinn, M., 1998. Before the fall: Were East Asian currencies overvalued? Working Paper 6491, NBER, Cambridge, MA (http://papers.nber.org/papers/W6491.pdf).

Choe, H., Masulis, R.W., Nanda, V., 1993. Common stock offerings across the business cycle: Theory and evidence. Journal of Empirical Finance 1, 3–31.

Chowdhry, B., Titman, S., 1999. Why real interest rates, cost of capital and price/earning ratios vary across countries. Working Paper, UCLA, Los Angeles, CA.

20 The Finance Minister of Mexico has promised to publish the information about the level of international reserves on the Internet. See http://www.inegi.gob.mx/economia/ingles/fieconomia.html.

Corsetti, G., Pesenti, P., Roubini, N., 1998. What caused the Asian currency and financial crisis? I. A macroeconomic overview. Working Paper, New York University, New York (http:// www.stern.nyu.edu/~nroubini/asia/AsianCrisis.pdf).

Diamond, D., Dybvig, P., 1983. Bank runs, liquidity, and deposit insurance. Journal of Political Economy 91, 401–419.

Edwards, S., 1997. The Mexican peso crisis: How much did we know? When did we know it? Working Paper 7233, NBER, Cambridge, MA (http://papers.nber.org/papers/W7233.pdf).

Edwards, S., 1999. Crisis prevention: Lessons from Mexico and East Asia. Working Paper 6334, NBER, Cambridge, MA (http://papers.nber.org/papers/W6334.pdf).

Fama, E.F., 1990. Stock returns, expected returns and real activity. Journal of Finance 45, 1089–1108.

Flood, R.P., Garber, P.M., 1984. Collapsing exchange rate regimes—some linear examples. Journal of International Economics 17, 1–13.

Frankel, J., Rose, A., 1996. Currency crashes in emerging markets: an empirical treatment. Journal of International Economics 41, 351–366.

Furman, J., Stiglitz, J.E., 1998. Economic crises: Evidence and insights from East Asia. Brookings Papers on Economic Activity (2), 1-135 (http://www.brookings.org/es/macroeconomics/ bpea/l.htm).

Ho, L.C., Burridge, P., Cadle, J., Theobald, M., 2000. Value at risk: Applying the extreme value approach to Asian markets in the recent financial turmoil. Pacific-Basin Finance Journal 8 (2), this issue.

Ito, T., 1999. Capital flows in Asia. Working Paper 7134, NBER, Cambridge, MA (http://papers.nber.org/papers/W7134.pdf).

Kaminsky, G., Lizondo, S., Reinhart, C., 1998. Leading indicators of currency crises. IMF Staff Papers 45, 1 -48 (http://www.imf.org/external/pubs/ft/staffp/1998/03-98/pdf/kaminsky.pdf).

Kaminsky, G., Reinhart, C., 1998. The twin crises: The causes of banking and balance-of-payments problems. American Economic Review, forthcoming (http://www.puaf.umd.edu/papers/reinhart/bank2.pdf).

Kane, E., 2000. Silent runs, capital movements, and banking policy in the Asian financial crisis. Pacific-Basin Finance Journal 8 (2), this issue.

Kho, B., Stulz, R., 2000. Banks, the IMF, and the Asian crisis. Pacific-Basin Finance Journal 8 (2), this issue.

Krugman, P., 1979. A model of balance of payments crises. Journal of Money, Credit and Banking 11, 311–325.

Krugman, P., 1998. What happened to Asia? Working Paper, MIT, Cambridge, MA (http:// web.mit.edu/krugman/www/DISINTER.html).

Kyle, A., 1985. Continuous auctions and insider trading. Econometrica 53, 1315–1335.

Lucas, D.J., McDonald, R.L., 1990. Equity issues and stock price dynamics. Journal of Finance 45, 1019–1043.

Obstfeld, M., 1984. The logic of currency crisis. Cahiers Economiques et Monetaires 43, 189–213.

Pindyck, R., 1988. Irreversible investment, capacity choice, and the value of the firm. American Economic Review 78, 969–985.

Pindyck, R., 1991. Irreversibility, uncertainty, and investment. Journal of Economic Literature 29, 1110–1148.

Radelet, S., Sachs, J., 1998. The onset of the East Asian financial crisis. Working Paper, Harvard Institute for International Development (http://www.hiid.harvard.edu/pub/other/eaonset.pdf).

Rodrik, D., Velasco, A., 1999. Short-term capital flows. Working Paper, Harvard University (http://www.ksg.harvard.edu/rodrik/stcapflows.pdf).

Sachs, J., Tomell, A., Velasco, A., 1996. Financial crises in emerging markets: the lessons from 1995. Brooking Papers on Economic Activity 1, 147-215 (http://www.brookings.org/pub/bpea/ oldtoc.htm\# 1996).

Tornell, A., 1999. Common fundamentals in the tequila and Asian crises. NBER Working Paper 7139 (http: //papers.nber.org/papers/W7139).

END-OF-CHAPTER QUESTIONS

1. What were the two key characteristics of the financial crisis in East Asia during the latter 1990s?

2. What was the event that appears to have triggered the crisis on July 2, 1997? Explain the role that contagion played as the crisis began to spread.
3. Explain the concept of "competitive devaluation." Why exactly would a devaluation cause havoc in certain Asian nations starting in 1997 and beyond?
4. Whereas Thailand, Malaysia, Philippines, Taiwan, Singapore, South Korea, and Indonesia were incapable in preventing their currencies from losing value, Hong Kong was able to successfully defend its currency against speculative attacks. What made Hong Kong different than other nations in having been able to maintain the value of its currency?
5. It has long been argued that currency crises are usually preceded by a gradual deterioration in economic fundamentals. What exactly happened in the Thai economy that likely caused its currency crisis?
6. What are the two important variables that have proven particularly useful in anticipating currency crises?
7. Explain how a rise in the real exchange rate may indicate a loss of international reserves.
8. The level of external debt and lending activity—often measured by short-term debt and capital flows and domestic credit and/or M2—may also indicate impending financial trouble. What is the intuition behind these alternative variables serving as indicators of impending crises?
9. Four broad categories of theoretical explanations to the Asian crisis have been thoroughly discussed in the economics literature. The first one deals with a collapse of the fundamentals in an economy. The second one emphasizes tensions between maintaining a fixed exchange rate regime or abandoning it. The third revolves around problems of asymmetric information and the fourth, on liquidity problems. Briefly summarize the principal features of each one of these explanations.
10. Explain the reasons why the policy responses for crises that are better explained by liquidity problems or moral hazard are diametrically opposite. If a crisis is the result of both liquidity runs and asymmetric information, what should the policy response be? Explain.
11. Explain why the authors argue that equity capital flows may not have played an important role in generating or deepening the crisis in East Asia. Is their argument convincing? Why?

PART III

Financial Crises in Specific Countries

READINGS

CHAPTER 5

Inflation and Inflation Uncertainty in Bolivia

Antonio N. Bojanic

ABSTRACT

This paper estimates a GARCH-M model of inflation for Bolivia and investigates its linkages with resulting measures of inflation uncertainty in a bivariate VAR framework. Utilizing a consumer price index constructed by combining six different official indices, the main findings are as follows: inflation and inflation uncertainty have both declined steadily since the late 1980s and early 1990s, when the hyperinflation period finally ended. These variables are cointegrated and ECM-causality tests indicate bidirectional causality. However, the effect of inflation on uncertainty is stronger, which supports the hypothesis formulated separately by Friedman and Ball. An implication of this finding is that the Central Bank of Bolivia can achieve lower inflation uncertainty by lowering the inflation rate.

RESUMEN

Este trabajo propone un modelo GARCH-M de inflación para Bolivia e investiga la relación entre inflación y un indicador de incertidumbre inflacionaria en el contexto de un modelo VAR de dos variables. Utilizando un índice de precios al consumidor construido a partir de seis índices oficiales, los principales resultados son los siguientes: inflación e incertidumbre inflacionaria se han reducido consistentemente desde finales de los 1980s y principios de los 1990s, cuando el periodo de hiperinflación finalmente terminó. Estas variables están cointegradas y tests de causalidad de tipo ECM indican causalidad bi-direccional. Sin embargo, el efecto de la inflación sobre la incertidumbre inflacionaria es más fuerte, lo que apoya la hipótesis planteada de manera separada por Friedman y Ball. Una implicación de este resultado es que el Banco Central de Bolivia podría reducir la incertidumbre inflacionaria a través de una reducción de la tasa de inflación.

JEL: E31, E52, C22

Keywords: Inflation, inflation uncertainty, GARCH models

Antonio N. Bojanic, "Inflation and Inflation Uncertainty in Bolivia," *El Trimestre Economico*, vol. 80, no. 318, pp. 401-426.

1. INTRODUCTION

The economic history of Bolivia is inexorably tied to dramatic monetary disequilibriums that have resulted in wild price fluctuations. Perhaps the better known episode of price instability occurred between 1982 and 1985, when the country suffered the first recorded hyperinflation that was not the result of a foreign war, a civil war, or an internal political revolution. Between January 1982 and January 1986—which roughly marks the beginning and end of the worst stage of the hyperinflation period—prices rose by more than 4 million percent. Only in the last few months of this period, May 1985 through January 1986, prices rose by over a 1,000 percent.

Despite the notoriety of the hyperinflation period, Bolivia has experienced other episodes of severe inflation—notably between January 1953 and December 1956, when inflation neared 3,000 percent—though nothing as traumatic as what occurred during the 1980s. Political instability due to weak governments, badly managed monetary and fiscal policies, and difficulties in trying to please a diverse and conflictive electorate are all reasons that may explain the troublesome economic evolution of this country. Since approximately 1990, however, and surely due in part to the lessons of the hyperinflation period, Bolivia has enjoyed a relatively long spell of price stability.

This paper analyzes the relationship between inflation and inflation uncertainty from 1937 to 2011. Inflation uncertainty refers to unpredictable behavior of prices in the future and is not to be confused with variability in prices, which, by definition, creates no true economic uncertainty if this variability is predictable. Uncertainty about future prices makes the planning of all economic agents—firms, consumers, and government—harder, as they are unable to predict the real value of goods and services, of money, of loans, and generally of any obligation that must be met in the future. Several authors[1] have demonstrated that uncertainty about what inflation will be in the future hurts economic performance, leads to misallocation of resources, and creates inefficiencies throughout an economy, hence the calls for greater transparency and accountability from monetary and fiscal authorities about economic policies and their possible impact on prices.

Bolivia lends itself to close scrutiny on how inflation and inflation uncertainty have affected and reinforced each other over time. The objective of this paper is to determine the nature of the relationship between inflation and uncertainty. If it is determined that causality exists, be it from inflation to uncertainty, the other way around, or bidirectionally, the findings should help monetary authorities in designing policies that may tame inflation and lower uncertainty about future prices.

As most studies on the general subject of inflation in Bolivia focus exclusively on the 1980s, here I expand the time horizon significantly and analyze inflation and inflation uncertainty in this country since 1937. In addition to focusing on a longer time period, the present study contributes to this area of the literature in several other ways: (i) it uses a consumer price index that was constructed by combining different indices produced by the Bolivian entities in charge of recording official economic statistics. The result is the longest available index in the country, and this is the first time that it is placed for further examination; (ii) in contrast with most previous

1 A small sample of authors that have studied the effect of price uncertainty on economic performance includes Friedman (1977), Ball (1992), Grier and Grier (1998), Kontonikas (2004), and Caporale, *et al.* (2010).

studies with limited time series data, here I use monthly observations that span more than eight decades, and conduct analysis for the whole data set and for subsets of it to test the robustness of the results; (iii) it estimates a time-varying GARCH-M model of inflation with the aim of producing measures of inflation uncertainty and investigating the linkages between inflation and inflation uncertainty in a VAR framework; and (iv) it represents the first time that a study of this kind focuses exclusively on Bolivia.

The paper is structured as follows. Section 2 contains a brief literature review. Section 3 describes the data and how the price index was constructed from this data set. Section 4 describes the advantages of using GARCH techniques to measure uncertainty. Section 5 presents the empirical results, and Section 6 offers some concluding remarks, including the policy implications of the findings.

2. LITERATURE REVIEW

Inflation uncertainty, its linkages with actual inflation, and its potential impact on real economic activity have been extensively analyzed in the literature. Friedman (1977) was the first to suggest that higher average inflation could result in higher inflation uncertainty, an idea formalized by Ball (1992) in the context of a model in which higher inflation leads to increasing uncertainty over future monetary policies. Pourgerami and Maskus (1987) and Ungar and Zilberfarb (1993) pointed out from different angles that a negative effect of inflation on uncertainty may occur as agents in an environment of accelerating inflation tend to invest more resources on inflation forecasting, thus reducing uncertainty. Causality in the opposite direction, namely from inflation uncertainty to inflation, is a property of models based on the Barro-Gordon setup, such as the one described in Cukierman and Meltzer (1986), who show that increases in inflation uncertainty raise the optimal average inflation rate by increasing the incentives for the policy maker to create inflation surprises.

Concerning the relationship between inflation uncertainty and real economic activity, some authors suggest that the former reduces the rate of investment by hindering longterm contracts. Fischer and Modigliani (1978) are representatives of this line of research. Others—such as Pindyck (1991)—argue that inflation uncertainty increases the option value of delaying an irreversible investment. Friedman (1977) describes how inflation uncertainty reduces the allocative efficiency of the price system, while Dotsey and Sarte (2000), offering an alternative view on Friedman's position, show that inflation variability may increase investment through its impact on precautionary savings. Finally, Cecchetti (1993) suggests that a general equilibrium, representative agent model, is not likely to yield a convincingly unambiguous result on the impact of uncertainty on real economic activity.

On the empirical side, a number of studies have investigated the relationship between inflation and inflation uncertainty, typically adopting an econometric framework of the GARCH type. The evidence of these models is mixed (for a survey, refer to Davis and Kanago, 2000). Some specific contributions for individual and for a cross section of countries are found in Engle (1982), Della Mea and Peña (1996), Grier and Perry (2000), Fernández (2001), Kontonikas (2004), and Caporale, *et al.* (2010).

The studies on Bolivia and inflation have focused exclusively on the hyperinflation episode of the 1980s. Representative works are Sachs (1987), who analyzes the chronology of the hyperinflation and the stabilization mechanism that was put in place between 1980 and 1986, and Morales (1987) who describes the economic and political events that led to hyperinflation and the new political economy that emerged from the stabilization process. Asilis, *et al.* (1993), also on the 1980s decade, examine the demand for money and find that expected inflation and inflation uncertainty both matter for money demand.

In this work, I analyze the relationship between average inflation and inflation uncertainty during the 1937-2011 period. In order to achieve this objective, GARCH-M methods are utilized to estimate measures of inflation uncertainty; cointegration techniques are used to determine whether a long-run relation exists between these variables; and finally causality between inflation and inflation uncertainty is determined with Error Correction Models (ECMs).

3. DATA—COMPILING A PRICE INDEX

The Central Bank of Bolivia (CBB) started compiling a consumer price index for the the city of La Paz[2] in the late 1930s (http://www.bcb.gob.bo/?q=indicadores/inflacion). As time passed, other price indices began to be constructed which were better and more representative of market fluctuations in the country.[3] In all, nine indices were developed over the course of approximately seventy years, though in this paper only six of these indices have been utilized.[4] The reason behind the utilization of six indices lies in the fact that the Central Bank discontinued construction of older indices when a new index began to be collected, hence a single, unified index from the 1930s to the present is not available. Here, I fill that gap by presenting a single, unbroken monthly consumer price index between January 1937 and December 2011, which was built out of six indices that were constructed during this period of time.[5]

2 Bolivia is divided into 9 Departments or Provinces. The city of La Paz is the capital of the Department of La Paz and the seat of government of the country. The city of El Alto, also located in La Paz, is an important urban sprawling and, along with the other 9 capitals, is considered one of the most important economic centers of the country.

3 Until the late 1960s price indices constructed by the CBB only covered the city of La Paz. During the latter years of that decade a new index added the city of El Alto. From 1992 onwards the indices began covering the cities of La Paz, El Alto, Cochabamba and Santa Cruz. The latest index, which only began to be compiled in the first decade of this century, covers the nine capital cities and El Alto.

4 The first index runs from January 1937 through 1956. Its base month is December 1936 and its coverage is the city of La Paz. The second index begins in 1956 and ends in 1965. Its base month is January 1956 and its coverage is the city of La Paz. The third index runs from 1957 through 1967. The base month is January 1957 and the coverage is the city of La Paz. The fourth index runs from 1967 through 1992. The base year is 1966 and the coverage includes the cities of La Paz and El Alto. The fifth index begins in 1992 and it is still being compiled. The base year is 1980 and it covers the cities of La Paz, Cochabamba, Santa Cruz and El Alto. The sixth index runs from 2007 through the present. The base year is 2007 and it covers the 9 capital cities plus El Alto.

5 The aggregation of different indices is problematic for a host of technical reasons, including the (incorrect) assumption that each index has the same degree of measurement error. Though aware of these difficulties, the single index presented in this work is an aggregation of various indices and I address the technical problems by performing the same statistical analysis for different subperiods between 1937 and 2011. The similarity (or discrepancy) of results obtained for various subperiods should be a good indicator of the consistency of the index.

TABLE 5.1 Summary inflation rates by decade*

DECADE	MEAN π	MEDIAN π	MONTHLY MAXIMUM	MONTHLY MINIMUM	Q1 π	Q2 π	Q3 π	Q4 π	AVERAGE π**
1940s	1.18	0.66	12.14	−2.71	1.18	0.74	0.89	1.89	291.98
1950s	4.10	2.30	71.59	−30.83	2.24	4.47	2.21	7.49	8,182.67
1960s	0.48	0.50	8.21	−6.81	0.55	0.51	0.46	0.39	72.83
1970s	1.42	0.58	23.66	−2.11	1.18	0.79	1.12	2.61	407.87
1980s	12.00	2.49	182.77	−2.33	14.90	10.44	12.93	9.70	12,683,466.35
1990s	0.76	0.55	5.84	−1.05	0.87	0.55	0.68	0.94	144.72
2000s	0.43	0.37	2.68	−2.55	0.38	0.35	0.48	0.38	59.56

* All rates expressed in %
** Estimated between January of first year and December of last year of decade
All calculations based on CPI compiled by author

The methodology for putting together a single index out of the six indices that were utilized is fairly straightforward: the single index is built on the values that the initial index—the one that begins in 1937—would have if monthly rates of change of the other indices were applied to this initial index after it ceased to be compiled in 1956. The resulting values are then standardized by setting January 2000 as the base month. The Appendix presents the price index, along with yearly inflation rates.

A continuous, unbroken price index series since 1937 offers a unique glimpse into the evolution of Bolivia over several decades of experimenting with economic policy. Table 5.1 reports summary statistics for the inflation rate in each of the decades covered by the index.

As Table 5.1 illustrates, the country experienced significant fluctuations in inflation rates throughout the years. The worst decade—unsurprising since only in 1985 the yearly inflation topped 4,800%—was the 1980s, when monthly rates consistently hit two and three figures, and the decade-long inflation rate was nearly 13 million percent. When inflation is calculated for the period January 1937 to December 2011, the rate is even more astonishing: 366 billion percent![6] The 1950s were also a decade of significant price fluctuations but paled compared to the 1980s. Since 1990 rates have consistently been in the lower 1-digit figures, matching and often outperforming those of neighboring countries. Figure 5.1 plots the monthly inflation rate, together with the corresponding year-on-year growth rate, for the period 1938-2011.

Visual inspection suggests significant variability in inflation rates up until the mid 1980s, when the hyperinflation period finally ended. The mid 1950s and 1980s are characterized by dramatic peaks in inflation, consistent with the two periods of greatest monetary disequilibrium. Since the latter part of the 1980s, inflation rates in single digits have been the norm, as

6 The unit of account of the country changed twice during the period 1937–2011: On July 13, 1962, the 'Boliviano' became the 'Peso Boliviano'. This new currency was created by eliminating 3 zeros from the Boliviano, that is, 1 Peso Boliviano = 1000 Bolivianos. On January 1, 1987, and as a result of the hyperinflation of previous years, a new currency was introduced. The new 'Boliviano' came into existence and now the exchange rate with the old currency was set at 1 Boliviano = 1,000,000 Pesos Bolivianos.

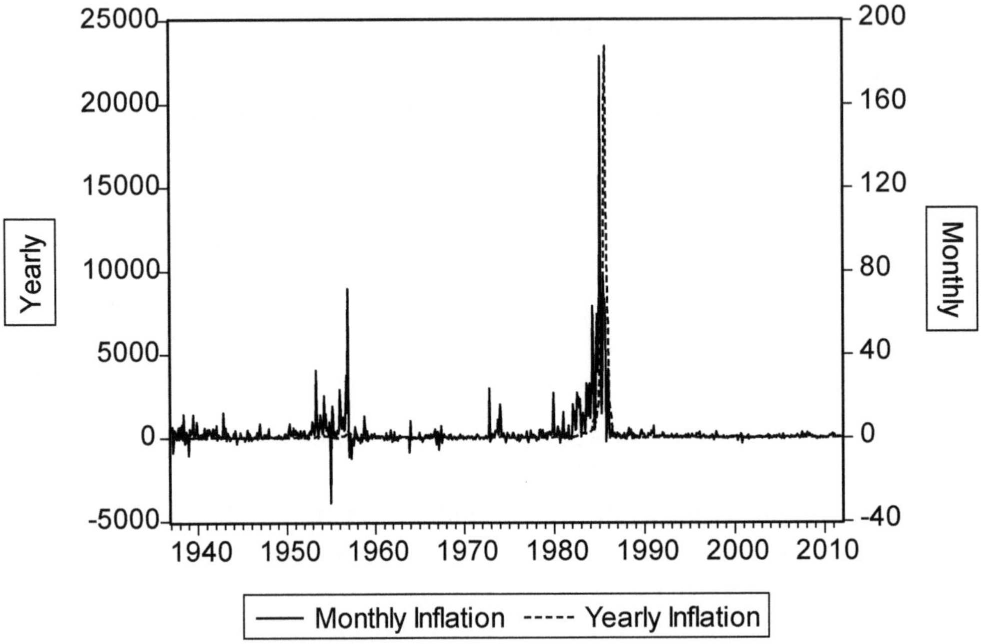

FIGURE 5.1 Yearly and Monthly Inflation, 1938–2011

successive governments placed price stability at the center of monetary policy and the country entered a self-enforcing cycle of low inflation and low uncertainty. Interestingly, even with the current administration of Evo Morales, the strict stance against inflation of his predecessors has been maintained, which stands in stark contrast with economic and political events in the 1950s and in the 1980s, when other populist administrations-in many ways, very much like the current one—carried out significant structural reforms without regard to public finances, which generated severe episodes of hyperinflation and abrupt ends to their regimes. It seems that the current populist reformers will embark on ambitious social and political projects, but aware of the fate of those who did not learn the economic lessons of their time, will not compromise on the monetary stability of the country.[7]

7 A qualification is needed regarding this last statement and it concerns the commitment of the Morales administration to price stability. The new Constitution, approved and ratified by the National Congress in October 2008, establishes that (Article 236) the Executive branch determines the objectives of monetary and exchange rate policy, implicitly revoking the autonomy of the Central Bank established in Law 1670 (Central Bank of Bolivia Law) of October 1995. With the new Constitution, the Ministry of Economy and Public Finance—part of the Executive branch—supervises and controls the activities of the Central Bank. Time will tell whether this renewed effort by the current political class to control monetary policy will bring the same economic collapse observed in Bolivia during the 1950s and 1980s, when the government elites at the time held the Central Bank hostage to political whims.

4. USING GARCH TECHNIQUES TO MEASURE UNCERTAINTY

Testing the effect of inflation uncertainty on average inflation requires the construction of a specific measure of uncertainty. GARCH techniques have proven to be useful in generating estimates of uncertainty as they estimate a model of the variance of unpredictable innovations in a variable, rather than simply calculating a variability measure from past outcomes. As is well known, there can be large differences between variability and uncertainty, depending on whether the variability is predictable or not. GARCH estimates correspond well to the notion of uncertainty and will not be blurred by the possibility that predictable fluctuations do not create true economic uncertainty. Due to the utilization of parametric models, GARCH techniques are useful for at least three other reasons. First, GARCH estimation provides an explicit test of whether the movement in the conditional variance of a variable over time is statistically significant. That is, a test can be devised to test the null hypothesis that uncertainty is constant over the sample period. Second. GARCH allows simultaneous estimation of the conditional variance equations and the mean equations for the variables under consideration, and as Pagan (1984) shows, when working with generated regressors, simultaneous estimation is more efficient than a two-step process. Finally, and as Engle (1982) demonstrates, when the variable of interest exhibits significant conditional heteroscedasticity—as is the case with the measure of uncertainty utilized in this work—the gains of utilizing GARCH over OLS are indeed very large.

In most widely used GARCH models, the conditional variance is defined as a linear function of lagged conditional variances and squared past values of the residual of the mean equation. Formally, let π_t be a sequence of monthly inflation values, ε_t be a series of innovations that are assumed to be independent and identically distributed (i.i.d.) zero-mean random variable, σ_t^2 be the variance of π_t given the information at time *t*, the GARCH *(p,q)* model for inflation π_t is defined as follows:

$$\pi_t = \beta_t \varepsilon_t \qquad \sigma_t^2 = \alpha_0 + \sum_{i=1}^{p} \alpha_i \sigma_{t-i}^2 + \sum_{j=1}^{q} \alpha_j \varepsilon_{t-j}^2 \tag{1}$$

where $p, q = 0, 1....$ are integers, and $\alpha_0 > 0$, $\alpha_i \geq 0$, $\alpha_j \geq 0$, $i = 1, ... q$, $j = 1, ...$ are model parameters.

The sign of σ_t^2 in the GARCH-in-mean inflation equation would determine the type of effect that uncertainty has on average inflation.

5. RESULTS

First, a single-equation OLS model for inflation is specified to test the null hypothesis that each variable has a unit root and a constant conditional variance. The sample is monthly data from 1937:08 through 2011:12. Inflation is the annualized monthly difference of the log of the consumer price index [$\pi_t = \log(CPI_t/CPI_{t-1})* 1200$]. Table 5.2 reports an OLS inflation equation with six lags of inflation and a twelfth-order moving average term as regressors.[8]

8 Several specifications were tested and the one with the highest adjusted R^2 was chosen. The optimal number of lags varies slightly depending on the sample period analyzed. The results obtained about the effect of inflation uncertainty on inflation are not sensitive to a particular specification. Specifically, while the

TABLE 5.2 OLS regressions for inflation, August 1937–December 2011

$$\underset{}{\pi_t} = \underset{(1.80)}{3.85} + \underset{(13.42)}{0.45\pi_{t-1}} + \underset{(0.16)}{0.01\pi_{t-2}} + \underset{(0.76)}{0.03\pi_{t-3}} + \underset{(5.25)}{0.19\pi_{t-4}} + \underset{(2.40)}{0.09\pi_{t-5}} + \underset{(3.32)}{0.11\pi_{t-6}} - \underset{(-2.44)}{0.08\varepsilon_{t-12}} + \varepsilon_t$$

Adj. $R^2 = 0.501$

Log likelihood function = –4971.16

Ljung-Box Q(4) = 0.19

Ljung-Box Q(12) = 10.95

Ljung-Box $Q^2(4) = 176.03$

Ljung-Box $Q^2(12) = 309.60$

Notes: Sample is 893 monthly observations, π_t is the inflation rate calculated from the Consumer Price Index. T-statistics are in parentheses. Q(4) and Q(12) are the Ljung-Box statistics for fourth- and twelfth-order serial correlation in the residuals. $Q^2(4)$ and $Q^2(12)$ are the Ljung-Box statistics for fourth- and twelfth-order serial correlation in the squared residuals. All data are from the Central Bank of Bolivia (www.bcb.gob. bo/?q=indicadores/).

The OLS results indicate that inflation is best explained by the most immediate episode of price fluctuations. Inflation with a one-lag period is significant, positive, and the coefficient (0.45) indicates its strong influence on current average inflation. Inflation with lags four, five, and six are also significant and positive, but their combined effect is not as important as the effect of π_{t-1}. The residuals are uncorrelated (Q-statistic = 0.19 at 4 lags and 10.96 at 12 lags), but the squared residuals show the classic volatility clustering of an ARCH process.

The stationarity of the inflation process is tested with the augmented Dickey-Fuller (ADF) test. A constant is included but no time trend, as recommended by Dickey, *et al.* (1986). In addition to testing the price index, monthly average inflation and the measure of inflation uncertainty are tested for four different time periods: the full sample period (1937:08–2011:12), the pre-hyperinflation period (1937:08–1981:12), the hyperinflation period (1982:01–1989:12), and the current period (1990:01–2011:12). Table 5.3 reports these results.

According to the test statistics by MacKinnon (1991), the ADF test shows that nonstationarity cannot be rejected for the levels of all variables.[9] When the data are differenced, nonstationarity can be rejected for all data series studied. This indicates that all data series are integrated of order one, or *I*(1).

Since the correlation of squared residuals is somewhat persistent, a GARCH(1,1) specification of the error variances in n_t is utilized. The bivariate GARCH(1,1)-M model for inflation is:

$$\pi_t = \beta_0 + \sum_{i=1}^{6} \beta_i \pi_{t-1} + \beta_7 \sigma_t^2 + \beta_8 \varepsilon_{t-12} + \varepsilon_t \tag{2}$$

---

moving average terms are necessary to ensure clean residuals, dropping them does not affect the results in any way.

9 Inflation for the whole period is stationary in levels at the 5% level of significance.

TABLE 5.3 Augmented Dickey-Fuller Unit Root Tests

	LAGS	LEVEL	AIC (n)	FIRST DIFFERENCE	AIC (n)
Price Index	4	−0.6474	−3.0005	−5.4875**	−3.0163
π 1937:08–2011:12	29	−3.2960*	11.1613	−7.7276**	11.1735
π 1937:08–1981:12	29	−2.5687	10.7206	−8.1241**	10.7300
π 1982:01–1989:12	4	−1.8049	12.8767	−6.8074**	12.8993
π 1990:01–2011:12	14	−2.7397	7.1116	−7.2501**	7.1406
σ^2 1937:08–2011:12	30	−2.8191	1.4959	−6.4961**	1.5040
σ^2 1937:08–1981:12	19	−2.6931	2.0110	−7.4303**	2.0232
σ^2 1982:01–1989:12	2	−1.3335	2.3596	−6.8095**	2.3596
σ^2 1990:01–2011:12	32	−2.7678	0.8751	−4.7443**	0.9175

Notes: ** and * denote significance at the 1% and 5% level, respectively.
All variables expressed in logs

$$\sigma_t^2 = \alpha_0 + \alpha_1 \varepsilon_{t-1}^2 + \alpha_2 \sigma_{t-1}^2 \quad (3)$$

Equation (2) describes the mean inflation rate as a function of six lags of inflation, a twelfth-order moving average term and the conditional variance of inflation. It is assumed that the error term, ε_t, has zero mean. Equation (3) gives the conditional variance of inflation (σ_t^2), which is the time-series measure of inflation uncertainty. The GARCH(1,1) specification implies that the conditional error variance of inflation follows an ARMA(1,1) process. The system is estimated using the Berndt *et al.* (1974) numerical optimization algorithm to calculate the maximum likelihood estimates of the parameters. Bollerslev (1986) demonstrates that under the assumptions of this work, the BHHH estimate of the asymptotic covariance matrix of the coefficients will be consistent. Given that there are more than 500 observations in the full sample, the estimated asymptotic *t*-statistics should be relatively accurate. The effect of inflation uncertainty on inflation is tested by looking at β_7, the coefficient on the conditional variance of inflation in equation (2). A positive and significant coefficient would support the Cukierman and Meltzer hypothesis while a negative and significant coefficient would show that increases in uncertainty lead to lower inflation rates.

Table 5.4 reports estimates of the GARCH(1,1)-M model shown above for four different time periods: the full sample period (1937:08–2011:12), the pre-hyperinflation period (1937:08–1981:12), the hyperinflation period (1982:01–1989:12), and the current period (1990:01-2011:12). The mean and conditional residual variance equations are reported in equations (1) and (2) for each period.

The results for each period are similar, evidence that the unified price index is indeed a good indicator of price fluctuations in the country since 1937. In all cases, inflation is best explained by the most recent episode of price fluctuations, that is, inflation with a one-lagged period, which

TABLE 5.4 GARCH(1,1)-M System for inflation, 1937:08–2011:12

A. Full Sample. 1937:08–2011:12

(1a) $$\pi_t = 5.08 + 0.43\pi_{t-1} - 0.11\pi_{t-2} + 0.00\pi_{t-3} + 0.04\pi_{t-4} - 0.08\pi_{t-5} + 0.05\pi_{t-6} + 0.03\varepsilon_{t-12} + 0.000\,{}^{2}_{\varepsilon t} + \varepsilon_t$$

(3.98) (4.69) (−1.01) (0.01) (0.54) (−0.74) (0.57) (0.61) (1.08)

(2a) $$\sigma^2_{\varepsilon t} = 99.35 + 0.634\varepsilon^2_{t-1} + 0.576\sigma^2_{\varepsilon t-1}$$

(1.27) (2.74) (9.10)

Q(4) = 6.17	$Q^2(4) = 0.19$
Q(12) = 31.90	$Q^2(12) = 1.71$

Log likelihood function = −4315.08

B. Pre-hyperinflation period. 1937:08–1981:12

(1b) $$\pi_t = 11.98 + 0.14\pi_{t-1} - 0.14\pi_{t-2} - 0.01\pi_{t-3} - 0.03\pi_{t-4} - 0.08\pi_{t-5} - 0.08\pi_{t-6} + 0.01\varepsilon_{t-12} + 0.000\sigma^2_{\sigma t} + \varepsilon_t$$

(3.52) (2.01) (−2.13) (−0.27) (−0.60) (−1.38) (−1.67) (0.11) (0.14)

(2b) $$\sigma^2_{\varepsilon t} = 322.38 + 0.966\,\varepsilon^2_{t-1} + 0.339\sigma^2_{\varepsilon t-1}$$

(1.59) (2.57) (4.02)

Q(4) = 24.86	$Q^2(4) = 0.47$
Q(12) = 72.06	$Q^2(12) = 3.28$

Log likelihood function = −2686.08

C. Hyperinflation period. 1982:01–1989:12

(1c) $$\pi_t = 3.95 + 0.89\,\pi_{t-1} - 0.00\,\pi_{t-2} + 0.08\,\pi_{t-3} - 0.04\,\varepsilon_{t-11} - 0.001\varepsilon^2_{\varepsilon t} + \varepsilon_t$$

(0.33) (5.41) (−0.02) (1.16) (−0.41) (−2.76)

(2c) $$\sigma^2_{\varepsilon t} = 870.57 + 1.260\,\varepsilon^2_{t-1} + 0.203\sigma^2_{\varepsilon t-1}$$

(1.85) (2.43) (1.42)

Q(4) = 2.18	$Q^2(4) = 1.54$
Q(12) = 18.72	$Q^2(12) = 28.00$

Log likelihood function = −556.42

D. Current period. 1990:01–2011:12

(1d) $$\pi_t = 2.71 + 0.32\pi_{t-1} + 0.01\pi_{t-2} + 0.06\pi_{t-3} + 0.06\pi_{t-4} - 0.01\pi_{t-5} - 0.16\pi_{t-6} + 0.15\,\varepsilon_{t-12} + 0.019\sigma^2_{\varepsilon t} + \varepsilon_t$$

(4.22) (4.71) (0.17) (0.77) (0.70) (−0.11) (2.87) (2.33) (−1.82)

(2d) $$\sigma^2_{\varepsilon t} = 9.69 + 0.302\,\varepsilon^2_{t-1} + 0.596\sigma^2_{\varepsilon t-1}$$

(2.46) (2.73) (7.32)

Q(4) = 2.57	$Q^2(4) = 5.26$
Q(12) = 8.37	$Q^2(12) = 10.47$

Log likelihood function = −907.96

TABLE 5.5 Johansen cointegration tests between inflation rate and inflation uncertainty

	TRACE STATISTIC	CRITICAL VALUE (5%)	CRITICAL VALUE (1%)
(1) Period: 1938:05–2011:12 (VAR lag = 8)			
$H_0: r=0$	98.76**	18.17	23.46
$H_0: r\leq 0$	17.99**	3.74	6.40
(2) Period: 1937:10–1981:12 (VAR lag = 1)			
$H_0: r=0$	304.73**	18.17	23.46
$H_0: r\leq 0$	91.47**	3.74	6.40
(3) Period: 1982:03–1989:12 (VAR lag = 1)			
$H_0: r=0$	59.50**	18.17	23.46
$H_0: r\leq 0$	8.05**	3.74	6.40
(4) Period: 1990:03–2011:12 (VAR lag = 1)			
$H_0: r=0$	118.89**	18.17	23.46
$H_0: r\leq 0$	30.29**	3.74	6.40

Notes:
1. ** denotes significance at the 1% level.
2. The Schwartz criteria (SC) is used to select the number of lags required in the cointegrating test.
3. Critical values are taken from Johansen and Juselius (1990); r denotes the number of cointegrating vectors.
4. In the 4 cases, the Trace test indicates 2 cointegrating equations at both the 1% and 5% levels of significance.

is positive and significant at standard levels, demonstrating that in Bolivia inflation is mostly explained by short-term expectations. This finding is consistent with the OLS results reported in Table 5.2. Inflation rates in other periods, on the other hand, were found to be largely insignificant, though in those cases where they were statistically significant, their effect was never as important as π_{t-1}, as reflected in the size of the coefficients. The GARCH (1,1) parameters in the residual variance equations are largely significant, with the notable exception of the hyperinflation period, where the GARCH term is insignificant. Further, the coefficients are generally large, signifying that inflation shocks create persistent inflation uncertainty.

Inflation uncertainty as measured by the GARCH-in-mean variable (σ_t^2) is only significant in explaining inflation during the hyperinflation period, though the findings suggest that higher uncertainty leads to lower inflation. This result is not as surprising if one considers the period analyzed. As the country was experiencing a decade of never-before-seen inflation rates, the expectations were that regardless of what happened in the future—inflation uncertainty—it could never be as bad as what was happening during the 1980s. In that sense, the Cukierman and Meltzer theory is confirmed working in the opposite direction.[10]

The Ljung-Box Q-statistics are also reported at 4 and 12 lags for the levels and squares of the standardized residuals for the four GARCH (1,1)-M systems analyzed in this paper. The test results show that the time series models for the conditional mean and the GARCH (1,1) model for the residual conditional variance adequately capture the distribution of the disturbances.

10 It should also be noted that the coefficient of σ_t^2 is almost zero, which indicates that uncertainty may not be as important in explaining inflation during tins period.

TABLE 5.6 Causality tests for inflation and inflation uncertainty

1. Period: 1938:05–2011:12 (FPE lag = 8)		
Inflation (π)	1.00	–389.48 (–18.54)
Inflation Uncertainty (σ^2)	–0.003 (–21.41)	1.00
• Bidirectional causality		
2. Period: 1937:12–1981:12 (FPE lag = 3)		
Inflation (π)	1.00	–500.67 (–12.19)
Inflation Uncertainty (σ^2)	–0.002 (–12.31)	1.00
• Bidirectional causality		
3. Period: 1982:10–1989:12 (FPE lag = 8)		
Inflation (π)	1.00	–312.05 (–5.41)
Inflation Uncertainty (σ^2)	–0.003 (–7.74)	1.00
• Bidirectional causality		
4. Period: 1990:08–2011:12 (FPE lag = 6)		
Inflation (π)	1.00	–7.430 (–3.62)
Inflation Uncertainty (σ^2)	–0.135 (–6.39)	1.00
• Bidirectional causality		

FPE = Final Prediction Error criterion

Next, a bivariate VAR model is estimated for inflation and inflation uncertainty to test for causality between these variables. Having confirmed the existence of unit roots for all data series, there remains the task of determining whether there exists a long-run equilibrium relationship between inflation and inflation uncertainty. Following the Johansen and Juselius method (1990). a VAR model is estimated and the Johansen Cointegration Test results are presented in Table 5.5. Cointegration tests are reported for each of the four periods analyzed here.

Cointegration results for the four different time periods demonstrate there is indeed a long-run equilibrium relation between inflation and inflation uncertainty. The Trace statistics for each of the four time periods produce results suggesting that there are two cointegration equations at the 5 and 1 percent levels of significance.[11]

Once cointegration has been confirmed for the four time periods, error-correction models (ECMs) are utilized to determine causality between inflation and inflation uncertainty. As

11 The Maximum Eigenvalue test corroborates the results found with the Trace test for each of the four time periods tested in this work.

Granger-causality tests are known to be very sensitive to lag length, in this work the Akaike's (1974) minimum Final Prediction Error (FPE) criterion is utilized to address this concern. Table 5.6 reports these test results.

The results suggest bidirectional causality between inflation and inflation uncertainty for the four time periods tested. However, the effect of inflation on inflation uncertainty is stronger in all cases, a finding consistent with the Friedman-Ball hypothesis and with the findings of Pourgerami and Maskus (1987) and Ungar and Zilberfarb (1993), who found that in environments with significant inflation, agents invest on inflation forecasting, thus reducing inflation. In any case, in a country like Bolivia, where inflation is so intimately tied to its economic history, bidirectional causality between inflation and uncertainty should not be surprising, as past experience forces agents to continually adjust expectations to current inflation, a process that produces a continuous feedback between inflation and expectations about future inflation. This finding seems to suggest that a disciplined monetary policy, aimed at reducing the levels of inflation is the most effective way to tackle inflation uncertainty in Bolivia.

Finally, it is important to point out that the results are consistent regardless of whether the whole period from 1937 to 2011 is considered, or sub-periods within these years. This consistency of findings adds credence to the price index presented in this work and to its capacity to reflect true price variations in the country since 1937.

6. CONCLUSIONS

This paper estimates a time-varying GARCH-M model of inflation for Bolivia and investigates its linkages with resulting measures of inflation uncertainty in a bivariate VAR framework. The analysis is done observing—and isolating—the hyperinflation period that the country experienced during the 1980s decade.

Obtaining accurate measures of inflation uncertainty is crucial for monetary authorities, since higher uncertainty requires more active policies, a position substantiated by Söderström (2002). The main findings are as follows: inflation and inflation uncertainty have both declined steadily since 1990, when the hyperinflation period finally ended. These variables are cointegrated and ECM-causality tests indicate bidirectional causality. However, the effect of inflation on uncertainty is stronger, which supports the hypothesis formulated separately by Friedman and Ball. Finally, the price index that was utilized—which runs from January 1937 through December 2011—was constructed by combining six different official indices that were collected by the CBB. This is the first time that this index is used in the context of obtaining reliable measures of inflation and inflation uncertainty, and the consistency of results obtained for the whole period and for sub-periods between 1937 and 2011 provides confidence on the dependability of the price index.

The analysis suggests that a tough anti-inflation stance seems to be the most conducive way to reducing uncertainty about future inflation. Hence, it appears that the CBB, in accordance to the Friedman-Ball link, might be able to reduce inflation uncertainty by maintaining low and stable inflation rates.

REFERENCES

Akaike, Hirotsugu (1974), A New Look at the Statistical Model Identification, *IEEE Transactions on Automatic Control* AC-19: 716–23.

Asilis, Carlos Manuel, Patrick Honohan, and Paul McNelis (1993). Money Demand during Hyperinflation and Stabilization: Bolivia, 1980–88, *Economic Inquiry,* 31:2, pp, 262–73.

Ball, Laurence (1992). Why Does Higher Inflation Raise Inflation Uncertainty ? *Journal of Monetary Economics,* 29:3, pp. 371–378.

Caporale, Guglielmo Maria, Luca Onorante, and Paolo Paesani (2010). Inflation and Inflation Uncertainty in the Euro Area, European Central Bank Working Paper Series No. 1229, pp. 1–22.

Cecchetti, Stephen (1993). Inflation Uncertainty, Relative Price Uncertainty and Investment in US Manufacturing: Comment, *Journal of Money, Credit, and Banking.* 25, pp. 550–556.

Cukierman, Alex and Allan Meitzer (1986). A Theory of Ambiguity, Credibility and Inflation under Discretion and Asymmetric Information, *Econometrica,* 54, pp. 1099–1128.

Davis, George and Bryce Kanago (2000). The Level of Uncertainty of Inflation: Results from OECD Forecasts, *Economic Inquiry,* 38, pp. 58–72.

Della Mea, Humberto and Alejandro Peña (1996). Explorando la Incertidumbre Inflacionaria: 1973-1985, *Revista de Economía, Banco Central del Uruguay,* 3:2, pp. 19–40.

Dickey, David, A, William Bell, and Robert. Miller (1986). Unit Roots in Time Series Models: Tests and Implications, *The American Statistician,* 40:1, pp. 12–26.

Dotsey, M., and P. D. Sarte (2000). Inflation Uncertainty and Growth in a Cash-in-Advance Economy, *Journal of Monetary Economics,* 45, pp. 631–655.

Engle, Robert (1982). Autoregressive Conditional Heteroskedasticity with Estimates of the Variance of United Kingdom Inflation. *Econometrica,* 50, pp. 987–1007.

Fernández Valdovinos, Carlos (2001). Further Evidence on Friedman's Hypothesis: The Case of Paraguay, *Cuadernos de Economía,* 38:115, pp. 257–273.

Fischer, Stanley and Franco Modigliani (1978). Toward an Understanding of the Real Effects and Costs of Inflation, *Weltwirtschaftliches Archiv,* 114, pp. 810–833.

Friedman, Milton (1977). Nobel lecture: Inflation and Unemployment, *Journal of Political Economy,* 85:3, pp. 451–472.

Glosten. L. R., R., Jagannathan, and D. E., Runkle (1993). On the Relation Between the Expected Value and the Volatility of the Nominal Excess Return on Stocks. *Journal of Finance,* 48, pp. 1779–1801.

Grier, Kevin and Mark Perry (2000). The Effects of Real and Nominal Uncertainty on Inflation and Output Growth: Some Garch-m Evidence. *Journal of Applied Econometrics,* 15:1, pp. 45–58.

Johansen, Soren and Katarina Juselius (1990). Maximum Likelihood Estimation and Inference on Cointegration—with Applications to the Demand for Money, *Oxford Bulletin of Economics and Statistics, 52,* pp. 169–210.

Kontonikas, Alexandras (2004). Inflation and Inflation Uncertainty in the United Kingdom, Evidence from GARCH Modelling. *Economic Modelling,* 21:3, pp. 525–543.

MacKinnon. James (1991). Critical Values for Cointegration Tests in Long-Run Economic Relationships, in *Readings in Cointegration* (Eds), Engle, Robert and Clive Granger, Oxford University Press, New York, pp. 267–76.

Morales, Juan Antonio (1987). Estabilización y Nueva Política Económica en Bolivia, *Trimestre Económico,* 54, pp. 179–211.

Pagan, Adrian (1984). Econometric Issues in the Analysis of Regressions with Generated Regressors, *International Economic Review,* 25, pp. 221–247.

Pindyck, Robert (1991). Irreversibility, Uncertainty, and Investment, *Journal of Economic Literature,* 29, pp. 1110–1148.

Pourgerami, Abbas and Keith Maskus (1987). The Effects of Inflation on the Predictability of Price Changes in Latin America: Some Estimates and Policy Implications, *World Development,* 15:2, pp. 287–290.

Sachs, Jeffrey (1987). The Bolivian Hyperinflation and Stabilization, *American Economic Review,* 77:2, pp. 279–283.

Söderström, Ulf (2002). Monetary Policy with Uncertain Parameters, *The Scandinavian Journal of Economics,* 104:1, pp. 125–145.

Ungar, Meyer and Ben-Zion Zilberfarb (1993). Inflation and its Unpredictability—Theory and Empirical Evidence. *Journal of Money, Credit, and Banking,* 25:4, pp. 709–720.

Zakoian, Jean Michel (1990). Threshold Heteroskedastic Models. Mimeo, CREST.

APPENDIX

Bolivia: Monthly Consumer Price Index, 1937–2011 (Base Month: January 2000)*

	JANUARY	FEBRUARY	MARCH	APRIL	MAY	JUNE	JULY	AUGUST	SEPTEMBER	OCTOBER	NOVEMBER	DECEMBER	YEARLY INFLATION (%)
1937	5,00E-08	5,12E-08	5,40E-08	5,03E-08	4,94E-08	5,12E-08	5,28E-08	5,28E-08	5,24E-08	5,37E-08	5,65E-08	5,62E-08	12,35
1938	5,92E-08	6,08E-08	6,14E-08	6,54E-08	6,51E-08	7,25E-08	7,44E-08	7,25E-08	7,10E-08	7,31E-08	7,40E-08	7,53E-08	27,08
1939	6,91E-08	7,22E-08	7,34E-08	7,53E-08	7,71E-08	8,18E-08	9,10E-08	9,16E-08	9,29E-08	9,44E-08	9,81E-08	1,06E-07	53,13
1940	1,08E-07	1,08E-07	1,08E-07	1,09E-07	1,11E-07	1,11E-07	1,13E-07	1,14E-07	1,17E-07	1,23E-07	1,24E-07	1,24E-07	14,90
1941	1,24E-07	1,29E-07	1,31E-07	1,37E-07	1,42E-07	1,45E-07	1,47E-07	1,50E-07	1,57E-07	1,58E-07	1,60E-07	1,67E-07	35,16
1942	1,71E-07	1,82E-07	1,81E-07	1,82E-07	1,85E-07	1,86E-07	1,88E-07	1,88E-07	1,88E-07	1,91E-07	2,14E-07	2,16E-07	26,31
1943	2,19E-07	2,30E-07	2,28E-07	2,28E-07	2,33E-07	2,35E-07	2,37E-07	2,34E-07	2,33E-07	2,34E-07	2,34E-07	2,34E-07	7,19
1944	2,40E-07	2,41E-07	2,50E-07	2,51E-07	2,44E-07	2,44E-07	2,45E-07	2,45E-07	2,45E-07	2,51E-07	2,52E-07	2,52E-07	5,28
1945	2,53E-07	2,53E-07	2,54E-07	2,51E-07	2,51E-07	2,52E-07	2,62E-07	2,66E-07	2,63E-07	2,69E-07	2,71E-07	2,72E-07	7,31
1946	2,69E-07	2,70E-07	2,70E-07	2,70E-07	2,72E-07	2,74E-07	2,76E-07	2,83E-07	2,82E-07	2,83E-07	2,95E-07	3,15E-07	17,20
1947	3,23E-07	3,23E-07	3,25E-07	3,25E-07	3,28E-07	3,33E-07	3,36E-07	3,41E-07	3,46E-07	3,47E-07	3,49E-07	3,65E-07	13,19
1948	3,68E-07	3,70E-07	3,72E-07	3,74E-07	3,75E-07	3,76E-07	3,76E-07	3,76E-07	3,78E-07	3,81E-07	3,85E-07	3,85E-07	4,61
1949	3,88E-07	3,94E-07	3,97E-07	3,97E-07	4,01E-07	4,02E-07	4,01E-07	4,02E-07	4,04E-07	4,12E-07	4,14E-07	4,22E-07	8,83
1950	4,25E-07	4,29E-07	4,32E-07	4,53E-07	4,85E-07	4,91E-07	4,99E-07	5,14E-07	5,20E-07	5,47E-07	5,63E-07	5,73E-07	34,93
1951	5,95E-07	6,06E-07	6,21E-07	6,39E-07	6,39E-07	6,49E-07	6,61E-07	6,84E-07	6,86E-07	6,92E-07	7,06E-07	7,27E-07	22,18
1952	7,54E-07	7,59E-07	7,63E-07	7,74E-07	7,86E-07	7,95E-07	7,93E-07	8,14E-07	8,35E-07	8,65E-07	8,82E-07	9,52E-07	26,32
1953	1,02E-06	1,05E-06	1,07E-06	1,15E-06	1,52E-06	1,73E-06	1,84E-06	1,84E-06	1,92E-06	2,00E-06	2,23E-06	2,40E-06	135,59
1954	2,53E-06	2,59E-06	2,66E-06	3,20E-06	3,37E-06	3,77E-06	3,91E-06	4,06E-06	4,28E-06	4,33E-06	4,67E-06	4,77E-06	88,44
1955	3,30E-06	3,42E-06	3,94E-06	4,37E-06	4,45E-06	4,59E-06	4,64E-06	4,65E-06	4,76E-06	4,95E-06	5,07E-06	5,43E-06	64,58
1956	6,70E-06	7,80E-06	8,23E-06	8,64E-06	9,06E-06	9,97E-06	1,04E-05	1,08E-05	1,24E-05	1,62E-05	1,82E-05	3,12E-05	366,26
1957	3,16E-05	2,87E-05	2,94E-05	2,84E-05	2,57E-05	2,52E-05	2,52E-05	2,43E-05	2,44E-05	2,58E-05	2,64E-05	2,69E-05	–14,68
1958	2,72E-05	2,69E-05	2,70E-05	2,69E-05	2,63E-05	2,68E-05	2,64E-05	2,67E-05	2,67E-05	2,95E-05	3,13E-05	3,20E-05	17,53
1959	3,17E-05	3,28E-05	3,24E-05	3,27E-05	3,27E-05	3,28E-05	3,32E-05	3,38E-05	3,38E-05	3,40E-05	3,44E-05	3,52E-05	11,02
1960	3,55E-05	3,58E-05	3,61E-05	3,65E-05	3,68E-05	3,71E-05	3,75E-05	3,78E-05	3,81E-05	3,85E-05	3,88E-05	3,89E-05	9,70

Bolivia: Monthly Consumer Price Index, 1937–2011 (Base Month: January 2000)* *(continued)*

	JANUARY	FEBRUARY	MARCH	APRIL	MAY	JUNE	JULY	AUGUST	SEPTEMBER	OCTOBER	NOVEMBER	DECEMBER	YEARLY INFLATION (%)
1961	3,86E-05	3,87E-05	3,87E-05	3,96E-05	3,94E-05	3,96E-05	3,99E-05	3,98E-05	4,02E-05	4,18E-05	4,25E-05	4,18E-05	8,35
1962	4,19E-05	4,15E-05	4,27E-05	4,26E-05	4,22E-05	4,23E-05	4,25E-05	4,20E-05	4,22E-05	4,25E-05	4,30E-05	4,32E-05	3,04
1963	4,34E-05	4,36E-05	4,38E-05	4,40E-05	4,43E-05	4,45E-05	4,47E-05	4,49E-05	4,52E-05	4,54E-05	4,56E-05	4,25E-05	2,04
1964	4,60E-05	4,65E-05	4,61E-05	4,63E-05	4,61E-05	4,63E-05	4,63E-05	4,65E-05	4,64E-05	4,65E-05	4,65E-05	4,69E-05	2,04
1965	4,81E-05	4,79E-05	4,81E-05	4,81E-05	4,73E-05	4,68E-05	4,69E-05	4,69E-05	4,75E-05	4,81E-05	4,86E-05	4,92E-05	2,23
1966	4,98E-05	4,98E-05	4,97E-05	5,06E-05	5,07E-05	5,13E-05	5,19E-05	5,23E-05	5,37E-05	5,60E-05	5,53E-05	5,37E-05	7,70
1967	5,53E-05	5,65E-05	5,33E-05	5,40E-05	5,36E-05	5,66E-05	5,54E-05	5,58E-05	5,60E-05	5,70E-05	5,72E-05	5,75E-05	3,89
1968	5,78E-05	5,78E-05	5,77E-05	5,74E-05	5,82E-05	5,89E-05	5,99E-05	5,96E-05	5,92E-05	5,91E-05	5,94E-05	5,95E-05	2,86
1969	5,97E-05	5,93E-05	5,89E-05	5,88E-05	5,91E-05	5,92E-05	5,96E-05	6,06E-05	6,07E-05	6,11E-05	6,17E-05	6,14E-05	2,85
1970	6,14E-05	6,16E-05	6,16E-05	6,13E-05	6,17E-05	6,21E-05	6,26E-05	6,27E-05	6,27E-05	6,31E-05	6,35E-05	6,39E-05	4,08
1971	6,35E-05	6,32E-05	6,34E-05	6,30E-05	6,32E-05	6,42E-05	6,51E-05	6,59E-05	6,63E-05	6,59E-05	6,59E-05	6,60E-05	3,94
1972	6,60E-05	6,60E-05	6,56E-05	6,56E-05	6,56E-05	6,61E-05	6,66E-05	6,64E-05	6,66E-05	6,71E-05	8,29E-05	8,15E-05	23,50
1973	8,13E-05	8,15E-05	8,30E-05	8,40E-05	8,45E-05	8,48E-05	8,77E-05	9,09E-05	9,34E-05	1,02E-04	1,03E-04	1,10E-04	35,08
1974	1,27E-04	1,43E-04	1,46E-04	1,47E-04	1,48E-04	1,51E-04	1,52E-04	1,52E-04	1,49E-04	1,48E-04	1,51E-04	1,53E-04	19,80
1975	1,55E-04	1,55E-04	1,54E-04	1,54E-04	1,55E-04	1,58E-04	1,62E-04	1,64E-04	1,64E-04	1,64E-04	1,63E-04	1,62E-04	4,79
1976	1,64E-04	1,66E-04	1,63E-04	1,62E-04	1,63E-04	1,66E-04	1,67E-04	1,68E-04	1,68E-04	1,69E-04	1,69E-04	1,71E-04	4,22
1977	1,76E-04	1,76E-04	1,72E-04	1,73E-04	1,73E-04	1,79E-04	1,81E-04	1,84E-04	1,84E-04	1,86E-04	1,87E-04	1,89E-04	7,03
1978	1,90E-04	1,87E-04	1,87E-04	1,88E-04	1,86E-04	1,93E-04	2,01E-04	2,04E-04	2,05E-04	2,13E-04	2,13E-04	2,14E-04	12,98
1979	2,16E-04	2,20E-04	2,19E-04	2,18E-04	2,23E-04	2,27E-04	2,34E-04	2,39E-04	2,42E-04	2,46E-04	2,56E-04	3,12E-04	44,34
1980	3,17E-04	3,18E-04	3,24E-04	3,26E-04	3,36E-04	3,55E-04	3,60E-04	3,72E-04	3,63E-04	3,68E-04	3,73E-04	3,86E-04	21,78
1981	4,34E-04	4,43E-04	4,41E-04	4,42E-04	4,52E-04	4,52E-04	4,59E-04	4,86E-04	4,84E-04	4,87E-04	4,86E-04	4,83E-04	11,28
1982	4,96E-04	5,75E-04	6,22E-04	7,00E-04	7,29E-04	7,63E-04	9,28E-04	1,09E-03	1,31E-03	1,50E-03	1,78E-03	1,92E-03	286,74
1983	1,93E-03	2,13E-03	2,38E-03	2,58E-03	2,81E-03	2,90E-03	3,20E-03	4,03E-03	4,72E-03	5,23E-03	6,52E-03	8,21E-03	325,95
1984	9,00E-03	1,11E-02	1,34E-02	2,18E-02	3,21E-02	3,34E-02	3,52E-02	4,04E-02	5,55E-02	8,84E-02	1,16E-01	1,87E-01	1.978,48
1985	3,16E-01	8,92E-01	1,1149	1,2463	1,6908	3,0175	5,0182	8,3533	13,0728	12,8300	13,2407	15,4657	4.800,75
1986	20,5637	22,1988	22,2134	23,0117	23,2344	24,2241	24,6560	24,8132	25,3785	25,5282	25,5012	25,6674	24,82
1987	26,2960	26,6195	26,8047	27,2317	27,3243	27,2646	27,2501	27,5207	27,6796	28,2576	28,1773	28,4040	8,02

1988	28,2759	28,8259	29,0680	30,4446	30,8749	31,5101	32,7685	33,5545	33,4302	34,1245	34,0599	34,5123	22,06
1989	34,6791	34,8694	35,1625	35,2020	35,4220	35,3583	35,5216	36,6347	37,9983	38,7883	39,4650	40,2285	16,00
1990	40,6488	40,6107	40,7525	40,8852	41,1116	41,9362	42,6851	43,1543	43,6627	45,1694	46,4506	47,4737	16,79
1991	50,2447	50,3800	50,6999	50,9488	51,3506	51,7397	52,1752	52,7111	52,9316	53,4434	53,8870	54,3670	8,20
1992	55,7626	57,0131	57,3115	57,4614	57,8591	58,2363	58,6754	59,2126	59,2520	59,5601	59,8579	60,0554	7,70
1993	61,0764	61,6566	61,6258	61,6997	62,1687	62,7282	63,4245	64,5344	64,8764	65,2073	65,3312	65,6448	7,48
1994	66,1896	66,5471	66,4938	66,8197	67,2273	67,5499	68,1815	69,0202	69,4412	69,9738	71,1465	71,2389	7,63
1995	71,8302	72,2325	72,9006	74,0306	74,3785	74,8918	75,1838	75,5748	75,9602	77,3913	78,7766	80,1946	11,64
1996	81,4376	83,6853	83,5012	83,3175	83,6383	84,0816	85,0317	85,9160	86,0535	85,9847	86,4258	86,5701	6,30
1997	86,5615	86,7259	86,5182	86,9943	87,6246	88,4487	89,5655	90,1541	89,2105	89,5525	89,6607	92,3963	6,74
1998	93,6878	94,4660	94,6600	94,9280	95,2237	95,4454	95,6579	95,6856	95,6394	96,5819	96,6096	96,4525	2,95
1999	96,5962	96,9637	96,5580	96,4084	96,4911	96,8480	97,0399	97,5424	98,1214	98,8300	98,8966	99,4753	2,98
2000	100,0000	100,4152	101,0271	102,0019	100,7287	100,9250	101,6500	102,0537	103,9318	105,3281	102,6399	102,8674	2,87
2001	103,0987	103,0713	102,8315	103,0525	102,8692	103,6286	104,8733	104,1820	103,9063	103,9835	103,7490	103,8169	0,70
2002	103,8065	104,0296	103,7100	103,6821	103,7235	103,8376	104,2633	104,4917	104,9714	105,5402	106,1112	106,3604	2,46
2003	106,7805	106,5518	106,6156	106,9560	106,9751	107,1900	107,8282	108,5195	108,7744	110,1362	109,5725	110,5542	3,53
2004	111,2385	111,4478	111,1512	111,1733	111,6332	112,4612	113,0549	113,4507	113,4220	114,3351	114,9708	115,6618	3,98
2005	117,2510	117,3054	117,4924	117,0497	117,8362	119,6562	119,1013	119,5176	119,6973	120,1432	120,6666	121,3391	3,49
2006	121,8289	122,2086	121,8695	122,0404	123,0612	123,8279	124,5246	124,7594	124,8612	125,4440	126,3871	127,3395	4,52
2007	129,1663	130,2433	130,6294	130,2959	130,8872	131,9939	135,5268	137,6826	137,9438	139,6636	141,3786	142,2720	10,15
2008	143,8233	147,5925	149,0315	150,1319	152,9343	154,8574	155,5718	156,5883	157,9620	158,2505	158,4565	159,1297	10,64
2009	159,7066	159,5967	158,8137	158,1269	157,8246	158,1406	157,8246	158,8137	158,9786	159,4868	159,1846	159,5555	0,09
2010	159,8302	160,0913	159,8989	160,0500	160,0226	160,2424	161,2314	162,9348	164,1849	166,1905	168,0450	171,5754	7,35
2011	173,2238	176,0949	177,6609	177,7021	178,0593	178,3065	179,2544	179,9412	180,4907	181,3424	181,9331	182,8123	5,54

*Notes: Values on table reflect author's calculations based on data from Central Bank of Bolivia (CBB)

END-OF-CHAPTER QUESTIONS

1. Explain the Friedman-Ball hypothesis concerning inflation and inflation uncertainty.
2. Why does the author argue that the economic history of Bolivia is inexorably linked to dramatic monetary disequilibriums?
3. What is the difference between inflation and hyperinflation? When, according to Phillip Cagan, does hyperinflation commence?
4. What is inflation uncertainty, and how does it differ from variability in prices?
5. What are some of the consequences of inflation uncertainty?
6. Provide a brief chronology of the hyperinflation in Bolivia during the 1980s, with an emphasis on the stabilization mechanism that was put in place in the latter part of 1985.
7. Utilizing the price index included in the Appendix, graph the monthly inflation rates for each decade starting in 1937 (one graph per decade). Based on those graphs, which decade shows the greatest price stability? Which one shows the greatest price instability?
8. Why would the unit of account in Bolivia change twice between the 1930s and the 2000s? What did policy makers want to accomplish by introducing a new currency?
9. Explain the reasons why the current administration of Evo Morales has not (yet) fallen on the inflation trap that besieged previous populist governments.
10. What are some of the advantages of using GARCH models to estimate inflation uncertainty?
11. What is the meaning behind the assertion that inflation and inflation uncertainty are cointegrated? What are the implications of such cointegration?
12. A principal finding of the article is the existence of bidirectional causality between inflation and inflation uncertainty. What is the significance of this finding?
13. If, in fact, there is bidirectional causality between inflation and inflation uncertainty, what could the Central Bank of Bolivia do to prevent inflation uncertainty?

CHAPTER 6

Iceland's Rise, Fall, Stabilisation and Beyond

Robert H. Wade and Silla Sigurgeirsdottir*

Iceland is an unusually pure example of the dynamics that blocked regulation and caused financial fragility across the developed world for 20 years. This essay describes the statist-and-corporatist political economy of the country as it soared from near the bottom of the Western European income hierarchy at the end of the World War II to up near the top by the 1980s. It illustrates how a group of neoliberal politicians and allied civil servants drove through selective deregulation and privatisation in the 1990s and 2000s. In the space created for newly privatised banks, Icelandic financiers grew the banks and linked private equity firms through mergers and acquisitions abroad to the point where by 2007 tiny Iceland supported three banks in the world's biggest 300 banks, with assets eight times the GDP—second highest in the world after Switzerland. As profits from these overseas operations were partly redistributed back to Iceland the economy boomed, in the grip of super-Minsky processes. The government, the banks and the media interpreted the boom as testimony to the validity of neoliberal policies and went out of their way to hide increasing financial fragility from view, preventing a negative or self-correcting policy feedback loop. The accident waiting to happen happened in the wake of the Lehman collapse in September 2008. The essay charts the zigzags of the government's response and the citizens' response, and discusses the prospects for a resumption of growth on a more sustainable basis. It suggests that Iceland illustrates in miniature the ratcheting down

---

Manuscript received 21 September 2011; final version received 2 November 2011.
Address for correspondence: (Sigurbjörg) Silla Sigurgeirsdottir, Department of Political Science, School of Social Sciences, University of Iceland, Gimli v/Sæmundargötu, 101 Reykjavik, Iceland; email: silla@hi.is

*London School of Economics and University of Iceland. Robert Wade is professor of political economy at the London School of Economics and winner of the Leontief Prize in 2008. Silla Sigurgeirsdottir is lecturer in public policy at the Department of Political Science, School of Social Sciences, University of Iceland. This paper builds on their 'Iceland's loud no', *Le Monde Diplomatique* (English), August 2011; 'Lessons from Iceland', *New Left Review*, vol. 65, Sept–Oct 2010, 5–29; 'Iceland's meltdown: the rise and fall of international banking in the North Atlantic', *Real-world Economic Review*, vol. 56, February 2011 58–71; and 'Iceland's rise and fall', in Michell, J. and Toporowski, J. (eds), *A Handbook of Critical Issues in Finance*, Cheltenham, Edward Elgar, 2012 (forthcoming).

of mass living standards underway across the Western world now that the cushion of debt has been removed, even as financiers and others in the top few percentiles of national income distributions increase their share of national income. But economic institutions and politics matter: in Iceland the large devaluation spread the cut in a relatively 'apolitical' way; the government let the banks go bust rather than bail them out at taxpayers' expense; it imposed capital controls on outflows; and it used fiscal transfers to protect the bottom half of the population from disproportionate cuts.

Key words: Financial crisis, Minsky, Liberalisation, Privatization, Policy feedbck loop, Corporatism

JEL classifications: G20, F50

> *Iceland should be a model to the world. (Laffer, 2007)*
>
> *They [the Icelandic banks] shouldn't be worried about the fundamental soundness of their business model. I think it is very sound and very good. Any market turmoil is just prompted by some misplaced misunderstandings of market analysts. (Richard Portes, professor at the London Business School; Portes, 2008)*
>
> *It was absolutely obvious that its banking model was not viable. (Buiter and Sibert, 2008)*[1]

Iceland recovered from a near-death experience. The sense of fear and shock were palpable [when the IMF mission arrived in October 2008]—few, if any, countries had ever experienced such a catastrophic economic crash . . . The scale of the uncertainty was staggering. (Poul M. Thomsen, Deputy Director of the IMF's European Department, October 2011; Thomsen, 2011)

1. INTRODUCTION

The small North Atlantic island of Iceland has lessons for the world. Its experience of a financial boom and bust over the 2000s provides an unusually pure example of the dynamics that caused financial fragility and blocked regulation across the developed world for 20 years.

These larger dynamics can be thought of as operating on three levels. First, the level of broad-based Minsky-like processes that make positive, self-reinforcing feedback loops across the economy, such that asset price inflation feeds upon itself.[2] Second, the level of globally concentrated corporate power. A recent analysis identifies a global 'superentity' with a high proportion of total corporate revenues and dense cross-ownership between its constituents, comprising 147 global companies; in the top 50, only one is not a financial firm (Coghalan and MacKenzie, 2011). Such superconcentration provides a platform for subgroups of firms to capture the state and secure public policy in line with their preferences.

1 The report was written at the start of 2008 for an Icelandic bank, which kept it confidential until October 2008.

2 Pro-cyclicality comes partly from the use of short-term performance measures in managers' compensation schemes, resulting in higher appetite for risk and increased leverage (Minsky, 1992; Columba *et al.*, 2009; Goodhart, 2009).

Third, the level of second-round Minsky effects within the state, as public policy comes to amplify rather than counter the larger positive feedback loops (Baumgartner and Jones, 2002). One channel of these second-round effects is the actions of individuals and networks of individuals able to manipulate positions across the private/public sector divide. Janine Wedel, in *Shadow Elite*, describes an expanding class of people she calls 'flexians', who perform overlapping and not-fully-disclosed roles (consultants to private companies, official advisors, unofficial advisors, lobbyists, academics and television pundits). Flexians often operate in 'flex nets', whose members are more loyal to each other than to the organisations for which they work at any one time (Wedel, 2009).[3] The reform movement known as New Public Management, based on the premise that governments should operate more like private businesses and encourage more interchange of personnel between private and public sectors, has created vast new opportunities for flexians and flex nets to gain access to strategic public sector information and policymaking and deploy their influence for private profit and ideological advantage. New information technologies create many new unregulated spaces for their operations.

As the boom rolled on and came to be accepted as 'the new normal', the three-level dynamics described above all operated to raise the level of financial fragility. Corporations reduced their cushions against risk; the ratings agencies and Big Four audit firms increasingly took bank financial statements at face value;[4] corporate concentration and interconnection rose; and governments eased up on regulation, bewitched by the 'efficient markets hypothesis' and forgetting that self-regulation is to regulation as self-importance is to importance. Governments also took less care over rules governing relations between public officials and private actors.

This is the phenomenon of "state capture" (Hellman and Kaufmann, 2001). In the general case, state capture tends to be a zero-sum game. However, the financial boom of the 2000s saw the public at large apparently benefiting from the boom even as the share of national income accruing to the top few percentiles soared (Palma, 2011). The galloping growth of lightly regulated finance enabled large-scale consumer borrowing on the back of inflating asset prices, despite stagnant median incomes. Debt became the way to live.

Iceland is tiny, only 319,000 people in an area 42% that of the UK (whose population is 62 million). It might be thought that in such a small society government would be extra accountable, through greater transparency of both formal and informal processes; wrongdoing would be difficult to hide. In fact, this turns out not to be the case. It was relatively easy for the leadership class to eliminate or marginalise sources of information critical of the direction of policy; in other words, to ensure that positive information feedback loops dominated, supporting pro-cyclical trends. And it was easy for blatant conflicts of interest to be redefined as mere 'coincidences of interest'; for what critics might call 'cronyism' to be defended as 'family values'.

---

3 For an application to Iceland's power networks see Logason, 2011.

4 See, for example, Norris (2011). The US Public Company Accounting Oversight Board wrote a report on Deloitte & Touche's audit of a major US bank, in late 2007, saying that its inspections revealed 'a [D & T] firm culture that allows . . . audit approaches that do not consistently emphasize the need for an appropriate level of critical analysis . . . and that rely largely on management representations'. The rules of disclosure allowed D & T to keep the report confidential for 41 months.

This essay traces the institutions and processes that generated the growth of the financial sector and the resulting economic boom over the 2000s and, then, post-crisis in late 2008, the zigzags of the government's response and the citizens' response. It discusses the prospects for a resumption of growth on a more sustainable basis and assesses the IMF's role.

2. ICELAND'S ROLLERCOASTER

In 2007, just before the financial crisis, Iceland's average income was the fifth highest in the world, 60% above US levels; Reykjavik's shops were laden with luxury goods, its restaurants made London seem cheap, SUVs choked the narrow streets. Icelanders were the happiest people in the world, according to an international study in 2006 (World Database of Happiness, 2006). They also had one of the least corrupt public administrations in the world, according to Transparency International.

Much of Iceland's success rested on the superfast growth of three Icelandic banks, which rose from small, public utility organisations in 1998 to being, after privatisation and mergers, among the world's top 300 banks eight years later, increasing their assets from 100% of GDP in 2000 to more than 800% by 2007, second only to Switzerland.

They borrowed massively on the back of implicit government guarantees, and lent to private equity firms owned by the bankers themselves or their close friends and relatives, against little or no real collateral.[5] The equity firms went on an exuberant mergers and acquisitions spree, buying up firms in several parts of Europe with borrowed money. They extracted vast profits for themselves and also for paying salaries, wages and taxes back home in Iceland.

In essence, Iceland's success, which earned the country the sobriquet of 'Nordic Tiger' (to match Ireland's 'Celtic Tiger'), was based on a mechanism whereby a small group of financiers backed by the state borrowed colossal sums from international capital markets, bought foreign assets, restructured the assets and redistributed profits back to tiny Iceland, booming the economy. The Icelandic elite and masses cheered them on, much as the populations at home in Norway and Denmark had cheered on the old Vikings as they returned from their marauding raids up and down the west coast of Europe a millennium ago.

This, of course, is not how the success was interpreted in Iceland and in the rest of the world at the time. Instead, the success was said to prove the validity of free-market economics as the route to prosperity. The leading Icelandic champion of free-market economics declared in the *Wall Street Journal*: '[Prime Minister] Oddsson's experiment with liberal policies is the greatest success story in the world' (Gissurarson, 2004).[6] Arthur Laffer, the Reagan-era guru of supply-side economics, declared on a visit to Iceland in November 2007 that fast economic growth with a large

5 For similar machinations elsewhere see Black (2005).

6 He is a professor of political theory at the University of Iceland, and also affiliated with the Instituto Millenium Rio de Janeiro and Friedrich Nauman Stiftung Sao Paulo. He was a member of the Locomotive Group, a member of the board of the Mont Pelerin Society from 1998 to 2004, and organiser of a meeting of the society in Iceland in August 2005. He published the book *How Iceland Could Be the Richest Country in the World in 2002*. He retains his university position even after being convicted of gross plagiarism in a unanimous judgement of the Icelandic Supreme Court, March 2008.

trade deficit and ballooning foreign debt were signs of success: 'Iceland should be a model to the world', he announced (Laffer, 2007).

The crisis came in September 2008 when money markets seized up after the Lehman meltdown. Within a week Iceland's three big banks collapsed and were taken into public ownership. They then entered a less glorious league—Moody's list of the 11 biggest financial collapses in history.

The economy experienced the third biggest fall in output and the fourth biggest fall in employment among the 30 OECD countries. The contraction stopped in late 2010, at 11% below the peak in the first quarter of 2008. At the time of writing, real GDP is expected to grow by just over 2% in 2011 and a little higher in 2012. Thanks to increases in welfare spending, only 14% of the population say they are finding it 'very difficult' to make ends meet, well below the European Union (EU) average, though rising since 2008 (Ólafsson, 2011). The government re-entered capital markets for the first time in June 2011 when it sold $1 billion worth of bonds at a spread of only 3.2 percentage points above LIBOR (London Interbank Offered Rates), much less than the other crisis-hit governments are having to pay, which testifies to the credibility of the government's stabilisation performance in the eyes of financial markets.

Now that the economy has stabilised, let us step back and consider how Iceland came to enjoy such economic success as to be dubbed the 'Nordic Tiger' and how the increasing financial fragility was hidden from view. Then we consider how the crisis was handled and the prospects for a resumption of growth on a more sustainable basis.

3. ICELAND MODERNISES

After more than 600 years of foreign (Norwegian and Danish) rule, Iceland's social structure was the most feudal of all Nordic countries at the beginning of the twentieth century. Agriculture dominated the economy and the majority of the population in 1900 worked as subsistence farmers or as agricultural wage labourers effectively tied to the landowners in semi-serf conditions (half the cultivated area was owned by the Danish crown or the Lutheran church; the other half by a small number of landlords who owed their wealth to the exploitation of their tenants or wage workers). It was about the poorest place in Western Europe, its bleakness vividly described by Iceland's Nobel Laureate in literature, Halldor Laxness, in the novel *Independent People*. Around the turn of the twentieth century commercial fishing developed (previously only foreign boats had fished on a commercial scale, because most of the population was tied to the land). As the twentieth century lengthened fishing came to generate most of the foreign-currency earnings. It allowed the development of an import-based commercial sector in towns: fish factories, boat construction, building construction, retail and light industry.

At the start of World War II the population was divided between those who thought the country should stay out of the war altogether and 'those who preferred the Germans [to occupy the country] because of the implicit promise of a privileged status under the Nazis [on account of the German perception of Iceland as the home of pure Aryans]' (Boyes, 2009, p. 19). To general dismay the British invaded in 1940 and were then replaced by the Americans in 1941.

After World War II, with the country newly independent from Danish rule, the economy grew strongly thanks to: Marshall Plan aid (the US–NATO military base provided 15%–20% of foreign exchange earnings between 1954 and 1960); an abundant export commodity, cold-water fish, unusually blessed with high income elasticity of demand; and a small, literate, hard-working and ethnically homogeneous population with a strong sense of national identity. At the same time the capitalist economy was heavily regulated, with elaborate trade protection and multiple exchange rates. Around 1955 about half of imports were subject to quantitative restrictions or rationing, a useful tool of patron–client politics (Jóhannesson, 2010).

In 1960 the government began cautiously to liberalise. It unified and devalued the exchange rate, reduced tariffs and quantitative restrictions, raised interest rates, and banned the indexing of wages to prices. But the government retained a large role in managing the economy, especially through rationing credit via the state-owned banks and directing investment to particular sectors. Growth zoomed ahead at an average of 4% a year from 1960 to 1989, though with high variability from year to year (related to fish yields). 1960–89 was the period of the 'Icelandic miracle' (Ólafsson, 2011).

By the 1980s Iceland had shot up from one of the poorest places in Western Europe at the start of World War II to one of the most prosperous. It established a welfare state in line with the tax-financed Scandinavian model and by the 1980s had attained a level and a distribution of disposable income equal to the Nordic average. Yet it remained both more regulated and more patron–client-dominated than its European neighbours; a local oligopoly restricted the political and economic opportunities. As recently as 1975 it was ranked 53rd in the Economic Freedom of the World index.

There is a path-dependent line of ascent from the quasi-feudal power structures of the nineteenth century to the modernised Icelandic capitalism of the later twentieth century, when a bloc of 14 families, popularly known as The Octopus, constituted the economic and political ruling elite, living like chieftains. They controlled imports, transport, banking, insurance, fishing and supplies to the US–NATO base, and provided most top politicians. A firm controlled by people prominent in the two dominant right-of-centre political parties made particularly good profits through its effective monopoly of much of the commerce between the US–NATO base and the domestic economy. The story is told that when the firm presented its bill for building a fence around the base the Americans exclaimed, 'We could build a fence around France for this amount!', but they paid it anyway.

The Octopus controlled the right-wing Independence Party (IP), which dominated the media and decided on senior appointments in the civil service, police and judiciary. The other right-wing party was the Centre Party (CP), also known as the Progressive Party, based in the rural economy and controlled by its business arm (sometimes known as The Squid). These two parties provided most of the governments for the past 60 years. They effectively ran the state-owned banks and prominent figures within them owned the two main daily newspapers.

The small left-wing parties spent most of their time at each other's throats, to the benefit of the right-wing bloc. However, they regularly got 15%–20% of the vote, which was enough to get one or other of them occasionally into power as junior coalition partner, and that plus ideology gave them enough patronage to sustain their electoral base.

Party membership was a standard part of a person's identity, together with parentage, occupation and schooling. The parties provided access to careers in both the public and private sectors. Political cleavages went right down to small units at the base, like firms, university departments and men's choirs. Ordinary people had to go through party functionaries to get loans to buy a car or foreign exchange to travel abroad. Power networks operated as webs of bullying, sycophancy and distrust, permeated with a macho culture, resembling the former Soviet Union.

While left-wing parties were weak, trade unions were strong. One of their main aims was to defend real wages from the effects of the government's main tool of macroeconomic management: devaluation to secure profitable conditions for the export industries (mainly fish and, later, aluminium in the 1970s). All through the fast growth period of 1960–89 Iceland experienced high inflation driven by price–wage spirals and intense labour conflict, sometimes coming close to general strikes.

Not only was the work force strongly unionised, the agricultural and fisheries sectors were strongly corporatised in the sense that their collective organisations decided what they wanted to see by way of government policy for the sector, and the government mostly obliged (Thorhallsson, 2010).

Looking through neoliberal eyes, Iceland at this time was a paradox: on the one hand, a highly statist and corporatist economy with a relatively 'closed access' political and economic elite run by a right-wing bloc, which also controlled the media; on the other hand, a strong union movement; and on the other hand again, high economic growth accompanied by falling post-tax income inequality (as the right-wing bloc had no choice but to negotiate with the unions). Today's neoliberals resolve the paradox by denying it: by claiming that Iceland's fast growth dates from 1995, when the big push to apply the precepts of Reagan, Thatcher and New Zealand's Roger Douglas began. This is false.

Iceland's statist and corporatist political economy began to be challenged from within by a neoliberal faction. It coalesced in the early 1970s when some law and business administration students at the University of Iceland took over a journal, *The Locomotive*, and they became known as the Locomotive Group. Their aim was not just to promote free-market policies but also to open career opportunities for themselves, rather than wait for Octopus patronage. At the end of the Cold War their position strengthened materially and ideologically, as 'statism' and left-wing parties lost public support. Over the decades the Locomotive members took senior positions in politics, law, the judiciary, business and academia. In Wedel's terms the group functioned as a flex net.

The future IP prime minister, Davíð Oddsson, was a prominent member from the beginning. Born in 1948 into a middle-class family, he was elected as an IP councillor to the Reykjavik municipal council in 1974, then mayor of Reykjavik in 1982. In that capacity he led privatisation campaigns, including selling of the municipality's fishing industry to the benefit of members of the Locomotive. In 1991 he led the IP to victory in the general election and reigned (not too strong a word) as prime minister for 14 years, overseeing the growth of the financial sector, before installing himself as governor of the Central Bank in 2004. He had little experience or interest in the world beyond Iceland. His Locomotive protégé Geir Haarde, finance minister from 1998 to 2005 (with a degree in economics from Brandeis University in Boston (MA, USA) in the early 1970s), took over as prime minister shortly after.

These two men most directly steered Iceland's respecialisation strategy to create an international financial centre cum tax haven in the North Atlantic, conveniently midway between Europe and America.

4. ICELAND LIBERALISES

The following figures summarise Iceland's growing financial 'success'—and fragility. Figure 1 shows the build-up of Iceland's gross foreign long-term and short-term debts from 1989 to 2008 and then beyond, together with some of the accompanying events. Figure 2 shows the build-up of the three biggest banks' assets relative to GDP from 2003. Figure 3 shows household debt in local currency and the share of different kinds of lending institutions in that debt, 1991–2008.

The story behind these trends is as follows. Liberalisation of the economy accelerated after 1994, when accession to the European Economic Area, the free-trade bloc of EU countries, plus Iceland, Lichtenstein and Norway, required lifting restrictions on cross-border flows of capital, goods, services and people. The Oddsson government then sold off state-owned assets and

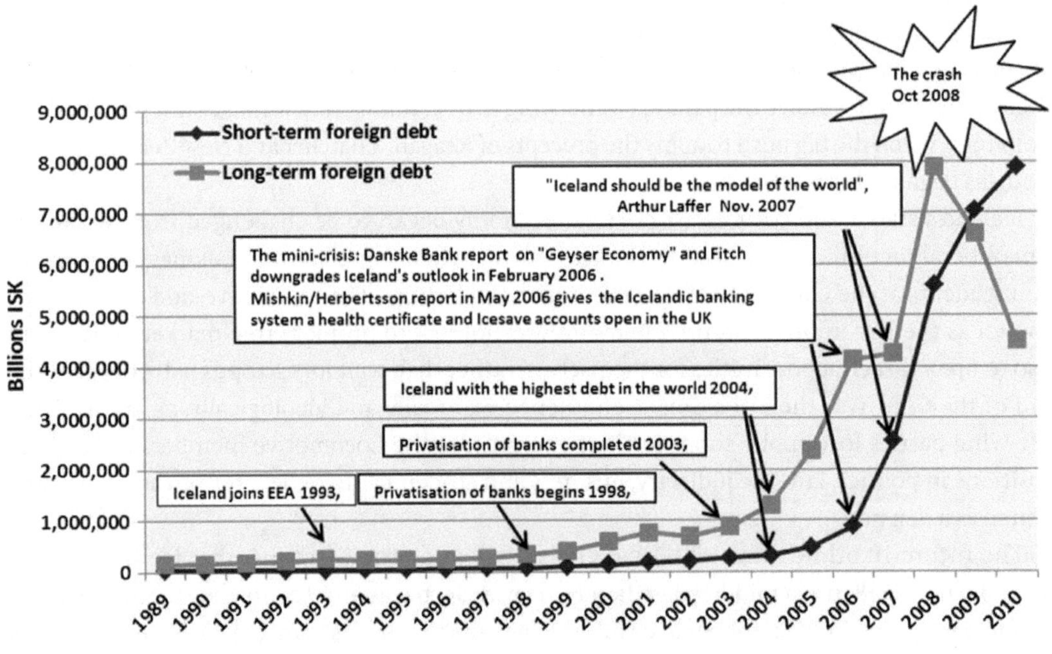

FIGURE 6.1 Iceland's long- and short-term foreign debt: 1989–2010. Source: Central Bank of Iceland Statistics Website [date last accessed, October 2011]. Authors' labelling of events.

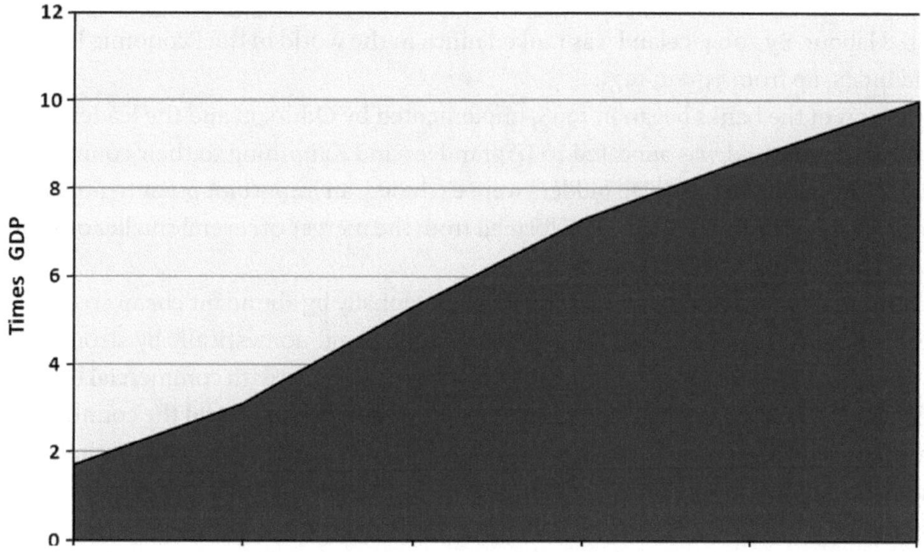

FIGURE 6.2 The three largest banks' end-of-year assets, relative to Icelandic GDP. Source: Special Investigation Report, April 2010, Annex 3 Viðauki 3 Mynd 9 at http://www.rannsoknarnefnd.is/ [date last accessed December 2011].

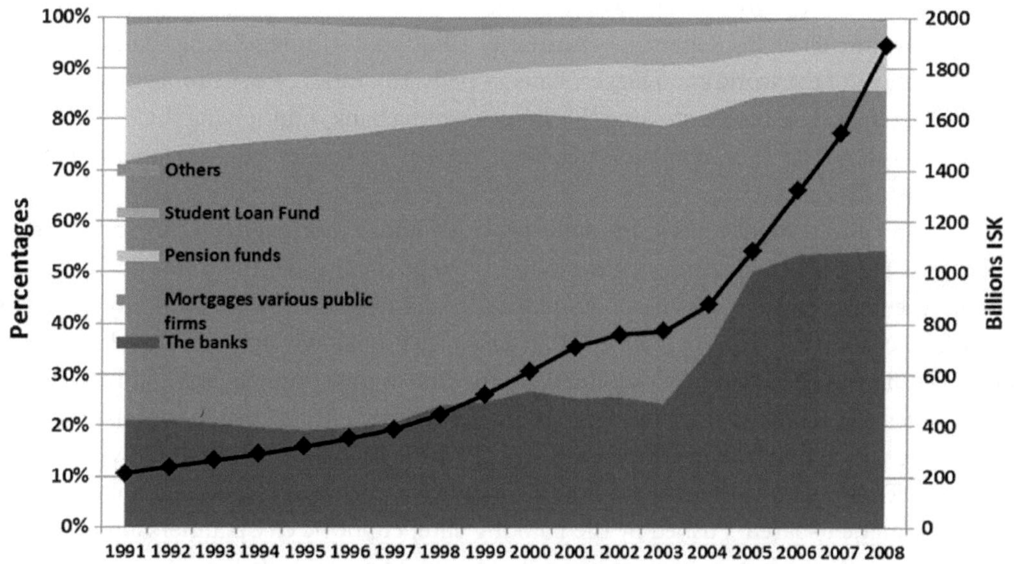

FIGURE 6.3 Household debts (right axis) and the share of lending institutions in household debts (left axis): 1991–2008. Source: Special Investigation Report April 2010. Chapter 4, Volume I, Website Figures in Chapter 4 (Kafli 4; Mynd 42) at http://www.rannsoknarnefnd.is/ [date last accessed December 2011].

deregulated labour. By 2004 Iceland was ranked ninth in the world in the Economic Freedom of the World index, up from 53rd in 1975.

Privatisation of the banks began in 1998, implemented by Oddsson and the leader of the CP. Of the banks, Landsbanki was allocated to IP grandees and Kaupthing to their counterparts in the CP, its coalition partner. Foreign bidders were excluded, an important point to note for what was to come. Later, Glitnir, a private bank formed from the merger of several smaller ones, joined the league.

So Iceland roared into international finance aided globally by abundant cheap credit (thanks to US loose monetary policy during the 1990s and 2000s) and domestically by strong political backing for the banks. The new banks merged investment banking with commercial banking, so that the former shared the implicit government guarantee of the latter. And the country had low sovereign debt, which gave the banks high marks from the international credit-rating agencies. The major shareholders of Landsbanki, Kaupthing, Glitnir and their spin-offs reversed the earlier political dominance of finance: finance now dominated government policy.

Here the established format of Iceland's corporatism was helpful. As noted, from the start Iceland's statism had been integrated with a form of corporatism in which both agriculture and the fishing industry more or less regulated themselves. When aluminium smelting began in the 1970s the government extended the same governance dispensation to the (foreign-owned) aluminium firms. It was only 'natural', then, that when finance emerged as the big new growth sector after 2000, both it and the IP-led government *expected* that it would tell the government what it wanted and the government would oblige. The result was very light regulation and a regulatory body (the Financial Supervisory Authority, FME) that—for regulating a financial system including three of the world's 300 biggest banks—had a total staff of 45 in 2006, many of whom were biding their time before crossing the street to join a bank, multiplying their salary several times. It was largely a 'shop-window' operation, justified by general euphoria and the efficient markets hypothesis.

Oddsson's government relaxed the state-provided house mortgage rules in 2004, allowing 90% loans. The post-crash government inquiry into the bubble identified this one decision as perhaps the most serious economic policy blunder of many, given that the economy was already in the grip of bubble dynamics (SIC, 2010). It prompted the newly privatised banks to rush to offer even more generous terms, accelerating the house price bubble (see Figure 3). Brokers criss-crossed the country urging people to refinance their house mortgages in Swiss francs and Japanese yen to get much lower interest rates. At the same time the government lowered income tax and VAT rates with the aim of turning Iceland into a low-tax international financial centre. The stock market soared. Pushed by the banking elite, euphoric city planners aimed to move Reykjavik from the trajectory of an ordinary city to that of a world city (despite its small population of 110,000), and approved several grandiose new public and private buildings. 'If Dubai, why not Reykjavik?' was the spirit.

Meanwhile, Iceland's small banking elite was driving through mergers and acquisitions at home and abroad, competing and cooperating with each other. Using their shares as collateral, some took out large loans from their own banks and bought more shares in their own or related banks, inflating share prices. It worked like this: Bank A lent to shareholders in Bank B, who bought more shares in B using shares as collateral, raising B's share price. Bank B returned the favour. The share prices of both banks rose without new money coming in. The banks not only grew bigger, they grew more and more interconnected.

The owners and managers of financial firms and law firms remunerated themselves on an ever more extravagant scale. The richer they became the more political support they attracted. Their private jets, roaring in and out of Reykjavik's domestic airport, provided visual and auditory proof of their success to the part-admiring, part-envious population below. The bankers made large financial contributions to the governing parties and giant loans to key politicians.[7] Below the surface several flex nets competed and cooperated at the top level of the state, incorporating varying combinations of bankers, lawyers, politicians, judges, civil servants and academics.

Income and wealth inequality surged, helped by government policies that shifted the tax burden to the bottom half of the distribution (Ólafsson and Kristjánsson, 2010). In 1995 the Gini coefficient of disposable income including capital gains was about 0.26; by 2000 0.31; by 2005 0.39 and by 2007 0.43. Then, as capital gains collapsed, the Gini fell back to 0.34 by 2009.

But the Gini hides as much as it reveals. Most of the rise of inequality happened in the share of the top few percentiles of the distribution as they galloped away from the rest. The share of the top 10% increased over the 2000s at an even faster rate than in the USA, though from a much lower base. Increasing concentration at the top triggered a 'consumption cascade', thanks to easy access to credit. Those below the top borrowed to keep within sight of the top, and so on down. Against the background of the earlier decades of credit rationing, people saw themselves as fully independent at last as they consumed with abandon, which may help to explain their happiness ranking over the 2000s. They lived in the spirit of Plautus, the third century BC Roman playwright, who had one of his characters declare, 'I am a rich man, as long as I do not repay my creditors'.

In the euphoria the dangers of a strategy of 'economic growth with vast foreign borrowing' were overlooked (Pereira, 2010). With almost all the media controlled by the IP and CP, there were few cautionary voices. The Chamber of Commerce told its members in 2006 that Iceland should 'stop comparing itself with the other Nordic countries—after all we are in many ways superior to them' (Icelandic Chamber of Commerce, 2006).

5. THE MINI-CRISIS

In 2006 worries began to be expressed in the foreign and domestic financial press about the stability of the big banks, which were starting to have problems raising funds in the short-term money markets (on which their business model depended). Iceland's current-account deficit had

7 Ten out of 63 MPs had 100 million ISK (Icelandic Krónas) loans from the banks in September 2008. At this time the average household debt was 18–20 million ISK.

soared from 5% of GDP in 2003 to 20% in 2006, one of the highest in the world. The stock market multiplied itself nine times over between 2001 and 2007. You did not have to be a rocket scientist to see that things were unstable.

Landsbanki, Kaupthing and Glitnir were operating far beyond the capacity of Iceland's central bank to support them as lender of last resort; their liabilities were real, but many of their assets were dubious. In February 2006 Fitch downgraded Iceland's outlook from stable to negative and triggered the 2006 'mini-crisis': the krona fell sharply, the value of banks' liabilities in foreign currencies rose, the stock market fell and business defaults rose, and the sustainability of foreign-currency debts became a public problem. The Danske Bank of Copenhagen described Iceland as a 'geyser economy', on the point of exploding (Danske Bank, 2006). The IMF wrote an alarmed Article IV consultation report in 2006. Its private version to the government described the imbalances as 'staggering', toned down in the public version to 'remarkable'.

Icelandic bankers and politicians brushed aside the crisis. The central bank took out a loan to double the foreign exchange reserves, while the Chamber of Commerce, run by representatives of Landsbanki, Kaupthing, Glitnir and their spin-offs, responded with a PR campaign. The Chamber and the University of Iceland invited a string of conservative economists to come to Iceland to assure the audience of the stunning success of the neoliberal model. The Chamber paid the American monetary economist Frederic Mishkin $135,000 to lend his name to a report attesting to the stability of Iceland's banks (Mishkin and Herbertsson, 2006).[8] It allegedly paid the London Business School economist Richard Portes £58,000 to do the same on a later report (Portes and Baldursson, 2007).[9] Either these economists did not know how to identify a bubble, in which case they took the money under false pretences, or they did know but ignored the signs because they accepted an implicit contract to endorse the Chambers' conclusions. With their blessing no one paid attention to the Danske Bank and IMF reports.[10]

In the elections of May 2007, the Social Democratic Alliance (SDA) entered a coalition government with the still-dominant IP. To the consternation of many supporters, SDA leaders ditched their election pledges to assert greater control over macro stabilisation policy and, instead, left it to the IP side of the coalition; and gave enthusiastic support to continued expansion of the financial sector, while knowing next to nothing about conditions in the financial market. They were happy to sit at the top table of government at last and were not about to rock the boat.

8 After the crash the title mysteriously changed to 'Financial instability in Iceland', as listed on his web site: (see Charles Ferguson, the director of the documentary film, Inside Job, interviewing Frederic S. Mishkin here http://movieclips.com/KCct-inside-job-movie-financial-stability-in-iceland/ [date last accessed *December 2011]*. Mishkin's fee is given in 'Mishkin resigns: a look back', *Wall Street Journal*, 28 May 2008; 'Ex-Fed governor's report on Iceland stability missed crisis', *Wall Street Journal*, 17 October 2008.

9 Portes's fee is given in the SIC Report, April 2010, vol. 8, annex III, p. 3. See here http://www.rannsoknarnefnd.is/html/vidauki1.html [date last accessed December 2011].

10 Nor did people pay attention to Wade's warnings in semi-public lectures from summer 2005 onwards, in which he drew attention to parallels with the build up to the East Asian crisis of 1997. Wade's *Financial Times* article (2008) FT.com July 1st http://www.ft.com/cms/s/0/061070b8-4781-11dd-93ca-000077b07658.html#axzz1fxUjMkxW [date last accessed December 2011] and published in the printed version July 2nd 2008, 'Iceland pays the price for financial excess' (2 July 2008) promoted a letter to the editor from Portes and Baldursson, which began 'Robert Wade gets Iceland very wrong' (4 July 2008).

Though they survived 2006, Landsbanki, Kaupthing and Glitnir had trouble raising money to fund their asset purchases and repay existing debts, largely denominated in foreign currencies. So Landsbanki pioneered Icesave, an Internet-based service that aimed to win retail savings deposits by offering more attractive interest rates than high-street banks. Established in Britain in October 2006 and in the Netherlands 18 months later, Icesave caught the attention of best-buy Internet finance sites and was soon flooded with deposits. The staff of the bank could scarcely believe their eyes as the deposit numbers kept rising on their computer screens week after week, month after month. Millions of pounds rolled in from Cambridge University, the London Metropolitan Police Authority, even the UK Audit Commission, responsible for overseeing local government funds, as well as 300,000 Icesave depositors in the UK alone.

At the insistence of Landsbanki, Icesave entities were legally established as branches rather than subsidiaries, so they were under the (more colludable) supervision of the Icelandic authorities rather than their hosts. No foreigner noticed the tiny size of the Icelandic regulatory agency. No one worried that, because of Iceland's obligations as a member of the EEA (European Economic Area) deposit insurance scheme, its population of 319,000 would be responsible for compensating the depositors *abroad* in the event of failure. Landsbanki's employees and shareholders reaped the short-term profits, while the general public in Iceland knew nothing about Icesave and the obligations it was imposing on them.

6. LOVE LETTERS

The second 'solution' to difficulties in raising new funds was to get more access to liquidity without pledging real assets as collateral. The Big Three sold debt securities to smaller regional banks, which took these bonds to the central bank and borrowed against them without having to supply further collateral; they then lent back to the initiating big bank. The bonds were called 'love letters'—mere promises. By participating in this game and accepting as collateral claims on other Icelandic banks, the central bank was conniving in the banks' strategy of gambling for resurrection.

Then the banks internationalised the process: the Big Three established subsidiaries in Luxembourg and sold love letters to them. The subsidiaries sold them on to the Central Bank of Luxembourg or the European Central Bank and received cash in return, which they could pass back to the parent bank in Iceland or use themselves. The OECD calculates that just the domestic love letters, between the central bank and the Icelandic banks, incurred losses to the central bank and the treasury of 13% of GDP (OECD, 2011).

7. THE FINANCIAL COLLAPSE AND POLITICAL RESPONSE

The Icelandic banks fell two weeks after Lehman Brothers. On 29 September 2008, Glitnir approached Oddsson at the central bank for help with its looming liquidity problem. To restore confidence Oddsson suggested that the treasury should buy 75% of Glitnir's shares. The effect was not to boost Glitnir but to undermine confidence in Iceland. The country's rating plunged, and credit lines were withdrawn from Landsbanki and Kaupthing. A run on Icesave's overseas branches began.

On 7 October 2008 governor Oddsson made a characteristic decision. Consulting no one and informing only the prime minister (as far as is officially known), he ordered the krona pegged to a basket of currencies at close to the pre-crisis value. When the central bank's chief economist heard about it on the Internet he threw up his hands and exclaimed, 'Oh no, now we are really going down the tubes!' Pegging the krona in a falling market offered an opportunity for those in the know to make a short-seller's fortune. The peg lasted only a few hours, when billions of krona fled the currency. Then, with the reserves exhausted, the governor ordered the krona to be floated, and it sank like a stone. On 8 October the then UK prime minister, Gordon Brown, froze Landsbanki's UK assets under anti-terrorism laws. The stock market, bank bonds, house prices and average income went into free-fall, along with the currency.

The IMF arrived in Reykjavik in October 2008 to prepare a crisis-management programme, the first time the Fund had been called in to rescue a developed economy since Britain in 1976. It found a country in a 'near-death experience', in the words of a senior IMF official (see epigraphs). It offered a conditional loan of $2.1 billion to stabilise the krona; it supported the government's decision to let the banks go bust rather than be bailed out by the taxpayers (which, given the size of the banks' liabilities, was impossible in any case); and it supported the imposition of temporary capital controls on outflows. It also backed the British and Dutch governments' demands that Iceland should honour the obligations of the European deposit-guarantee scheme and recompense them for their bailouts of Icesave depositors.

Meanwhile, Iceland's normally placid population erupted in an angry protest movement, principally targeted at Haarde, Oddsson and the IP, although the SDA's foreign minister was considered tarnished too. Thousands of people assembled in Reykjavik's main square on freezing Saturday afternoons between October 2008 and January 2009, banged saucepans, linked arms around the parliament building to demand the government's resignation and pelted the building with food.

In January 2009, the IP–SDA coalition broke. To date, Iceland is the only country to have shifted distinctly to the left after the financial crisis. An interim SDA–Left Green Movement (SDA–LGM) government was formed in January 2009 to lead into April's election. In the election the IP was reduced to 16 seats despite the bias of the electoral system in its favour, its worst result since its formation in 1929. Remarkably, this was the first time since World War II that Iceland had a left-wing government, which has been the standard governing power bloc in the other Nordic countries during this time.

8. ICESAVE DEBT REJECTED

The SDA–LGM government came under immediate pressure to repay the Icesave debt; much of the IMF loan was withheld until Reykjavik agreed. The new government was also divided on whether to apply for full membership of the EU and eurozone, with most of the SDA strongly in favour. After long negotiations the government presented the terms they had agreed on the Icesave debt to the parliament in October 2009: €5.5 billion, or 50% of Iceland's GDP, was to be paid to the British and Dutch treasuries between 2016 and 2023 (a high but uncertain part of this would be recovered from the sale of the failed bank's assets).

The government's health minister resigned in protest and five dissidents refused to vote with the government. The bill was forced through on 30 December 2009, against high feelings in the country. On 5 January 2010 President Grímsson announced that he would not sign it into law, out of respect for the national sentiment. In the ensuing referendum (the second in the republic's history) the bill was decisively rejected by 93% of the voters. In the May 2010 Reykjavik municipal elections the SDA slumped to 19% and a comedian was elected as the city's mayor. In October 2010 protests resumed and the coalition conceded the election of a constitutional assembly to draw up a new constitution (the existing one having been inherited from Denmark on independence in 1944). When the (IP-linked) Supreme Court invalidated the election, the parliament reconvened it as a constitutional council.

The British and Dutch negotiators put a new deal on the table, which was put to a referendum in April 2011 and rejected by 66% of the voters. After the 'no' vote, the Icesave case has been referred to the EFTA Court. But in the meantime it seems that the failed bank's assets, slowly being recovered, may cover more than 90% of the outstanding principal. The Icesave debt is no longer a burning issue.

9. THE POSTPONED CRISIS

The cost of losses on loans and guarantees, added to the cost of restructuring financial organisations, brings the total direct fiscal costs of the crisis to about 20% of GDP, higher than in any other country except Ireland (OECD, 2011).[11] But the cuts to the national purchasing power have been more hidden in Iceland than in other crisis-affected countries, because the steep devaluation of the krona (90 to the euro in early 2008 to 160 today) carried more of the burden of adjustment and cuts in public spending relatively less. Krona devaluation raised consumer prices in an import-dependent economy and cut aggregate spending, while the indexing of loans to the consumer price index further lowered household and business purchasing power. The devaluation helped to generate a trade surplus for the first time in many years, due mainly to import compression.

GDP contraction stopped in late 2010 at 11% down from the peak, and modest growth is expected for 2011 and 2012. The unemployment rate, only 2% in 2006, has been between 7% and 9% since 2009, relatively low by European standards; but the rate of outmigration, of Icelanders and other European workers (predominantly Polish), has been the highest since the

11 Other estimates suggest the total cost is more like 60% of GDP, the amount by which public debt is estimated to rise over the medium term after the crash.

late nineteenth century. Inflation is around 5%, net public debt is manageable, fiscal consolidation is proceeding. The fall in the krona boosted the domestic profits of export firms.

However, the SDA–LGM government announced more cuts in public spending for 2011 and beyond, with the aim of generating an overall budget surplus (including interest payments) by 2013. Local governments have no budget for fresh projects. Hospitals and schools are cutting salaries and sacking employees. The freeze on house repossessions expired in 2010.

Political resistance is rising. People say, 'We have been in this crisis for three years. Surely we can't be expected to take more cuts. This government is working for the financial sector and failing us.' In contrast, the big public spending slashers like Ireland, Estonia and Lithuania now have a worse economic situation to deal with than Iceland, but an easier political one—because their governments cut deeply when the population was too shocked to resist.

10. WHERE IS GROWTH TO COME FROM?

What comes after stabilisation? Sustainable economic growth faces at least three big obstacles. The first is that more than half of Iceland's exports are lightly processed natural resources (aluminium and fish) and their response to the now sharply devalued exchange rate faces volume constraints. The overvalued exchange rate of the boom years hindered the growth of non-natural-resource-based export firms or induced them to move abroad. There is certainly scope for the growth of intellectual property-based exports in the information industries and on the margins of the natural resource industries (in fishing services, geothermal turbines, higher value-added food, etc.), but starting from a low base. For now, the potential for an export-led recovery on the back of the depreciated exchange rate is limited.

Second, domestic investment is constrained by weak corporate balance sheets. The simultaneous banking, stock market, property and currency collapses plunged about a third of firms into or close to insolvency. Of the biggest 120 firms, more than half are now (October 2011) controlled by banks. It may take years for enough debt to be written down and enough equity rebuilt to permit significant new investment. Investment was 13% of GDP in 2010, as compared with the long-term average of around 24%, the lowest since records began.

Third, investors face high uncertainty about market conditions. One source is the exchange rate. The currency restrictions imposed after October 2008 have sustained a higher-valued exchange rate than the market rate. Pressure is growing, including from export firms, to remove the restrictions and let the krona further depreciate. But the powerful labour federations are opposed (their members include 85% of the work force). Also, the government is worried that non-residents will seek to convert large holdings of krona-denominated bonds and deposits (about 30% of GDP) into foreign exchange, resulting in not just further devaluation but collapse. The upshot is that potential investors have little idea of what the exchange rate will be in two or three years.

The other source of uncertainty is political. The governing coalition of the SDA and the LGM stuck together during the crisis, but now that stabilisation is assured it is at loggerheads on some key issues. For example, the SDA, backed by the pension funds, wants to stimulate investment in roads, hospitals and other public assets via public–private partnerships; however, the LGM interior minister will have none of it, being opposed to public–private partnerships in principle.

Meanwhile, the right-of-centre IP, which enabled the bubble to grow through the 2000s, is impatiently waiting to regain its rightful place as the ruling party (for almost all of the past 60 years). Polls show that it has succeeded in convincing a majority of the population that the current government (which took office in April 2009) is somehow responsible for their troubles and it would be re-elected if an election were called tomorrow. Majority opinion in the IP continues to believe that 'alpha Iceland was hit by a perfect storm from abroad', meaning that 'the crisis was not our fault', and it continues to believe in the vision of Iceland as an international tax haven in the North Atlantic and earner of rents from the sale of long-term franchises to the private use of natural resources.

Still, all things considered, the governments of Ireland and the Southern European countries would surely sooner face Iceland's problems than their own.

11. FINANCE IN THE DRIVING SEAT

Iceland illustrates what can happen when banker capitalism gets the state and democracy over a barrel, reworking them to be its useful idiots—while redistributing enough to other elites and the population at large to buy their support. As the boom continued over the 2000s a Minsky effect occurred in banks and non-financial companies as they cut their cushions of reserves, and a second-round Minsky effect occurred in the public administration. The boom induced civil service complacency about the government's regulatory role and a general loosening of civil service procedures (meetings with no minutes, the appointment of senior civil servants on the basis of one-on-one meetings with the minister, etc.). Concern about the appointment of people to public positions with a clear conflict of interest—e.g. a state prosecutor in the line of responsibility for a case involving his son—tended to be anaesthetised with a shrug of the shoulders and the claim that it was merely a 'coincidence of interest'. Then as the banks got into trouble the preexisting shadow elite gained even more room to manoeuvre as the government tried to rescue them without imposing conditions, telling itself and the public that protecting the private interests of the banks was in the interest of the public.

The IP–SDA government's decision in 2008 to provide *unlimited* bank deposit guarantees to domestic savers illustrates its debt to the financial elite and the strength of financial corporatism. Had it limited the guarantee to five million krona ($70,000), it would have protected the entire deposits of 95% of depositors; only the wealthiest 5%, including many politicians, benefited from the unlimited guarantee, which now further constrains public spending.

Iceland's tiny scale seemed to make it easier for the public to challenge the government's financial deregulation and then its denial of impending crisis, but the opposite was true. The predominance of positive feedback mechanisms generated bandwagon effects and herding behaviour; the few economists and others who raised concerns were marginalised (Baumgartner and Jones 2002). The main media were controlled by people close to the dominant political parties supporting the financial project. The Oddsson government abolished the National Economic Institute in 2002, which had established a reputation for independent thinking, sometimes critical of the government. From then on the banks, international rating companies and the Chamber of Commerce provided almost the only information and running commentary on the economy; in effect, the supply of relevant public information was privatised (Wedel, 2009). The powerful Confederation of Labour might have been a cautionary voice, but for decades it has been the co-manager, with the Federation of Employers, of the enormous pension funds[12] (Baldvinsdóttir, 1998) and, as such, inclined to favour people and policies promising high rates of return to assets. While the boom lasted it was all too willing to buy in to the bankers' claims that Iceland had discovered a new sustainable growth model.

Paradoxically, a number of critical reports were published when the bubble was in the early stages, including one by the central bank. However, by 2007–08, when the dangers were acute, reports became noticeably softer in tone, including those from the IMF. It seems that the official financial organisations understood that the situation was so fragile that just to speak of it might trigger a crisis. From the perspective of the top politicians the less they knew about negative information the more easily they could escape accountability (Logason, 2011).

What has been the follow-up? In terms of holding people to account, in October 2010, the parliament decided to charge Prime Minister Haarde for breach of ministerial responsibility. The permanent secretary of the finance ministry (and former member of the Locomotive group) has been given two years in prison for using inside information for his personal advantage when selling his shares in Landsbanki in September 2008. But the special prosecutor in charge of the investigation of the banks has been working with a team of 60 lawyers and others for more than two years and so far brought no charges. He does not expect to finish until 2014, by which time the IP will probably be back in power and concerned to 'let bygones be bygones'. 'Iceland's talent pool is so small, we should harness the skills of the bankers rather than prosecute them', is the commonly heard sentiment.

Meanwhile, Oddsson was appointed in September 2009 as editor-in-chief at *Morgunblaðið*, the leading Iceland daily newspaper, and orchestrated the coverage of the crisis. A commentator said that was like appointing Nixon editor of the *Washington Post* after Watergate. The elite looks after its own.

The government has driven through impressive reforms to the financial regulatory regime, but has so far managed to do little to make the public administration work in a more bureaucratic, less informal, less clientelistic way.

The constitutional council presented a draft constitution in July 2011, after intense Internet-based consultation with the population at large. The draft helps to crystallise out what the saucepan-banging protestors were protesting *for*. It directly tackles the reform of public administration and the ownership of natural resources. If approved in a national referendum

12 The pension funds now equal 130% of GDP.

it would provide a constitutional obstacle to the modus operandi of the dominant political parties—which may try to stall its approval indefinitely (Gylfason, 2011A, 2011B).

The IMF comes out of its Icelandic experience if not smelling of roses, then certainly as a more user-friendly organisation than the one that in 1997–99 dictated harsh austerity and market opening to countries swept up in the East Asia/Russia/Brazil crisis (Grabel, 2011; Wade, 1998). It did not press for quick 'fiscal consolidation' (knowing that the steep devaluation was helping to spread the downward adjustment of purchasing power quickly over both the public and private sectors in an 'apolitical' way); it went out of its way to consult widely and transparently; it supported controls on capital outflows; and it brought in technical experts to help restructure the banks. At the same time the left-wing government in power since 2009 has made it a high priority to use the welfare state and employment legislation to protect people at the lower end of the income scale, as reflected in the low proportion (14%) of the population who say they are finding it 'very difficult' to make ends meet, well below the European average. Whether the government will reap electoral rewards for doing so is another question, as the IP and its shadow elite wait impatiently to reclaim their rightful place at the centre of power and resources. But so far, at least, Iceland stands as a rebuke to the new classical economics prescription for bank bailouts and steep public spending cuts as the way to satisfy financial markets and create jobs.

BIBLIOGRAPHY

Baldvinsdóttir, H. D. 1998. Networks of financial power in Iceland: the labour movement paradox, PhD thesis, Lancaster University

Baumgartner, F. R. and Jones, B. D. (eds) 2002. *Policy Dynamics*. Chicago, University of Chicago Press

Black, W. K. 2005. *The Best Way to Rob a Bank is to Own One: How Corporate Executives and Politicians Looted the S&L Industry*, Austin, University of Texas Press

Boyes, R. 2009. *Meltdown Iceland*, London, Bloomsbury

Buiter, W. and Sibert, A. 2008. 'The Icelandic Banking Crisis and What to do About it: the Lender of Last Resort Theory of Optimal Currency Areas', Centre for Economic Policy Research Policy Insight no. 26

Coghalan, A. and MacKenzie, D. 2011. Revealed—the capitalist network that runs the world, *New Scientist*, 19 October

Columba, F., Cornacchia, W. and Salleo, C. 2009. *Financial Sector Developments and Procyclicality*, http://www.voxeu.org/index.php?q=node/3722 [date last accessed December 2011]

Bank, Danske 2006. *Iceland: Geyser Crisis*, http://www.mbl.is/media/98/398.pdf [date last accessed December 2011]

Gissurarson, H. H. 2004. *Miracle on Iceland, Wall Street Journal*, 29 January

Goodhart, C. 2009. *Procyclicality and Financial Regulation*, http://www.bde.es/webbde/Secciones/Publicaciones/InformesBoletinesRevistas/RevistaEstabilidadFinanciera/09/May/Fic/ief0116.pdf [date last accessed December 2011]

Grabel, I. 2011. Not your grandfather's IMF: global crisis, 'productive incoherence', and developmental policy space, *Cambridge Journal of Economics*, vol. 85, 805–30

Gylfason, T. 2011A. *From Crisis to Constitution*, VoxEU, 11 October, http://www.voxeu.org/index.php?q=node/7077 [date last accessed December 2011]

Gylfason, T. 2011B. Crowds and Constitution, VoxEU, 13 October at http://www.voxeu.org/index.php?q=node/7090 [date last accessed December 2011]

Hellman, J. and Kaufmann, D. 2001. Confronting the challenge of state capture in transition economies, *Finance & Development*, vol. 38, no. 3, http://www.imf.org/external/pubs/ft/fandd/2001/09/hellman.htm [date last accessed December 2011]

Icelandic Chamber of Commerce. 2006. *Vidskiptathing Islands 2015*, p. 22, http://www.vi.is/files/1612898009%C3%8Dsland%202015%20Vi%C3%Boskipta%C3%BEing%202006.pdf [date last accessed December 2011], Reykjavík, Icelandic Chamber of Commerce.

International Monetary Fund. 2006. *Staff Report: Iceland*, 13 July

Jóhannesson, G.Th. 2010. Gunnar Thoroddsen - Ævisaga. Reykjavík, Forlagið. Laffer, A. 2007. Overheating is not dangerous, *Morgunblaðið*, 17 November

Logason, T. 2011. Power elites and corruption: corruption as a cause of the collapse in Iceland in 2008, MSc thesis, University of Iceland

Minsky, H. P. 1992. 'The Financial Instability Hypothesis', Working Paper no. 74, Prepared for Handbook of Radical Political Economy, edited by Philip Arestis and Malcolm Sawyer, Edward Elgar: Aldershot, 1993

Mishkin, F. and Herbertsson, T. 2006. *Financial Stability in Iceland*, Reykjavik, Iceland Chamber of Commerce

Norris, F. 2011. Secrecy lets auditor duck scrutiny, *International Herald Tribune*, 21 October, p. 20

OECD. 2011. *OECD Economic Surveys: Iceland*, June, http://www.oecd.org/document/16/0,3746,en_2649_34569_43946384_1_1_1_1,00.html [date last accessed December 2011]

Ólafsson, S. 2011. Icelandic Capitalism–From Statism to Neoliberalism and Financial Collapse, in Lars Mjøset (ed.), *The Nordic Varieties of Capitalism (Comparative Social Research, Volume 28)*, Emerald Group Publishing Limited, pp. 1–51

Ólafsson, S. and Kristjánsson, A. S. 2010. Income Inequality in a Bubble Economy: The Case of Iceland 1992–2008, paper presented at the Income Study Conference, Luxemburg, 28–30 June, http://www.lisproject.org/conference/papers/olafsson-kristjansson.pdf [date last accessed December 2011]

Palma, J. G. 2011. Homogeneous middles vs. heterogeneous tails, and the end of the 'inverted U', *Development and Change*, vol. 42, no. 1, 87–153

Pereira, L. C. B. 2010. *Globalization and Competition: Why Some Emergent Countries Succeed while Others Fall Behind*, New York, Cambridge University Press

Portes, R. 2008. An interview on Icelandic television, May, reprised in *Maybe I Should Have*, directed by Gunnar Sigurdsson

Portes, R. and Baldursson, F. 2007. *The Internationalisation of Iceland's Financial Sector*, Reykjavik, Iceland Chamber of Commerce, http://faculty.london.edu/rportes/Iceland%20final.pdf [date last accessed December 2011]

Portes, R. and Baldursson, F. 2008. Letter, *Financial Times*, 4 July

SIC. 2010. *Special Investigation Report to Parliament in April 2010*, vol. 1, section 4.4.5, p. 117, http://sic.althingi.is/an English summary and excerpts of the report's findings [date last accessed December 2011]

Thomsen, P. 2011. http://blog-imfdirect.imf.org/2011/10/26/how-iceland-recovered-from-its-near-death-experience/ [date last accessed December 2011]

Thorhallsson, B. 2010. The corporatist model and its value in understanding small European states in the neo-liberal world of the twenty-first century: the case of Iceland, *European Political Science*, vol. 9, 375–86

Wade, R. 1998. From 'miracle' to 'cronyism': explaining the Great Asian Slump, *Cambridge Journal of Economics*, vol. 22, no. 6, 693–706

Wade, R. 2008. Iceland pays the price for financial excess, *Financial Times*, 2 July

Wade, R. 2011. Global trends in income inequality: what is happening, and should we worry? *Challenge*, September–October

Wedel, J. 2009. *Shadow Elite: How the World's New Power Brokers Undermine Democracy, Government, and the Free Market*, New York, Basic Books

World Database of Happiness. 2006. www.worlddatabaseofhappiness.eur.nl [date last accessed December 2011]

END-OF-CHAPTER QUESTIONS

1. Briefly, explain the statist-and-corporatist political economy of Iceland between the end of World War II and the late 1980s.

2. Describe how a global "superentity" could capture a state and secure public policy in line with its preferences. What exactly do the authors mean by superentity?
3. In the same vein, describe the role of a shadow elite—referred to as "flexians"—and their role in generating political instability and havoc in financial markets.
4. What is the New Public Management paradigm, and how is it able to influence public policy for private profit and ideological advantage?
5. How do the work of flexians and the New Public Management advocates translate into less regulation in markets and industries?
6. Describe the concept of "state capture" by powerful elites and conglomerates and how this capture many generate financial crises.
7. Explain how a lightly regulated financial sector enabled large-scale consumer borrowing on the back of inflating asset prices despite insignificant increases in real incomes—in other words, explain how "debt became the way to live."
8. How could three small Icelandic banks—Landsbanki, Kaupthing, and Glitnir—grow within less than 10 years, 1998 to approximately 2007, to among the world's top 300 banks, increasing their assets from 100% of GDP in 2000 to more than 800% by 2007?
9. Explain the mechanism of Iceland's success before 2007, which earned the country the sobriquet of "Nordic Tiger." Why was this mechanism unsustainable and bound to eventually collapse?
10. Who is Arthur Laffer, and why was he so cheerful and giddy about Iceland's apparent success prior to 2007?
11. The crisis erupted in September 2008 after the Lehman Brothers meltdown in the US. Explain what happened to three banks referred to in Question 8.
12. Describe Iceland's economy at the turn of the twentieth century, its passage through both World Wars, its miracle-growth era after 1960, and its ascent to becoming one of the world's richest nations today. What role did the "Octopus" and the Locomotive Group play in making Iceland what it is today? What exactly are the Octopus and the Locomotive Group?
13. Describe the role of Davíð Oddson and Geir Haarde in creating an international financial crisis in Iceland between the early 1990s and the crisis years of the latter 2000s.
14. Explain the role that economists Frederic Mishkin and Richard Portes may have played in not shedding light on the true financial condition of the country in mid-2000s.
15. Describe Icesave, a Landsbankin invention that, though highly successful at the beginning, may have been a principal reason for the collapse of the economy—and the bank—in the fall of 2008.
16. Explain the role of so-called "love letters" in the financial crisis of the late 2000s. How exactly did these "love letters" work?
17. Describe the role the IMF played in stabilizing the country after 2008.
18. What are the principal lessons from the experience of Iceland, both pre- and post-crisis?

CHAPTER 7

Are Economic Crises Necessary for Trade Liberalization and Fiscal Reform? The Mexican Experience

Aaron Tornell

> The bourgeoisie confesses that . . . in order to save its purse it must forfeit the crown, and the sword that is to safeguard it must at the same time be hung over its own head as a sword of Damocles.
>
> K. Marx, "Eighteenth Brumaire of Louis Bonaparte"

INTRODUCTION

In 1979, one of the oil boom years, President Lôpez Portillo announced Mexico's intention to adhere to the General Agreement on Tariffs and Trade (GATT). In 1980, having engaged in consultations with major interest groups, he then reversed this decision. Under President de la Madrid (1982–88), Mexico experienced several negative shocks, namely the collapse of the oil price and the interruption of foreign credit influx at a time when around 5% of the GDP was being used to service foreign debt. To make matters worse, the country suffered one of the severest earthquakes of the century. Still, in 1985, in the midst of this crisis, Mexico finally did accede to GATT. By 1987, it had transformed itself from an extremely closed economy into one of the most open ones in the world. And in 1993, it signed the North American Free Trade Agreement (NAFTA) with Canada and the United States. This transformation occurred notwithstanding the fact that trade liberalization implied significant adjustment costs for the private, import-competing sector, and that the state-owned sector had seen its subsidies vanish. Nonetheless, the import-competing sector, which had opposed trade liberalization in 1979, did not oppose it in 1985. It was curious that it should have been President de la Madrid, typically portrayed as weak and indecisive, who initiated the change, rather than President Lôpez Portillo, who tended to be seen as the strong leader.

Following the liberalization of trade, the government implemented a far-reaching fiscal reform. The majority of state-owned companies were privatized, bringing their number down from 1,155 in 1982 to less than 220 in 1993; the income tax rate was reduced from 42% to 34%

Aaron Tornell, "Are Economic Crises Necessary for Trade Liberalization and Fiscal Reform? The Mexican Experience," *Reform, Recovery, and Growth: Latin America and the Middle East*, ed. Rudiger Dornbusch and Sebastian Edwards, pp. 53-73.

and tax compliance was enforced, resulting in increased tax collection; and government subsidies were significantly reduced. This reform changed the sign of the primary fiscal balance from negative during the period 1970–82 to positive for each year of the period 1983–93. It is worth noting that the reform took place in a context of deteriorating terms of trade. As can be seen in Figure 7.1, the index fell around 50% between 1981 and 1986.

The Mexican experience raises the question of why the reforms were implemented at a time of economic crisis rather than at a time of bonanza, when the country might have been able to "afford" the short-term costs more easily. One may look at this puzzle in at least two ways. A first perspective would be that the government has the latitude to act as if it were a central planner who maximizes some objective function and does not face any pressure from interest groups. According to this view, in the Mexican case, Presidents Echeverría (1970–76) and Lôpez Portillo (1976–82) either did what they deemed best, or what was in fashion throughout the world at that particular time, while Presidents de la Madrid (1982–88) and Salinas (1988–94) decided to follow the reformist vogue of the eighties. For this perspective, the story ends here.

By contrast, the second view would be that governments do not act in a vacuum, but in a jungle of rent-seeking groups. In this view, economic policy ceases to be the design of a central planner and becomes the result of interaction by rent-seeking groups. Thus in order to understand changes in economic policy, we would have to analyze the gains and losses of each interest group.

In all likelihood, the correct explanation is a combination of both these perspectives. However, for the purpose of shedding some light on the aforementioned puzzle, I will make the extreme contention that only interest-group interaction matters. That is, even if a government is concerned about social welfare, it will be able to implement structural reforms, such as trade liberalization, *only if* it does not encounter opposition from interest groups that have the power to block the reform.

In Mexico, the two major interest groups that blocked trade liberalization during the seventies were the import-competing, private sector elite and the state-owned companies (parastatal elite). Through the political process, these groups had almost unlimited access to fiscal revenue. They enjoyed subsidized inputs and profited from convoluted regulations and high trade barriers, which had the effect of increasing the profitability of the fixed factors in these sectors. Trade liberalization left both groups in a worse situation than the one they enjoyed under the status quo. Why is it, to reiterate the puzzle, that the private elite supported trade liberalization during bad times, even if it preferred the status quo over trade liberalization? And why is it that it would not support trade liberalization during good times?

The first point I make in this paper is that, when fiscal revenue was high in Mexico, subsidies to interest groups were high. Thus a "cohabitation equilibrium" existed between these two groups, and both were unanimously blocking trade liberalization. However, when fiscal revenue plummeted, the cohabitation equilibrium broke down, as it became profitable for each group to undertake actions to diminish the power of the other group, and thus secure a greater share of

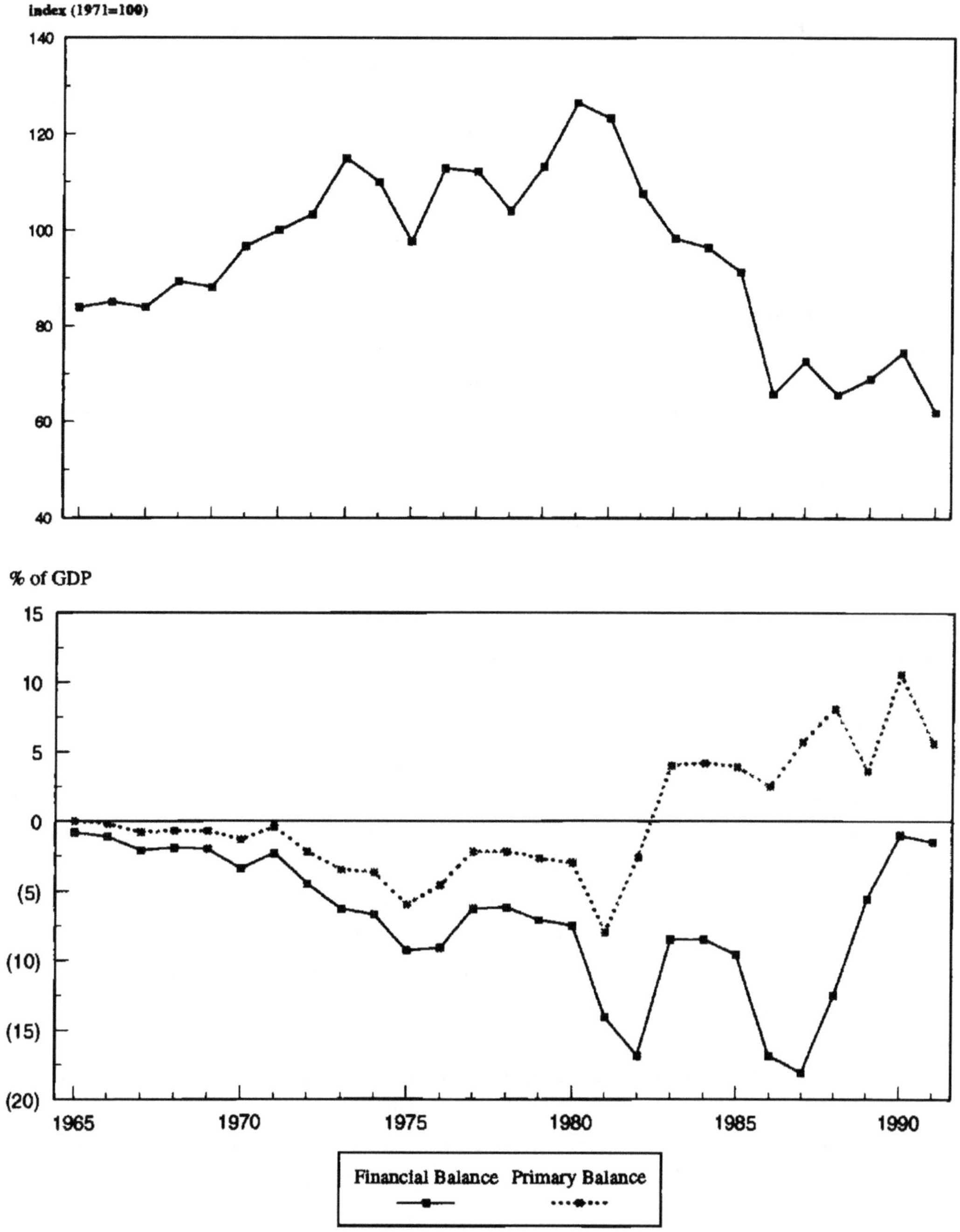

FIGURE 7.1 Mexican terms of trade and fiscal balance

Nores: The primary balance includes interest payments, while the financial balance excludes them. In both cases the revenue from privatization is excluded.

fiscal revenue for itself. In other words, previously friendly rivals switched to an attitude of "if I don't shoot, he will shoot." Support of trade liberalization was one such action

As fiscal revenue collapsed in the early eighties, the parastatal elite took the first action. It induced the expropriation of all private banks in 1982. This move took everyone by surprise, and it was rumored that more expropriations were to follow. However, to the astonishment of many, the next move was trade liberalization. This time trade liberalization was supported by the private elite even though it faced severe costs in terms of reallocation of factors of production. It supported trade liberalization because *the choice for the private elite was not between the status quo and trade liberalization, as in the seventies, but between more expropriations and trade liberalization*.

Trade liberalization reduces the risk of further expropriation because it entails what one might call a "discipline effect." This effect has two components, foreign and domestic. The foreign component derives from the fact that under free trade it is no longer easy for the government to expropriate, since it has to fear that foreigners will retaliate by withdrawing investment or erecting trade barriers. Moreover, international agreements such as NAFTA penalize the imposition of regulations that protect some sectors. Thus, when seeking protection and subsidies, interest groups have to face the potential retaliation from foreigners. The domestic component in turn has two aspects; first, free trade generates new strong groups, that is, exporters who have an interest in maintaining free trade. Second, under free trade, regulations become simpler and more transparent. The previous involved system of import licensing and multiple tariffs is replaced by a much more straightforward law mandating only one or two rates to be applied across all industries. These new rules expose rent-seeking behavior by individual groups more effectively. As a result, other groups may block it at inception.

The second point of the paper is that, as the major interest groups had been weakened by their internecine struggles (which were reflected in bank expropriation and trade liberalization), the governments of Presidents de la Madrid and Salinas achieved a temporary *autonomy* from the established elites. This enabled them to press on with further reforms that had been deemed impossible just a few years back, such as the privatization of the majority of state-owned companies, including the banks, a radical deregulation process that eliminated monopolistic rents on items ranging from jelly jars to ports, and a major tax reform.

In sum, trade liberalization was supported by the private elite in order to save itself from the parastatal elite. Under free trade, the parastatal elite has to face new interests: exporters and foreigners. However, free trade also limits the ability of the private elite to obtain monopoly rents. Referring to the quote from Marx's "Eighteenth Brumaire of Louis Bonaparte," we might say that in the Mexican case trade liberalization acted as the sword of Damocles.

In order to make these points more precise, I present in section 7.3 a game-theoretic model that analyzes the interaction between the two interest groups. I explain why in good times trade liberalization is blocked unanimously by all powerful interest groups, and why in bad times this unanimity breaks down, with some groups supporting trade liberalization, even if all groups end up worse off than under the status quo.

The model is based on the observation that each group has the potential to reduce the power of the second group by temporarily using part of its fixed factors in activities other than production. This entails a short-run cost in terms of forgone profits, and a long-term gain derived from a weaker second group. For example, consider the case of trade liberalization. When it is implemented, some of the fixed factors remain temporarily idle because they have to be reallocated. Although this involves a short-term loss, the future power of rent-seeking groups to expropriate will be reduced because of the discipline effect of trade liberalization.

The cohabitation equilibrium breaks down when one group finds it profitable to incur the short-run cost and displace the second group. If in addition the payoff of matching is greater than the payoff of staying put, the second group will also incur the short-run cost and eliminate the power of the first group. In these circumstances, both groups lose their power, and reform might take place. I show that this occurs when fiscal revenues, and thus subsidies, are sufficiently small. This is because the profitability of fixed factors goes down, making it less costly to have part of them idle during the short run, and raising the incentives to displace other groups and having access to a greater share of the smaller fiscal revenue. This situation is similar to the game of musical chairs. If there are two chairs for Helen and Mary, they have no reason to fight even when the music stops. If we remove a chair, however, Helen and Mary will scream and fight for that chair even before the music stops.

I would like to point out that this paper *does not* suggest that the reforms that took place in Mexico would have happened regardless of who was the president. The autonomy to act can be used in various ways, and the protagonists as well as fashionable academic ideas will influence the course chosen. It might well be that if the government had been headed by persons other than de la Madrid and Salinas, they would have misused their temporary autonomy. What is clear, however, is that the mutual weakening of the major interest groups gave the government the latitude to implement the reforms.

Finally, a few words about how this paper relates to the literature. The model I present is a two-period version of a preemption game. These games are used in industrial organization to study the adoption of a new technology or the introduction of a new product. Since such a move entails a cost, any firm would prefer to adopt as late as possible, provided the other firms also wait. However, since introducing the product first gives a monopolistic advantage, at some point in time each firm would find it optimal to preempt, if the other firms were waiting to adopt at a later date. Therefore, there might be early adoption even if it is against the interest of the industry as a whole.

Alesina and Drazen (1991) use a war-of-attrition model to analyze delays in stabilizations. In a war of attrition, the game ends when one player concedes, and as long as the war continues both groups incur a cost. In contrast to preemption games, in a war of attrition each player wants the game to end as soon as possible, and prefers the other to concede first. In the model of Alesina and Drazen, delays occur because players are *uncertain* about the payoffs of the other players. By waiting they induce the weaker players to concede first.

Femandez and Rodrik (1991) present a model where *uncertainty* regarding the probable winners and losers from reform leads to a bias toward the status quo. Thus reforms that would have been blocked might find support if they could be implemented.

Lastly, Velasco (1993) presents an argument along the same lines as mine to explain the reforms that took place in Chile during the seventies. Unlike Mexico, in Chile it was not a drastic collapse in the terms of trade that induced the breakdown of the status quo, but rather "the arrival of several new guests at the dinner table of the distributive state" in the sixties. Among them were the traditional urban labor movement, the shanty-town dwellers, and rural labor. However, the effect was the same as in Mexico: less available fiscal revenue for each group. This increased the incentives to incur the short-run costs necessary to eliminate the power of the other groups. The results were the wave of expropriations and strikes of 1970–73 and the trade liberalization of 1975. As established interest groups weakened one another, Pinochet acquired autonomy to act as he saw fit.

This paper is structured as follows. In section 7.2 I review the Mexican experience in detail. In section 7.3 I present the model. In section 7.4 I analyze the role of politics. In section 7.5 I address the issue of whether the reforms should outlast the crisis that generated them. Lastly, in section 7.6 I present the conclusions.

7.2 THE MEXICAN EXPERIENCE

During the fifties and sixties, Mexico followed an import substitution policy and a tight fiscal policy. The economy experienced an extraordinary average GDP growth of almost 7% per year and annual inflation rates of less than 5%. However, industrialization had been attained by way of very protectionist trade policies and heavy regulation.[1] By the end of the sixties, the emerging consensus held that the import substitution strategy had been exhausted and that a reform was needed. At the same time, there was mounting pressure from the left for a reduction in poverty and income inequality

In order to address these demands, the administration of President Echeverría (1970–76) increased the emphasis on redistributive policies and increased its involvement in production. Thus the administration started an ambitious program of building state-owned enterprises in sectors that had been private in the past, such as steel. Increased government expenditures were not matched by higher taxes because opposition from the private sector did not allow the government to implement a tax increase. As a result, the fiscal deficit increased from 4% of GDP in 1970 to 10% in 1976. This in turn led to higher inflation, higher foreign debt, and higher current account deficits. It is interesting to note that, prior to becoming president, Echeverría was the minister of the interior, and at that time he was considered an economic conservative.

1 For an analysis of the "Desarrollo Estabilizador," see Ortiz Mena (1970). For an analysis of the period 1970–82, see Bazdresch and Levy (1991).

Echeverría's six years ended with a depreciation of the currency of 60%, tense relations between government and private sector, and the emergence of the parastatal elite as a strong new interest group. Indeed, this group had benefited the most from the new investment projects initiated by the government. Unfortunately, contrary to expectations, indicators of income distribution had not improved.[2] It should be emphasized that, despite its antibusiness rhetoric, the Echeverría government did not introduce trade and fiscal reforms, even though these had been deemed necessary since the early seventies.

When President López Portillo took office in 1976, he tried to reestablish cordial relations with the private sector. Although in 1977 the government announced intentions of a structural reform, and a fiscal contraction was begun, these plans were soon abandoned. This was due to the discovery of significant oil reserves and the increase in the price of oil. A free-for-all fiscal policy was implemented, meaning that the increase in the fiscal revenue was matched by a more than proportional increase in government expenditures. The investment program in government-owned enterprises was accelerated; prices of electricity, oil, and gas were heavily subsidized; and a very ambitious program to reduce poverty was implemented. An indicator of the increase in fiscal transfers is the evolution of expenditures of the parastatal sector, which represented 9.8% of GDP in 1970 and reached 22.2% in 1982. An indicator of the transfers to the private sector is the half-billion-dollar bailout in 1981 of Grupo Alfa, one of the biggest private companies in Mexico. As a result of these policies, the fiscal deficit jumped from 10% in GDP in 1977 to 17% in 1982.

Since fiscal revenue was sufficient to give transfers to almost every group—to the parastatal and private elites, to the urban middle class and to the rural poor—it is fair to say that every powerful group was satisfied with the status quo, and no incentive existed to implement the reforms contemplated since 1970. That is, high subsidies led to high profitability of fixed factors owned by powerful groups. Therefore no group found it profitable to incur the short-run cost necessary to weaken the other groups, and secure for itself a greater share of future fiscal revenue. Hence in those years of bonanza, all powerful groups blocked reform. An example, mentioned in the introduction, is the 1979 presidential announcement of Mexico's intentions to adhere to GATT. This plan generated criticism from the private and the parastatal elite, and in 1980 the decision not to accede to GATT was made public. It should be noted that, were one to embrace the central-planner view of policy making, another plausible explanation for this outcome is that the members of the economic cabinet did not consider free trade to be welfare improving.

The populist transfer policies had to be halted at the beginning of the eighties due to the fall in the price of oil and the interruption in foreign lending. As a result, fiscal resources were no longer sufficient to satisfy all interest groups. Thus there was an increase in the net payoff that a group could expect from inducing a change in the status quo. The first move was made by the parastatal elite. In September 1982, just three months before he left

2 See Aspe and Beristain (1984).

office, President López Portillo announced the expropriation of all the Mexican private banks during his last and very dramatic address to Congress. The bank owners were considered one of the strongest groups within the private elite, and the banks an important conduit of fiscal revenue to the private sector (through subsidized credit and through implicit guarantees of their borrowings from foreign banks). The expropriation occurred simultaneously with the imposition of capital controls, and with the resignation of the orthodox governor of the Central Bank, Miguel Mancera. He was replaced by Carlos Tello, an economist with interventionist ideas, who was close to José A. de Oteyza, the extremely influential minister of energy, mines, and parastatal industry. The reaction of the private sector representatives was to call a national strike for September 8. However, on September 7, this strike was canceled.

In the midst of this crisis, President de la Madrid took office in December 1982. There were fears that under his tenure expropriations would continue and statism would increase, since after all he had been the minister of budget and planning during the administration of President López Portillo. However, the opposite occurred. During his tenure, three important decisions were made: not to interrupt debt service to foreign banks, to open the economy by joining GATT in 1985, and to privatize the parastatal sector. Confirming the commitment to monetary austerity, Miguel Mancera was reappointed governor of the Central Bank (a position he holds until the present).

Trade liberalization was painful for the private sector. The puzzle is why it did not oppose trade liberalization this time around, given that it had opposed reform in the past. The argument of the paper is the following: The reversion of lending flows from inflows to outflows and the deterioration in the terms of trade resulted in a reduction in the fiscal revenue available for rent-seeking groups. In order to eliminate the access that the private sector had to fiscal revenues via subsidized credit, the parastatal elite decided to induce the expropriation of the banks. The private sector matched this move by incurring the adjustment costs associated with trade liberalization. Adherence to GATT and later to NAFTA had a double effect. First, it blocked the access of the parastatal group to fiscal revenues because these treaties required Mexico to deregulate and to eliminate the bulk of fiscal subsidies. Second, expropriation of private industries was more difficult in an open economy. In other words, the private elite did not oppose trade liberalization because its choice was not between trade liberalization and the status quo, but between trade liberalization and becoming the follower. It chose the first because it thereby could weaken the parastatal elite and stop further expropriations.

The moves undertaken by the parastatal and the private elites were costly to these groups, and reduced their access to fiscal revenue. Indeed, it is very likely that for these groups (not for the economy as a whole) the status quo would have been more advantageous than the free trade regime, deregulation, and reduction in subsidies. The question is why they nonetheless acted the way they did, given that they were rational and had perfect foresight. The answer is simple: As fiscal revenues shrank, the payoff of becoming the "leader" and displacing the other group became greater than the payoff of retaining the status quo. Thus the implicit agreement not to take any action against the other group was not sustainable anymore, and was broken by the parastatal elite with the expropriation of the banks. For the private sector the expected payoff of matching by supporting trade liberalization was greater than the expected value of not liberalizing and becoming the follower (with the risk of being further expropriated by the leader). Therefore, the private elite decided to match the move by the parastatal elite.

The result was that both groups lost their power, giving autonomy to the government to implement further reforms. Thus the de la Madrid administration was able to implement the whole package of reforms that had been considered necessary since the late sixties. Foreign trade liberalization was completed, the privatization and deregulation processes were initiated, and the primary fiscal balance, which had been in deficit during the last decade, was transformed into a surplus. Figures 7.1 and 7.2 show the evolution of the Mexican terms of trade and of the primary fiscal surplus. As can be seen, the reforms of 1983–87 coincided with the sharp decline in the terms of trade. We might also note the sharp swing in the primary fiscal balance, which was transformed into a surplus in 1983 and remains positive.

In the political arena, the private sector reacted to trade liberalization partly by becoming more active in party politics. This broke the pattern of lack of political competition involving private interests noted by Skidmore and Smith (1984). According to Maxfield and Anzaldua (1987), before 1982 an implicit agreement had obliged businessmen to stay out of party politics, while in return the government promised to ensure a profitable investment climate.[3] The bank nationalization of 1982 dealt a blow to this accord and induced a structural shift. Since then some businessmen became involved in electoral politics by supporting Partido Acción Nacional (PAN), an opposition party from the right, and by running as candidates of the Partido Revolucionario Institucional (PRI), the party in power. For example, in the presidential elections of 1988, the candidate of the PAN was Clouthier, a former member of PRI who was the leader of the business association when the banks were expropriated.

Some members of the parastatal sector reacted by splitting from the PRI a few months before the presidential elections of 1988. Combining with leftist parties, a group headed by Cuauhtemoc Cárdenas and Porfirio Munoz Ledo formed the Partido de la Revolución Democratica (PRD) and obtained a third of the votes. Cárdenas is the son of the former president who founded the modern PRI, and was the manager of the Sicarsa steel plant (built during the seventies) and a governor of the state of Michoacan. Munoz Ledo was a cabinet minister and head of the PRI.

3 For an insightful analysis of the Mexican political system, see Cosio Villegas (1972).

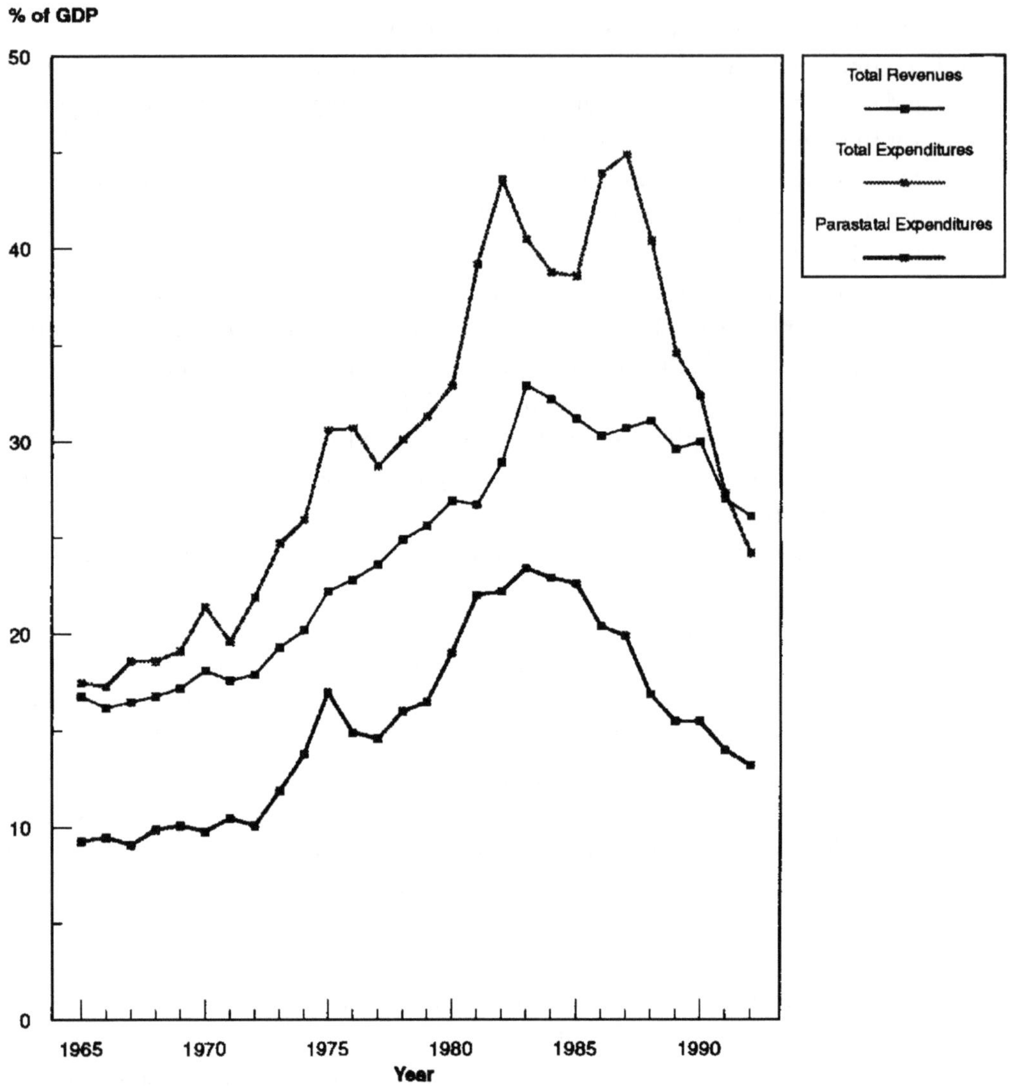

FIGURE 7.2 Revenues and expenditures of the Mexican government

7.3 THE MODEL

I present a two-period model where, under the status quo, all rent-seeking groups have common access to fiscal revenue. During good times none of the groups has incentives to change the status quo, while during bad times, it is optimal for each group to incur the costs necessary to bar the other groups from access to fiscal revenue. The model contains three ingredients: rent-seeking groups that compete to appropriate fiscal revenue; a sector that is not organized politically, that is the source of fiscal revenue; and a rule describing how one group can bar another group from access to fiscal revenue. There is neither capital accumulation nor depreciation in the model[4]

The rent-seeking sector is composed of two groups (a and b), which live for two periods and which produce a consumption good that is traded internationally and is the numeraire. This good is produced using capital and a variable input provided by the government at a subsidized price. The objective of each group is to maximize the present value of its profits. For each period the profits of group *i* are given by

$$\pi(g_i, z) = g_i^{\beta} k_i^{\gamma} - z g_i, \qquad 0 < \beta \leq 1, \qquad \gamma > 0, \tag{1}$$

where g_i is the amount of government input used by group *i*, *z* is the unit price of this input, and k_i is the capital stock of group *i*. The *g*'s may also have a more indirect interpretation as import tariffs. In this case, *z* would represent bribes to the bureaucracy that administers trade policy or patronage payments to politicians.

Setting up the problem in this way captures the fact that in many countries fiscal transfers to rent-seeking groups take the form of government inputs, such as electricity, gas, and soft credit, provided at subsidized rates. For instance, in the case of Mexico, transfers from the federal government to the national electric utility (in order to sell cheap electricity) represented 0.3% of GDP in 1971 (when President Echeverría took office), 0.5% in 1977, and 1.7% in 1983, (when President López Portillo left office). At present, following the fiscal reform, these subsidies represent only around 0.1% of GDP.

Next, we will describe the nonorganized sector, which is the source of fiscal revenue. This sector is composed of investors that live for only one period. During each period, the representative investor is born with an endowment of W units of the consumption good. She can invest it abroad and receive a fixed tax-free rate of return *r*, or she can invest it domestically to produce a good that is not consumed domestically, using a decreasing returns technology. The government cannot tax foreign source income. Thus the investor must pay only taxes equal to a proportion τ of the profits on her domestic investment. The investor spends all of her after-tax income on the importable consumption good.

Since the exportable good is produced using the consumption good as the only input, it follows that the representative investor has an after-tax income equal to

$$Y = [1 - \tau] p w^{\alpha} + [1 + r][W - w], \qquad 0 < \alpha < 1, \tag{2}$$

where τ is the tax rate, *w* is the amount of working capital invested domestically, and *p* represents the terms of trade (i.e., the price of the exportable good produced by the nonorganized sector, in terms of the importable consumption good). If instead the nonorganized sector produced the consumption good, then *p* would be a shift parameter measuring the profitability of investing domestically.

4 In Tornell (1992), I characterize the evolution of a similar economy, in which there is capital accumulation and property rights switch endogenously between private and common access.

Lastly, we consider the government. It produces the input used by rent-seeking groups at a cost of one in terms of the consumption good. However, it sells this input at $z < 1$. To cover the costs, the government collects taxes from the nonorganized sector. I assume that the government cannot issue debt, so that the fiscal budget has to be balanced during each period. I also assume that payments made by rent-seeking groups for government inputs are not used to cover the fiscal budget. They are made for purposes of patronage or corruption. It follows then that

$$g_a(t) + g_b(t) = T(t), \tag{3}$$

where $T(t)$ is total fiscal revenue during period t.

The objective of the government is to maximize income in the nonorganized sector. Thus, if it were unconstrained, it would set g_a, g_b, and τ equal to zero during each period. However, the government's power is limited by the power of rent-seeking groups. I will consider three possible regimes under which τ is determined:

1. "Common access": under this regime the government is powerless, and both groups have equal power. The tax rate is set equal to the revenue maximizing level ($\hat{\tau}$).[5]
2. "Leader-follower": under this regime all power is concentrated in one group, "the leader." The government and the other group ("the follower") are powerless. As in the previous regime, τ is set equal to $\hat{\tau}$.
3. "Autonomous": under this regime both groups are weak. The only constraint faced by the government is to transfer to the groups a small proportion $\underline{\tau}(< \hat{\tau})$ of the nonorganized sector's domestic income.

Tax rates are derived assuming the following sequence of events. During each period, conditional on $p(t)$ and on the prevalent regime, the government sets $\tau(t)$. Then, conditional on $p(t)$ and $\tau(t)$, investors choose $w(t)$ and each group is allocated its respective share of $T(p(t))$, $g_a(t)$ and $g_b(t)$. Under the leader-follower and common access regimes, the government sets τ so as to maximize tax revenues, taking as given that the representative investor allocates her working capital so as to equalize after-tax rates of return. I show in the appendix that tax revenue is maximized at $\hat{\tau} = 1 - \alpha$. Therefore, under these regimes the tax revenue function is

$$\hat{T}(p) = p\hat{w}(\hat{\tau}(p), p)^{\alpha}\hat{\tau}(p) = Bp^{1/(1-\alpha)}, \qquad B > 0. \tag{4}$$

Under the autonomous regime, the government sets $\tau = \underline{\tau} < 1 - \alpha$. Thus

$$T_{aut}(p) = pw(\tau, p)^{\alpha}\,\underline{\tau}. \tag{5}$$

---

5 Aizenman (1992) and Tornell and Velasco (1992) analyze the common access regime in a dynamic setup.

Since $T(p, \tau)$ is concave in τ (see equation [A3]), and since $\underline{\tau} < 1 - \alpha$ it follows that $\hat{T}(p) > T_{aut}(p)$ for all p.

Consider the following two-stage game between both rent-seeking groups. In the first stage, both groups have common access to fiscal revenue. At time 0, after $p(0)$ and $p(1)$ are revealed and after $\tau(0)$, $g_a(0)$, and $g_b(0)$ are chosen, each group decides whether or not to lose a proportion q of its profits, in order to eliminate the access to fiscal revenue that the other group will have at time 1. In the second stage, $\tau(1)$, $g_a(1)$, and $g_b(1)$ are chosen.[6]

The preceding sequence of moves is meant to capture the two effects of trade liberalization that I identified in the introduction. To see this, let the two groups be the import-competing elite and the parastatal elite. On the one hand, the efficiency effect of trade liberalization implies that productive factors must be reallocated. This entails a short-run cost to the import-competing elite. On the other hand, the discipline effect of trade liberalization implies a reduction in the ability of the parastatal elite to expropriate the assets of other groups in the future.

There are three possible outcomes in this game.

1. Status quo: neither group incurs the cost $q\neq$, and common access to fiscal revenue prevails.
2. Matching: both groups incur the cost $q\neq$, both lose their power, and a shift to the autonomous regime takes place.
3. Leader-follower: one group incurs the cost $q\neq$ and becomes the leader, while the other group does not and becomes the follower. The leader gets the government input for free, and it can expropriate all the wealth of the follower.

Next, I determine the equilibrium levels of g_a and g_b. To make precise the idea that rent-seeking groups are inefficient in production, and that the government subsidizes them through low input prices, I make two assumptions that hold for all regimes and for all realizations of p. First, neither group finds it profitable to buy an extra unit of the input at a price of one (recall that the inputs' marginal cost of production is one). Second, there exists an excess demand for the government input at the price z. Since p takes values in the interval $[\underline{p}, \overline{p}]$, since the leader gets the government input for free, and since $\beta \leq 1$, these conditions hold if and only if

$$\beta[T_{aut}(\underline{p})/2]^{\beta-1} k^{\gamma} < 1, \quad \beta[\hat{T}(\overline{p})/2]^{\beta-1} k^{\gamma} \geq z. \tag{6}$$

I assume that in the case of the autonomous and the common access regimes half of total fiscal revenue is allocated to each group. Condition (6) implies that it is not optimal for any group to buy the input at its market price. Consequently, we have that the g's are given by

$$g_l(p) = \hat{T}(p), \quad g_f(p) = 0, \quad g_{ca,i} = \hat{T}(p)/2, \quad g_{aut,i} = T_{aut}(p)/2. \tag{7}$$

6 The same results could be obtained if the cost was a proportion q of revenues, or of the capital stock.

To determine which of the three possible outcomes mentioned above will be equilibrium outcomes, I derive the payoffs associated with each. Using (1) and (7), the payoffs of the follower and the leader are

$$F(p_0) = \pi(\hat{T}(p_0)/2, z), \tag{8}$$

and

$$L(p_0, p_1) = [1 - q]\pi(\hat{T}(p_0)/2, z) + \delta\pi(\hat{T}(p_1), 0), \tag{9}$$

where δ is the discount factor.

Under the status quo, the common access regime prevails in both periods.
Thus the payoff of each group is

$$SQ(p_0, p_1) = \pi(\hat{T}(p_0)/2, z) + \delta\pi(\hat{T}(p_1)/2, z). \tag{10}$$

Lastly, in the matching case, both groups incur the short-run cost, and their power to set the tax rate is eliminated. The payoff of each group is

$$M(p_0, p_1) = [1 - q]\pi(\hat{T}(p_0)/2, z) + \delta\pi(T_{aut}(p_1)/2, z). \tag{11}$$

In order to characterize the Nash equilibria of the game, it is useful to represent it in the following strategic form,

		Group a	
		I	NI
Group b	I	(M, M)	(F, L)
	NI	(L, F)	(S, S)

where I stands for incurring the short-run cost, NI for not incurring it, M for matching, S for status quo, F for follower, and L for leader. The first and second terms in parentheses are the payoffs to groups a and b, respectively; they are given by equations (8)–(11).

The size of L relative to S and the size of M relative to F determine which of the three possible outcomes (status quo, leader-follower, or matching) will be an equilibrium outcome. For instance, if $L \geq S$ and $M \geq F$ the unique Nash equilibrium is matching (i.e., that both groups incur the short-run cost q). On the one hand, given that group a incurs the cost, the best response of group b is to match because the payoff of matching is greater than that of becoming the follower. On the other hand, regardless of group b's action, group a finds it profitable to incur the cost. It either gets L, which is greater than S if b does not move, or M, which is greater than F if b moves. For future reference, the equilibrium outcomes are summarized here.

Payoffs		*Equilibrium Outcomes*
$L \geq S$	$M \geq F$	shift to autonomous regime
	$M < F$	shift to leader-follower regime
$L < S$	$M \geq F$	status quo prevails, or shift to autonomous regime
	$M < F$	status quo prevails

As can be seen in equations (8)–(11), the relative sizes of the payoffs depend on the values of p_0 and p_1. In order to address the issue of when trade liberalization will take place, I let p_0 vary while keeping p_1 constant. I will show that for sufficiently small p_0 the only equilibrium outcome is matching (i.e., a shift to the autonomous regime), while for sufficiently high p_0 the only equilibrium outcome is the status quo. That is, trade liberalization is an equilibrium outcome during bad times, but not during good times.

The key to this result is that, as p_0 goes up, the value of remaining in the status quo increases more rapidly than the value of becoming the leader, and the value of following increases more rapidly than the value of matching. To illustrate we use figure 2.3, which depicts the payoffs F, L, M, and S as functions of p_0(p_1, is held constant). All payoffs are increasing in p_0 because higher terms of trade increase the profitability for the nonorganized sector to invest domestically. This in turn increases total tax collection, and thus increases government subsidies at time 0. The higher the government subsidies are, the higher the profits of rent-seeking groups are under each regime.

To see why the payoff function of leading is flatter than that of the status quo, note that at time 0 the leader loses a share q of its profits (profits are $[1 - q]\pi(0)$), while under the status quo no cost is incurred (profits are $\pi(0)$). Thus an increase in $p(0)$ has a greater impact on the payoff of the status quo than in the payoff of leading, because $\pi(0)$ is increasing in $p(0)$ and because the future reward, in terms of a greater share of government subsidies, remains unchanged ($p(1)$ is fixed). In other words, at very low levels of $p(0)$ it is "cheap" to engage in nonproductive activities in order to induce change.

As can be seen in Figure 7.3, during normal times ($p(0) = p$) the status quo is preferred to leading and following is preferred to matching. Thus at p the status quo is the only equilibrium outcome. However, during bad times ($p(0) \leq p'$) the only equilibrium outcome is matching. In this equilibrium, both groups lose $\neq q$ at $t = 0$ and both lose their access to fiscal revenue. During good times ($p(0) > p''$), the only equilibrium outcome is the status quo. I analyze the case in which $p(0)$ is in $(p', p'']$ in the next section.[7]

7. There is another case in which $p' > p''$. In this case matching is the only equilibrium outcome for $p(0) < p''$, leader-follower is the only equilibrium outcome for $p(0) \in (p'', p']$, and the status quo is the only equilibrium outcome for $p(0) > p'$.

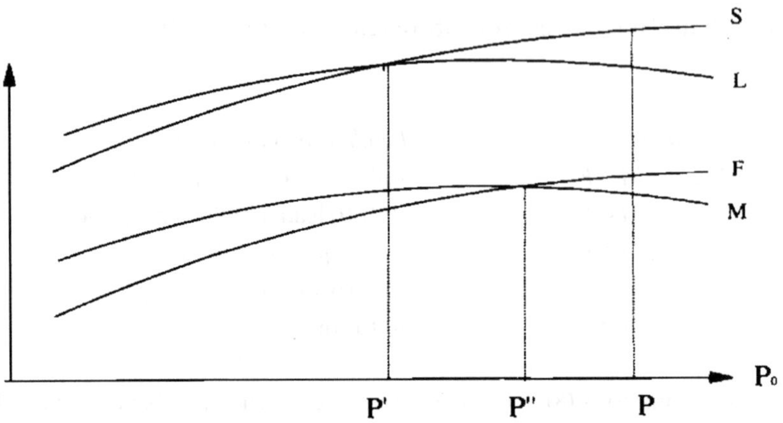

FIGURE 7.3 Pair of functions

7.4 DOES THE GOVERNMENT MATTER IN THIS MODEL?

Up to now we have assumed that under the status quo interest groups can block any government decision. While maintaining this assumption, let us now suppose that the government has the ability to influence a group's expectations concerning the move that the other group will make. Let us define "political manipulation" as the act of influencing these expectations. It follows that political manipulation matters when there are multiple Nash equilibria in the game played by interest groups. In this case there is room for the government to induce interest groups to end up in the Nash equilibrium that is best for the economy as a whole, although it may be bad for the interest groups.

To illustrate this point, suppose that in the status quo both groups have common access to fiscal revenue, and consider the case in which $p(0)$ is between p' and p''. In this case the value of remaining in the status quo is greater than that of becoming the leader, and the value of matching is greater than that of following. Therefore, there are two Nash equilibria: In the first, neither group incurs the short-run cost $q\neq$, and the status quo prevails. In the second, both groups incur the cost, and there is a shift to the autonomous regime. Both groups are better off under the first equilibrium. However, the second equilibrium is sustained by the fear of each group that the other group will make the move. In this case, the role of political manipulation would be to bring about the second equilibrium. That is, the government would induce expectations among groups, that the other group will make the move. This is likely to be a difficult task for the government because the status quo is the Pareto-superior outcome.

The role of political manipulation as defined above is limited to this case. If p_0 were outside the interval (p', p'') or if p' were greater than p'', there would be a unique Nash equilibrium, as is clear from Figure 7.3. Therefore, in these cases the outcome is independent of the government's political manipulation.

I should note that in the model we are considering groups that move simultaneously. In the real world, by contrast, groups can move sequentially and can follow more complicated strategies that depend on the history of the game. However, to the extent that there exists an advantage to moving first, the results of this paper should remain valid.

7.5 REVERSION OF THE REFORMS AND POLICY IMPLICATIONS

A question often asked is whether or not trade liberalization and fiscal reform will outlast the crisis that generated them, or whether there will be a reversion to the old ways if good times return.

In the case of Mexico, beginning in 1989, the wind started to blow in a favorable direction. There was a 35% reduction in foreign debt, exports were more diversified than in 1982, and financial capital started to flow in again. The reforms initiated by President de la Madrid were not undone, however, but were deepened to an extent that was considered impossible a few years back: NAFTA has been signed, all the big companies except for oil, electricity, and railroads have been privatized, and a radical deregulation program has been implemented, eliminating many monopolies and sources of corruption.

We can analyze the reversion of reform using a model similar to the one in section 7.3. Suppose that the autonomous regime prevails under the status quo (i.e., rent-seeking groups do not have access to fiscal revenue and $\tau = \underline{\tau}$), and consider the following two-stage game: In the first stage, after $p(0)$ and $p(1)$ are announced, and after $\tau(0)$, $g_a(0)$, and $g_b(0)$ are chosen, each group decides whether or not to incur a loss $q'\pi(T_{aut}(p_0)/2, z)$ at time 0, in order to become more powerful at time 1. In the second stage, $\tau(1)$, $g_a(1)$, and $g_b(1)$ are chosen. Again, there are three possible outcomes.

1. Only one group incurs the loss, and it becomes the leader. Thus the other group becomes the follower.
2. Both groups incur the loss, and both get common access to fiscal revenue.
3. Neither group incurs the loss, and the status quo prevails.

As in section 7.3, under the common access regime $g_i = \hat{T}(p)/2$, and under the leader-follower regime $g_f = 0$ and $g_t = \hat{T}(p)$. Therefore, the payoffs of the leader and the follower are

$$L = [1 - q']\pi(T_{aut}(p_0)/2, z) + \delta\pi(\hat{T}(p_1), 0), \tag{12}$$

and

$$F = \pi(T_{aut}(p_0), z). \tag{13}$$

Under the status quo, the autonomous regime prevails in both periods. Thus the payoff of each group is

$$S = \pi(T_{aut}(p_0)/2, z) + \delta\pi(T_{aut}(p_1)/2, z). \tag{14}$$

Lastly, in the matching case the payoff of each group is

$$M = [1 - q']\pi(T_{aut}(p_0)/2, z) + \delta\pi(\hat{T}(p_1)/2, z). \tag{15}$$

In terms of this model, a reform is not undone if the status quo is the only equilibrium outcome. Recall that this is the case if and only if the status quo is preferred to leading, and following is preferred to matching. Subtracting (14) from (12) and (13) from (15), $L - S$ and $M - F$ are increasing in $p(1)$ and decreasing in $p(0)$. Thus, at high levels of $p(1)$, the status quo ceases to be an equilibrium outcome. There is a shift to common access or to the leader-follower regime.

Let us now consider the policy implications of this model. Suppose that the costs of getting access to fiscal revenues (q') can be affected by the government. Since $L - S$ and $M - F$ are decreasing in q', it follows that, if during the period that the government enjoys autonomy it implements policies that lead q' to increase at a faster rate than potential fiscal revenue, then the likelihood of a reversion to the old system of privileges diminishes. On the contrary, if potential fiscal revenue were to grow faster than q', the likelihood of a failed reform would increase because of the heightened temptation of the groups to gain back their old privileges.

We might identify policies that alter q' as those that have to do with structural and judicial reform. For instance, signing a free trade agreement limits the possibility that groups will gain back import protection or production subsidies. Eliminating complicated regulations, introducing clear bankruptcy laws, and creating an independent judicial system will make the reestablishment of a patronage network much more expensive, since there will be no room for "interpretation of the law."

Increases in the parameter p can be identified with events that increase the ability of the government to obtain more fiscal revenue or that allow the government to borrow more. These events include an increase in foreign aid, discoveries of natural resources such as oil, and improvements in the terms of trade. These events might increase the cost a rent-seeking group is willing to pay in order to get access to this enlarged source of revenue.

For instance, if after a crisis foreign aid were granted, with no conditions of change in the regulatory framework or in the subsidization scheme, then the temptation of rent-seeking groups to gain back their old privileges would increase. Thus, foreign aid packages might have the unintended effect of preventing growth-enhancing structural change.

7.6 CONCLUSIONS

In Mexico, since the late sixties it became evident that the protectionist development strategy was not beneficial for the country anymore. However, trade liberalization did not take place until 1985, and the badly needed fiscal reform did not take place until 1989.

In this paper, I offer an explanation of why these reforms were delayed until an economic crisis took place and were not implemented during the 1970s, when the country could afford the costs associated with these reforms. My premise is that welfare-improving reforms for the country can be blocked by powerful interest groups that stand to lose from these reforms.

The interest groups that blocked the reforms during the seventies were the private import-competing elite and the parastatal elite. In the seventies, both groups were interested in keeping the status quo. Since fiscal resources were plentiful, both groups enjoyed high subsidies, which kept the profitability of their fixed assets at a high level. Under these circumstances, it was not profitable for either group to redirect its assets away from productive activities in order to reduce the power of the other group and to guarantee for itself a greater share of fiscal revenue. Hence the status quo prevailed.

The equilibrium between these two powerful groups broke down when the debt crisis erupted in 1982, since the government could no longer maintain high levels of subsidies. The struggle between interest groups took place in the spheres of private bank expropriation and trade liberalization. The short-run costs of trade liberalization were the adjustment costs implied by the efficiency effects of free trade. The private elite benefited because the power of the parastatal elite to expropriate and obtain studies was reduced. This mutual weakening gave temporary autonomy to the government to implement a fiscal reform.

APPENDIX A

Here I derive the fiscal revenue function (4). During each period, given the realization of $p(t)$ and the tax rate $\tau(t)$, the representative investor maximizes equation (2) by allocating her working capital so as to equalize after-tax rates of return:

$$p[1-\tau]\alpha\hat{w}^{\alpha-1} = 1+r. \tag{A1}$$

In order to derive the fiscal revenue function, I further assume that the size of the investors' population is one. Thus, from (A1),

$$T(\tau, p) = p\tau\hat{w}(\tau, p)^{\alpha} = \frac{\tau}{[1-\tau]^{\alpha/\alpha-1}}Ap^{\frac{1}{1-\alpha}}, \quad A = \left[\frac{1+r}{\alpha}\right]^{\frac{\alpha}{\alpha-1}} > 0, \tag{A2}$$

where T is total fiscal revenue. Under the common access and the leader-follower regimes, the tax rate is set so as to maximize tax revenue. The first and second order conditions are

$$\frac{dT}{d\tau} = \left\{[1-\tau]^{\alpha/(1-\alpha)} - \tau[1-\tau]^{(2\alpha-1)/(1-\alpha)}\frac{\alpha}{\alpha-1}\right\}Ap^{1/(1-\alpha)} = 0 \tag{A3}$$

and

$$\begin{aligned}\frac{d^2T(p,\tau)}{d\tau^2} &= \frac{\alpha}{1-\alpha}[1-\tau]^{(2\alpha-1)/(1-\alpha)}\left[\frac{2\alpha-1}{1-\alpha}\frac{\tau}{1-\tau} - 2\right]Ap^{1/(1-\alpha)} \\ &= -\frac{2\alpha A}{1-\alpha}p^{\frac{1}{1-\alpha}}[1-\tau]^{\frac{3\alpha-2}{1-\alpha}} < 0.\end{aligned} \tag{A4}$$

Since the solution to (A3) is $\tau = 1 - \alpha$, and since $T(p, T)$ is concave in τ, the fiscal revenue function under the leader-follower and the common access regimes is obtained by substituting $\tau = 1 - \alpha$ in (A2).

$$\hat{T}(p) = Bp^{1/(1-\alpha)}, \qquad B \equiv [1-\alpha][\alpha^2/(1+r)]^{\alpha/(1-\alpha)} > 0 \tag{A5}$$

APPENDIX B

TABLE 7.A1 Mexican Fiscal Indicators (% of GDP)

Year	Terms of Trade	Financial Balance	Primary Balance	Total Revenue	Total Expenditure	Parastatal Expenditure
1965	83.9	−0.8	0	16.8	17.5	9.3
1966	85.0	−1.1	−0.2	16.2	17.3	9.5
1967	83.9	−2.1	−0.8	16.5	18.6	9.1
1968	89.3	−1.9	−0.7	16.8	18.6	9.9
1969	88.0	−2.0	−0.7	17.2	19.1	10.1
1970	96.7	−3.4	−1.3	18.1	21.4	9.8
1971	100.0	−2.3	−0.4	17.6	19.6	10.5
1972	103.2	−4.5	−2.2	17.9	21.9	10.1
1973	114.8	−6.3	−3.5	19.3	24.7	11.9
1974	109.8	−6.7	−3.7	20.2	25.9	13.8
1975	97.5	−9.3	−6.0	22.2	30.6	17.0
1976	112.7	−9.1	−4.6	22.8	30.7	14.9
1977	112.0	−6.3	−2.2	23.6	28.7	14.6
1978	103.9	−6.2	−2.2	24.9	30.1	16
1979	113.1	−7.1	−2.7	25.6	31.3	16.5
1980	126.5	−7.5	−3.0	26.9	32.9	19.0
1981	123.3	−14.1	−8.0	26.7	39.2	22.0
1982	107.5	−16.9	−2.6	28.9	43.6	22.2
1983	98.2	−8.5	4.0	32.9	40.5	23.4
1984	96.3	−8.5	4.2	32.2	38.8	22.9
1985	91.1	−9.6	3.9	31.2	38.6	22.6
1986	65.6	−16.9	2.5	30.3	43.9	20.4
1987	72.5	−18.1	5.7	30.7	44.9	19.9
1988	65.5	−12.5	8.1	31.1	40.4	16.9
1989	68.9	−5.6	3.6	29.6	34.6	15.5
1990	74.3	−1.0	10.6	30.0	32.4	15.5
1991	61.8	−1.5	5.6	27.0	27.3	14.0
1992	—	—	—	26.1	24.2	13.2

Sources: Banco de México; Secretariat de Hacienda y Credito Publico.

REFERENCES

Aizenman, J. 1992. Competitive Externalities and the Optimal Seignorage Segmentation. *Journal of Money Credit and Banking*.

Alesina, A., and A. Drazen. 1991. Why Are Stabilizations Delayed? *American Economic Review* 81 (5): 1170–88.

Aspe, P., and J. Beristain. 1984. Towards a First Estimation of the Evolution of Inequality in Mexico. In *The Political Economy of Income Distribution in Mexico*, ed. P. Aspe and P. Sigmund. New York: Holmes and Meier.

Bazdresch, C., and S. Levy. 1991. Populism and Economic Policy in Mexico, 1970–1982. In *The Macroeconomics of Populism in Latin America*, ed. R. Dornbusch and S. Edwards. Chicago: University of Chicago Press.

Cosio Villegas, D. 1972. *El Sistema Politico Mexicano*. Mexico City: Joaquin Mortiz.

Fernandez, R., and D. Rodrik. 1991. Resistance to Reform: Status Quo Bias in the Presence of Individual-Specific Uncertainty. *American Economic Review* 81 (5): 1146–55.

Maxfield, S., and R. Anzaldua Montoya, eds. 1987. *Government and Private Sector in Contemporary Mexico*. San Diego: University of California.

Ortiz Mena, A. 1970. El Desarrollo Estabilizador. *El Trimestre Economico* no. 146.

Skidmore, Thomas E., and Peter H. Smith. 1984. *Modern Latin America*. New York: Oxford University Press.

Tornell, A. 1992. The Rise and Decline of Economies with Endogenous Property Rights. NBER Working Paper no. 4354. Cambridge, MA: National Bureau of Economic Research.

Tornell, A., and A. Velasco. 1992. The Tragedy of the Commons and Economic Growth: Why Does Capital Flow from Poor to Rich Countries? *Journal of Political Economy* 100 (6): 1208–31.

Velasco, A. 1993. The State and Economic Policy: Chile 1952–1992. In *The Chilean Economy: Policy Lessons and Challenges*, ed. B. Bosworth, R. Dornbusch, and R. Labán. Washington, D.C.: Brookings Institution.

End-of-Chapter Questions

1. Describe Mexico's evolution from being one of the closest economies to trade in the Americas during the 1950s, 1960s, and 1970s, to becoming one of the most open countries in the world by the late 1980 and early 1990s. What were the driving forces for this turnaround?
2. What is the meaning of so-called import-competing sectors? Why are these sectors usually opposed to any opening up of a country's economy?
3. Following its liberalization of trade during the late 1980s and early 1990s, describe Mexico's structural reforms during the succeeding years. Were these reforms successful in launching Mexico's economy forward?
4. Why were the reforms in Mexico began to be implemented right after the crisis of 1982 rather than during a time of economic bonanza, when the country might have been able to afford short-term costs more easily?
5. Explain what the author means by stating that a government 'will be able to implement structural reforms, such as trade liberalization, only if it does not encounter opposition from interest groups that have the power to block the reform'.
6. What two interest groups might have been able to block the liberalization and structural reforms adopted during the 1980s and 1990s? Why didn't they oppose these reforms?
7. Why did these two interest groups engage in the zero-sum game of 'if I don't shoot, he will shoot' that paved the way for trade liberalization?

8. Explain what are the benefits of trade liberalization and why liberalization may have averted further expropriations that began to happen in or around 1982. What are the costs of trade liberalization?
9. Explain why trade liberalization was supported by the private elite in order to save itself from the parastatal elite
10. Describe the game-theoretical model that analyzes the interaction between two powerful interest groups. Explain why in good times trade liberalization is blocked unanimously by all, and why in bad times this unanimity breaks down, with some groups supporting trade liberalization even if all groups end up worse off than under the status quo.
11. Explain how the growth of the state-owned oil industry during the 1970s prevented any significant structural reforms and increased the power of the parastatal elite. Might this explain why Mexico chose not to adhere to GATT in 1980? Why?
12. In September 1982 President Lopez Portillo announced the expropriation of all the Mexican private banks. What drove President Portillo to that decision? Was this move proof that one powerful interest group – the parastatal elite – was trying to outpace the other interest group – the private elite – in order to maintain its benefits intact? Explain in detail your reasoning
13. When President de la Madrid took office in December 1982, three important decisions were made: not to interrupt debt service to foreign banks, to open the economy by joining GATT in 1985, and to privatize the parastatal sector. Explain the ramifications of each

CHAPTER 8

Thailand's Financial Crisis: Its Causes, Consequences, and Implications

Jonathan E. Leightner

The Asian financial crisis began in Thailand in 1997 and then spread throughout Asia and around the world. Before the crisis passed, Thailand, South Korea, Indonesia, Brazil, and Russia accepted large loans from the International Monetary Fund (IMF). Some feared that the entire international financial system might collapse. On all corners of the globe, governments now fear facing a similar fate as evidenced by the European Union (EU) recently developing an emergency plan to deal with a possible European financial crisis. In the *Financial Times* article, "Ministers Plan Simulation of EU Financial Crisis" (May 16, 2005), George Parker explained, "[a]lthough there are no signs that such a problem is likely to appear in the foreseeable future, European regulators are haunted by the Asian financial crisis in 1997-98, which shook the whole region." In addition to producing systemic fear, the crisis set in motion profound shifts in Thai economic, political, and social systems.

This paper explains the causes and consequences of Thailand's financial crisis. It begins with a brief summary of the literature. Afterwards, this paper goes beyond the current literature on Thailand's crisis by extending the story to the current year and explicitly presenting some of the most important institutional consequences of the crisis.

A BRIEF SURVEY OF THE LITERATURE: THE CAUSES OF THE CRISIS

The literature on Thailand's financial crisis includes Leightner 1999, 2000, 2002, forthcoming; Alam and Leightner 2001; and Leightner and Alam 2002. The story of the Thai crisis has parallels in the Japanese stories told by Ozawa (1999; 2003) and in the South Korean stories told by Zalewski (1999a; 1999b; 2002). The risks that Grabel (1999; 2000) warns of for Asia, the invidious distinction and conspicuous consumption that Elliott and Harvey (2000) warn of for Jamaica, and the problems with absentee ownership and the menace of competition that Atkinson (1999) warns of for globalization have counterparts in the Thai story. After summarizing the literature on the relationship between capital account liberalization and crises, Eichengreen (2004) argues that capital account liberalization is "unavoidable"; however, the pace of liberalization needs to be controlled and correctly sequenced to minimize the risks of future crises. Specifically,

Jonathan E. Leightner, "Thailand's Financial Crisis: Its Causes, Consequences, and Implications," *Journal of Economic Issues*, vol. 41, no. 1, pp. 61-76.

domestic financial markets need to be liberalized first and prudential supervision strengthened; foreign direct investment liberalized second; stock and bond markets third; and offshore banking last. The Thai case started with Thailand setting up an offshore banking center.

In the early 1990s, wages in Thailand increased much faster than wages increased in its neighbors—Cambodia, Laos, Malaysia, Burma (Mayamar), Vietnam, and Southern China. The Thai government was concerned that Thai manufacturers would move their production facilities to neighboring countries. In response to this concern, the Thai government decided to help those neighbors grow. The theory was that if Thailand could be the older brother (patron) that helped its younger siblings (clients), then when the siblings grew enough to threaten Thailand, they would be grateful for past help and be responsive to their older brother's needs. Therefore the Thai government established tax breaks and other incentives for Thai businesses to invest in Thailand's neighbors (Leightner 1999).

A good older brother also provides financing. Thus, Thailand decided to establish the Bangkok International Banking Facility (BIBF) which began operating in 1993. The intent of the BIBF was to attract money from the United States, Japan, and Europe to lend to Thailand's neighbors. However, the government's good intentions were subverted by business realities.[1] Since Thailand had much higher interest rates than its neighbors did, the foreign money was loaned to native Thais. Part of this foreign money fueled a speculative bubble in the Thai property market. Speculators purchased property because they expected the price of the property to rise in the near future. Their increased purchasing of the property caused the price of the property to rise, which caused even more speculative buying. When it became obvious that the current price greatly exceeded the real value of the property, speculators quickly sold, causing the price to collapse - the bubble burst (Leightner 1999).

In 1996, the Bangkok Bank of Commerce (BBC) experienced serious cash flow problems due to delinquent loans to the property sector. In an effort to solve its cash flow problems, the BBC asked politicians to whom it had made loans, to start paying on those loans for the first time. Apparently, some politicians saw BBC loans as bribes and had not intended to ever make payments on them. The Bank of Thailand (BOT), foreseeing a major political scandal, tried to cover up the BBC problems. When these problems were revealed to the public, the Bank of Thailand's reputation had been tarnished. Prior to 1996, the BOT had the reputation of being above corruption.

On March 3, 1997, the BOT increased reserve requirements on all financial institutions and named ten weak finance companies. Banks that *hold* higher reserves are viewed as stronger but *adjusting* to higher reserve requirements reduces the profits of banks and decreases the domestic money supply. Thus, the BOT was worried that announcing higher reserve requirements would cause a panic and snowball dumping of Thai financial institutions' stocks and bonds. Therefore, immediately prior to announcing the higher reserve requirements, the Thai government suspended (for one day) the trading of all bank and finance company stocks on the stock market. This was the first time in the 21 year history of the Thai stock market that trade was suspended. In spite of the BOT's good intentions, panic began.

These events created a run on all finance companies, especially the ones cited for being weak. The speculative bubble in the Thai property market affected finance companies much more than banks because a relatively high percentage of finance company loans were to the property market. Furthermore, the BIBF licenses held by all Thai banks made it possible for them to obtain funds (from overseas) much cheaper than Thai finance companies could, (because finance companies could only raise funds from domestic deposits). Even prior to the BIBF, the playing field between Thailand's 15 commercial banks and its 91 finance/securities companies was biased in favor of the banks. The BIBF made this bias worse and there was serious concern that all 91 of Thailand's finance and securities companies would go bankrupt (Leightner 1999; forthcoming; see also Atkinson 1999, on the menace of competition; and Elliott and Harvey 2000, on invidious distinction).

George Soros used the above events and concerns in order to lead a speculative attack on the Thai baht—the official currency of Thailand. To understand speculative currency attacks, one must understand how fixed exchange rates are maintained. If an exchange rate is fixed above equilibrium, then a surplus of the currency emerges and the government must buy up this surplus (paying for it with foreign reserves) in order to keep the exchange rate from falling. If an exchange rate is fixed below equilibrium, then a shortage of the currency emerges and the government can maintain the fixed exchange rate by printing more currency and exchanging it for additional foreign reserves.

This author does not know the actual amounts of money used in George Soros' speculative attack against the Thai baht in the spring of 1997; therefore, the numbers used in this paragraph to illustrate how a speculative attack is conducted are hypothetical. First, George Soros bought forward currency contracts on the baht in the spring of 1997. Forward currency contracts are legal agreements to exchange currency at an agreed upon rate at some date in the future. Perhaps these forward contracts gave Soros the option of selling baht at the rate of one US$ for 26 baht in January of 1998. Next Soros sells all of his baht, convinces all of his friends to sell their baht, and advertises the current problems of the Thai economy (see above) in an effort to get others to sell their baht. Soros advertised Thailand's problems because he wanted to create a panic where all foreign investors would want to sell their baht immediately for fear its value was on the verge of collapse. As everyone begins selling baht (and no one wants to buy it), the Thai government must buy up the resulting surplus in order to maintain the fixed exchange rate. Thailand spent US$6.8 billion and committed at least an additional US$23.4 billion in forward obligations in an effort to maintain the fixed exchange rate (Leightner 1999; note Thailand had US$39 billion of foreign reserves in January 1997). On July 2, 1997, the BOT gave up its fixed exchange rate and floated the baht (stopped buying and selling to keep the baht's value fixed). By January 1998, the baht had fallen to US$1 for 54 baht. In January 1998, George Soros could exchange US$1 billion for 54 billion baht on the spot market (the market using current prices). He could then use his forward contracts to exchange the 54 billion baht for more than US$2 billion - more than doubling his money.[2] Soros took advantage of Thailand's problems to make a huge personal profit and in the process Thailand was devastated.

INSTITUTIONAL CONSEQUENCES OF THE CRISIS: CREDIT

When the value of the baht fell from US$1 for 25 baht in June of 1997 to US$1 dollar for 54 baht in January of 1998, the dollar value of Thai exports was halved and the price Thailand had to pay for imports doubled. Thailand fell into a serious recession. On August 19, 1997, Thailand accepted a US$17.2 billion from the IMF and the World Bank. This loan came with conditions, which would cause the Thai economy to contract further, but had the implicit goal of improving foreign investor confidence in the Thai economy.[3] One condition of the loan was that the Thai government not rescue additional financial institutions. By May of 1998, only 35 finance and securities companies remained of the original 91 and the Thai government took over seven of the remaining firms. The Thai government also took over four of Thailand's fifteen commercial banks (Leightner 2002).

The managers were fired at most of the financial firms that were shut down or taken over and the value of the shares of these companies was decreased to 1/1000th of their previous value. The Thai government issued a stern warning that if other financial firms did not get their delinquent loans under control, they would face the same fate. Out of fear, Thai financial institutions seriously curtailed the making of new loans (Leightner 2002). When financial firms stopped making loans, many debtors stopped paying on their current debts (called the strategic non-payment of loans). Debtors saw no financial advantage of paying on their current debts because not paying debts usually resulted in their being able to negotiate with desperate banks for more favorable payment options and maintaining a good credit rating is not advantageous if banks are not loaning. When the first prominent case of a non paying debtor was taken to bankruptcy court, the court threw the case out because the debtor had the money to pay its debts and, thus, was not bankrupt. Vongvipanond and Wichitaksorn (2004) show the bankruptcy court's top priority was avoiding the liquidation of firms. The strategic non-payment of loans and the reaction of the bankruptcy court caused banks to be even more reluctant to make new loans. The restructuring of corporate debt did not make significant progress until 2000 (Boonlai 2001) but even then the amount of new delinquent loans almost equaled the amount successfully restructured (Bunyamanee 2001).

The shortage of credit continues to haunt the Thai economy (Ingsrisawang 2001; Leightner 2002). State owned banks resumed some lending in 2001 under direct pressure from the government, but the private banks did not (Chudasri 2002; 2004). Even in 2005, Thai banks continue to hold more deposits than needed for the loans they make. Compounding the problem is the fact that extremely low interest rates do not give banks much incentive to lend. Most importantly, the Thai crisis caused possibly permanent changes in the institutional relationships underlying the giving and receiving of credit by (1) changing the number and types of financial institutions, (2) transforming previously cooperative relationships between borrowers and lenders into adversarial relationships, (3) undermining trust, and (4) creating a pervasive fear of government take over among financial intermediaries.

INSTITUTIONAL CONSEQUENCES OF THE CRISIS: POLITICAL

Chavalit, Thailand's prime minister when the crisis began, resigned under tremendous pressure on November 3, 1997. Chuan Leekpai, who had been prime minister from September 1992 to May 1995, took over as Thailand's new prime minister. Chuan had the reputation for being a cautious and incorruptible leader. This change in leadership improved international expectations and the Thai baht increased in value for a short amount of time. However, the depth of the domestic problems caused by the recession-producing IMF program and Chuan's reputation for cautiousness caused the Thais to embrace a new, more daring, political party in the January 2001 elections. This new political party was created by a billionaire Thai businessman named Thaksin Shinawatra. Thaksin was one of the few Thais who gained financially from the collapse of the Thai baht (McCargo and Pathmanand 2005). The political party that Thaksin created was called the "Thai Love Thai" (Thai Rak Thai) party.

Immediately prior to the Thai crisis, the Thais had spent a considerable amount of time and effort writing a new constitution. One of the major improvements in this new constitution was much stronger safeguards against political corruption. Under this new constitution, a Counter-Corruption Commission examined the assets of all politicians. Any politicians found guilty of corruption were outlawed from politics for five years. Prior to the January 2001 elections, the Counter-Corruption Commission found that Thaksin had hid some of his assets. Thaksin was not immediately thrown out of politics because the Constitutional Court began investigating his case. Thaksin won the January 2001 election with the biggest landslide victory in Thai history. In August 2001, the Constitutional Court acquitted Thaksin (with an extremely controversial 8 to 7 decision). Two of the casualties of these events were the credibility of the Counter-Corruption Commission and of the Constitutional Court.[4]

The Thai Love Thai political party of Thaksin won the 2001 election by promising huge increases in government spending. One million baht (approximately US$25,000) was promised to each of Thailand's 77,000 villages for a total of US$1.925 billion. A promise was made to small farmers (who owed less than 100,000 baht each) that their interest payments would be suspended for three years. The banks were promised that an asset management company would take over their delinquent loans. On the eve of the election, a final promise was made that every Thai citizen would have to pay only 30 baht (less than US$1) for medical care (Leightner 2002; Sirithaveeporn 2002).[5] Having made these promises, the Thai Love Thai party enjoyed the biggest land-slide victory in Thai history. For the first time in Thai history, a single party had won enough votes to form a government without having to form a coalition with other political parties.

With the important exception of the Democratic party, most of Thailand's other political parties negotiated with the Thai Love Thai party to merge in the wake of the January 2001 election. The result of these negotiations is that Thailand changed from a multi-party system where coalition governments were a necessity, to a two-party system with the Democratic and Thai Love Thai parties being the only viable remaining parties. The February 2005 election further consolidated the political domination of the Thai Love Thai political party. After this last election, all opposition members of parliament combined do not have the votes to initiate a motion to censure the prime minister or a cabinet minister. Time will tell whether or not Thailand will become a single party state.

The breaking of a dominating party into factions can threaten a single party rule in many democracies. However, Thailand's new constitution gives Thaksin a trump card, which he is using to prevent breakaway factions. Prior to the new constitution, Thailand had a two-tier vote buying system. Political parties often paid famous politicians huge sums to run under their party banner. The paid politicians would then distribute this money to voters in an effort to buy votes. The writers of the new constitution wanted to stop this practice and to reduce the number of political parties. Toward these ends, the writers included many provisions in the new constitution, including one that politicians who leave one political party cannot participate in an election under a different political party for 90 days. The *Bangkok Post* (Dec. 31, 2005) explains how Thaksin is using this provision to maintain a single party rule as illustrated in the case of Sanoh Thienthong.

Sanoh is the leader of the Wang Nam Yen faction of Thaksin's political party. In the 2001 election, the Wang Nam Yen faction won more than 80 Member of Parliament seats (MPs), but was awarded only three cabinet positions by Thaksin. When Sanoh threatened to take his 80 MPs and either join another political party or establish a new political party, Thaksin said that such an action might result in a dissolving of parliament. If parliament was dissolved, then new elections would have to be called and MPs from the break away faction could not run. In the wake of the February 2005 election, Thaksin allocated minister positions in such a way as to reduce the power of potential competitors (including Sanoh) and to increase the power of his closest friends. The Thai Love Thai political party is clearly a one-man show with the Prime Minister, Thaksin, in firm control.

Thaksin appears to have even the Bank of Thailand (BOT) under his thumb. When Thaksin became prime minister in January 2001, M.R. Chatumongol Sonakul was the governor of the BOT. In late May 2001, M.R. Chatumongol Sonakul was "sacked." The government argued that the firing "was due to a lack of coordination and co-operation, not interest-rate policy" (Yuthamanop 2001). Chatumongol had argued that low interest rates were needed to help debt restructuring and economic growth (a position supported by the IMF). Thaksin and his Minister of Finance wanted higher interest rates to stabilize the Thai exchange rate and to increase foreign reserve levels. When this author expressed concerns about what the sacking meant for central bank independence to officials at the BOT in June of 2001, he was told that the duty of the BOT is to support the government of Thailand.

In the summer of 2005, the Ministry of Finance proposed a two-step process that would remove from the BOT its role of supervising commercial banks (a role that it has had since 1941). In the first step, a new agency, directly under the control of the Ministry of Finance, would be established to supervise banks and insurance companies. In the second step, a consolidated umbrella agency would be set up to control banks, non-bank financial companies, the stock exchange, and insurance companies. Again, this umbrella agency would be under the direct control of the Ministry of Finance, with no supervising role left for the BOT. Officially, the BOT would be left managing the money supply and interest rate policy, but it would have no credible threats to use for moral suasion. As of the writing of this article, this two-step process has not been approved at the cabinet level of Thailand's government. However, the BOT continues to be relatively passive, even in light of this serious threat - a passivity that began when its governor was sacked in May of 2001.

Thaksin also controls Thailand's police force. In 2001, Thaksin told Thailand's police to eradicate drugs from Thailand. When questioned about the 1700 to 2500 extra judicial killings that occurred in Thaksin's campaign against drugs (McCargo and Pathmanand 2005, 245), Thaksin was unrepentant. Thaksin's efforts to use similar strong-arm tactics against Muslim rebels have been less successful in Thailand's deep south, where over 1000 died between January 2004 and December 2005. Thaksin repeatedly says things that further alienate the Muslims. For example, Veera Prateepchaikul of the *Bangkok Post* (Nov. 7, 2005) reports that, Thaksin said that provinces that voted wholly for his party "would get special attention from the government while the others would have to wait in the queue." In the 2005 elections, the deep south voted overwhelmingly for the Democratic party, not for Thaksin's Thai Love Thai party. All evidence to date shows that Thaksin insists on absolute control; will use whatever methods it takes to get that control; and gets very angry when criticized.

Thaksin has tried several methods to silence criticism from the press. Immediately prior to the 2001 elections, one of Thaksin's companies "purchased a controlling interest in iTV, an 'independent' television station with a reputation for strong and critical news coverage. More than 20 of the more outspoken iTV journalists were immediately fired" (McCargo and Pathmanand 2005, 189). After the iTV purchase, Thaksin controlled all Thai TV networks. Critics cannot use radio waves because the Thai military controls all radio waves and Thaksin controls the military. When the newspaper, *Manager Daily*, published the sermon of an important Buddhist monk, which compared Thaksin to one of Buddha's most evil adversaries, Thaksin sued the paper for 500 million baht (US$12 million). The *Bangkok Post* (Oct. 12, 2005) explained that the monk, who accused Thaksin of ruining the country, being ungrateful and arrogant, and wanting to abuse his power, could not be sued due to his religious position. The Thai press is scared—Thaksin is extremely rich and powerful and, if you dare to criticize him, he sets out to destroy you. Thirayuth Boonmi, a student activist from the 1970s and now a sociology lecturer at Thammasat University, is one of Thaksin's most vocal critics. Thirayuth coined words like "Thaksinisation," "Thaksinocracy," and "Thaksinocronies" (McCargo and Pathmanand 2005).

Since the February 2005 election gave the Thai Love Thai political party so much of a majority that censure motions are not possible and since the scrutiny role of the press has been squelched, some could argue that the checks and balances necessary for a democracy have been short circuited in Thailand. However, perhaps having a CEO run a developing country like a corporation may produce good results—the economy has greatly improved. The key issues are: (1) can Thaksin successfully run Thailand as a corporation; and (2) will Thaksin's desire to create a legacy for himself as Thailand's savior keep his desire for personal profit sufficiently in check? No matter what Thaksin's ultimate legacy, the crisis has caused Thai political institutions to evolve by:

(1) replacing coalition governments with a single party rule; (2) discrediting the new constitution and the anti-corruption institutions it set up; (3) moving away from free press and free speech towards censorship and government control of the media; and (4) moving from a parliamentary form of government toward the domination of the entire political system by one man—the prime minister.

HIS MAJESTY KING BHUMIBOL ADULYADEY AND PRIME MINISTER THAKSIN

On January 1, 2006, Thaksin appeared invincible. By March 1, 2006, Thaksin's position looked much more vulnerable. The change is primarily due to His Majesty King Bhumibol Adulyadey and to Thaksin's family selling their telecommunications assets. Thailand's king is forbidden by law from interfering in politics. However, the Thais adore this king because he has spent his adult life helping Thailand. He developed better hybrids of rice, ways to revitalize Bangkok's canals, and flood/drought control methods. He brought electricity to remote villages, medicine to the sick, and education to the poor. He is the ultimate, loving, father figure for the Thais. Because of their love for King Bhumibol, the Thais study his every word and deed to try to discern his views and then whole-heartedly support him.

For example, the King stopped the April Fool's Day coup of 1981 by leaving the capital with the then current prime minister, Prem Tinsulanonda. The Thais interpreted the King's presence with the current prime minister as showing his tacit support (Wright 1991). In 1992, when two powerful men started shooting at each other in Bangkok and some of the King's citizens were killed, the King interrupted Thai television to demand that the two leaders come to his audience chamber immediately. Within the hour, Thai television showed both men on their knees in front of the King who was condemning them for being immature. The king then commanded them to stay in an adjacent room until they found a way to live in peace.

The King has several times checked Thaksin's power. Thitinan Pongsudhirak of the *Bangkok Post* (Sept. 20, 2005) reported that the latest military promotion list underwent major revisions before the King would approve it. In the past, Thaksin used the military promotion process to place his former military classmates in key military positions. The 1977 coup, the 1981 and 1985 coup attempts, and the 1991 coup were all based on the domination of the military of specific classes from the Armed Forces academy (McCargo and Pathmanand 2005).

The King is also suppose to endorse the appointments of key political figures including Thailand's Auditor-General. After being appointed by the Senate and endorsed by the King, Auditor-General Jaruvan Maintaka started investigating accusations of corruption against Thaksin's government. Subsequently, the Constitutional Court found that Jaruvan's selection had been incorrect and the Senate appointed a replacement for Jaruvan. Pongsudhirak, in the above-mentioned *Bangkok Post* article, reported that the King ignored the Senate's request that he endorse the new Auditor-General. Jaruvan argued that this implied the King wanted her to remain as the Auditor-General. The person appointed by the Senate to replace Jaruvan withdrew his name because the King did not endorse him. The Senate had the locks changed on the Auditor-General's door to keep Jaruvan out, but she kept in contact with her staff via phone. Because the King, in his 2005 birthday speech, called on everyone to accept criticism, the senate ultimately re-instated Jaruvan.

The Economist ("A New Order" 2002) reported that in the King's birthday speech of December 2001, he warned of "disaster" facing the country due to the failure to listen to criticism. "There was no doubt about the intended target of his comments, but they were phrased ambiguously enough to save Mr. Thaksin's face" (16). According to the *Bangkok Post* (Dec. 5, 2005), the King, in his December 2005 birthday speech, explicitly told Thaksin "to be open to criticism and not to overreact when countering his critics." After the King's speech, Thaksin withdrew his three civil cases against Sondhi Limthongkul and nine others. Thaksin had sought two billion baht (and 7.5 percent interest) in compensation, or US$49 million, for "libel" from these members of the press. The Thais interpreted the above events as indicating that the King disapproved of Thaksin. The king's disapproval gave Thaksin's critics credibility and power with the Thai population. Then Thaksin's son and daughter selling the telecommunications firm (Shin Corp) that had made Thaksin a billionaire, gave Thaksin's critics an issue around which they could focus their attacks.

The *Bangkok Post* (Feb. 1, 2006), reported that on January 20, 2006, Ample Rich Investments Ltd. (which Thaksin says is owned by his son) sold 392 million shares of Shin Corp to Thaksin's son and daughter for one baht per share. On January 23, 2006, these siblings sold all of their holdings in Shin Corp to Singapore's Temasek Holdings at 49.25 baht per share. *The Wall Street Journal* (March 1, 2006, p. Al) reports this sale cost Singapore US$1.9 billion. In order to attract foreign investors, Thai law makes the sales of stocks tax free. Thus, Thaksin's family paid no tax on this US$1.9 billion sale. The sale was made "legal" only one working day before it occurred when the Thai legislature increased the foreign ownership limits on Thai telecommunications firms from 25 to 49 percent.

Anucha Charoenpo in a *Bangkok Post* article (Feb 9, 2006) reports that Prem Tinsulanonda, the President of the Kings Privy Council, gave a speech on February 8, 2006 to doctorial candidates, which quoted the king at length. Prem said, "Being smart and intelligent is a good thing, but if there is no morality and ethics it is not so good." Prem claimed that his comments were not aimed at anyone, but the Thai people interpreted his speech as implying that the king thinks that Thaksin is immoral. Several major demonstrations have occurred in Bangkok since Prem's speech (with 100,000 protesters or more), in which Sanoh and other Thaksin critics accuse Thaksin of being immoral and demanding that he resign.

On February 4, 2006, "Thaksin said that he will not quit unless, 'His Majesty the King tells him to go'" (*Bangkok Post*, Feb. 4, 2006). On February 24, 2006, Thaksin dissolved the Thai parliament and called for snap elections on April 2, 2006, three years early. The opposition political parties, dominated by the Democrats, are boycotting the April 2 election. Their reasons for the boycott include: (1) not enough time was given for them to field candidates; (2) the real problem is Thaksin, not the current parliament; (3) real political reform should occur first; and (4) under Thaksin's influence, the election is unlikely to be fair. However, if the opposition does not participate, the perceived legitimacy of the resulting government will be greatly diminished. Mongkol Bangprapa, in a *Bangkok Post* article (March 5, 2006), reports that a candidate in an uncontested district must get the votes of at least 20 percent of the eligible voters in order to take a seat in parliament. Thus, if not enough people vote (or if enough people mark the "no vote" box on their ballots) then the 500 members of parliament required by law may not be obtained.

Thaksin vowed not to return to office if his Thai Love Thai political party failed to get more than 50 percent of the votes cast in the April 2, 2006 election (*Bangkok Post*, March 4, 2006). Subsequently, the opposition urged all voters to go to the polls and mark the "no vote" option on their ballots. The author of this paper sees no way out of the current situation that would not damage democracy in Thailand. Indeed, he believes that it is likely that Thailand's King will feel forced to get even more involved.

THAILAND'S RECOVERY

The Democrats argue that Chuan Leekpai's government started Thailand on the road to recovery prior to the January 2001 election. The Thai Love Thai party argues that the Thai economy did not begin recovering until after they won the January 2001 election. Although Thaksin tried to begin his administration with rapid change, his efforts were impeded by his corruption case before the Constitutional Court, which was not resolved until August. Almost immediately, the terrorist attack against the World Trade Center in New York on September 11, 2001 produced a worldwide economic slow down.

The major concern about Thaksin's policies was that his social programs would "bankrupt the public purse" without producing sustainable growth (Ingsrisawang 2002). The 2001 budget under Thaksin predicted a 105 billion baht deficit, not including the refinancing costs of 500 billion baht of bonds for the liabilities of the Financial Institutions Development Fund (Sirithaveeporn 2001). The 2002 budget deficit was projected to be 200 billion baht (Sirithaveeporn 2002). The 2003 budget deficit was originally projected to be 174 billion baht, but a 13.6 percent increase in state revenues produced an actual budget deficit of only 40 billion baht. There was hope that the state budget should be balanced in 2005, for the first time in almost a decade (Savanayana 2005). However, preliminary figures indicate that the 2005 budget ended up with an approximately 18 billion baht deficit.

Government spending provided the sole hope for economic recovery in Thailand between 1997 and 2001. The hope of sustained recovery grew significantly brighter in 2002 and 2003 when consumers started to spend again and exports rose (Maneerungsee 2003; Yuthamanop 2004). Consumer spending rose: (1) as consumer confidence increased, (2) as interest rates stayed low, (3) as consumer credit increased,[6] (4) as the stock market improved creating wealth effects, and (5) as tax breaks for the purchase of real estate drew to an end. The increase in Thai exports did not come from Thailand's traditional export markets (especially the United States); instead exports rose significantly to China and to other ASEAN (Association of Southeast Asian Nations) countries (Yuthamanop 2004; Maneerungsee 2004). The shift away from trade with the United States and toward trade with China and ASEAN countries is likely to continue for the foreseeable future, and this shift has direct consequences for the political clout of countries like the United States.[7] The December 2004 tsunami, southern unrest, bird flu, drought, and a surge in oil prices all dampened demand in 2005. However, there is hope that additional government investment and exports will help Thailand's economy in 2006 (Yuthamanop 2006).

IMPLICATIONS

Asia's fantastic growth from 1985 to 1996 earned the title of the "Asian Miracle" and was praised by the IMF and world leaders. Economists and political scientists eagerly studied successful Asian countries to see how this miracle could be replicated elsewhere. In 1997, this miracle turned into a catastrophe in the small country of Thailand. By 1998, South Korea and Indonesia—also Asian miracle countries—joined Thailand in utter disarray.

Financial crises, caused by a rapid retreat of foreign investors, can happen almost anywhere in our globally connected world. All that is needed is enough bad news to cause a panic among foreign investors. Countries can reduce the risk of a financial crisis by: (1) exporting more than importing; (2) not using foreign capital inflows that can be quickly stopped to fund projects that require long time periods to be profitable; (3) maintaining flexible exchange rates or at least frequently adjusting their fixed exchange rates; (4) maintaining balanced government budgets; and (5) keeping large amounts of stable foreign currencies. These "risk-reducing" goals are not easy to achieve and maintain. However, even if these goals could be achieved, they provide no guarantee that a financial crisis will not occur. All that is needed to start a financial crisis is enough bad news (of any kind) that someone like George Soros can advertise to create an international panic among foreign investors who then, in a snow-balling fashion, dump the currency of the crisis country. Furthermore, people like Soros have a powerful profit motive to do this.

Some institutionalists, like Crotty and Epstein (1999) and Grabel (1999; 2000), advocate stronger constraints on short-term capital flows, however, even if only long term capital was allowed, a massive withdrawal of that capital can cause a crisis. Those opposed to apartheid successfully encouraged a significant exodus of long-term capital from South Africa in the 1980s. The nationalization of foreign assets (physical and financial) is another alternative. Unfortunately, nationalized industries usually become inefficient and deteriorate over time and additional foreign investment becomes scarce when nations begin nationalizing. There is no method that can be universally applied to all countries that would eliminate all risk of a financial crisis.

The Thai case shows that crises can set in motion events that cause institutions to evolve, where "evolve" does not necessarily imply an improvement. Indeed, in the wake of its crisis, Thailand suffers from an increase in distrust and fear and a significantly weakened democracy. Thailand's political landscape will never be the same again. Thailand's current Prime Minister, Thaksin, used the crisis to propel himself into power and he has left a permanent mark on Thailand. Perhaps most disturbing, Thailand's crisis was set in motion by good intentions of the government—a desire to help Thailand's neighbors. These "good intentions" were subverted by those seeking greater profits—many of Thailand's financial institutions and currency speculators like George Soros.

NOTES

1. Ozawa (2003) gives examples of the Japanese government's good intentions being distorted by market realities and changes.
2. Stiglitz (2003, 95) tells how loans can be used in a speculative attack, instead of using forward contracts. Both were probably used in the Thai case, but with different speculators.
3. Zalewski (2000) argues that political stability affects expectations as much, or more, than monetary stability. He implies that political stability is not adequately considered by the IMF when it makes conditional loans to crisis countries.
4. Stiglitz (2003, 131) lists Thailand's new constitution as one of the few positive changes brought about by the crisis. However, the new constitution was written in the years leading up to the crisis. The first election under the rules of the new constitution was the 2001 election swept by Thaksin. Thus, the perceived unjust resolution of Thaksin's corruption case significantly weakened the new constitution in its first major application.
5. This has resulted in a dualistic medical system. The state subsidized hospitals, to which patients only pay 30 baht, are overwhelmed with patients, under staffed, and under funded. Many medical workers, especially doctors and nurses, are leaving the state hospitals to go work for private hospitals where their pay rates are higher and their work loads are easier. Many private hospitals flush with cash are attracting major international investment, and are targeting the rich Thai population and foreign market (Kittikanya 2006). "Pongsak Viddayakorn, president of Bangkok Dusit Medical Services Pic which operates Bangkok Hospital, said the 30 baht scheme and the need for effective cost management could shrink the existing 350 hospital groups in Thailand to about 10 over the next decade" ("Hospital Care Divide Widens" 2005).
6. In South Korea, consumption has also increased in the wake of the crisis. Zalewski (2002, 807) says "South Korean banks have responded to weak corporate loan demand by increasing their lending to households . . . half of all new bank loans went to consumers."
7. The *Bangkok Post* article, "Military Sale to Thailand means 'Russia Controls Region'" (Dec. 18, 2005) cites the *Moscow Times* as reporting that Thailand had agreed to purchase US$ 500 million of Russian made jets. According to Konstantin Makiyenko (deputy head of the Russian Center for Analysis of Strategies and Technologies), "[tjhis is good news for Russia, we haven't sold a single cartridge to Thailand ... It also means that Russia has taken over the region - we have fighter jets in China, Malaysia, Indonesia, Vietnam and now Thailand" (as reported in "Military Sale . . ." 2005). Subsequently, the *Bangkok Post* (Dec. 20, 2005) reported that Panitan Wattanayagor (a security analyst) asked the Thai government "to clarify if Thailand was planning a military and political shift from the United States, its long-time ally, to Russia." The Thai government insists that no final decision will be made until April or May of 2006.

REFERENCES

"A New Order." *The Economist* (March 2, 2002): 3–16.

Alam, Ila Semenick, and Jonathan E. Leightner. "The Impact of the Financial Crisis on the Productivity of Thailand's Financial Institutions." *Singapore Economic Review* 46, no. 2 (2001): 153–177.

Atkinson, Glen. "Developing Global Institutions: Lessons to be Learned from Regional Integration Experiences." *Journal of Economic Issues* 33, no. 2 (1999): 335–341.

Boonlai, Kochakorn. "Finally Cleaning up the Mess." Bangkok Post Economic Review: Year-end 2000 (http://www.bangkokpost.com/yereview2000/corporate.html), 2001.

Bunyamanee, Soonruth. "Slow Road to Recovery." Bangkok Post Economic Review: Year-end 2000 (http://www.bangkokpost.com/yereview2000/industry.html), 2001.

Chudasri, Darana. "House-cleaning and caution set the Trend." Bangkok Post Economic Review: Year-end 2001 (http://www.bangkokpost.com/yearend2001/banking.html), 2002.

______. "Outlook not Necessarily Rosy." Bangkok Post Economic Review: Year-end 2003 (http:// www.bangkokpost.com/yearend2003/economy2.html), 2004.

Crotty, James, and Gerald Epstein. "A Defense of Capital Controls in Light of the Asian Financial Crisis." *Journal of Economic Issues* 33, no. 2 (1999): 427–433.

Eichengreen, B. *Capital Flows and Crises*. Cambridge, Massachusetts: MIT Press, 2004.

Elliott, Dawn R., and John T. Harvey. "Underdevelopment in Jamaica: An Institutionalist Perspective." *Journal of Economic Issues* 34, no. 2 (2000): 393–401.

Grabel, Ilene. "Identifying Risks, Preventing Crises: Lessons from the Asian Crisis." *Journal of Economic Issues* 34, no. 2 (2000): 377-383.

______. "Mexico Redux? Making Sense of the Financial Crisis of 1997–98." *Journal of Economic Issues* 33, no. 2 (1999): 375-381.

"Hospital Care Divide Widens." Bangkok Post Economic Review: Mid Year 2005 (http:// www.bangkokpost.com/midyear2005/healthcare.html), 2005.

Ingsrisawang, Cholada. "Recovery or False Dawn?" Bangkok Post Economic Review: Year-end 2000 (http:// www.bangkokpost.com/yereview2000/ economy.html), 2001.

______. "Jury still out on Thaksinomics." Bangkok Post Economic Review: Year-end 2001 (http:// www.bangkokpost.com/yearend2001/ economy.html), 2002.

Kittikanya, Charoen. "State hospitals left behind in race." Bangkok Post Economic Review: Year-end 2005 (http://www.bangkokpost.com/yearend2005/ page 52.html), 2006.

Leightner, Jonathan E. "Globalization and Thailand's Financial Crisis." *Journal of Economic Issues* 33, no. 2 (1999): 367-373.

______. "Asia's Financial Crisis, Speculative Bubbles, and Under-Consumption Theory." *Journal of Economic Issues* 34, no. 2 (2000): 385–392.

______. "The Domestic Effects of Tight Monetary Policy in the Wake of Thailand's Financial Crisis." *Journal of the Asia Pacific Economy* 7, no. 2 (2002): 242–266.

______. "Returns to Market Power in Financial Institutions." *Journal of Asia-Pacific Economy*, forthcoming.

Leightner, Jonathan E., and Ila M. Semenick Alam. "Financial Crisis Hypotheses and the Productivity of Thailand's Financial Institutions." In *Productivity and Economic Performance in the Asia-Pacific Region*, edited by Tsu-tan Fu, Cliff J. Huang, and C.A. Knox Lovell, 287-307. Northampton, MA: Edward Elgar Publishing, 2002.

Wright, Joseph J, Jr. *The Balancing Act: A History of Modern Thailand*. Bangkok: Asia Books, 1991.

Yuthamanop, Parista. "Acrimony over new direction." Bangkok Post Economic Review: Mid-Year 2001 (http://www.bangkokpost.com/midyear2001/ monetary.html), 2001.

______. "Planning for the Long Term." Bangkok Post Economic Review: Year-end 2003 (http://www.bangkokpost.com/yearend2003/ economyl.html), 2004.

______. "Smoother sailing after the storm." Bangkok Post Economic Review: Year-end 2005 (http://www.bangkokpost.com/yearend2005/page06.html), 2006.

Zalewski, David A. "Brothers, Can you Spare $58 Billion? Regulatory Lessons from South Korea's Currency Crisis." *Journal of Economic Issues* 33, no. 2 (1999a): 359–366.

______. "Regulatory Lessons from the South Korean Currency Crisis: A Reply to Jai S. Mah." *Journal of Economic Issues* 33, no. 2 (1999b): 367–373.
______. "Political Confidence and Monetary Stability in the Age of Globalization." *Journal of Economic Issues* 36, no. 3 (2002): 804–809.

ADDENDUM

The *Journal of Economic Issues* has graciously allowed me to write this addendum to catch the reader up on what has happened politically in Thailand between March 2006 and October 2006. The April 2, 2006 election occurred with Thaksin's political party, the Thai Love Thai party, fielding candidates and the Democratic and Chart Thai parties boycotting the election. A candidate must receive the votes of 20 percent of the eligible voters in uncontested districts to be officially elected. In several uncontested districts in Bangkok and in the Muslim dominated south, the Thai Love Thai candidate did not get enough votes to take office. The Thai constitution requires that a new parliament convene within 30 days of an election and that all districts be represented in the new parliament. The April 2, 2006 election created a situation where both of these constitutional requirements could not be simultaneously met.

Meanwhile, the Democratic party accused the Thai Love Thai party of paying some small parties to field candidates in some districts (which would make those districts contested) so the Thai Love Thais could avoid the 20 percent rule. Moreover, the accusation was leveled (and later proved) that the election commission backdated the credentials of some small party candidates to make them appear legitimate when they were not. The Thai Love Thais countered by accusing the Democratic party of pressuring some small parties to not field candidates and of hurting democracy by boycotting the election. The pending court cases based on these and other accusations could result in the Thai Love Thai and/or the Democratic parties being dissolved.

Many of Thaksin's critics petitioned the King to replace Thaksin as the caretaker prime minister so fair elections could be held. The King met with the judges from Thailand's three highest courts. He told the judges he would not appoint an interim prime minister because that would not be democracy. He also said that an election with only one political party is not democracy. The King told the judges that it is their job to fix Thailand's current political problems in such a way that democracy is preserved. He told them if they could not solve the problems, they should resign and cover their heads with chamber pots to hide their shame. Soon after this meeting, the judges annulled the April 2, 2006 election. Without the King's speech the judges would not have interfered—they would not have had the power to interfere and, even if they had the power, they would not act against Thaksin.

Following the annulment of the April 2 election, two of Thailand's five election commissioners resigned. The Thai courts found the three remaining commissioners guilty of malfeasance and sentenced them to four years in prison - thus ending their positions as commissioners. New election commissioners were selected and plans were made to hold the next election on October 15, 2006, or as soon thereafter as possible.

Due to Thaksin's overwhelming support from Thailand's rural poor, most experts believed that Thaksin's Thai Love Thai party would dominate the planned election. The People's Alliance for Democracy (PAD), which organized anti-Thaksin street protests in Bangkok in early 2006, called for a new round of street protests to start on September 20, 2006. PAD's purpose for the new round of protests was to force Thaksin to commit to not taking the Prime Minister's position if his party won the Fall 2006 election.

Meanwhile, Thaksin's continued efforts to place his previous classmates into top military positions were often opposed by the Chairman of the King's Privy Council, Prem Tinsulanonda. Thaksin personally threatened to move top military leaders into inactive posts, including General Sonthi Bunyaratkalin (the Army Commander-in-Chief) who had strong connections to Prem. In August, the National Park Forest Rangers, who are staunch supporters of Thaksin, refused to return approximately 1,000 rifles to the army that were loaned to them several years previously. Rumors spread that the Forest Rangers would forcefully suppress the planned anti-Thaksin street protest of September 20, 2006. Thaksin could then use the resulting bloodshed to declare a state of emergency and to replace top military leaders with his supporters.

To preempt bloodshed and prevent Thaksin from seizing more power through a state of emergency, top military leaders staged a bloodless coup d'etat September 19, 2006. At the time, Thaksin was in New York attending a meeting of the United Nations. The leader of the coup was General Sonthi. Sonthi promised that the government would be handed over to a civilian interim prime minister within two weeks, that a new constitution would be written, and that new elections would be held within a year. The King quickly endorsed the coup makers. As promised, an interim prime minister, retired General Surayud Chulanont, was appointed within two weeks. Surayud had been a strong vocal critic of past military involvement in politics and he was a member of the King's Privy Council. Surayud's stated priorities are to end conflicts between Thais, especially in the deep South, and to promote the King's economic philosophy of sufficiency.

The King's sufficiency philosophy grew out of the 1997 Thai financial crisis. The foundation of this philosophy is being satisfied with enough. This policy is anti greed, anti-accumulation for the sake of accumulation, and anti-excessive risk taking. It emphasizes being moral, transparent, and helpful to others. Although it encourages increasing self-sufficiency, it is not isolationist or anti-trade. When applied to economics, it emphasizes sustainable growth, instead of maximizing growth. It is the opposite of what Thaksin represents.

Surayud also appears to have the goal of uncovering the depths of Thaksin's corruption. As of today, there is strong proof that many of Thaksin's cronies are guilty, but direct proof of Thaksin's involvement has been illusive. It is likely that those who have evidence will not reveal it because it would be self-incriminating and because they fear retaliation from Thaksin if he returns. If Thaksin is not ultimately incarcerated based on strong evidence of his guilt, there is a significant chance that he will return to power and domination of Thai politics. Due to Thaksin's populous policies, Thailand's rural poor love Thaksin and they have the votes needed to return him to power.

What is democracy? Surely democracy cannot be defined as the majority voting to do whatever they want. If democracy involves protecting minority rights, the rule of law, and institutional checks and balances to prevent the abuse of power, then Thaksin destroyed Thai democracy. He controlled the press; Election Commission, courts, Anti-Money Laundering Office, Counter Corruption Commission, legislature etc. and he used these institutions to destroy anyone who dared oppose him. The irony is that a coup, which deposed an elected prime minister, is Thailand's best hope of regaining a democracy that is complete with all the working checks and balances needed to protect freedom, liberty, and justice for all. Let us hope that the coup fulfills its promises and that Thai democracy thrives.

END-OF-CHAPTER QUESTIONS

1. Explain why some argue that in our globalized world, capital account liberalization is "unavoidable," but to prevent financial crises, the pace of liberalization has to be controlled. What is the capital account, and how does it apply to the Thai situation?
2. Explain how Thailand's government's efforts to help its poorer neighboring countries in the early 1990s—through tax breaks and other incentives for Thai businesses to invest in these countries—may have contributed to the Thai crisis that erupted in 1997.
3. Explain how the establishment of the Bangkok International Banking Facility (BIFB) may have contributed to a speculative asset price bubble in the Thai property market. What is an asset price bubble, and why is it dangerous for the financial system?
4. When and why did the property asset price bubble burst, and what were the consequences of the collapse in the property market of the country?
5. Explain the relationship among the Bangkok Bank of Commerce (BBC), the Bank of Thailand (BOT—the country's central bank—and politicians and their combined effort to cover up the significant cash flow problems that the BBC was having in 1996.
6. In March 1997, the Thai government suspended, for one day, trading of all bank and finance company stocks on the securities market. What were the consequences in the general economy of this suspension of trade in the Thai stock market?
7. Explain how the establishment of the BIBF made the playing field even more biased in favor of Thailand's commercial banks at the expense of the country's investment banks.
8. According to the author, George Soros used the unfolding financial crisis to lead a speculative attack on the country's currency, the Thai Baht. Does this assertion make any economic sense? Why would Soros do this?
9. How did the BOT try to defend the fixed exchange rate regime against the speculative attack initiated by Soros? Did it succeed? Why?
10. What were the roles of the IMF and the World Bank during and after the crisis? What were the IMF's conditions for accessing loans from it? Were these conditions sensible, and did they help attenuate the crisis?

11. Explain the role that Thaksin Shinawatra and his newly formed political party, "Thai Love Thai," have played since 2001 when he won the presidential elections. Has his role as president made the country more or less prepared to confront future crisis? Explain.
12. Describe some of the policy proposals made by Shinawatra on the eve of Thailand's elections in 2001. Are these proposals the foundation of a healthy financial system in Thailand or anywhere?
13. Describe the role that King Bhumibol Adulyadey has played in Thailand during his tenure as King. Describe the King's relationship with Thaksin Shinawatra and how this relationship eventually came to an end.
14. According to the author, what five actions can be pursued by a government to prevent financial crises? Are these actions sensible in light of the country's crisis in 1997? Why?

CHAPTER 9

Argentina's Fall

Lessons from the Latest Financial Crisis

Martin Feldstein

Argentina's 35 million citizens will not be the only ones to pay a heavy price for that country's latest economic crisis. The fallout may also radically alter economic policies and political relations both within Latin America and with the United States. It is already clear that Argentina will reverse at least some of the favorable economic reforms introduced by President Carlos Menem in the early 1990s. Although Menem's reforms are not responsible for the current chaos, they are a politically convenient scapegoat. Blaming them also provides a rationale for renationalizing Argentine firms, erecting barriers to imports and foreign investment, and increasing government spending.

The current crisis will weaken the prospects for the Mercosur trading arrangement among Argentina and its neighbors (Brazil, Paraguay, and Uruguay) and may kill any chance of a general Free Trade Area of the Americas. Many Argentines are already blaming their troubles on Washington, claiming that U.S. policies got them into this mess and that the United States then abandoned Argentina because, unlike Turkey, it is not of geopolitical significance.

If other emerging-market governments misinterpret Argentina's experience, they too might move away from the promarket policies that hold the best promise of raising future living standards. Gaining a better understanding of the real reasons for the Argentine crisis is therefore essential. Doing so might help Argentina and other emerging countries avoid making the wrong policy choices in the future and reduce the risk of further financial crises.

PEGGED ALL WRONG

An overvalued fixed exchange rate (locked at one peso per dollar since 1991) and an excessive amount of foreign debt were the two proximate causes of the Argentine crisis. Because the exchange rate was fixed at too high a level, Argentina exported too little and imported too much. This trade imbalance made it impossible for the country to earn the foreign exchange it needed to pay the interest on its foreign debt. Instead, Argentina had to borrow to meet those interest payments, causing the debt to grow ever larger. The country's foreign debt, most of which was owed by the central and provincial governments, eventually reached 50 percent of GDP by late

Martin Feldstein, "Argentina's Fall: Lessons from the Latest Financial Crisis," *Foreign Affairs*, vol. 81, no. 2, pp. 8-14.

2001 and included $30 billion due in 2002. Once it finally became clear that Argentina could no longer borrow to roll over those debts and pay the interest, Buenos Aires was forced to default and to devalue the peso.

Although the devalued peso will eventually raise Argentine exports, in the near term the weakening of the currency will cause widespread bankruptcies. This is because most local businesses borrowed in dollars. A company that took a loan for one million dollars expected to repay it with one million pesos. But if the peso is devalued by 50 percent, the firm will have to find two million pesos to repay its obligation. Companies unable to afford such an increase in the peso value of their debt will wind up in bankruptcy. Corporate failures will then weigh heavily on the Argentine banks and may cause them to collapse too. The country's already high unemployment rate will increase as a result.

The havoc that an overvalued exchange rate and excessive foreign debt caused in Argentina is certainly not unique. These two conditions, either singly or together, have been the cause of every currency crisis during at least the past 25 years. Similarly, the painfuil effect that dollar-denominated debt can have when a sharp devaluation occurs was dramatically demonstrated in several Southeast Asian countries during the late 1990s. All of this was well known to Argentine economists and policymakers. Why then did they allow the crisis to develop? Why did Argentina not end its fixed link to the dollar several years ago, allowing the peso to float down to a more competitive level that could improve the trade balance and start to shrink its foreign debts? Had Buenos Aires done so, the current crisis would probably have been avoided.

GREENBACKED

The reason Argentina retained its fixed exchange rate too long is fairly simple, however: such a peg had cured hyperinflation at the end of the 1980s and brought a decade of price stability that provided the framework for strong economic growth. Policy officials feared that breaking the link to the dollar would bring back high inflation and all of the accompanying economic problems of the 1970s and 1980s.

This fear seemed justified. After all, at the beginning of the 1990s—before the currency was pegged—consumer prices in Argentina were rising at a rate of 200 percent per month, or more than 5,000 percent per year. Markets ceased to function and productivity declined. Street riots led President Raúl Alfonsín to step down sooner than normal after the election of his successor, Carlos Menem. With his economy minister, Domingo Cavallo, Menem moved Argentina from an internationally isolated and state-dominated economy to one that encouraged foreign trade and investments and privatized state-owned industries.

In taking such steps, Argentina followed the lead of Chile and Mexico as well as the Southeast Asian nations, all of which had shown that such liberalization would lead to strong economic growth. Argentina's response was thus no exception. Buenos Aires' new policies caused the country's economy to grow at a real rate of more than 7 percent a year from 1991 to 1994, one of the highest growth rates anywhere during those years.

Argentina went further than any of those other countries, however, when it enacted a "convertibility law" that pegged the peso to the dollar at a one-to-one exchange rate and stipulated that everyone had the right to convert as many pesos to dollars as they wanted. To give credibility to that promise, the government provided that each peso in circulation would have to be backed by a dollar (or similar hard currency) at the central bank, the so-called currency board system.

If Menem and Cavallo's strategy had succeeded, Argentina today would be enjoying strong growth, low inflation, and financial stability. The fixed exchange rate could have succeeded, however, only if the peso became competitive enough to generate more exports than imports, so that the net foreign-exchange earnings could be used to pay interest on the outstanding international debt. Although the one-to-one exchange rate made Argentine products uncompetitively expensive, this could still have been remedied if productivity had risen faster than wages, permitting Argentine prices to decline relative to those abroad. Cavallo correctly foresaw that the combination of low inflation and market liberalization would lead to a rapid growth of productivity. Although this was sufficient at first to lead to both rising real wages and increased international competitiveness, eventually rigid labor laws and strong union pressures prevented the further reduction in production costs that Argentina needed to become competitive.

The pegged exchange rate prevented the adjustment necessary to shrink the current-account deficit, but the combination of the currency peg and the rule against creating pesos without foreign-exchange backing did achieve the price stability that was its original purpose. To the average Argentine, the convertibility law made a peso "as good as a dollar"; the two were fully interchangeable in everyday transactions.

WARNING SIGNS

Not everyone was convinced that the peso would remain fixed, however. Some worried about what would happen if investors who saw Argentina's rising current-account deficit and its increasing foreign debt became nervous and wanted to convert their pesos to dollars. (See, for instance, my skeptical comments about the currency board system in my "Self-Help Guide for Emerging Markets," *Foreign Affairs,* March/April 1999.) Although the government had enough dollars at the central bank to back the currency in circulation, it didn't have nearly enough to cover the total amount in checking and savings accounts that individuals might want to convert.

Still, in principle that disparity was not a problem. The currency board rules ensured that as individuals began to convert their pesos into dollars, the central bank would shrink the money supply and cause interest rates to rise sharply. Long before the central bank ran out of dollars, the interest rates on peso deposits would get so high that people would be encouraged to keep their funds in pesos. In that way, the central bank would never exhaust its supply of dollars. Moreover, the high interest rates would weaken domestic demand, causing wages and prices to fall until the peso became competitive again, eliminating the reason for the original investor nervousness.

Although this logic seemed impeccable, a problem remained. If the government was not willing to push interest rates high enough to prevent speculation because of the damage that those high rates would do to the economy, and if wages did not fall sufficiently in response to economic weakness, the current-account deficit would remain and investors would lose confidence in the exchange rate's long-term viability.

Cavallo hoped that the currency board would never be put to this test. In his view, the productivity gains that he foresaw would make Argentine goods competitive internationally. Once confidence in the peso became established, sound monetary policy would then prevent inflation—even if the peso were allowed to float. Ideally, the shift from the pegged rate system to a floating rate would occur when the peso was undervalued, causing the peso to rise when the peg was ended, thereby giving a further boost to price stability.

PRESSURE BUILDING

Unfortunately, these conditions never occurred. Wage increases kept the cost of production in Argentina high, depressing exports and encouraging imports. Argentina's competitiveness worsened as the dollar strengthened relative to most other currencies, pulling the peso up with it. The dollar rose sharply against the Japanese yen after 1995, against the currencies of Southeast Asia after their crises of 1997 and 1998, and against the European currencies in 1999 and 2000. The terms of trade also moved against Argentina, with world prices for its exports declining relative to the prices of its imports. But the biggest blow to Argentine competitiveness came when Brazil's currency, the real, fell sharply in 1999.

To keep the peso-dollar peg intact as the economy became less competitive, Buenos Aires tightened macroeconomic policy, raising interest rates and pushing the economy into recession. But despite unemployment rates of close to 15 percent, wages did not decline and competitiveness did not improve. The fixed exchange rate made it impossible to increase competitiveness by a traditional currency devaluation (as a variety of countries did, ranging from the United Kingdom in 1992 to South Korea in 1998 and Brazil in 1999) and the resistance of unions to lower wages prevented a fall in production costs that could have achieved the same real devaluation without a change in the exchange rate.

The inevitable result was increasing current-account deficits, which reached nearly five percent of GDP, and therefore mounting foreign debt. The growth of the foreign debt also reflected the combination of low private savings rates, which reduced the domestic pool of investment, and substantial deficits in the budgets of the central and provincial governments. These budget deficits were due to wide spread tax evasion and to an inability to control government spending, particularly at the provincial level. The provincial deficits continued despite a constitutional rule requiring revenue sharing, which turned any increase in central government tax revenue into an extra source of finance for provincial spending. Even with these funds, the provinces still required financing through substantial capital inflows from abroad.

As the debt grew, the interest rate that Argentina had to pay foreign creditors also rose, further increasing the annual imbalance and accelerating the growth of the foreign debt. Default became unavoidable. When Argentina finally defaulted on $155 billion of central and provincial government debt in December 2001, it was the largest sovereign debt default ever.

PEG HEADED?

Sophisticated Argentines and foreign investors knew that the peso had to be devalued if future current-account deficits were to be reduced without a continued massive recession. The convertibility law allowed them to shift pesos into dollars and then to take the dollars out of the country. The result was a loss of dollar reserves at the Argentine central bank, making it all the more likely that a devaluation would be necessary. Although a loan from the International Monetary Fund (IMF) in 2001 gave a temporary boost to confidence that stemmed the run on the central bank, this lasted only a few months and the peso was devalued sharply in January 2002.

Why did Argentina not devalue sooner—in 1997, 1998, or even 1999—so that the default could have been avoided, the devaluation smaller, and the adverse effects of devaluation on domestic firms and banks limited? There were three reasons. First was a fear that breaking the peg and devaluing the peso would bring back the high rates of inflation that had plagued the economy before the two currencies were tied. Brazil's experience in 1999 had shown that a country with a long history of high inflation could abandon a fixed exchange rate and avoid inflation by an explicit "inflation targeting" approach to monetary policy—i.e., raising interest rates whenever inflation increased above a low "target" rate. But Argentina's history and the centrality of the convertibility law understandably made officials nervous that its inflation was more sensitive to any departure from the fixed peg.

Second, because Argentine house-holds and businesses had so much. dollar-denominated debt, the government feared that a devaluation would prompt widespread bankruptcies and personal defaults by raising the peso value of outstanding debts. This problem would also affect the central and provincial governments themselves, which also had large dollar-denominated debts to foreign creditors that would become more of a burden after devaluation, since tax revenue was collected in pesos.

Finally, there was always the hope that the situation would improve over time. The large U.S. trade deficit suggested that the dollar might experience a sharp decline relative to the yen and the European currencies. If that happened, Argentine products would become much more competitive internationally. But that did not happen. The dollar (and therefore the peso) continued to strengthen in 2000 and 2001.

What was the role of the IMF in all of this? Critics of the fund charge three things: its staff did not adequately warn Argentina of the danger of its policies; it forced Argentina to adopt contractionary policies that led to three years of recession before the crisis hit; and it encouraged the continuation of bad policies by providing a series of large loans.

In reality, the Argentines understood the risk that they were taking at least as well as the IMF staff did. Theirs was a calculated risk that might have produced good results. It is true, however, that the IMF staff did encourage Argentina to continue with the fixed exchange rate and currency board. Although the IMF and virtually all outside economists believe that a floating exchange rate is preferable to a "fixed but adjustable" system, in which the government recognizes that it will have to devalue occasionally, the IMF (as well as some outside economists) came to believe that the currency board system of a firmly fixed exchange rate (a "hard peg," in the jargon of international finance) is a viable long-term policy for an economy. Argentina's experience has proved that belief wrong.

The contractionary policies that Argentina pursued during the past few years were exactly what the currency board system required. They may have been bad and painftil policies, but they were inherent in the currency board approach. The real problem with the IMF "conditionality" in Argentina is that it did not achieve the changes that were really needed, especially the changes in such things as the constitutional revenue-sharing rule and the level of provincial spending that continued to contribute to the budget deficit.

The multi-billion-dollar loans that the IMF gave to Argentina, furthermore, permitted Buenos Aires to postpone dealing with its fundamental problems and abandoning the currency board. The IMF clung too long to the belief that the currency board system was viable. It also wanted to show support for Argentina because of that country's previous shift to favorable market-oriented policies. It should be possible, however, for the IMF to show support for a country's promarket reforms without pouring tens of billions of dollars into a losing battle.

LOOKING AHEAD

What lessons can be learned from the Argentine experience? First, a fixed exchange-rate system, even one based on a currency board or other "hard" fix, is a bad idea that is likely to lead to an overvalued exchange rate, a currency crisis, and widespread defaults. A market-determined floating exchange rate is the only way to avoid these problems.

Second, substantial foreign borrowing in dollars is a very risky strategy. This is particularly true of short-term debt but is also a problem with longer-term borrowing. It is a problem regardless of whether the borrower is the government or the private sector. Other forms of capital inflow, in particular portfolio equity investments and direct investments in plant and equipment, do not raise the problems associated with debt.

Third, the opening of the economy to trade, the encouragement of foreign direct investment, and the privatizing of state-owned firms are desirable policies. Those policies did not cause or contribute to Argentina's crisis, and it would be a serious mistake to reverse them now in Argentina or any other emerging market.

END-OF-CHAPTER QUESTIONS

1. Explain how the Argentinian crisis of 2001 affected its relationship with the US and with the rest of Latin American nations

2. Describe the structural reforms carried out in the country prior to the crisis, during the presidency of Carlos Menem in the 1990s, and whether these reforms played a role in the crisis of the 2000s.
3. Explain how an overvalued fixed exchange rate (locked at one peso per dollar since 1991) and an excessive amount of foreign debt were two of the principal causes of the Argentine crisis.
4. On the fixed exchange rate, why is it that the one-peso-one-dollar fixed rate became out of sync in the late 1990s and into the 2000s? Whose fault was it? Explain your reasoning.
5. What were the consequences of an overvalued peso? Who benefitted, and who got hurt by the 1-to-1 exchange rate between the peso and the dollar?
6. Explain the role that central and provincial governments had in the accumulation of the country's foreign debt.
7. When the peso was finally allowed to float and depreciate in currency markets, explain what happened to the country's balance of trade and why this depreciation caused widespread bankruptcies.
8. What are the three principal reasons often cited to explain why Argentina retained its fixed exchange rate even after most analysts determined that the parity rate had become untenable.
9. Explain the purpose of the so-called "convertibility law" and why this law may have inadvertently placed the government in a fiscal straight jacket.
10. Explain why, in combination with the convertibility law, Argentina adopted a currency board. What golden rule must always be respected in order for a currency board to properly function?
11. Explain how the devaluation of Brazil's real in 1999 and high real wages—supported by strong unions—affected Argentina's competitiveness and may have accelerated the country's currency crisis.
12. Describe the reasons why Argentina finally defaulted on its foreign debt in December of 2001, and explain the immediate consequences of the default.
13. What role did the IMF play during and after the crisis finally ended in late 2002? Is it reasonable to think that the IMF's loans worsened the problem of moral hazard and, hence, contributed to deepening the crisis in the country? Explain your reasoning.
14. What are the most important lessons that come from the Argentina experience?

PART IV

The Recent Financial Crisis

READINGS

DEEPAK LAL (2010)
The Great Crash of 2008: Causes and Consequences

ROSA LASTRA AND GEOFFREY WOOD (2010)
The Crisis of 2007–09: Nature, Causes, and Reactions

CHAPTER 10

The Great Crash of 2008: Causes and Consequences

Deepak Lal

In the early 1980s, I was working as the research administrator at the World Bank, while the Third World was engulfed by a debt crisis. The current global financial crisis has eerie similarities, but different outcomes. Why?

First, both the crises arose because there was a surplus of savings in a number of countries—the oil producers in the 1970s, the Asian economies and commodity exporters today—which was recycled through the international banking system. Second, highly liquid banks imprudently funneled cheap credit to uncreditworthy borrowers: the fiscally challenged and inflation-prone countries of Latin America and Africa in the 1970s, the *ninja* (those with no income, no jobs, no assets) subprime mortgagees of the current crisis. Third, there was a rise in commodity prices and a worsening of the terms of trade of the OECD, posing the stagflation dilemma for their central banks, having aided and abetted the earlier asset boom. Fourth, the imprudent banks sought bailouts from taxpayers, claiming their demise would fatally damage the world's financial system.

But, the outcomes have been different. The 1980s crisis was finally solved after a prolonged cat-and-mouse game when the banks accepted substantial write-downs of their Third World debt, sacked their imprudent mangers, and shareholders suffered large losses. But no systemic threat to the world's financial system (or the global economy) emerged. By contrast, today the Western financial system seems to be dissolving before our eyes, and with the U.S. Federal Reserve's ever expanding balance sheet, bailouts are no longer the exception but the norm. Many now foretell a deep and perhaps prolonged recession, with deflation, rising unemployment, and Keynes' famed liquidity trap about to engulf the world's major economies.

CHANGING FINANCIAL STRUCTURES

What explains this difference in outcomes? It cannot be purported "global imbalances," which were the origins of both crises. It is the differences in financial structures within which these temporally separated but largely similar crises occurred. In the 1970s the recycling of the global surpluses was undertaken by the offshore branches of Western money center banks, which were neither supervised nor had access to the lender of last resort facilities of their parent country's

Deepak Lal, "The Great Crash of 2008: Causes and Consequences," *Cato Journal*, vol. 30, no. 2, pp. 265-277.

central bank. Hence, when their Third World Euro dollar loans went into "default," there was no direct threat to the Western banking system.

The present crisis emerged in a radically different financial structure: the rise of universal banks from the United Kingdom's "Big Bang" financial liberalization in the 1980s, and the Clinton era abolition of the Glass-Steagall Act, which had kept a firewall between the commercial and investment banking parts of the financial system since the 1930s. The former had implicit deposit insurance and access to the central banks' lender of last resort facilities. The latter did not. It is worth explaining why this matters.

This distinction between what were previously nonbank financial intermediaries and banks is important because it is only clearing banks that can add to (or reduce) the stock of money. A clearing bank holds deposits in cash (legal tender base money) from nonbanks, repaying deposits in notes and making payments for depositors by settlements in cash through an account in the central bank. When a clearing bank extends a loan it adds to its assets and simultaneously creates deposit liabilities against itself, increasing the broad money supply at "the stroke of a pen." This ability to create money out of thin air is limited by the bank's capital and cash. As cash can be borrowed from the central bank, the ultimate constraint on its ability to create money is its capital. But it is only because banks take in cash deposits—Keynes's "widow's cruse"—that they can create money.

By contrast, a nonbank financial intermediary, say a mortgage lender, when it takes deposits or makes a mortgage loan has to "clear" these through deposits held at the clearing banks. Thus, when someone deposits "cash" at an S&L, this comes out of the depositor's bank account with a clearing bank. Similarly, when the S&L makes a loan to a mortgagee, this comes from the S&L's bank account with a clearing bank. Thus, the essential difference between nonbank financial institutions and clearing banks is that they cannot create the bank deposit component of broad money (M2 or M4).

When the FDIC was created as part of Roosevelt's New Deal to prevent the bank runs that the earlier universal banks' gambling had engendered, Marriner Eccles, who redesigned the Federal Reserve system for FDR in the Great Depression, insisted that with deposit insurance the banking industry must be split in half: the public utility part of the financial system, which constitutes the payments system, must be kept separate from the gambling investment banking part, which is an essential part of a dynamic economy. For these gambles impart the dynamic efficiency through the cleansing processes of creative destruction. But if these gambles are protected against losses by taxpayers, as the payment system activities have to be because of deposit insurance, the gamblers will always win: keeping their gains when their gambles are correct and passing their losses onto taxpayers when their gambles turn sour. Hence, the Glass-Steagall Act.

Given this "moral hazard," many classical liberals have favored free banking. Banks combining the payment and investment functions and issuing their own notes should be *monitored by their depositors*, who would stand to lose if their banks undertook imprudent lending. But with the near universality of deposits as a means of payment, there is little likelihood of this monitoring function being effectively exercised. While the rise of Demos precludes any government being able to resist pressures to bail out imprudent banks to protect their depositors. This makes deposit insurance inevitable, and to prevent investment banks from gambling with the taxpayer insured deposit base, something akin to Glass-Steagall remains essential.

POLICY ERRORS

The recent emergence of universal banking was followed by a number of public policy mistakes on the path to the current crisis. The *first* was the bailout of LTCM in 1998. Its failure posed no obvious systemic threat. Its public salvation changed expectations of market participants that nonbank financial institutions could also hope for bailouts. Next, the infamous Greenspan "put," which put a floor to the unwinding of the dotcom stock market bubble, promoted excessive risk taking. Third, the promotion of "affordable" housing for the poor by the Clinton administration, through the unreformed and failed Freddie mortgage twins, led to the development of sub-prime mortgages. Fourth, the Basle II capital adequacy requirements led banks to put their risky assets into off-balance sheet vehicles—the structured investment vehicles or SIVs—leading to the opacity currently being bemoaned. Fifth, when the housing bubble burst, and the credit crunch began with the gambles taken during it turning sour, the Fed chose to bail out Bear Sterns, sending the signal that the Fed's balance sheet was open to nondeposit taking "banks" as signaled by the earlier LTCM bailout. Sixth, and most heinously given all that had gone before, the U.S. authorities then chose *not* to bail out Lehman's—like a fallen woman suddenly finding virtue. This dashing of the bailout expectations that the authorities had endorsed only in the spring, led to the intensification of the credit crunch. Seventh, as the authorities finally seemed to tackle the toxic subprime infected financial assets that caused the crisis through TARP, it calmed the markets. When TARP was changed to be used only to recapitalize banks, markets went into free fall. The essential step, of forcing banks to come clean on their balance sheets, and then removing the toxic assets they reveal into a newly created institutional *cordon sanitaire,* has still not been taken. Worse, instead of recreating a firewall between the payment part and the gambling part of the banking system, even the pure investment banks, like Goldman Sachs, were pushed into becoming universal banks with access to the Fed's balance sheet and thence taxpayer's money.[1]

Given these public shortcomings, the near universal calls for greater regulation and state intervention is astounding. Public agents, not private ones—who reacted rationally to the implicit or explicit "rules of the game" promoted—are to blame for the crisis. It would be foolish to blame the puppets for the failings of the puppeteer.

1 The recent embrace by President Obama of the Volcker Rule, which seeks to create a new Glass-Steagall type firewall between investment and commercial banks, is a step in the right direction in my view. But it remains to be seen whether it will be passed by a Congress facing intensive lobbying against it by Wall Street.

REMEDIES

What of the remedies? In answering this question, it is essential to be clear about the nature of the crisis, and to view it from the correct theoretical perspective. Because of the association of Keynes's name with the Great Depression, the crisis and its cures are being seen through "crass Keynesian" lenses. Is this appropriate? To answer this question, I briefly outline the alternative theoretical perspectives, which seek to explain the current crisis as well as the remedies.

Here a personal note is in order. When I got my first academic job as a lecturer at Christ Church, Oxford, my senior colleague was Sir Roy Harrod—Keynes's first biographer and keeper of his flame. On having to provide a reading list for my tutorials on "economic fluctuations and growth," I asked him what I should ask my pupils to read. I expected him to say Keynes, and his own work on trade cycles and growth. But after some reflection he said: Wicksell. So before I prescribed this to my pupils, I immersed myself in *Interest and Prices* and *Lectures on Political Economy*. Since then I have been pleasantly surprised that most of the macro economic perspectives on offer really hark back to Wicksell.[2]

Wicksell asked: How could the price level be anchored in a pure credit economy? Bagehot had observed in *Lombard Street* that the whole of the Bank of England's note issue depended on a slender and declining gold ratio. What if this ratio went to zero? asked Wicksell. His answer was that, if the Bank rate were set at the *natural* rate of interest, which balances productivity with thrift, the price level could be kept constant. This is, of course, the theory underlying inflation targeting, as embodied in the Taylor Rule. As John Taylor (2009) has noted, it was the failure of the Greenspan Fed to follow this rule that led to the credit bubble after the dotcom bust.

The reasons for this failure are provided by Hayek's refurbished Austrian theory of the trade cycle. Hayek saw divergences between the Wicksellian natural and market rates of interest as causing booms and slumps. If increased bank credit led to market interest rates below the natural rate, businesses will undertake relatively more capital-intensive projects with relatively low rates of return. There will also be an unsustainable boom, with more projects undertaken than can be completed, leading to resource scarcities that end the boom. The financial crash which follows will lead to the liquidation of these "maladjustments," followed by an economic recovery with resources being reallocated in line with intertemporal consumer preferences and resource availabilities. While broadly accepting the quantity theory of money, Hayek argues that it assumed the absence of "injection" effects, which even with prices stable could lead to false signals in the pattern of intertemporal prices, and thence to maladjusted investments. The recent U.S. housing boom, with a stable general price level, provides an example of these maladjustments.

But Hayek's prescription that the slump should be allowed to run its course came to be disowned even by his LSE circle led by Robbins in the 1930s. As Gottfried Haberler (1986: 422), a close friend and member of Hayek's Austrian circle, noted in his astute appraisal of Hayek's business cycle theory: "Keynes, Robbins, and many others were correct: if a cyclical decline has

2 The following section has benefited from a paper by my UCLA colleague Axel Leijonhufvud (2009). I had in Lal (1995) applied the Wicksellian theory to examine alternative monetary regimes for Brazil.

been allowed to degenerate into a severe slump with mass unemployment, falling prices, and deflationary expectations, government deficit spending to inject money directly into the income stream is necessary. Moreover, Hayek himself has changed his mind on this point."

Though Keynes, unlike Hayek, provides no explanation for the boom preceding the slump, he was right in emphasizing "effective demand" failures in the face of a financial crash, and the need for deficit spending. Though not, as advocated by many current Keynesians, through counter cyclical public works. Thus, Keynes (1942: 122) wrote: "Organized public works at home and abroad, maybe the right cure for a chronic tendency to a deficiency of effective demand. But they are not capable of sufficiently rapid organization (and above all cannot be reversed or undone at a later date), to be the most serviceable instrument for the prevention of the trade cycle." A point reinforced by the Congressional Budget Office's assessment of the planned Obama infrastructure spending.

Friedman, unlike Hayek, was closer to Wicksell in concentrating on the effects of divergences between the natural and market rate of interest on the *general* price level and not as Hayek's theory presupposes on *relative* prices. With the *real* (natural) rate being determined by productivity and thrift, monetary expansion will only raise nominal interest rates through inflationary expectations. Given the natural rate of interest, there will also be a corresponding *natural rate of unemployment.* Monetary policy can only lead to transitory deviations from these natural rates, if capital and labor markets are efficient. There is little about credit markets in Friedman, or in his successors of the New Classical and Real Business cycle schools. As the current New Neoclassical synthesis is based on these models (with some twists of Keynesian "imperfections"), but contains neither money nor finance, it is useless in explaining or providing curcs for the current crisis.

Thus, though Hayek provides the best diagnosis of the cause of the current crisis, neither he nor Keynes provides an adequate explanation of the financial aspects of business cycles, assuming these are endogenous to the fluctuations in the real economy. It is Irving Fisher who provides the correct diagnosis of the nature and cures for the current crisis. Fisher saw a "balance sheet recession" as an essential element in the Great Depression. He argued that, while there were many cyclical factors behind trade cycles, for Great Depressions the two dominant factors are "*over-indebtedness* to start with and *deflation* following soon after" (Fisher 1933: 341). Like the Austrians, he saw over-indebtedness as caused by "easy money" (p. 348). This provides a succinct explanation of the current crisis and pointers to its cure. We have a Hayekian recession with Fisherian consequences.[3]

Having learned the lessons of Friedman and Schwartz's work on the Great Depression, Ben Bernanke has made sure that the second leg of a Fisherian debt deflation will not occur. But, past and present U.S. authorities have failed to adequately restore the balance sheets of over-leveraged banks, firms, and households. U.S. banks urgently need to be restored to health, perhaps through temporary nationalization as in Sweden in 1992.[4] Meanwhile, stimulus packages have failed to

3 This was also my diagnosis of the Japanese slump in Lal (2003).

4 Though there is considerable doubt that it would work in the much larger and more diverse U.S. market. Also public choice rightly warns us not to rely on nationalization: witness the continuing travails of AIG and Freddie Mac and Fannie Mae.

adopt the obvious means to restore household and firm balance sheets—namely, by a massive across-the-board tax cut accompanied by an equivalent fiscal deficit. It is argued that most of this extra income will be saved not spent. But this is to be bewitched by the wholly inappropriate Keynesian income-expenditure analysis, which fails to deal with balance sheets. If this Fisherian aftermath of a Hayekian recession is caused by attempts to reduce unsustainable debt, the "savings" generated by the tax cut (i.e., reducing liabilities to the government)[5] will allow the necessary deleveraging, without a downward spiral in income and increased bankruptcies. By facilitating households to pay off their mortgage and credit card debts, it will prevent further impairment of bank assets.[6] Instead, we have the dog's breakfast of the Obama stimulus package and a dubious Geithner "plan" to clean up the banking sector. This, like Nero, is to fiddle while Rome burns.

A NEW FINANCIAL OLIGARCHY?

Finally, I want to consider who are the winners from this ongoing global financial crisis. The answer is: China, India, and Goldman Sachs!

Let us consider the latter. This also provides a clue to the political economy behind the current crisis in its epicenter—the United States. As in the numerous Third World financial crises, the question to be asked is: Who are the "rent-seekers" who created the crisis, and whose reluctance to take a "haircut" prevents the domestic polity from accepting the obvious cures? So that, ultimately, the intervention of an external agency like the IMF is needed to administer the necessary cures.

The current crisis was caused by financiers taking ever more risky gambles with the complicity of the government. This is reflected in the changing share of U.S. domestic corporate profits that have gone to the financial sector. From 1973 to 1985, it was 16 percent. In the 1990s, it oscillated between 21 and 30 percent. In the last decade it reached 41 percent. This was accompanied by a dramatic increase in pay, which rose from 108 percent of the average for all domestic private industries in 1999 to 181 percent in 2007. This great increase and concentration of wealth has created a new financial oligarchy similar to the one in the early years of the last century, which has great political weight in the United States. At its head is Goldman Sachs. It has provided the Treasury secretaries under the last two U.S. presidents and numerous alumni have held and continue to hold influential posts in devising and implementing U.S. economic policy (see Johnson 2009).

5 Unlike the 1930s, governments in developed countries have much more leeway to do this as the share of general government revenue (their tax cut) as a share of GDP had increased from about 20 percent in the United States and Great Britain to about 32 percent in the United States and 38 percent in Britain in 1997 (Tanzi and Schuknecht 2000: 52).

6 As Guha (2009: 9) reported, the parts of the Obama stimulus package that have worked were the "fast acting tax breaks and transfer payments [that] largely explain why disposable income rose 2.9 percent from January to May, even as earned income fell 0.7 percent, allowing the savings rate to rise without a collapse in spending." If the whole of the $787 billion stimulus package had consisted of an across-the-board tax cut, there would have been a large deleveraging of the economy with an increase in private savings without an equivalent cut in private spending—the increased private savings being matched by public dis-savings reflected in the increased budget deficit. Also the tax cut could be reversed once the economy recovered, providing an easy "exit strategy" from the fiscal stimulus.

This explains some of the bailouts. Why for instance was Lehman allowed to go the wall but AIG was "saved"? Lehman had the misfortune of both being a major competitor to Goldman's and being run and staffed by the "barrow boys" from the Bronx rather than the Ivy League gentlemen manning its rival. AIG was saved, I suspect because, as appeared when Congress forced AIG to disclose what it had done with its bailout money, it had to disclose that most if it was to pay off its counter-parties, the major one being Goldman! It is ironic that just as the century-old rise, decline, and now fall of GM, which marked the era of American industrial ascendancy, with one of its chairman claiming that "what was good for GM was good for America," should now be followed by an era in which seemingly "what is good for Goldman is good for America," or more generally Wall Street.

GEOPOLITICAL CONSEQUENCES

What of China and India? Though their growth rates have fallen with the backwash from the U.S. crisis on global trade, they are still likely to grow robustly. This suggests some important geopolitical consequences of the current crisis.

The last two centuries have been dominated by two Anglo-Saxon empires—the British and the United States—whose liberal international economic orders have allowed the wholly benign processes of globalization to bring untold global prosperity (Lal 2004, 2006). The interwar imperial interregnum saw a period of grave disorder and the emergence of fascism and communism. Today, will the United States be able and willing to maintain its hegemony, allowing globalization to continue?

On October 10, 1916, in the middle of a British financial crisis, Keynes wrote a memorandum to the Treasury, noting that financial hegemony had passed across the Atlantic (Skidelsky 1983: 335).[7] Is the collapse of Lehman Brothers on September 15, 2008, a similar turning point? For with the three high-savings countries—China, Japan, and India—as the major source of funding for the exploding U.S. public debt, will the United States have to adopt the policy Keynes recommended for Britain: "not only to avoid any form of reprisal or even active irritation but also to conciliate and please?" And which of these countries is likely to replace or help U.S. hegemony?

Japan because of its continuing reluctance to match its economic with military power and with its stagnant economy and demographics is an unlikely candidate. This leaves the two emerging Asian giants.

China, which has signaled that it is not planning to sell its holdings of U.S. debt, along with the Gulf State sovereign funds, is the most likely source of finance for the exploding U.S. budget deficit. So expect talk of Chinese "currency manipulation" and lectures on human rights to diminish as the U.S. *faut mieux* has to follow Keynes' advice. Though, at present, it is impossible for China to take over America's hegemonic role, it will undoubtedly have increasing leverage over U.S. foreign and domestic policy as the financier of the United States.

7 It however took another 40 years and another World War for the United States to replace Britain as the world's financial hegemon.

This is likely to make the U.S. war against the current totalitarian threat from militant Islam more difficult. For given China's desire to assure supplies of primary products—particularly oil—for its rapid industrialization, China's foreign policy is unlikely to antagonize many natural resource producing countries, like Iran and Sudan, which continue to aid and abet international terrorism. Nor, given China's historical support of the current crucible of jihadists, Pakistan, as a counterweight to its emerging Asian rival, India, can much help be expected in this quarter.

This leaves India, which even more than the United States (as the Mumbai attacks demonstrated), has to fear the rise of militant Islam and the impending implosion of the Pakistani state. George W. Bush's most notable achievement was the strategic partnership he established with India, cemented by the Indo-U.S. nuclear deal. But India's economic and military power is at present dwarfed by China's. It is unlikely to be able to take over the U.S. burden.

In many ways it would be the natural partner of the United States with its large army to accompany the technological wizardry of the U.S. military. But is it able or willing to take on the role of a partner in the U.S. Imperium? This is unlikely. For though it also faces the threat from militant Islam, the fear that its large indigenous minority Muslim population, which hitherto has been largely uninfected by jihadism, could be radicalized if Indian troops were actively participating in the "war on terror," would lead it to forbear.

Meanwhile, as the other potential partners of the United States in sharing its imperial burden—the Europeans—have (apart form the British) clearly signaled, with their refusal to send more troops to Afghanistan, that they are going to continue to be free riders, the United States stands alone in maintaining global order. Will the aftermath of the current crisis leave it with the means and will to do so?

The parallel with Rome is instructive. The causes of Rome's decline were ultimately economic. As the past rents acquired during the empire's growth had been in part committed to a vast expansion of a welfare state without extending the domestic tax base, the empire faced an endemic fiscal crisis. It tried to close the deficit by levying the inflation tax by debasing the currency. Not being enough, taxes had to be raised, leading by the middle of the fourth century to tax evasion and avoidance by high officials and large landowners. The fiscal crisis also led to problems in maintaining the old military organization. Without the means to provide the *Italici* satisfactory treatment, recruitment was expanded to the provincials and in the late Empire to the barbarians. Having let them inside the gates the empire sealed its doom.

That the U.S. Imperium is on a similar primrose path was pointed out in a dire warning by the former U.S. comptroller general David Walker in August 2007, when the U.S. budget deficit was only projected to be under $500 billion. He explicitly drew parallels with Rome, including "declining moral values and political civility at home, an over confident and over extended military in foreign lands and fiscal irresponsibility by the central government" (Grant, 2007).

This irresponsibility has increased manifold with the current crisis. The 2007 GAO budget report (Walker 2007: 6) noted that it was primarily the health entitlements that made the U.S. budget unsustainable. This is the entitlement Obama is planning to enlarge. Walker also warned that the crisis could not be solved by growing out of the problem, eliminating earmarks, wiping out fraud, ending the Iraq war or cutting defense expenditures, restraining discretionary spending or letting the Bush tax cuts expire (Walker 2007: 18). These are the very policies that Obama is hoping will reverse exploding future deficits. With projected reductions in military spending, it seems likely that the United States like its Roman predecessor will find it difficult to maintain the sinews of the forces that have maintained global order. With no obvious alternative to provide this global public good, I fear the ensuing erosion of global order, so essential for the processes of globalization to work, is likely to be the most serious long-term consequence of the global financial crisis.

REFERENCES

Fisher, I (1933) "The Debt-Deflation Theory of Great Depressions." *Econometrica* 1 (4): 337–57.

Grant, J. (2007) "Learn from the Fall of Rome, U.S. Warned." *Financial Times* (14 August).

Guha, K. (2009) "White House Hit in Skirmishes over Spending." *Financial Times* (9 July): 9.

Haberler, G. (1986) "Reflections on Hayek's Business Cycle Theory." *Cato Journal* 6 (2): 421–35.

Johnson, S. (2009) "The Quiet Coup." *The Atlantic* (May). Available at www.theatlantic.com/doc/200905/imf-advice#at.

Keynes, J. M. (1944) *Collected Writings of John Maynard Keynes,* vol. 27: *Activities 1940–46: Shaping the Postwar World.* Edited by D. E. Moggridge. Cambridge: Cambridge University Press.

Lal, D. (1995) "Notes on Money, Debt and Alternative Monetary Regimes for Brazil." *Revista de Economica Politica* 15(4): 99–111.

_________ (2003) "The Japanese Slump." In R. Pethig and M. Rauscher (eds.) *Challenges to the World Economy.* Berlin: Springer.

_________ (2004) *In Praise of Empires: Globalization and Order.* New York: Palgrave-Macmillan.

_________ (2006) *Reviving the Invisible Hand.* Princeton, N.J.: Princeton University Press.

Leijonhufvud, A. (2009) "Wicksell, Hayek, Keynes, Friedman: Whom Should We Follow?" Paper presented at the Special Meeting of the Mont Pelerin Society, "The End of Globalizing Capitalism? Classical Liberal Responses to the Global Financial Crisis," New York (March).

Skidelsky, R. ([1983]1994) *John Maynard Keynes: Volume 1: Hopes Betrayed, 1883–1920.* London: Macmillan; New York: Penguin Books.

Tanzi, V., and Schuknecht, L. (2000) *Public Spending in the 20th Century.* Cambridge: Cambridge University Press.

Taylor J. B. (2009) *Getting Off Track: How Government Actions and Interventions Caused, Prolonged and Worsened the Financial Crisis.* Stanford, Calif.: Hoover Institution Press.

Walker D. M. (2007) "Long-Term Budget Outlook: Deficits Matter—Saving Our Future Requires Tough Choices Today." U.S. Government Accountability Office, Testimony before the Committee on the Budget, House of Representatives, GAO-07-389T. Available at www.gao.gov/new.items/d07389t.pdf.

END-OF-CHAPTER QUESTIONS

1. Explain four principal similarities between the recent financial crisis of the late 2000s and the debt crisis in the developing world during the 1980s.
2. What are the principal differences between these two financial crises? Why was the recent financial crisis considered to be a systemic threat to the world financial system, whereas, the crisis in the 1980s never quite rose to that threat level?

3. Why was the Fed engulfed in a so-called liquidity trap through early in 2016? What exactly is a liquidity trap?
4. In the late 1990s, the Clinton Administration abolished the Glass-Steagall Act. What were the major provisions of this act, and why was it enacted in the 1933? Why was it mostly abolished in 1999, with the passing of the Gramm-Leach-Bliley Act? Do you think the abolition of the Glass-Steagall Act contributed to the financial crisis during the late 2000s? Explain your answer.
5. Explain how traditional banking institutions—those that accept deposits and make loans—are able to create money with "the stroke of a pen."
6. The rationale for the Glass-Steagall Act and for the creation of the FDIC insurance program was that the public-utility part of the financial system had to be kept separate from the gambling-investment part. Explain the meaning of this assertion.
7. Explain the concept of "free banking" and whether this theoretical possibility has any real chance to be implemented in today's world.
8. The author mentions several policy errors that, in his view, contributed to the crisis in the 2000s. Briefly, comment on how the bailout of Long-Term Capital Management (LTCM) in 1998 is considered the initial error that preceded the crisis.
9. A second policy error concerns Alan Greenspan's "put," which put a floor to the unwinding of the dotcom stock market bubble. Explain why, according to the author, this was a second policy error.
10. His next target is the Clinton Administration promotion of affordable housing for the poor. How and why is this a policy error for the author?
11. Basle II capital adequacy requirements is also listed as a (international) policy error. Explain how these adequacy requirements are related to the financial crisis of the 2000s.
12. The bailing out of Bear Sterns and, then, the bankruptcy of Lehman Brothers are also considered grave policy errors but for different reasons. Why are these two events considered policy errors by the author?
13. The Trouble-Asset-Relief Program (TARP) is also considered a significant policy error that deepened the financial crisis. Why does the author think so?
14. Explain the so-called Volcker Rule and how its application may decrease the problem of moral hazard in financial markets.
15. What is the Taylor rule, and why does the author think that Greenspan's inability to adhere to this rule led to the credit bubble after the dotcom bust.
16. As part of the solutions for the crisis, the author argues that the balance sheet of all economic agents—banks, firms, and households—urgently need to be restored to health. With banks, he even argues for temporary nationalizations. What exactly does he mean by this?
17. Who, according to the author, are the winners of the crisis, what he calls the new financial oligarchy? Why does he think so?

CHAPTER 11

The Crisis of 2007–09: Nature, Causes, and Reactions

Rosa M. Lastra and Geoffrey Wood

ABSTRACT

This article analyses the nature and causes of the financial crisis of 2007–09 as well as the regulatory responses. There are two types of crises: banking crises, which affect the money stock and thus threaten the economy, and financial crises, which may destroy wealth but do not endanger the economy as a whole. Banking crises can be precipitated by a shortage of capital or by a shortage of liquidity. The 2007–09 crisis was a banking crisis, caused by a capital shortage. Numerous explanations have been given for this crisis. In this article these explanations are organized into ten groups. The main factors were easy money, excessive leverage, risk-management failures, bad lending, too-big-to-fail (TBTF) policies, inadequate supervision, and ill-thought-out regulation. The flurry of responses to the crisis is then summarized. Some are welcome, but the article concludes that unless the fear of failure returns to banking, so that management, shareholders, bondholders, and all creditors (except small depositors) suffer in a failure, then all other reforms will ultimately be pointless.

I. INTRODUCTION

Financial crises are of two types: liquidity crises and capital crises. One type rapidly merges with the other, so that beyond the initial stage of a crisis there are both liquidity and capital problems, but it is useful to start with a sharp distinction. That will help us to examine the numerous explanations given for the crisis of 2007–09.[1]

A. A LIQUIDITY CRISIS

A liquidity crisis is what might be described as the classic type of banking crisis: a bank for some reason cannot meet all its payment obligations. Given the imperfect knowledge that customers have of their banks, and the links through the interbank market and the payment system, other banks experience runs. These other banks get into difficulties because, by the nature of fractional

1 This does not mean that the crisis ended in 2009, but that financial sector difficulties ceased to be acute. That said, in 2009 and 2010, the crisis eventually mutated into a sovereign debt crisis in some countries.

Rosa M. Lastra and Geoffrey Wood, "The Crisis of 2007–09: Nature, Causes, and Reactions," *Journal of International Economic Law*, vol. 13, no. 3, pp. 531-550.

reserve banking, they cannot immediately pay out on all deposits. In the extreme the entire banking system collapses like a row of dominoes.[2]

It is a liquidity crisis that is modelled in the famous Diamond and Dybvig paper.[3] It could not be otherwise, for their model of a bank is of a bank without capital (and, incidentally, in a world without money). Nevertheless that model does describe one of the most famous banking crises in history—that which occurred in England at the outbreak of the wars with France in 1793. That crisis has become famous partly because, thanks to Francis Baring, it led to the emergence of the term 'lender of last resort' or *dernier resort*.[4] The concept was developed by Henry Thornton (1802)[5] and further explained by Walter Bagehot, notably in his book Lombard Street (1873)[6] but also in his journalism in The Economist and elsewhere. How a lender of last resort operation by the central bank can stop a liquidity crisis and, indeed, what consitutes a liquidity crisis, is best clarified by two quotations. In 1802, Thornton explains that: 'If any bank fails, a general run upon the neighbouring banks is apt to take place, which if not checked in the beginning by a pouring into the circulation of a very large quantity of gold, leads to very extensive mischief'.[7]

Bagehot in 1873 explained why this policy worked: 'What is wanted and what is necessary to stop a panic is to diffuse the impression that though money may be dear, money is still to be had. If people could really be convinced that they would have money . . . they would cease to run in such a herd-like way for money'.[8] A liquidity crisis, then, originates with a sudden demand for cash—for central bank money, to use the modern term. Fractional reserve banks by their nature cannot meet this demand. So unless the central bank meets it, many, perhaps all, banks in a system may fail.

---

2 Gary Gorton believes that it was the [wholesale] run on the sale-and-repurchase market (the repo market) during 2008, a bank run not so much on depository institution, but on the shadow banking system, which caused the crisis. In Gary Gorton and Andrew Metrick, 'Securitized Banking and the Run on the Repo', National Bureau of Economic Research Working Paper No w15223, August 2009, http://papers.ssrn.com/sol3/papers.cfm?abstract_id = 1454939 (visited 9 August 2010), the authors argue that the panic of 2007–08 was a run on the repo market which is a very large short-term market that provides financing for a wide range of securitization activities and financial institutions. Repo transactions are collateralized, frequently with securitized bonds. They refer to the combination of securitization plus repo finance as securitized banking, and argue that these activities were at the nexus of the crisis. Concerns about the liquidity of markets for the bonds used as collateral led to increases in repo haircuts—the amount of collateral required for any given transaction. With declining asset values and increasing haircuts, the US banking system was, the authors suggest, effectively insolvent. Although the authors single out the repo market, other markets, such as the commercial paper market, also suffered a run.

3 Douglas W. Diamond and Philip H. Dybvig, 'Bank Runs, Deposit Insurance and Liquidity', 91(3) Journal of Political Economy 401 (1983).

4 See Francis Baring, *Observations on the Establishment of the Bank of England and on the Paper circulation of the Country*, 1797 ed. (New York: A.M. Kelly, facsimile reprint 1967) 19–23. Baring both imported the term *dernier resort* and used it in a new, metaphorical way—in France, *dernier resort* referred to the final court of appeal. It is truly remarkable how accurately Baring's description of the 1793 crisis also describes that of 1929–33 in the USA. That latter episode is discussed further below.

5 Henry Thornton, *An Enquiry into the Nature and Effects of the Paper Credit of Great Britain* (London: J. Hatchard and F. and C. Rivington, 1802).

6 Walter Bagehot, *Lombard Street: A Description of the Money Market* (London: Henry S. King & Co., 1873).

7 See Thornton, above n 5, at 182.

8 See Bagehot, above n 6, at 63–64.

B. A CAPITAL CRISIS

The second type of crisis is when there is a sharp decline in the value of a bank's capital. This could come about if one large loan suddenly collapsed in value. As bank balance sheets are opaque to customers (and apparently often to management too, judging by recent experience), this leads to fears about the solvency of other banks, runs take place on them, and again in the extreme the whole system fails.[9]

The archetypal capital crisis also occurred in England, but this time in the 19th century. This episode was confined to one bank, and thus was not a banking-system crisis, but it could easily have spread to the entire system and perhaps beyond. This was the 'Baring Crisis' of 1890.

Barings was a bank of high reputation. Driven by competition from newer banks, it had invested substantially in Argentina. In April 1890, the Argentinian government defaulted. Next, and partly in consequence, the Argentinian national bank suspended interest payments on its debts. This precipitated a run on the Argentinian banking system. By November 1890, its directors realized that Barings could not survive unaided, and on 8 November, they revealed this to the Bank of England. The Bank was horrified, fearing a run on the British banking system, and perhaps on sterling, if Barings defaulted. After a hurried inspection of the books of Barings, it was decided that the situation could be saved by an injection of capital. A consortium was organized—the Bank was too small to have sufficient funds on its own—and Barings was saved.

That is a perfect example of a capital crisis. A firm is short of capital and cannot pay its debts. If this brings down other banks, or if depositors in the original bank lose their deposits, a system-wide liquidity crisis may start. But the injection of capital can stop the crisis short. Note that central bank provision of liquidity would not suffice, because, to continue with the example of Barings, Barings did not have the assets to offer in exchange for the capital.

Until the 20th century, only problems in the banking system were regarded as crises. Even the failure of merchant banks (the traditional term in the UK for what are now called investment banks) was not regarded as a crisis unless the event led to a run on the banks whose liabilities were part of the money stock. This view was restated in the 20th century by Anna Schwartz.[10] She distinguished between 'real' and 'pseudo' crises. A real crisis she defined as follows: 'Such a crisis is fuelled by fear that means of payment will be unavailable at any price, and in a fractional reserve banking system leads to a scramble for high powered money'.[11] These real crises are often referred to as 'banking crises'. Pseudo crises, meanwhile, involve 'a decline in asset prices, of equity stock, real estate, commodities; depreciation of the exchange value of the national currency; financial distress of a large non-financial firm, a large municipality, a financial industry, or sovereign debtors'.[12] A common term for such pseudo crises is 'financial crises'.

---

9 These runs may well, in modern circumstances, be what are called 'silent runs'. We set out this concept later, and also propose that a better name might be 'private runs'.

10 Anna J. Schwartz, 'Real and Pseudo-Financial Crises', in Forrest Capie and Geoffrey Wood (eds), *Financial Crises and World Banking Policy* (New York: St. Martin's Press, 1986).

11 Ibid, at 11.

This might seem to suggest that, if we accept Schwartz's definition of a crisis, the failure of investment banks or insurers (such as AIG) is of no importance.[13] But the definition most certainly does not suggest that. Failures of institutions whose liabilities are not part of *any* measure of the money stock matter if they trigger alarm or threats to the stability of the core banking system. For if they do, they can lead quickly to a banking crisis in the strict, Anna Schwartz, sense. They therefore fall within the scope of the present discussion.

With the distinction between the two types of crisis, banking and financial, and the two types of cause, capital and liquidity, clearly in mind, we can proceed to an examination of the 2007–09 crisis.

II. 2007–2009: LIQUIDITY OR CAPITAL?

A comparison between the 2007–09 crisis, the first major banking crisis of the 21st century, and the crisis of 1929–33, the first major banking crisis of the 20th century, helps answer the question.

What was the main cause of the crisis of 1929–33?[14] The US economy started to decline after the 1929 Stock Market Crash. The decline continued until 1933, by which time money income in the USA had fallen by 53% and real income by 36%. There had been wave after wave of bank failures. These did not end until the closure of all banks by President Roosevelt and the suspension of gold shipments abroad on 6 March 1933. Why did these waves of bank failures occur?

There are two primary, competing explanations: (i) banking practices of previous years which saw with banks getting into securities dealings, and (ii) the behaviour of the Federal Reserve. The first explanation has been examined by Peach,[15] Benston,[16] and Kroszner and Rajan,[17] among many others. All found that securities dealing did not bring the banks down. The cause was substantial pressure on bank liquidity, unrelieved by Federal Reserve action. Banks were forced to sell their holdings of government bonds at a big discount, thus adding shortage of capital to shortage of liquidity.

That was manifestly a liquidity crisis in its origin.[18] How did it spread? As the monetary approach to the balance of payments suggests, the monetary squeeze in the USA affected those countries pegged to the US dollar (through gold, at this time) but left countries without such a link substantially unaffected. Countries such as Sweden and the UK, which broke early from the

12 Ibid, at 24.

13 The whole range of definitions of financial stability is reviewed in William A. Allen and Geoffrey Wood, 'Defining and Achieving Financial Stability', 2(2) Journal of Financial Stability 152 (2006). They conclude by essentially concurring with the Schwartz definition.

14 A brief overview of these years can be found in the introductory essay to Forrest Capie and Geoffrey Wood (eds), *Critical Writings on the Great Depression* (Routledge, 2011) (forthcoming).

15 William N. Peach, *The Security Affiliates of National Banks* (Baltimore: Johns Hopkins Press, 1941).

16 George J. Benston, *The Separation of Commercial and Investment Banking: the Glass-Steagall Act Revisited and Reconsidered* (New York: Oxford University Press, 1990).

17 Randall S. Kroszner and Raghuram G. Rajan 'Is the Glass-Steagall Act Justified? A Study of the U.S. Experience with Universal Banking Before 1933', 84(4) The American Economic Review 810 (1994).

18 This is certainly not to deny that the banks also had other problems. Many banks were heavily involved in call loans to the New York Stock Exchange, and when the NYSE broke many of these loans would have gone bad. Thus they would certainly have experienced considerable losses on their earning assets.

gold standard, escaped the US problems, while those which stayed with the gold standard, such as France, experienced banking strains and severe recessions.

How did the recent crisis spread? The contrast with 1929–33 could not be sharper. The recent crisis spread between countries whose exchange rates were floating (the USA and the UK, for example). And it did not spread across all areas that used a single currency—the extreme case of fixed exchange rates—for the banking systems of some countries in the Eurozone were either unaffected or only slightly affected (for example, Finland). The crisis was not triggered by a scramble for liquidity. We can conclude that *the first crisis of the 21st century was a capital crisis, not a liquidity crisis*.[19]

There have been numerous explanations given for this recent crisis. We consider them in turn, and discuss in conclusion some of the consequences of the crisis, the increase in moral hazard and the reduction in competition that the policy response to the crisis has produced. Our starting point is a comparison of the recent crisis with some notable earlier ones. Time has allowed some firm conclusions about the origins of many previous crises, and this can help in understanding the most recent crisis.

III. A BRIEF HISTORICAL ACCOUNT

First, we examine the seasonal and cyclical pattern of early crises. It is widely accepted that in the 19th and early 20th centuries there was a seasonal pattern to banking crises.[20]

The still-accepted explanation for this seasonality is that given by Jevons in 1866. He observed a seasonal pattern, associated with the agricultural cycle, in asset demand. Reserve/deposit ratios for banks fell in the spring and the autumn when there was a seasonal upturn in the demand for both currency and credit. So it was in spring and autumn that banking systems were at their most vulnerable.[21] These were therefore manifestly all liquidity crises. In contrast, there was little cyclical regularity; Gary Gorton[22] found that crises usually occurred at business-cycle peaks, but not by any means at every business-cycle peak.

The East Asian crises of the mid-1990s were certainly not all identical, but they did have common features. There were asset-price booms, followed by crashes, problems in banking

19 Happily, in the 21st century, world trade rules ensured there was no outbreak of protectionism to make the situation worse. The role of protection in spreading the 1929–33 recession has been discussed many times—an outstanding and brief overview can be found in Forrest Capie, *Protection and Depression* (London: Macmillan, 1993). How it impeded recovery in the USA is set out clearly in Allan Meltzer, 'The Smoot Hawley Tariff and Economic Recovery', in Karl Brunner (ed), *The Great Depression Revisited* (London: Nijhoff, 1981, 1982) 148–63. The paper by Michael Gadbaw in this issue at 551–574, considers the role of trade regulation in detail.

20 Jeffrey A. Miron, 'Financial Panics, the Seasonality of the Nominal Interest Rate, and the Founding of the Fed', 76(1) The American Economic Review 125 (1986).

21 The seasonal pattern in interest rates largely vanished when central banks started smoothing the interest-rate cycle. They could do this only after 1914, with the founding of the Federal Reserve, as it was a worldwide cycle.

22 Gary Gorton, 'Banking Panics and Business Cycles', 40 Oxford Economic Papers 221 (1988).

systems, and flight from currencies.[23] The build-up of foreign currency indebtedness was encouraged by the pegged exchange-rate regime. Because of the guarantees, there was both undiversified lending and undiversified borrowing by banks. In addition, again because of the guarantees, the problem was large in scale.

None of the crises so far discussed necessitated an injection of capital.[24] Even the East Asian banks required liquidity, albeit in many cases in a currency their central banks could not supply. But Japan's problems of the 1990s were different and were on an altogether greater scale than those so far discussed. In the Great Depression, US banks lost capital equal to about 3–4% of the 1930 US gross national product (GNP). In the 1990s, Japanese banks lost capital equal to about 15–20% of the 1990 Japanese GNP.[25] Accordingly, the first point to emerge from the historical comparison is that while the recent crisis was not unprecedented, the Japanese crisis would appear to be the only precedent.

The Japanese crisis started with the bursting of an asset bubble at the end of the 1980s and culminated in 1997 with the failure of several major financial institutions. In the second-half of the 1980s, Japan had experienced above-trend growth and near-zero inflation. The resulting optimism led to a surge in the prices of most assets. There was financial market deregulation, and credit standards were eased. The stock market boomed, peaking at the end of 1989. Then the Ministry of Finance introduced limits on bank lending to the real estate sector. There was a fall in property prices and in the stock market. These damaged Japanese banks, since the fall in property prices undermined the real estate companies to which they had lent, and the decline in the value of banks' equity holdings also put pressure on their capital. The entire system was weakened. Then, in November 1997, Sanyo Securities declared bankruptcy. This resulted in Japan's first interbank loan default. Two weeks later Hokkaido Tokushoku was unable to borrow in the interbank market and had to declare bankruptcy—the first failure of a major Japanese bank since World War II. Only a week later Yamaichi Securities, one of the four biggest security dealers in Japan, failed. It soon emerged that the rumours of fraud that had led to its failure were true. Next, before the end of the month, Tokuyo City Bank failed. The three-month Eurodollar Tokyo Interbank Borrowing Rate rose sharply above its London equivalent. Spreads sharply widened in the domestic interbank market, and by late November 1997 some banks were finding even overnight borrowing difficult.

By the end of 1997 the government decided that 'something must be done'. They decided to inject taxpayers' funds, and also approved accounting changes which would allow banks to use either market or book value, whichever they wished, when valuing their share and real estate portfolios. There is plainly much in common between the background circumstances of the Japanese crisis and the recent, more widespread one.[26]

---

23 Ronald I. McKinnon and Huw Pill, 'Exchange-Rate Regimes for Emerging Markets: Moral Hazard and International Overborrowing', 15(3) Oxford Review of Economic Policy 19 (1999).

24 The same is true of the numerous 19th-century banking crises in France, and those in Italy from the middle of the 19th to the early 20th century.

25 We are indebted to Charles Calomiris of Columbia University for these noteworthy data.

IV. WHY THE RECENT CRISIS?

It is possible to divide the explanations for this crisis into 10 groups. These are not mutually exclusive; all may have played a part: (a) macro-economic imbalances; (b) lax monetary policy; (c) regulatory and supervisory failures; (d) too-big-to-fail (TBTF) doctrine and distorted incentives; (e) excesses of securitization; (f) unregulated firms, lightly regulated firms, and the shadow banking system; (g) corporate governance failures; (h) risk-management failures, excessive leverage, and excessive complexity; (i) the usual suspects: greed, euphoria, and others; and (j) faulty economic theories.

The first four groups of explanations put the blame mainly on the authorities (governments, regulators, central bankers). Groups (e)–(i) blame mainly the markets (financial products, managers, risk, greed, poor lending, leverage). The last group (faulty theories) blames economists.

A. MACROECONOMIC IMBALANCES NOTABLY BETWEEN THE USA AND CHINA

The linkage to trade liberalization and the trade imbalances (the so-called China factor) have been cited as causes of the crisis. 'Credit expansion in the US was financed by countries with sizable current account surpluses, notably China and oil exporting nations'.[27] Although there is nothing unusual about one country wanting to borrow and another to lend, large and persistent imbalances should prompt examination. Accordingly, the role of the IMF in the surveillance of macro-economic policies has come under greater scrutiny since the crisis.

B. LAX MONETARY POLICY IN THE USA AND OTHER COUNTRIES

Easy money and cheap credit fuelled the boom. Interest rates in the USA were for some years below what the Taylor Rule (the rule which has the central bank's policy rate set according to deviations from trend of nominal GNP) implied. The measurement of inflation essentially ignored asset prices, in particular house prices. This led in turn to the ignoring of the 'elephant in the room', the large asset-price bubble, including in particular a nationwide surge in house prices, which eventually burst in August 2007.[28] 'An asymmetric approach to managing interest rates, whereby policy is loosened when asset prices plunge but policymakers remain indifferent to asset prices until they burst' has been cited as a cause of the crisis.[29] In the phrase of the longest-serving chairman of the Federal Reserve (from 1951 to 1970), William McChesney Martin,

---

26 There is also much in common between the official responses to the episodes, but that is not a concern of this article.

27 See House of Lords' European Union Committee, 'The Future of EU Financial Regulation and Supervision', 14th Report of Session 2008–09, 17 June 2009, at 7, http://www.publications.parliament.uk/pa/ld200809/ldselect/ldeucom/106/106i.pdf (visited 9 August 2010).

28 This may be a variant of 'Goodhart's law': that any observed statistical regularity will tend to collapse once pressure is placed upon it for control purposes. See Charles Goodhart, *Monetary Theory and Practice: The UK Experience* (London: MacMillan, 1984) 96. See also Charles Goodhart, 'What Weight Should be Given to Asset Prices in the Measurement of Inflation?', 111(472) The Economic Journal F335 (2001), http://www.jstor.org/stable/2667880 (visited 9 August 2010).

'the role of the central bank is to take away the punch bowl just when the party is going'. Not, let it be emphasized, when the hangover has taken hold.

C. FAILURES OF REGULATION AND FAILURES OF SUPERVISION

There were plenty of regulatory and supervisory failures (as well as a degree of regulatory capture or, at the very least, excessive group-think). Rules regarding capital proved inadequate; accounting rules exacerbated problems; and the absence of rules on liquidity was unfortunate. Indeed, capital and accounting regulations actually made things worse by being procyclical, with rules on risk-weighting capital combining with mark-to-market accounting to reduce requirements in good times and raise them sharply in bad.[30] And the most glaring mistake and omission is that there was no appropriate legal framework to deal with cross-border financial crises. Supervision failed at the level of individual institutions (AIG being a notable example) and at the systemic level, where systemic risk considerations were not properly taken into account.

D. THE TBTF DOCTRINE AND DISTORTED INCENTIVES

The belief that some institutions were too-big-to-fail (and belief too in its variants, too interconnected to fail, too complex to fail, too many to fail) and other distorted incentives (a system that rewards short-term profits at the expense of long-term stability) triggered—and continue to trigger—huge moral hazard incentives. Huertas[31] has pointed out that the sudden and unpredictable reversal in resolution policy that marked the failure of Lehman Brothers profoundly changed market expectations and led to a general flight to quality. As straight after AIG was bailed out and a couple of weeks before Lehman Brothers failed, Fannie Mae and Freddie Mac had received support, and TBTF expectations were inflamed. The sudden change exacerbated instability in the financial system. This illustrates the need to remove or properly price the implicit guarantee that TBTF institutions (both banks and 'systemically significant' financial institutions) at the moment enjoy.[32]

---

29 See John Plender, 'Just Targeting Symptoms of the Crisis is too Neat', *Financial Times*, 25 February 2010.

30 The combination of Basel II and mark-to-market fair value accounting was almost a doomsday machine in itself—both reducing capital requirements under the wrong assumption that the system was extremely strong at the end of the asset price boom, and then reversing horribly during the crash.

31 Thomas Huertas, 'Resolution as a Source of Contagion', presented at the Financial Markets Group and Bank of England conference on Sources of Contagion, 25–26 February 2010, London. See also Thomas Huertas, *Crisis: Cause, Containment and Cure* (Basingstoke: Palgrave Macmillan, 2010).

32 Some authors have warned about the systemic impact of 'too-safe-to-fail' transactions (such as repo transactions), suggesting that macro-prudential supervision should be more concerned about 'seemingly fail-safe assets' which are typically beyond the radar of micro-prudential supervision. See Viral Acharya, 'Why Bankers Must Bear the Risk of "Too Safe to Fail" Assets', *Financial Times*, 18 March 2010: 'If a financial activity is viable only if its systemic risk must be borne by society while its profits in good times remain privatised in the financial sector, then it is time to revisit the desirability of the activity in the first place'.

E. EXCESSES OF SECURITIZATION

This was the 'causa proxima' of the crisis. The securitization market grew, encouraged by: accounting and capital rules, financial innovation, government housing and lending policies to encourage home ownership amongst the poor or less prosperous (sub-prime), mortgage policies and mortgage regulation (in the USA and in the UK) that proved inadequate given what some institutions did, the ratings method that ratings agencies applied to securitized products, and the reliance on those ratings both for regulatory purposes and as a substitute for due diligence by the financial institutions themselves. The term 'securitization' is often used as a shorthand for all these various factors—government policies, regulatory actions, and behaviour of the private sector—that combined to cause the securitization bubble. Much has been written about this, since the problems that commenced in the summer of 2007 were clearly related to the securitization market. But it would be wrong to describe securitization—a technique needed to bring market liquidity—as 'the cause' of the crisis. The mortgage market in the USA and its associated credit ratings were premised on the fact that there had been no significant fall in house prices *nationwide* in 50 years of data, and such a decline occurred.

F. THE PART PLAYED BY DERIVATIVES MARKETS, UNREGULATED FIRMS, LIGHTLY REGULATED FIRMS, AND THE SHADOW BANKING SYSTEM

The common denominator of these firms, markets, and products that now constitute a major part of the financial system is their lighter regulatory, clearing, and accounting structure. Unregulated firms (such as credit-rating agencies), lightly regulated firms (such as hedge funds), and the shadow banking system, generally, have also been blamed for the crisis. While credit-rating agencies have received much negative publicity,[33] hedge funds and other alternative investment funds have been relatively unscathed. According to Ken Scott, 'CDS or derivatives in general . . . created none of the losses. . . . They are an instrument for transferring, and thereby spreading, some of the risk, and they worked as designed'.[34] However, naked credit default swaps (CDS) have come under a great deal of scrutiny (with calls for their regulation) following the crisis in Greece. The expression 'shadow banking system' is imprecise and its contours are not clearly defined. According to Roubini,[35] broker-dealers, hedge funds, private equity groups, structured investment vehicles and conduits, money market funds, and non-bank mortgage lenders are all part of this shadow system. Other commentators relate the shadow banking system to the

---

33 A recent US Senate investigation into the role of the credit rating agencies (CRAs) in the financial crisis has exposed the conflicts of interest that riddle their business model. See 'Rating Agencies' Nixon Moment', *Financial Times*, 24 April 2010.

34 See Kenneth Scott, 'Criteria for Evaluating Failure Resolution Plans' (Mimeo presented at 'Ending Government Bailouts as We Know Them' Policy Workshop, Stanford University, 10 December 2009, on file with authors).

35 See Nouriel Roubini, 'The Shadow Banking System is Unravelling: Roubini Column in the Financial Times. Such Demise Confirmed by Morgan and Goldman Now Being Converted into Banks', http://www.roubini.com/roubini-monitor/253696/the_shadow_banking_system_is_unravelling_roubini_column_in_the_financial_times_such_demise_confirmed_by_morgan_and_goldman_now_being_converted_into_banks (visited 9 August 2010).

growth of the securitization of assets.[36] Gary Gorton and others believe that it was the (wholesale) run on the repo market during 2008—the bank run not so much on depository institutions as on the shadow banking system—that caused the crisis. Gorton explains that, while in the past depositors ran to their banks and demanded cash in exchange for their checking accounts, the 2008 panic involved financial firms 'running' on other financial firms by not renewing repo agreements or increasing the repo margin, thus forcing sudden deleveraging and leading to many banking insolvencies. Earlier banking crises have many features in common with the current crisis. History can help understand the current situation and guide thoughts about regulatory reform, by making the shadow banking system less vulnerable to panic.[37]

G. CORPORATE GOVERNANCE FAILURES

The misaligned incentives between the short-term interests of bankers (due to their compensation/bonus pay structure) and the long-term interest, and indeed the very survival, of their firms must be addressed. Pay structures, relationships between managers and shareholders, the relationships with other stakeholders and the respective responsibilities of each need to be reassessed. Crucial here is that shareholders acknowledge and act on their responsibilities.[38]

H. RISK-MANAGEMENT FAILURES, BAD LENDING, EXCESSIVE LEVERAGE, AND EXCESSIVE COMPLEXITY

Banks and the shadow banking system built up extraordinary leverage, which reached a historical maximum in June 2007. Over the preceding years, bank credit expansion was on average much faster than the growth rate of bank deposits. Banks achieved this through reducing their liquid assets, borrowing (massively and short term) in wholesale markets, securitizing, and increasing leverage. All these factors left them more exposed to any fall in asset prices. (The parallels with the Japanese crisis are particularly striking here.) The decline in lending standards also

36 See Tobias Adrian and Hyun Song Shin, 'The Shadow Banking System: Implications for Financial Regulation', Federal Reserve Bank of New York Staff Report No 382, 1 July 2009, http://papers.ssrn.com/sol3/papers.cfm?abstract_id = 1441324 (visited 9 August 2010). In this article, they argue that although securitization was intended as a way to transfer credit risk to those better able to absorb losses, instead, it increased the fragility of the entire financial system by allowing banks and other intermediaries to 'leverage up' by buying one another's securities.

37 See Gorton, above n 2, at 13. Gorton observes that the 'great panic' which commenced in August 2007 is no different from the Panics of 1907 or 1893, except that in 2007 'most people had never heard of the markets that were involved, did not know how they worked, or what their purposes were. Terms like subprime mortgage, asset-backed commercial paper conduit, structured investment vehicle, credit derivative, securitization, or repo market were meaningless'. And just like deposit bank runs earlier, the securitized banking system, which is in essence a real banking system, 'allowing institutional investors and firms to make enormous, short-term deposits', was vulnerable to a panic. What should be more troubling is that the events commencing with the August 2007 waterfall were not a retail panic involving individuals, but a wholesale panic involving institutions, where large financial firms 'ran' on other financial firms, making the system insolvent'.

38 Martin Wolf, 'The Challenge of Halting the Financial Doomsday Machine', *Financial Times*, 21 April 2010: 'The combination of state insurance (which protects creditors) with limited liability (which protects shareholders) creates a financial doomsday machine'.

contributed to the crisis.[39] Lord Turner (then and currently Chairman of the Financial Services Authority in the UK)[40] has claimed that some trading activities are socially useless.[41] Management failed to conduct appropriate due diligence, in particular with regard to subprime decisions, and relied unthinkingly on ratings. Complexity and opacity are risks per se, and were not properly priced in the build up of the crisis. In the words of Buchheit: 'When history looks back on this crisis, a big culprit will be the astonishing complexity of modern financial instruments and the drafting of their contracts'.[42] Scott and Taylor, who blame the toxic assets on banks' balance sheets as one of the causes of the crisis, emphasize how 'maddeningly complex' securitization was and suggest that 'mandated transparency is the only solution'.[43] One intriguing issue is the extent to which certain financial operations or vehicles are Ponzi schemes or other types of quasi-fraudulent transactions intended to mislead or to conceal losses.[44] While fraud is clearly a crime, and individuals such as Madoff should have been caught and prosecuted much earlier, there are other complex transactions or schemes which may be intended to obfuscate or disguise the real financial position of a firm. In this 'murky terrain', firms may sometimes exploit opportunities for regulatory arbitrage or 'forum shopping'. At other times they may be playing on the fringes of the law.[45] The report published by Anton Valukas on his investigations of Lehman Brothers raises eyebrows about the questionable use of the so-called Repo 105 transactions:

> Lehman's Repo 105 practice consisted of a two-step process: (1) undertaking Repo 105 transactions followed by (2) the use of Repo 105 cash borrowings to reduce liabilities, thus reducing leverage. A few days after the new quarter began, Lehman would borrow the necessary funds to repay the cash borrowings plus interest, repurchase the securities,

---

39 Conrad Voldstad (Chief Executive of the International Swaps and Derivatives Association, ISDA), 'We Have Failed to Address the Real Cause of the Financial Crisis', *Financial Times*, 7 July 2010: 'Bad lending, driven by poor underwriting standards and awful risk management, created and drove the crisis'.

40 Interview of Lord Turner, 'How to Tame Global Finance', *Prospect*, 27 August 2009.

41 Ibid. Lord Turner asserts that many of the financial activities which had proliferated in the City of London over the past 10 years were 'socially useless'. He neither defined the term nor provided any evidence for the assertion.

42 Lee Buchheit, 'We Made it Too Complicated', 27 International Financial Law Review 24 (2008), at 24, http://www.iflr.com (visited 9 August 2010): 'We ... reached the point where some financial engineers have managed to baffle even themselves. Along the way though, they seem to have befuddled their boards of directors, risk management committees, lawyers, accountants, customers and regulators'.

43 See Kenneth Scott and John Taylor, 'Why Toxic Assets Are so Hard to Clean Up', *Wall Street Journal*, 20 July 2009, http://online.wsj.com/article/SB124804469056163533.html (visited 2 October 2010).

44 William White, 'Modern Macroeconomics is on the Wrong Track', 46(4) Finance and Development 15 (2009), at 17, quoting Minsky: 'Minsky (1982) also spoke of stages of credit growth, with the horizon of the credit getting ever shorter, culminating into what was essentially Ponzi finance. Loans would, in the last stage of the boom, be made to pay the interest on previous loans.'

45 See Gillian Tett, 'Global Harmony a Distant Prospect Despite Lehman Outrage', *Financial Times*, 16 March 2010: 'The conditions which gave rise to the kind of regulatory arbitrage that Lehman exploited—namely a fragmented global regulatory and accounting regime—do not seem to be on their way out. . . .What drove Repo 105 . . . was a form of "forum shopping"'. Michael Lewis, *The Big Short: Inside the Doomsday Machine* (London: Allen Lane, 2010) 43, suggests that the line between gambling and investment is artificial and thin.

and restore the assets to its balance sheet. Lehman never publicly disclosed its use of Repo 105 transactions, its accounting treatment for these transactions, the considerable escalation of its total Repo 105 usage in late 2007 and into 2008 or the material impact these transactions had on the firm's publicly reported net leverage ratio.[46]

The use of an accounting artifice that allowed Lehman Brothers to move assets off the balance sheet to improve its results suggests that in some cases complexity and opacity can be intended to misrepresent the true financial implications of certain transactions or to conceal financial distress.

I. 'THE USUAL SUSPECTS'—GREED, EUPHORIA, ETC.

Human frailty is always a factor in both crisis and non-crisis situations. Furthermore, excessive 'groupthink' and 'herd behaviour' were also to blame. What was surely partly at fault is 'unbridled greed'—a system of incentives that rewarded the pursuit of excessive profits, while not appropriately internalizing the costs of losses. 'Too-big-to-fail' plainly contributed to this; but again, shareholders in institutions must surely take some responsibility for the contracts that they sign with their employees.

J. FAULTY ECONOMIC THEORIES

In the decades that preceded the great crash of 2008, some relied with almost unquestioning faith on the efficient market theory—markets as self-correcting mechanisms with rational expectations.[47] The existence of transaction and information costs was neglected, and it was forgotten that theory as well as much evidence says that markets tend to display these admirable efficiency properties *on average*, not all the time. Further, a certain belief in the superiority of mathematics, game theory and modelling over what were perceived as less rigorous disciplines—law, political science, psychology, sociology, history—permeated much research and teaching in economics and finance departments.[48] Utopian interpretations of economic theories can be construed as a 'causa remota' of the crisis. At times, a crude reliance on modelling with insufficient or incomplete data proved catastrophic. Particularly damaging was the neglect (and not just in the above-noted case of the housing market) of all but recent history. Any institution which based its risk modelling on even the preceding 10 years of daily data was drawing its data from what a longer perspective would have shown to be an unusually benign period; and many of those who looked at a longer perspective nonetheless behaved as if the change in the environment over the preceding few years would last forever. Cottier, in his excellent analysis of the challenges ahead for international economic law, suggests that the financial crisis 'epitomizes the failures of a

46 See Lehman Brothers Holdings Inc. Chapter 11 Proceedings Examiner's Report, 11 March 2010, at 733–734, http://lehmanreport.jenner.com (9 August 2010). For press coverage see *Financial Times*, 13–14 March 2010.

47 See White, above n 44, at 16: 'The recent crisis has demonstrated the inadequacy of models based on the assumption of rational expectations. . . . [T]he simplifying assumptions on which much of modern macroeconomics is based were not useful in explaining real world developments'.

48 See generally Financial Services Authority, 'The Turner Review: A Regulatory Response to the Global Banking Crisis', March 2009, http://www.fsa.gov.uk/pages/Library/Corporate/turner/index.shtml (visited 9 August 2010).

strictly disciplinary tradition of fragmentation and specialization, and the lack of truly interdisciplinary research', and suggests the need to deepen the relationship between international economic law, economics, and other social sciences, such as international relations theory.[49] Very few economists—with White[50] and Borio, at the Bank for International Settlements (BIS), and Roubini[51] as some of the most notable exceptions—predicted the magnitude of the crisis. In a visit to the London School of Economics (LSE) in November 2008, Queen Elizabeth II asked Luis Garicano why no economist had seen the crisis coming. Some had, but no one appeared inclined to listen. Westbrook wrote:

> Why was orthodox finance[52] so convincing, for so long, and yet so wrong? One might start by noting that finance has been oddly insensitive to law. Financial markets are essentially legal. Collateral is a form of property; derivatives are contracts; corporations and fiat money are creatures of law. Economics, however, has always aspired to be a natural science, and so has considered the social as if it were natural. This fundamental ontological error has led to fanciful pricing models, as if we could model the movements of legal instruments like we model the movements of the stars. When times are good, or trading intervals are very short, such conceits may be overlooked. But when times are bad, it becomes obvious that legal phenomena deform under political and social stresses, as holders of Greek debt or Lehman Brothers collateral ought to be amply aware.

V. A LONGER PERSPECTIVE

While *financial* crises ('pseudo' crises in Schwartz's terminology) are a fairly common feature of the economic cycle, *banking* crises ('real' crises) are much rarer. Banking crises are a subset of financial crises distributed differently in time and in space. Financial crises may well be inherent to the business cycle, or to human nature itself. Kindleberger[53] and Minsky[54] have both argued

49 Thomas Cottier, 'Challenges Ahead in International Economic Law', 12 Journal of International Economic Law 3 (2009), at 12.

50 William White was Economic Adviser and Head of the Monetary and Economic Department of the Bank for International Settlements from May 1995 to June 2008. His speeches and the BIS Annual Reports which included numerous warnings about the perils of the bubbles that were emerging in international financial markets were all but ignored.

51 Nouriel Roubini, known in some circles as Dr Doom, predicted the crisis as far back as 2006. See generally his archived articles on his website 'Roubini Global Economics' at http://www.rge.com. See e.g. Nouriel Roubini, 'Revisiting My July/August 2006 Prediction of a US Recession in 2007', *Roubini Global Economics*, http://www.roubini.com/roubinimonitor/160927/revisiting_my_july_august_2006_prediction_of_a_us_recession_in_2007 (visited 9 August 2010).

52 See generally David A. Westbrook, *Out of Crisis: Rethinking our Financial Markets* (Boulder: Paradigm Publishers, 2009). Westbrook explains that financial markets are like networks and that no firm should be too big to be resolved without substantial interruption to the trading operations of counter-parties. He also draws an analogy between financial markets and ecosystems. Economics, he argues, should abandon its claim to be like physics.

53 Charles P. Kindleberger, *Manias, Panics and Crashes: a History of Financial Crises* (London: Macmillan, 1978).

54 Hyman P. Minsky, 'The Financial Instability Hypothesis' (reprint), The Jerome Levy Economics Institute Working Paper No 74, May 1992.

that they are an inevitable part of the business cycle, and result from irrational reactions and myopia. Some banking theorists have argued, in a somewhat similar manner, that the structure of bank balance sheets makes panics inevitable.[55] If we are persuaded by one argument or the other (or both), then we should expect crises always to be with us. Perhaps we should have that expectation so far as financial crises are concerned; but the evidence is that we should not hold that expectation for banking crises.

Banking crises tend to occur (if they occur) around the time of cyclical downturns, and are closely associated with large declines in the value of bank loans, reflecting declines in the fortunes of the borrowers. Second, they have become more common in recent years, despite government interventions (such as government insurance of deposits) intended to achieve the opposite. Third, panics can happen without failures and failures without panics—the Panic of 1907 in the USA was not associated with a rise in the bank failure rate, and the wave of agricultural bank failures in the USA in the 1920s was not accompanied by a systemic panic. This suggests that uncertainty about small losses can cause panic without failure, while large losses with clear incidence cause failure without causing widespread panic. Most notable of all is that there are substantially different 'propensities' for crises at different times and places. The US banking system has historically been crisis prone.

Britain too was crisis prone, but that changed in the middle of the 19th century. After 1866 there was no crisis—even the outbreak of World War I did not provoke one. In the years 1875–1913, only four countries experienced severe waves of bank insolvency. This diverse pattern shows clearly that there must be more to banking crises than the inevitable features of human nature or bank balance sheets.

Changes in the fragility of banking systems usually result from changes in the 'rules of the banking game'. Such changes can be stability promoting, as was the Bank of England's adoption of and commitment to a lender of last resort role after 1866, or risk promoting, as were the pre-1893 Italian guarantees of the property lending of the Banca di Roma. The same story continues up to the present. Restrictions on structure have often proved perverse—for example, the protection of unit banking in the USA. In contrast, Canada's early allowing of nationwide branch banking contributed to stability. Getting the rules of the banking game wrong readily makes the game go wrong.

Did that happen this time? Looking at the USA, we certainly see a repetition of previous mistakes. There was pressure from the Congress on banks, on Fannie Mae, and on Freddie Mac, to promote house ownership by taking on more high-risk mortgages. There was Federal Housing Administration subsidy of high mortgage leverage. Foreclosures were discouraged. The legislation of 2006 encouraged rating agencies to relax standards on the rating of securitizations. Unsurprisingly, the US housing market boomed.

55 See e.g. James Tobin, 'Financial Intermediation and Deregulation in Perspective', 3(2) Bank of Japan Monetary and Economic Studies 19 (1985).

Banks elsewhere, some already caught up in their own housing booms, were drawn into the US boom. Regulators were defective. Preoccupied with individual banks, they did not see, or ignored, that securitization was simply spreading risk around the system, and focused instead on the illusory reduction in individual bank risk which it produced.[56] Problems spread round the world and systemic risk expanded.

In addition, it should be noted that the recent crisis was remarkably like the Japanese one. Easy money and steady growth followed by ill-thought-out regulatory policies were sufficient to cause the Japanese crisis. They were also present in the run-up to the present one.

VI. THE REGULATORY RESPONSES

We now turn to the flurry of regulatory responses, which can be divided into five groups.[57] The first looks at the substance of regulation, at the 'what to regulate', with new rules (or proposed rules) for capital, liquidity, and other indicators of banking and financial soundness. In this we can include the new Basel proposals (sometimes referred to as Basel III)[58] and others that look at ways of enhancing the quality or quantity of regulation (from dynamic provisioning and rules to prevent excessive leverage to rules regarding bonuses or compensation schemes, rules on insolvency and early intervention) at the national, European, or international level. With regard to the scope of institutions to be regulated, Andrew Crocket advocates the need to 'widen the net' beyond the three pillars upon which financial regulation has traditionally rested (i.e. banking, securities, and insurance) to a wider range of institutions that are now central to financial stability. In particular, he cites the players involved in the originate-to-distribute model of credit intermediation, service providers such as clearing and settlement systems, credit-rating agencies, auditing firms, and private pools of capital such as hedge funds and private equity funds.[59] Perhaps the answer in some cases—for example, with regard to derivatives markets—is not more regulation, but more transparency and accountability, a well-functioning clearing system, and on-balance-sheet accounting treatment.

The second group of proposals looks at the structure of supervision and regulation, at the 'how' and the 'who', and the intensity of supervision. It should be noted though that all national 'architectures', whether one authority, twin-peak, or many regulators, failed to prevent the

56 See Geoffrey Wood and Ali Kabiri, 'Firm Stability or System Stability: the Regulatory Delusion', in Dal Singh (ed), *Managing Systemic Risk* (Cheltenham: Edward Elgar, 2011) (forthcoming).
57 See Rosa M. Lastra, 'The Check Book that the Banks Cannot Bounce', *Parliamentary Brief*, 2 March 2010, 27–28, http://www.parliamentarybrief.com/articles/1/new/mag/83/1066/the-check-book-that.html (visited 9 August 2010).
58 The Basel Committee on Banking Supervision expects to adopt reforms to require banks to hold more and better capital in time for the November 2010 Seoul meeting of the Group of 20. Work on the first global liquidity standards may take longer, and implementation of both will include years of transition time. See http://www.bis.org/press/p100726.htm (visited 27 July 2010).
59 See Andrew Crocket, 'Rebuilding the Financial Architecture', 46(3) Finance & Development 18 (2009), at 18.

crisis.[60] Further, many of these proposals are nationally based. An 'international architecture' may have to be an essential part of any reform.

One of the major 'breakthroughs' in the response to the crisis is that a distinction is now made between macro-prudential supervision and micro-prudential supervision. According to the House of Lords' report on the Future of EU Financial Supervision and Regulation:[61] 'macro-prudential supervision is the analysis of trends and imbalances in the financial system and the detection of systemic risks that these trends may pose to financial institutions and the economy. . . . Micro-prudential supervision is the day-today supervision of individual financial institutions. . . . The same or a separate supervisor can carry out these two functions'.[62]

The third group of proposals concerns the behaviour of the banking industry and bank managers and the need to internalize the costs of protection. Here one can include the proposal by Deutsche Bank CEO Josef Ackermann (set out at Davos in January 2010) to establish a European Rescue and Resolution Fund largely financed by the banking industry and the proposal of IMF Managing Director Dominique Strauss-Kahn (on 19 March 2010) for a 'European Resolution Authority', an agency pre-financed by the banking industry as far as possible, to deal with failing cross-border banks in the EU.[63] Acknowledging the lack of adequate rules in this area, the European Commission published a Communication on 20 October 2009 proposing an EU framework for cross-border crisis management and a further Communication on bank resolution funds on 26 May 2010.[64]

A fourth group focuses on the fiscal side. In particular, 'extracting rents' (rather than merely profit taking) in a banking and financial market, which has been largely subsidized by governments' rescue packages and monetary and fiscal policies, raises controversy.[65] Acute moral hazard problems persist. The UK Government targeted compensation by imposing a one-off 50% tax on the bonus pools of a number of financial institutions in the UK. Some economists have advocated the imposition of a (global) tax on financial transactions, akin to the Tobin tax (a tax on the

60 See the paper by Luis Garicano and Rosa M. Lastra in this issue for further elaboration on this point, in particular with regard to the EU proposals. In the USA, President Obama signed the new financial legislation on 21 July 2010. The Dodd-Frank Wall Street Reform and Consumer Protection Act of 2010, H.R. 4173, Public L. 111–203, is the major financial reform in the USA since the New Deal legislation in the 1930s. In the UK, the new Government launched a consultation document spelling out the proposals that the Chancellor had outlined in his Mansion House Speech: 'A New Approach to Financial Regulation: Judgment, Focus and Stability', 26 July 2010, http://www.hm-treasury.gov.uk/d/consult_financial_regulation_condoc.pdf (visited 9 August 2010).

61 House of Lords' European Union Committee, above n 27.

62 Ibid, at para 27 and 28.

63 See 'IMF Seeks Bank Crisis Agency', *Financial Times*, 20 March 2010.

64 See European Commission, 'Communication from the Commission to the European Parliament, the Council, the European Economic and Social Committee and the European Central Bank: Bank Resolution Funds', COM(2010), 26 May 2010, http://ec.europa.eu/internal_market/bank/crisis_management/index_en.htm (visited 22 July 2010).

65 See Plender, above n 29: 'Bankers in the boom were being paid bonuses not for brilliance but for excessive risk taking via leverage and for oligopolistic super-profits. Now they have been offered a state safety net and a steep yield curve, whereby they borrow at low cost to invest in higher yielding assets. This guarantees easy, low risk profits, on which they nonetheless expect bonuses'.

value of foreign exchange transactions). The IMF issued a report on 27 June 2010 recommending that countries consider adopting two taxes: a Financial Stability Contribution and a Financial Activities Tax.[66]

A fifth group of proposals are bank structural reforms which aim to change the structure of the banking industry and the balance-sheet structure of commercial banks and other financial institutions so as to circumscribe the scope of institutions that receive governmental protection, to separate 'utility banking' from 'casino banking'. These proposals range from narrow banking to a full-scale mutualization of the financial industry.[67] The so-called Volcker rule adopted by the Dodd–Frank Act is also a structural reform, albeit more limited.[68] The Volcker rule prohibits federally insured 'banking entities' from engaging in proprietary trading (subject to certain exceptions) and restricts their relationships with hedge funds and private equity funds.

Given the multiplicity of proposals, it might be sensible to implement a simple approach that considers what is essential to maintain financial stability while preserving competition on the one hand, and what is desirable and feasible in the longer term on the other hand. The establishment of a robust and well-understood framework for the resolution of cross-border financial institutions, a framework which includes rules on burden sharing, is an essential policy priority.[69] The alternatives to an orderly resolution—either a chaotic resolution or a bail-out—would be disastrous. Capitalism relies on the lure of wealth (privatization of gains) and the discipline imposed by the fear of bankruptcy (privatization of losses). It is imperative to reinstate a credible fear of bankruptcy for banks and other systemically significant financial institutions so as to ensure that banks once more play their proper role in a market economy.

VII. CONCLUDING OBSERVATIONS

In this article, we have tentatively analysed the causes of the financial crisis of 2007–09 and outlined some of the responses. Following a distinction between liquidity crises and capital/solvency crises, we draw on the lessons of history to present the various culprits of the recent crisis. This

66 International Monetary Fund, 'A Fair and Substantial Contribution by the Financial Sector', Final Report for the G-20, 27 June 2010. The IMF's recommended financial stability contribution is similar to the financial stability fee that Sweden adopted in 2009, a direct levy on Swedish banks based on bank liabilities and equity. For a discussion of financial taxes generally see Alexander Kern in this issue at 893–910.

67 The narrow banking proposals have been again endorsed by John Kay, 'Narrow Banking: The Reform of Banking Regulation', Centre for the Study of Financial Innovation, 15 September 2009, http://www.johnkay.com/wp-content/uploads/2009/12/JK-Narrow-Banking.pdf (visited 9 August 2010); while Lawrence J. Kotlikoff has made a case for the mutualization of the financial industry in his book: Lawrence J. Kotlikoff, *Jimmy Stewart is Dead: Ending the World's Ongoing Financial Plague with Limited Purpose Banking* (Chichester: John Wiley & Sons, 2010).

68 Dodd-Frank Wall Street Reform and Consumer Protection Act of 2010, H.R. 4173, Public L. 111–203, §619.

69 See generally The International Monetary Fund, 'Resolution of Cross Border Banks—a Proposed Framework for Enhanced Coordination', Report of the Legal and Monetary and Capital Markets Departments, 11 June 2010 (to which one of the authors, Professor Rosa M. Lastra, contributed), http://www.imf.org/external/np/pp/eng/2010/061110.pdf (visited 22 July 2010).

is not the final story, since only with the benefit of hindsight will anyone be able to write an account of what happened akin to Milton Friedman and Anna Schwartz's authoritative Monetary History of the United States, which in 1963, three decades after the New Deal legislation introduced in the USA by President Roosevelt, provided the definitive analysis of that Depression.

This was a solvency/capital crisis, not a mere liquidity banking crisis. As for the culprits, the observation with which we conclude is that it is remarkable how people tend to side with 'one side of the story'. *Laissez-faire* proponents tend to argue that it is an unfettered free market that encourages virtue and government regulation that destroys it; markets are the solution, and government is the problem. In contrast, those who believe that markets are principally to blame advocate more intrusive and extensive regulation and intervention. Where both groups tend to agree is that finance needs to go back to being an instrument directed towards improved wealth creation and development.[70] To ensure this, the fear of failure needs to return to the business of banking.

END-OF-CHAPTER QUESTIONS

1. Briefly, explain the differences between banking crises and financial crises. Anna Schwartz, a famous American economist, referred to the former as a real crisis and to the latter as a pseudo crisis. Was she right?
2. Financial crises come in two varieties: liquidity crises and capital crises. What are the principal differences between these two types of financial crises?
3. Briefly explain what a repurchase agreement (referred to as "repo") is, a matched sale-purchase transaction (referred to as a "reverse repo"), and repo haircuts. Explain why some economists argue that the crisis of 2007–09 was the result of a collapse of the repo market.
4. Explain why fractional reserve banks are often unable meet a sudden increase in demand for cash and, hence, the need for a lender of last resort.
5. An example of a capital crisis was the Baring crisis of 1890. Explain what happened to that English bank more than a hundred years ago.
6. Why do the authors conclude that the crisis of 2007–09 was a capital crisis? Are they right in this assessment?
7. The authors argue that the Japanese crisis of the late 1980s and 1990s resembles the crisis of 2007–09. Briefly, discuss why these two crises are alike, and comment on the Japanese and US government response to each.

70 See Speech of Lord Turner, 'What Do Banks Do, What Should they Do and What Public Policies are Needed to Ensure Best Results for the Real Economy?', CASS Business School, 17 March 2010: 'A critical issue is . . . whether this increased financial intensity has delivered value added for the real economy—whether it has improved capital allocation, increased growth or increased human welfare and choice . . . And whether it has made the economy more or less volatile to shocks'. See also http://www.vatican.va/holy_father/benedict_xvi/encyclicals/documents/hf_ben-xvi_enc_20090629_caritas-in-veritate_en.html (visited 18 March 2010).

8. The authors argue that explanations for the crisis of 2007–09 fall into 10 groups which may not be mutually exclusive: (a) macroeconomic imbalances; (b) lax monetary policy; (c) weak regulatory structure; (d) too-big-to-fail (TBTF) doctrine; (e) securitization; (f) insufficient regulation of nonbanking institutions; (g) corporate governance failures; (h) risk-management failures; (i) greed; and (j) faulty economic theories. Briefly, explain the argument for each explanation, its main strengths and weaknesses.
9. When discussing faulty economic theories as an explanation for the crisis of 2007–09, the authors argue that an over reliance on the efficient markets theory and disdain for other social sciences may have led many economists to overlook important information that may have helped them predict the financial storm. What do the authors mean by this? Are they right?
10. In terms of regulatory responses to the crisis, describe the new (or proposed) rules for capital, liquidity, and other indicators of financial soundness, including the new Basel proposals, often referred to as Basel III.
11. Another response to the crisis deals with a distinction between macroprudential and microprudential supervision. What are the differences between the two, and why do they complement each other?
12. The Volcker rule—adopted by the Dodd-Frank Act of 2009—is another innovative response to the crisis. Explain what the Volcker rule is, and describe its main objectives.

9 781516 529803

Printed by Libri Plureos GmbH in Hamburg,
Germany